THE

ORGANON, OR LOGICAL TREATISES,

OF

ARISTOTLE.

WITH

THE INTRODUCTION OF PORPHYRY.

LITERALLY TRANSLATED, WITH NOTES, SYLLOGISTIC EXAMPLES, ANALYSIS, AND INTRODUCTION.

BY

OCTAVIUS FREIRE OWEN, M. A.

OF CHRIST CHURCH, OXFORD. RECTOR OF BURSTOW, SURREY; AND DOMESTIC CHAPLAIN TO THE DUKE OF PORTLAND.

IN TWO VOLUMES.

VOL. I.

LONDON:

HENRY G. BOHN, YORK STREET, COVENT GARDEN.

MDCCCLIII.

[illegible] principally the higher range of intellectual [illegible]
spiritual faculties peculiar to man. After life
he comes to living things in detail, first to Natural
Hist. which would include theoretically Botany
but we have nothing considerable from Aristotle
on that subject — Traces the period of vegetable
functioning through which the foetus of an animal
passes on its way to its fuller development
(See Dante Longfellow's trans 300. 330) from
Dante & Aquinas Lowell Lectures. for Comm-
ents on Poetic & Rhetoric see big notes on that [illegible]
— "Lastly, to crown all, come the treatises on
metaphysics. In studying material & still
more in studying vital phenomena, Aristotle
had become convinced that physical phenomena
point to something beyond themselves. In physics, motion, strictly speaking, never originates, because all bodily movement seems to be
produced by some body already moving &
consequently motion gives no account of its
origin, except in the soul of animals, such as
man, (see Dante Par [illegible]) [illegible] desiring & the
desired, therefore to dependence on which all movement can be ultimately traced, and both of them
immaterial. [illegible] remember the
where he sees a point of intensest light with rainbow
swirls around it [illegible] that "on that
point all heaven & Nature [illegible] Par. XXVIII, 41 Cary 54
Long. 54) He is repeating the phrase of Aristotle
literally & Dante recognizes that that point is God
& that the circling rainbow forms are the hierarchies
of Angels. Aristotle's study of meta-physics, was
the study of the immaterial principle on which
all heaven & Nature hang. It was his theology, his
examination of the ultimate nature of Being. The
Aristotle begins with motion, & is led by studying the
the motions of material things to believe in some
thing immaterial & unmoving on which material things depend. But when he comes to give
us, as he does in his physics, in the De Coelo & in
metaphysics, his idea of the nature & meaning of the
spiritual principle, we find that his conception
of far transcends anything that his mere inferences from the material world can cover.

JOHN CHILDS AND SON, BUNGAY.

or finding how Sharing with Parmenides & P[lato] to an exalted rapture, or a sense of awe, in contemplating the One & the Perfect, the Supreme Actuality unsupposed in all potentiality, which shows that he, too, is a Mystic, & which enables one to call from him something of the august emotion he experienced in that contemplation of the Truth which he regarded as at once the divinest life of man in itself & the truest suggestion to man of what must the life of God." Dakki & Aquinas

[Ar]istotle's fault lay in his finality. His Rationality was perfect; but where could Faith come in when every idea seemed symmetrically to arise only from the abstraction of the universal from the senses! Faith might come in as hypothesis" — See Summa 1. XLI. Bacon 143

INTRODUCTION.

The investigation of the science of Mind, especially as to its element, Thought, is of so interesting a character as in great measure to reconcile the inquirer to the abstruseness of formal reasoning. The beauty of the flower, whilst concealing the ruggedness, is apt to withdraw our attention from the utility, of the soil on which it grows; and thus in like manner the charms of Idealism, ending but too frequently in visionary speculation, have obstructed the clear appreciation of the design and use of Logic. Not that we deny the connexion which must ever subsist between Logic, as the science of the laws of reasoning, and psychology; indeed the latter is constantly introduced in several topics of the Organon; but if we would derive real practical benefit from logical study, we must regard it as enunciative of the universal principle of inference, affording a direct test for the detection of fallacy, and the establishment of true conclusion.

Wherefore, while primarily connected with the laws of Thought, Logic is secondarily and practically allied to language as enunciative of Thought. To enter into the mental processes incident thereto, though so tempting a theme as already to have seduced many from the direct subject of the science, would far exceed the limits of this Introduction. We shall therefore content ourselves with a few observations upon the utility of the study connected with the Organon itself.

It is a quaint remark of Erasmus, that the human understanding, like a drunken clown lifted on horseback, falls over on the farther side the instant he is supported on the nearer; and this is the characteristic of human praise and censure. From an ignorant and exaggerated notion of its purport, Logic, instead of being limited to its proper sphere, was supposed commensurate with the whole investigation of abstract truth in relation to matter, cause, and entity,—in fact, the substance of a folio volume, describing every phase of human life, compressed into a few pages of Boethius and Aldrich. Thus, not having effected what nothing short of a miraculous expansion of the understanding could effect, it sunk into insignificance, until recently vindicated, and placed upon its proper footing, by Whately, Mansel, and others.

It is true that, whether viewed as an art or a science,

2 Penetration by definition

Logic does not solve the origin of mental conception; but it furnishes the rules on which all reasoning is constructed; and it would be strange indeed if we refused the practical assistance of surgery because it does not exhibit in theory the operation of will upon matter. We may learn Logic and yet not be able to think; but the science cannot be blamed for the imperfection of the element worked upon, any more than the artificer for the inferiority of the only material within his reach. It is sufficient that Logic, without entering into all the phenomena of mind, provides certain forms which an argument, to be legitimate, must exhibit, certain tests by which fallacy may be detected, and certain barriers against ambiguity in the use of language.

Hence, the utility of a science which enables men to take cognizance of the travellers on the mind's highway, and excludes those disorderly interlopers verbal fallacies, needs but small attestation. Its searching penetration by definition alone, before which even mathematical precision fails,[1] would especially commend it to those whom the abstruseness of the study does not terrify, and who recognise the valuable results which must attend discipline of mind. Like a medicine, though not a panacea for every ill, it has the health of the mind for its aim, but requires the determination of a powerful will to imbibe its nauseating

[1] Prior Analyt. ii. 16. P. 216

yet wholesome influence: it is no wonder therefore that puny intellects, like weak stomachs, abhor and reject it. What florid declaimer can endure that the luxuriant boughs of verdant sophistry, the rich blossoms of oratorical fervour, should be lopped and pared by the stern axe of a syllogism, and the poor stripped trunk of worthless fallacy exposed unprotected to the nipping atmosphere of truth?

Like the science of which it treats, not only has the term "Logic" been variously applied,[1] but even the Organon, as a whole, presents no great claim to unity. The term is neither found, as belonging to an art or science, in Aristotle, nor does it occur in the writings of Plato, and the appellation "Organon," given to the treatises before us, has been attributed to the Peripatetics, who maintained against the Stoics that Logic was "an instrument" of Philosophy. The book, according to M. St. Hilaire, was not called "Organon" before the 15th century,[2] and the treatises were collected into one volume, as is supposed, about the time of Andronicus of Rhodes; it was translated into Latin by Boethius about the 6th century. That Aristotle did not compose the Organon as a whole, is evident from several portions having been severally regarded as logical, grammatical, and metaphysical, and even the Aristotelian names themselves, Analytic and Dialectic, are applica-

[1] Scotus super Univ. Qu. 3. [2] Cf. Waitz, vol. ii. p. 294.

ble only to certain portions of the Organon. Still the system is so far coherent in the immediate view taken of Logic, as conversant with language in the process of reasoning, that any addition to the structure of the Stagirite can never augment the compactness with which the syllogism, as a foundation, is built. The treatises themselves are mentioned under distinct titles by their author, and subsequent commentators have discussed the work, not as a whole, but according to its several divisions. It is remarkable also, that no quotations from the Categories, de Interpretatione, or Sophistical Elenchi, are found in the extant writings of Aristotle, since those given by Ritter[1] of the first and last must be considered doubtful.

In the present Translation my utmost endeavour has been to represent the mind and meaning of the author as closely as the genius of the two languages admits. The benefit of the student has been my especial object; hence in the Analysis, the definitions are given in the very words of Aristotle, and the syllogistic examples, introduced by Taylor, have been carefully examined and corrected. In order also to interpret the more confused passages, I have departed somewhat from the usual plan, and in addition to foot-notes have affixed explanations in the margin, that the eye may catch, in the same line, the word and its import. Wherever

[1] Vol. iii. p. 28.

further elucidation was necessary, I have referred to standard authorities, amongst whom I would gratefully commemorate the works of Mr. Mansel and Dr. Whately, not forgetting my solitary predecessor in this laborious undertaking, Thomas Taylor, whose strict integrity in endeavouring to give the meaning of the text deserves the highest commendation. For books placed at my disposal I have especially to express my sincere acknowledgments to the Rev. Dr. Hessey, Head Master of Merchant Tailors' School, and John Cuninghame, Esq. of Lainshaw.

By an alteration in the original plan, it has been found requisite, in order to equalize the size of the 609 volumes, to place Porphyry's Introduction at the close, instead of at the commencement, of the Organon.

O. F. O.

Burstow, June 23, 1853.
In Surrey

[illegible] for both matters, as fair & fare, bound [illegible] tended to words of like spelling but diff. pronunciation. Humboldt regrets Aristotle "was so averse to the grander views of the elder Pythagoreans, which indicated ideas so nearly approximating to truth, respecting the structure of the universe". Cosmos V1. 88

Nature only one particular genus of being. Possibly [illegible] nature has matter. Aristotle Metaphysics.

ARISTOTLE'S ORGANON.

Plato's works are preparatory exercises for the [illegible] Theaetetus 257) He leads you to see that propositions involving in themselves contradictions [illegible] therefore must belong to a logic — that of ideas. They are contradictory only in the Aristotelian logic, which is strictly of the understanding.

THE CATEGORIES.[1]

CHAP. I.—*Of Homonyms,[2] Synonyms, Paronyms.*

THINGS are termed homonymous, of which the name alone is common, but the definition (of substance according to the name) is different; thus "man" — 1. What are homonyms.

[1] Categories, or Predicaments, so called because they concern things which may always be predicated, are the several classes under which all abstract ideas, and their signs, common words, may be arranged. Their classification under ten heads was introduced by Archytas and adopted by Aristotle. The reason why, in this treatise about them, Aristotle does not begin from these, but from Homonyms, &c., is that he might previously explain what was necessary to the doctrine of the Categories to prevent subsequent digression. Vide Porphyr. in Prædicam. After comparing various opinions of Alexander Aphrodisiensis, Syrianus, Simplicius, and others, it appears agreed by all, that Aristotle's intention in this treatise was, *to discuss simple primary and general words, so far as they are significant of things; at the same time to instruct us in things and conceptions, so far as they are signified by words.* A recollection of this digested explanation, will much assist the student in the enunciation of the plan.

[2] "Homonyms," equivocal words,—"Synonyms," univocal,—"Paronyms," derivative. We may remark here, that analogous nouns constitute only one species of equivocal: that the synonyms of Aristotle must be distinguished from the modern synonyms, which latter are defined by Boethius, "those which have many names, but one definition;" and lastly, that paronyms have been limited by the schoolmen to certain concrete adjectives, a limitation which is not warranted by Aristotle, and is expressly rejected by his Greek commentators.—Mansel's Rudiments of Logic. See also Simplicius Scholia, p. 43, b. 5. "The reason," says Syrianus, "why things polyonomous, and heteronomous, are omitted by Aristotle, is because they rather pertain to ornament of diction, than to the consideration of things; they are therefore more properly discussed in the Rhetoric and Poetics."

and "the picture of a man" are each termed "animal," since of these, the name alone is common, but the definition (of the substance according to the name) is different;[1] as if any one were to assign what was in either, to constitute it "animal," he would allege the peculiar definition of each.

2. What are synonyms.

But those are called synonyms, of which both the name is common, and the definition (of the substance according to the name) is the same,[2] as both "a man" and "an ox" are "animal," for each of these is predicated of as "animal" by a common name, and the definition of the substance is the same, since if a man gave the reason of each as to what was in either, to constitute it "animal," he would assign the same reason.

3. Paronyms.

Again, things are called paronyms which, though differing in case, have their appellation (according to name) from some thing, as "a grammarian" is called so from "grammar," and "a courageous man" from "courage."

CHAP. II.—*Of the logical division of Things and their Attributes.*[3]

1. Subjects of discourse complex and incomplex.

OF things discoursed upon, some are enunciated after a complex, others after an incomplex, manner; the complex as "a man runs," "a man conquers," but the incomplex as "man," "ox,"

[1] Taylor translates λόγος sometimes "reason," at others "definition." It is better to preserve the latter as far as may be, though the student will do well to remember that it is capable of both significations. The brackets are retained from the Leipsic and other copies.

[2] Οὐσια, "a thing sufficient of itself to its own subsistence." Taylor. He translates it "essence," rather than "substance," because this latter word conveys no idea of self-subsistence. See his Introduction of Porphyry. It must be observed, however, that whilst by continued abstraction from the subject and different predicates of Propositions, the *predicates* arrive at the nine other categories, the *subject* will ultimately end in "substance." Cf. Phys. Ausc. lib. iii.

[3] This chapter, containing the several divisions of terms, into absolute and connotative, abstract and concrete, respectively, has presented endless difficulties to commentators; and the question of relation seems as far from being settled as ever. The whole subject may perhaps be properly condensed in the following manner. All ὄντα are divided by Aristotle into four classes, Universal and Singular Substances, and Universal and Singular Attributes; the former existing per se, the latter in the former. Universals are predicable of singulars, but attributes, in

"runs," "conquers." Likewise also some things are predicated of a certain subject, yet are in no subject, as "the man" is predicated of a subject, i. e. of 2. Varieties of predication.

their original state, are not predicable of substances; but by the mental act, we may so connect an attribute with a subject, as to render the former predicable of the latter, as a difference, property, or accident. When a predicate is thus formed from an attribute, it is called connotative, or, as Whately justly remarks, "attributive," and signifies primarily, the attribute, and secondarily, the subject of inhesion. Original universals or attributes, as "man," "whiteness," are called "absolute;" but terms may be made to cross, so that by an act of mind, that which signifies substance may be conceived as an attribute, and as no longer predicable of the individuals; in this sense they are called "abstract," as "humanitas" from "homo;" but when they are primarily or secondarily predicable of individuals, they become "concrete," e. g. "man" is concrete and absolute; "white," concrete and connotative; "whiteness," abstract and absolute; it must be remembered only, that no abstract term is connotative. Vid. Occam, Log. p. i. ch. 5, 10. Simplicius enumerates eleven modes of predication, arising from the relations of genus and species. Aristotle, in the Physics, divides substance in eight modes, omitting "time"—considering subject as both composite and individual. The division into universals and particulars was probably taken from the categorical scheme of Pythagoras.

We annex a scheme of the relation of subject to predicate, in respect of consistency and inhesion.

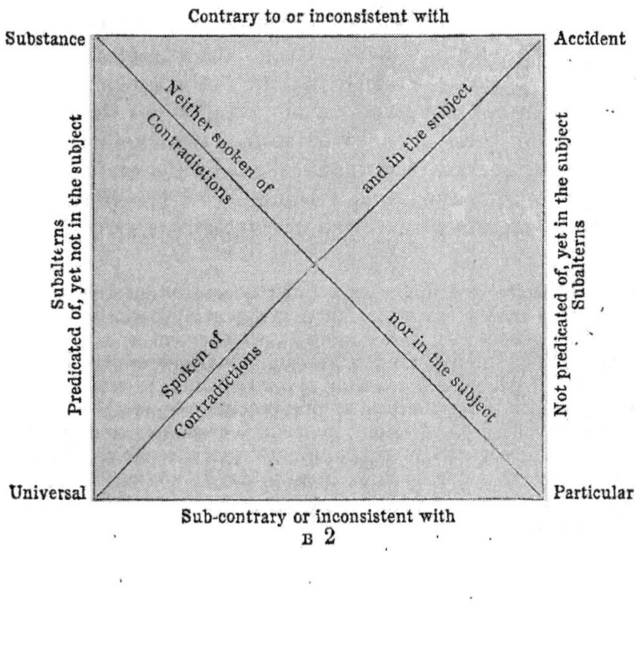

"some certain man," yet is in no subject. Others, again, are in a subject, yet are not predicated of any subject, (I mean by a thing being in a subject, that which is in any thing not as a part, but which cannot subsist without that in which it is,) as "a certain grammatical art" is in a subject, "the soul," but is not predicated of any; and "this white thing" is in a subject, "the body," (for all "colour" is in "body,") but is predicated of no subject. But some things are both predicated of and are in a subject, as "science" is in a subject—"the soul," but is predicated of a subject, namely, "grammar." Lastly, some are neither in, nor are predicated of, any subject, as "a certain man" and "a certain horse," for nothing of this sort is either in, or predicated of, a certain subject. In short, individuals, and whatever is one in number, are predicated of no subject, but nothing prevents some of them from being in a subject, for "a certain grammatical art" is amongst those things which are in a subject, but is not predicated of any subject.

3. Individuals, not predicated of a subject.

CHAP. III.—*Of the connexion between Predicate and Subject.*

1. Statement of argument in abstract.

WHEN one thing is predicated of another, as of a subject, whatever things are said of the predicate, may be also said of the subject,[1] as "the man" is predicated of "some certain man," but "the animal" is predicated of "the man," wherefore "the animal" will be predicated of "some certain man," since "the certain man" is both "man" and "animal." The differences of different genera, and of things not arranged under

2. Difference of distinct genera

[1] Genera, species, and differences, differ according to their predicaments, hence in each predicament, there are genera, species, and differences. Those genera also, have a mutual arrangement, one of which is under the other, as "flying" under "animal," but those are not mutually arranged, one of which, is not ranked under the other, as "animal" and "science." Upon the application of this general rule, see Whately and Hill's Logic, especially the latter, in respect to summa and subaltern genera, and their cognates, pages 56, 57. Properly speaking, there can be only one highest genus, namely, Being; though *relatively* a subaltern term, may at any time, be assumed as the summum genus, as "substance," "animal," etc.

each other, are diverse also in species,[1] as of "animal" and "science." For the differences of "animal" are "quadruped," "biped," "winged," "aquatic," but none of these, forms the difference of "science," since "science," does not differ from "science," in being "biped." But as to subaltern genera, there is nothing to prevent the differences being the same, as the superior are predicated of the genera under them; so that as many differences as there are of the predicate, so many will there also be of the subject.

induces difference in species under them.

3. Not so as to subaltern genera.

CHAP. IV.—*Enumeration of the Categories.*

1. Of incomplex universals.

OF things incomplex enunciated, each signifies either Substance, or Quantity, or Quality, or Relation, or Where, or When, or Position, or Possession, or Action, or Passion.[2] But Substance is, (to speak generally,) as "man," "horse;" Quantity, as "two" or "three cubits;" Quality, as "white," a "grammatical thing;" Relation, as "a double," "a half," "greater;" Where, as "in the Forum," "in the Lyceum;" When, as "yesterday," "last year;" Position, as "he reclines," "he sits;" Possession, as "he is shod," "he is armed;" Action, as "he cuts," "he burns;" Passion, as "he is cut," "he is burnt." Now each of the above, considered by itself, is predicated neither affirmatively nor negatively, but from the connexion of these with each other, affirmation or negation arises. For every affirmation or negation appears to be either true or false, but of things enun-

2. Categories by themselves, neither affirmative nor negative.

[1] Difference joined to genus constitutes species—it is called specific difference, when it constitutes the lowest species, as of individuals. Cf. Crakanthorpe Logica, lib. ii. The common definitions of the heads of the predicables, are those of Porphyry, adopted by subsequent logicians. Vide Porph. Isagoge.

[2] The principle of distinction above is shown to be grammatical, by Trendelenburg, Elementa, section 3rd. The six last may be reduced to Relation, see Hamilton on Reid, p. 688. The categories are enumerated and exemplified in the following verses, for the student's recollection.

> Summa decem: Substantia, Quantum, Quale, Relatio,
> Actio, Passio. Ubi, Quando, Situs, Habitus.
> Presbyter exilis, specie pater, orat et ardet,
> In campo, semper rectus, et in tunicâ.

ciafed without any connexion, none is either true or false, as "man," "white," "runs," "conquers."

CHAP. V.—*Of Substance.*[1]

1. Primary substance is neither in, nor is predicated of, any subject. 2. Secondary substances contain the first.

SUBSTANCE, in its strictest, first, and chief sense, is that which is neither predicated of any subject, nor is in any; as "a certain man," or "a certain horse." But secondary substances are they, in which as species, those primarily-named substances are inherent, that is to say, both these and the genera of these species;[2] as "a certain man" exists in "man," as in a species, but the genus of this species is "animal;" these, therefore, are termed secondary substances,

[1] On the various modes in which Aristotle employs the term *οὐσία*, cf. Metaphy. lib. iv., and Phys. lib. iii. Without entering into the dispute relative to the real existence of genera and species, as substances independent of us, between the old Realists and the modern Conceptualists, it will be sufficient to state that Aristotle here employs the term as the summum genus, under which, by continued abstraction of differences, all things may be comprehended as a common universal. Thus also Plato in Repub. lib. vii. Whether called Entity, Being, Substance, or Subsistence, it may be defined, "*That which subsists independently of any other created thing,*" and in this view may be affirmatively predicated of every cognate term, though no cognate term can be so predicated of it: thus all bodies, all animals, all lions, etc., are substances or things, according as we adopt either of these last as summum genus. Archytas places essence first; Plotinus and Nicostratus doubt its generic affinity altogether; but all regard the principle laid down, of some one, independent, existence, or conception.

[2] But in getting to this ultimate abstraction, the first common nature of which the mind forms conception from individual comparison, is called the lowest primary or most specific species, and of this, every cognate term may be universally predicated, though itself cannot be predicated of any cognate term. Between these extremes, all intermediate notions (and their verbal signs) are called subaltern, each of which, like the step of a ladder, is at once superior to some and inferior to others, and becomes a genus in relation to some lower species, and a species to some higher genera. The annexed "Arbor Porphyriana" is given by Aquinas, Opusc. 48. Tract. 2, cap. 3. In all the earlier specimens, "animal rationale" is placed between "Animal" and "Homo," as the proximum genus, divided into "mortale" and "immortale," in accordance with Porphyry's definition of man. We shall here observe also, that a summum genus can have no constitutive differences, which are represented at the side, though a summum genus may have properties.

as both "man" and "animal."[1] But it is evident from what has been said, that of those things which are predicated of a subject, both the name and the definition must be predicated of the subject, as "man" is predicated of "some certain man," as of a subject, and the name, at least, is predicated, for you will predicate "man" of "some certain man," and the

3. In predication the name and definition of the subject must be predicated.

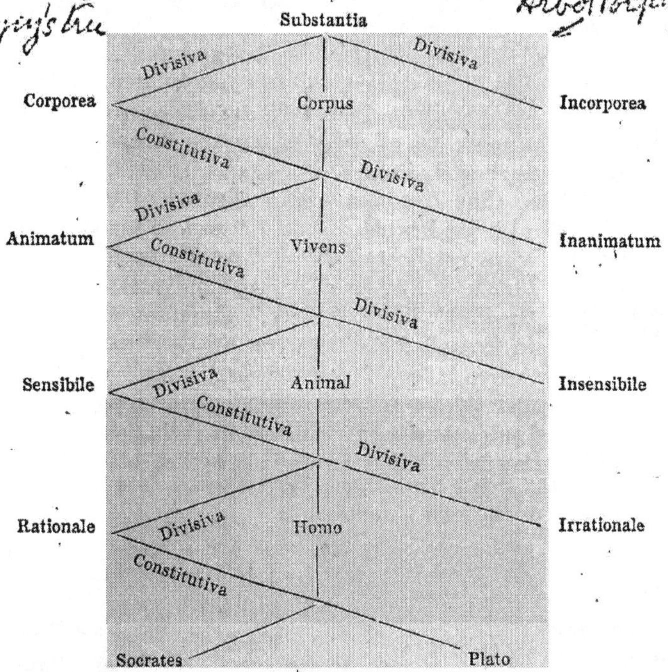

[1] For the method of predication, vide Huyshe, Aldrich, or Whately. Also compare the Topics iv. 2, Isagoge 2, Aquinas Opusc. 48, cap. 2. Genus and species are said "prædicari in quid," i. e. are expressed by a substantive; Property and Accident "in quale," or by an adjective. This whole chapter, brings forcibly to the mind, Butler's satirical burlesque of Hudibrastic acumen, in discovering

"Where entity and quiddity,
The ghosts of defunct bodies fly!"

Hudibras, Part i. Can. 1.

Though very necessary, the initiative processes of Logic, indeed present

"A kind of Babylonish dialect,
Which learned pedants much affect."

definition of man will be predicated of "some certain man," for "a certain man" is both "man" and "animal;" wherefore both the name and the definition will be predicated of a subject. But of things which are in a subject, for the most part, neither the name nor the definition is predicated of the subject, yet with some, there is nothing to prevent the name from being sometimes predicated of the subject, though the definition cannot be so; as "whiteness" being in a body, as in a subject, is predicated of the subject, (for the body is termed "white,") but the definition of "whiteness" can never be predicated of body. All other things, however, are either predicated of primary substances, as of subjects, or are inherent in them as in subjects;[1] this, indeed, is evident, from several obvious instances, thus "animal" is predicated of "man," and therefore is also predicated of some "certain man," for if it were predicated of no "man" particularly, neither could it be of "man" universally. Again, "colour" is in "body," therefore also is it in "some certain body," for if it were not in "some one" of bodies singularly, it could not be in "body" universally; so that all other things are either predicated of primary substances as of subjects, or are inherent in them as in subjects; if therefore the primal substances do not exist, it is impossible that any one of the rest should exist.

4. The contrary happens in the case of many inhesions.

5. The universal involves the particular.

6. Species more a substance than genus.

But of secondary substances, species is more substance than genus;[2] for it is nearer to the primary substance, and if any one explain what the primary substance is, he will explain it more clearly and appropriately by giving the species, rather than the genus; as a person defining "a certain man" would do so more clearly, by giving "man" than "animal," for the former is more the peculiarity of "a certain man," but the latter is more common. In like manner, whoever explains what "a certain tree" is, will define it in a more known and appropriate manner, by introducing "tree" than "plant." Besides the primary substances, because of their subjection to all other things, and these last being

7. Primary substances become subjects to all predicates;

[1] Plato, in the Philebus, observes, that a philosopher ought not to descend, below wholes, and common natures.

[2] Vide supra, note; also Metaph. lib. iv. and vi.

either predicated of them, or being in them, are for this reason, especially, termed substances. Yet the same relation as the primary substances bear to all other things, does species bear to genus, for species is subjected to genus, since genera are predicated of species, but species are not reciprocally predicated of genera, whence the species is rather substance than the genus.

hence their name.

8. Genus a predicate of species, but not *vice versâ*.

Of species themselves, however, as many as are not genera, are not more substance, one than another, for he will not give a more appropriate definition of "a certain man," who introduces "man," than he who introduces "horse," into the definition of "a certain horse:" in like manner of primary substances, one is not more substance than another, for "a certain man" is not more substance than a "certain ox." With reason therefore, after the first substances, of the rest, species and genera alone are termed secondary substances, since they alone declare the primary substances of the predicates; thus, if any one were to define what "a certain man" is, he would, by giving the species or the genus, define it appropriately, and will do so more clearly by introducing "man" than "animal;" but whatever else he may introduce, he will be introducing, in a manner, foreign to the purpose, as if he were to introduce "white," or "runs," or any thing else of the kind, so that with propriety of the others, these alone are termed substances. Moreover, the primary substances, because they are subject to all the rest, and all the others are predicated of, or exist in, these, are most properly termed substances, but the same relation which the primary substances bear to all other things, do the species and genera of the first substances bear to all the rest, since of these, are all the rest predicated, for you will say that "a certain man" is "a grammarian," and therefore you will call both "man" and "animal" "a grammarian," and in like manner of the rest.[1]

9. Infimæ species are equal in their not being substance.

10. Species and genera alone are secondary substances.

11. Equality of relation between cognate genera and species.

[1] Archytas adopts a different division of substance, into matter, form, and a composite of the two, and this division Aristotle shows in his Physics, and Metaphysics, and Physical Auscultation he knew, but does not employ it in this treatise, as not adapted for its subject matter, namely, logical discussion. Cf. Physica Ausc. lib. iii., and Metaph. lib. vi. and xi.

12. No substance in a subject. It is common however to every substance, not to be in a subject,[1] for neither is the primal substance in a subject, nor is it predicated of any; but of the secondary substances, that none of them is in a subject, is evident from this; "man" is predicated of "some certain" subject "man," but is not in a subject, for "man" is not in "a certain man." So also "animal" is predicated of "some certain" subject "man," but "animal" is not in "a certain man."

13. Of inhesives the name may be predicated of the subject, but not the definition. Moreover of those which are, in the subject, nothing prevents the name from being sometimes predicated of the subject, but that the definition should be predicated of it, is impossible. Of secondary substances however the definition and the name are both predicated of the subject, for you will predicate the definition of "a man" concerning "a certain man,"

14. The latter may be predicated of secondary substances. and likewise the definition of "animal," so that substance, may not be amongst the number, of those things which are in a subject.

15. Difference does not exist in subject. This however is not the peculiarity of substance, but difference also is of the number of those things not in a subject;[2] for "pedestrian" and "biped" are indeed predicated of "a man" as of a subject, but are not in a subject, for neither "biped" nor "pedestrian" is in "man." The definition also of difference is predicated of that, concerning which, difference is predicated, so that if "pedestrian" be predicated of "man," the definition also of "pedestrian" will be predicated of man, for "man" is "pedestrian."

16. Parts of substances are also substances. Nor let the parts of substances, being in wholes as in subjects, perplex us, so that we should at any time be compelled to say, that they are not substances; for in this manner,

[1] Simplicius observes that Aristotle discusses the things which substance has in common with the other predicaments; Iamblichus, what is common to it, and also its property and difference. Some may doubt how essence, will not be in a subject, as ideas according to Plato are, in intellect, yet these are neither as in a subject, but are as essence in another essence: Aristotle discusses this in the 12th book of the Metaphysics.

[2] Generic difference, it must be remembered, constitutes subaltern species—specific difference, forms the lowest species—the former difference is predicated of things different in species, the latter of things differing in number. In the scholastic theory, the properties of the summum genus were regarded as flowing from the simple substance, those of all subordinate classes, from the differentia. See Hill's Logic on the Predicables.

things would not be said to be in a subject, which are in any as parts. It happens indeed both to substances and to differences alike, that all things should be predicated of them univocally, for all the categories from them are predicated either in respect of individuals or of species, since from the primary substance there is no category, for it is predicated in respect of no subject. But of secondary substances, species indeed is predicated in respect of the individual, but genus in respect to species and to individuals; so also differences are predicated as to species and as to individuals. Again, the primary substances take the definition of species and of genera, and the species the definition of the genus, for as many things as are said of the predicate, so many also will be said of the subject, likewise both the species and the individuals accept the definition of the differences: those things at least were univocal, of which the name is common and the definition the same, so that all which arise from substances and differences are predicated univocally.

17. Difference and secondary substance predicated univocally.

18.

Nevertheless every substance appears to signify this particular thing:[1] as regards then the primary substances, it is unquestionably true that they signify a particular thing, for what is signified is individual, and one in number, but as regards the secondary substances, it appears in like manner that they signify this particular thing, by the figure of appellation, when any one says "man" or "animal," yet it is not truly so, but rather they signify a certain quality, for the sub-

19. All substance signifies some one thing.

20. Secondary substances sig-

[1] It was the opinion of Kant, as well as of Reid and Stewart, that in mind, as in body, substance and unity are not *presented* but *represented*, but what *the thing itself* is, which is the subject and owner of the several qualities, yet not identical with any one of them, can only be conceived, in as far as we can attain to any single conception of the τὸ ὂν—through its many modifications, which attainment is itself questionable. Vide some admirable remarks in Mansel's Prolego. Log. 277. Generally it suffices to retain the quaint form of the schools noticed above upon predication of genus and species. Vide Aldrich's Logic. Genus is a whole logically, but species metaphysically, or, as they may be better expressed, the first is Totum Universale, the second Totum Essentiale. Cf. Crakanthorpe Logica, lib. ii. cap. 5. Since writing the above, the striking illustration occurs to me, used by Lord Shaftesbury, of "the person left within, who has power to dispute the appearances, and redress, the imagination." Shaftesbury's Charac. vol. i. p. 325. The passage has more *sense* than, yet as much *sound* as, any of his Lordship's writing.

nify a certain "quale."

ject is not one, as the primary substance, but "man" and "animal" are predicated in respect of many. Neither do they signify simply a certain quality, as "white," for "white" signifies nothing else but a thing of a certain quality, but the species and the genus determine the quality, about the substance, for they signify what quality a certain substance possesses: still a wider limit is made by genus than by species, for whoever speaks of "animal," comprehends more than he who speaks of "man."

21. Primary substance admits no contrary.

It belongs also to substances that there is no contrary to them,[1] since what can be contrary to the primary substance, as to a certain "man," or to a certain "animal," for there is nothing contrary either at least to "man" or to "animal?" Now this is not the peculiarity of substance, but of many other things, as for instance of quantity; for there is no contrary to "two" cubits nor to "three" cubits, nor to "ten," nor to any thing of the kind, unless some one should say that "much" is contrary to "little," or "the great" to "the small;" but of definite quantities, none is contrary to the other.

22. Other instances.

23. Neither the greater nor less.

Substance, also, appears not to receive greater or less;[2] I mean, not that one substance is not, more or less, substance, than another, for it has been already said that it is, but that every substance is not said to be more or less, that very thing, that it is; as if the same substance be "man" he will not be more or less "man;" neither himself than himself, nor another "man" than another, for one "man" is not more "man" than another, as one "white thing" is more and less "white" than another, and one "beautiful" thing more and less "beautiful" than another, and "the same thing" more or less than "itself;" so a body being "white," is said to be more "white" now, than it was before, and if "warm" is said to be more or less "warm." Substance at least is not termed more or less substance, since "man" is not said to be more "man" now, than before, nor any

[1] This, says Simplicius, is doubted by some, and indeed in his Physics, lib. i., Aristotle apparently contradicts his own statement above by instancing Form as the contrary to Privation, both being substantial; but Form is but partly, substance, and partly, habit, and only in so much as it is the latter, is it contrary to Privation, not "quoad substantiam."

[2] This is true, discrete quantities being unchangeable, and definite in quantity.

one of such other things as are substances; hence substance is not capable of receiving the greater and the less.

24. Individually it can receive contraries, in which it differs from those which are not substances.

It appears however, to be especially the peculiarity of substance, that being one and the same in number, it can receive contraries, which no one can affirm of the rest which are not substances, as that being one in number, they are capable of contraries.[1] Thus "colour," which is one and the same in number, is not "white" and "black," neither the same action, also one in number, both bad and good; in like manner of other things as many as are not substances. But substance being one, and the same in number, can receive contraries, as "a certain man" being one and the same, is at one time, white, and at another, black, and warm and cold, and bad and good. In respect of none of the rest does such a thing appear, except some one should object, by saying, that a sentence and opinion are capable of receiving contraries, for the same sentence appears to be true and false; thus if the statement be true that "some one sits," when he stands up, this very same statement will be false. And in a similar manner in the matter of opinion, for if any one should truly opine that a certain person sits, when he rises up he will opine falsely, if he still holds the same opinion about him. Still, if any one, should even admit this, yet there is a difference in the mode. For some things in substances, being themselves changed, are capable of contraries, since cold, being made so, from hot, has changed, for it is changed in quality, and black from white, and good from bad: in like manner as to other things, each one of them receiving change is capable of contraries. The sentence indeed and the opinion remain themselves altogether immovable, but the thing being moved, a contrary is produced about them; the sentence indeed remains the same, that "some one sits," but the thing being moved, it becomes at one time, true, and at another, false. Likewise as to opinion,

25. Reply to objection by a reference to the mode.

26. Inherents in substances are, when changed, capable of contrariety.

Subject of change

[1] He does not mean that contraries exist in substance at one and the same time, as may be perceived from the examples he adduces. Archytas, according to Simplicius, admits the capability of contraries to be the peculiarity of substance; "thus vigilance is contrary to sleep, slowness to swiftness, disease to health, of all which, one and the same man, is capable." Simp. in Arist. Cat. Compare also Waitz, Organ. p. 291, Comment.

"A point is the principle of continuous quantity & the unity of discontinuous quantity" Aquinas

so that in this way, it will be the peculiarity of substance, to receive contraries according to the change in itself, but if any one admitted this, that a sentence and opinion can receive contraries, this would not be true. For the sentence and the opinion are not said to be capable of contraries in that they have received any thing, but, in that about something else, a passive quality has been produced, for in that a thing is, or is not, in this, is the sentence said to be true, or false, not in that itself, is capable of contraries.[1] In short, neither is a sentence nor an opinion moved by any thing, whence they cannot be capable of contraries, no passive quality being in them; substance at least, from the fact of itself receiving contraries, is said in this to be capable of contraries, for it receives disease and health, whiteness and blackness, and so long as it receives each of these, it is said to be capable of receiving contraries. Wherefore it will be the peculiarity of substance, that being the same, and one in number, according to change in itself, it is capable of receiving contraries; and concerning substance this may suffice.[2] Dec. 31. 19. Paper

27. Induction of passion in the example as to sentence and opinion.

CHAP. VI.—*Of Quantity.*[3]

1. Quantity two-fold, dis-

OF Quantity, one kind is discrete, and another continuous;[4] the one consists of parts, holding

[1] Simplicius alleges that certain Peripatetics asserted that matter itself was susceptible of πάθος. It must be remembered however that Aristotle's definition of πάθη (Rhet. lib. i.) is, that they are certain things added to substance, beyond its own nature. Vide Scholia ad Categorias, ed. Waitz, p. 32. Leip. 1844.

[2] The union between οὐσία and ὕλη is laid down in the treatise de Animâ, lib. ii. 1, sec. 2: the latter term was used by the schoolmen to signify the subject matter upon which any art was employed, in which sense, it was tantamount to primal substance.

[3] Some say that quantity, is considered in juxta-position with substance, because it subsists together with it, for after substance is admitted, it is necessary to inquire whether it is one or many; others, because among other motions, that which is according to quantity, viz. increase and diminution, is nearer to the notion of substance, viz. generation and corruption, than "alliation" is, which is a motion according to quality. Taylor. Vide ch. 8, and Sulpicius, concerning the nature of this last. See also, Arist. Phys. lib. iii. et v., also cf. Cat. ch. 14.

[4] Conf. Metaphy. lib. iv. cap. 13, Ποσὸν λέγεται τὸ διαιρετὸν εἰς ἐνυπάρχοντα, κ. τ. λ. The reader will do well to compare the above chapter, throughout, with that quoted from the Metaphysics, where these terms are all used equivocally.

crete and continuous; of parts occupying relative position, and the contrary.

position with respect to each other, but the other of parts, which have not that position. Discrete quantity is, as number and sentence, but continuous, as line, superficies, body, besides place and time. For, of the parts of number, there is no common term, by which its parts conjoin, as if five be a part of ten, five and five, conjoin at no common boundary, but are separated. Three, and seven, also conjoin at no common boundary, nor can you at all take a common limit of parts, in number, but they are always separated, whence number is of those things which are discrete. In like manner a sentence, for that a sentence is quantity is evident, since it is measured by a short and long syllable;[1] but I mean a sentence produced by the voice, as its parts concur at no common limit, for there is no common limit, at which the syllables concur, but each is distinct by itself. A line, on the contrary, is continuous, for you may take a common term, at which its parts meet, namely, a point, and of a superficies, a line, for the parts of a superficies coalesce in a certain common term. So also you can take a common term in respect of body, namely, a line, or a superficies, by which the parts of body are joined. Of the same sort are time and place, for the present time is joined both to the past and to the future. Again, place is of the number of continuous things, for the parts of a body occupy a certain place, which parts join at a certain common boundary, wherefore also the parts of place, which each part of the body occupies, join at the same boundary as the parts of the body, so that place will also be continuous, since its parts join at one common boundary.

2. Examples discrete.

1. Number.

2. Oratio.

3. Examples continuous.

1. A line.

2. A superficies.

3. Time and place.

Moreover, some things consist of parts, having position with respect to each other, but others of parts not having such position;[2] thus the parts of a line have relative position, for each of them lies

4. Relative position of some parts as to the above.

[1] Aristotle means by λόγος, a sentence subsisting in *voice*, not in intellect. Sulpic. He adds also, that Archytas, Athenodorus, and Ptolemy condemn the division of quantity into two kinds, and prefer that of number, magnitude, and momentum, but the reply is, that the last is a quality, the same as density.

[2] Plotinus, in his first book on the Genera of Being, says, if the continued, is quantity, discrete, cannot be; but he questions it as existing in

some where, and you can distinguish, and set out, where each lies, in a superficies, and to which part of the rest, it is joined. So also the parts of a superficies, have a certain position, for it may be in like manner pointed out where each lies, and what have relation to each other, and the parts of a solid, and of a place, in like manner. On the contrary, in respect of number, it is impossible for any one to show that its parts have any relative position, or that they are situated any where, or which of the parts are joined to each other. Nor as regards parts of time, for not one of the parts of time endures, but that which does not endure, how can it have any position? you would rather say, that they have a certain order, inasmuch as one part of time is former, but another latter. In the same manner is it with number, because one, is reckoned before two, and two, before three, and so it may have a certain order, but you can, by no means, assume, that it has position. A speech likewise, for none of its parts endures, but it has been spoken, and it is no longer possible to bring back what is spoken, so that there can be no position of its parts, since not one endures: some things therefore consist of parts having position, but others of those which have not position. What we have enumerated are alone properly termed quantities; all the rest being so denominated by accident, for looking to these, we call other things quantities, as whiteness is said to be much, because the superficies is great, and an action long, because of its time being long, and motion also, is termed, much. Yet each of these is not called a quantity by itself, for if a man should explain the quantity of an action, he will define it by time, describing it as yearly, or something of the sort; and if he were to explain the quantity of whiteness, he will define it by the superficies, for as the quantity of the superficies, so he would say is the quantity of the whiteness; whence the particulars we have mentioned are alone properly of themselves termed quantities, none of the rest being so of itself, but ac-

5. Parts have no relation in respect of number or time.

6. Oratio.

7. The above-named are the only proper quanta—all others reducible to these.—Examples.

the intellect, and confounds the distinction between order, in discrete, and position, in continued quantities. The point is touched upon also in lib. vi. of the Physics. Compare also ch. 12, on Priority, in the Categories, as to the relation in respect of number and time.

cording to accident. Again, nothing is contrary to quantity,[1] for in the definite it is clear there is nothing contrary, as to "two cubits" or to "three," or to "superficies," or to any thing of this kind, for there is no contrary to them; except indeed a man should allege that "much" was contrary to "little," or the "great" to the "small." Of these however, none is a quantity, but rather belongs to relatives, since nothing, itself by itself, is described as great or small, but from its being referred to something else. A mountain, for instance, is called "little," but a millet seed "large," from the fact of the one being greater, but the other less, in respect of things of the same nature, whence the relation is to something else, since if each were called "small" or "great" of itself, the mountain would never have been called "small," nor the seed "large." We say also that there are "many" men in a village, but "few" at Athens, although these last are more numerous, and "many" in a house, but "few" in a theatre, although there is a much larger number in the latter. Besides, "two cubits," "three," and every thing of the kind signify quantity, but "great" or "small" does not signify quantity, but rather relation, for the "great" and "small" are viewed in reference to something else, so as evidently to appear relatives. Whether however any one does, or does not, admit such things to be quantities, still there is no contrary to them, for to that which cannot of itself be assumed, but is referred to another, how can there be a contrary? Yet more, if "great" and "small" be contraries, it will happen, that the same thing, at the same time, receives contraries, and that the same things are contrary to themselves, for it happens that the same thing at the same time is both "great" and "small." Something in respect of this thing is "small," but the same, in reference to another, is "large," so that the same thing happens at the same time to be both "great" and "small," by which at the same moment it receives contraries. Nothing however appears to receive contraries simultaneously, as in the case of substance, for this indeed

8. Quantity, per se, has no contrary.

9. Reply to objection, founded upon the contrariety of great to small.

10.

11.

12. Simultaneous contrariety impossible.

[1] Ἰδιον τοῦ ποσοῦ ἀπέδωκαν τινες τὸ μηδὲν ἔχειν ἐναντίον, πρὸς ἀνατροπὴν δὲ τούτου οὐ χωρεῖ, διὰ τὸ προσεχῶς διδάξαι, ὅτι οὐδὲ τῇ οὐσίᾳ ἐστιν ἐναντιον.—Magent. Schol. ed. Waitz. Cf. Metaph. lib. ix. c. 4, 5, 6, and 7.

seems capable of contraries, yet no one is at the same time "sick" and "healthy," nor a thing "white" and "black" together, neither does any thing else receive contraries at one and the same time.

13\. It happens also, that the same things are contrary to themselves, since if the "great" be opposed to the "small," but the same thing at the same time be great and small, the same thing would be contrary to itself, but it is amongst the number of impossibilities, that the same thing should be contrary to itself, wherefore the great is not contrary to the small, nor the many to the few, so that even if some one should say that these do not belong to relatives, but to quantity, still they will have no contrary.

14\. The contrariety of quantity chiefly subsistent in space.

The contrariety however of quantity seems especially to subsist about place, since men admit "upward" to be contrary to "downward," calling the place toward the middle "downward," because there is the greatest distance from the middle, to the extremities of the world;[1] they appear also to deduce the definition of the other contraries from these, for they define contraries to be those things which, being of the same genus, are most distant from each other.

15\. Quantity is incapable of degree.

Nevertheless quantity does not appear capable of the greater and the less, as for instance "two cubits," for one thing is not more "two cubits" than another; neither in the case of number, since "three" or "five" are not said to be more than "three" or "five," neither "five" more "five" than "three" "three;" one time also is not said to be more "time" than another; in short, of none that I have mentioned is there said to be a greater or a less, wherefore quantity is not capable of the greater and less.

16\. But of equality and inequality.

Still it is the especial peculiarity of quantity to be called "equal" and "unequal,"[2] for each of the above-mentioned quantities is said to be

[1] The "upward" and "downward" do not signify place, but the predicament *where*, just as "yesterday" and "to-day" do not signify time, but the predicament *when*. Simplicius. Andronicus also assents to this. Compare the 4th book of Arist. Physics, where he defines place to be the boundary of that which it contains; the Pythagoreans, who in words agree with Aristotle, in effect differ most widely from him. Phys. lib. vi. and viii.

[2] This may be shown thus: Quantity, quoad se, is measurable: but the measurable can be measured by the same, or by more or by fewer measures; in the first case therefore, equality, in the second, inequality,

"equal" and "unequal," thus body is called "equal" and "unequal," and number, and time, are predicated of as "equal" and "unequal;" likewise in the case of the rest enumerated, each one is denominated "equal" and "unequal." Of the remainder, on the contrary, such as are not quantities, do not altogether appear to be called "equal" and "unequal," as for instance, disposition is not termed entirely "equal" and "unequal," but rather "similar" and "dissimilar;" and whiteness is not altogether "equal" and "unequal," but rather "similar" and "dissimilar;" hence the peculiarity of quantity will especially consist in its being termed "equal" and "unequal."

CHAP. VII.—*Of Relatives.*[1]

1. Definition of relatives, and instances.

SUCH things are termed "relatives," which are said to be what they are, from belonging to other things, or in whatever other way they may be referred to something else; thus "the greater" is said to be what it is in reference to another thing, for it is called greater than something; and "the double" is called what it is in reference to something else, for it is said to be double a certain thing; and similarly as to other things of this kind. Such as these are of the number of relatives, as habit,[2] disposition, sense, knowledge, position, for all these specified are said to be what they are, from belonging to others, or however else they are referrible to another, and they are nothing else; for habit is said to be the habit of some one, knowledge the knowledge of something, position the position of somewhat, and so the rest. Relatives, therefore, are such things, as are said to be what they are, from belonging to others, or which may somehow be referred to another; as a mountain is called "great" in comparison with another, for the mountain is called "great" in relation to something, and "like" is said to be like somewhat, and other things of this

subsists. Archytas divides the equal and unequal triply, according to the three differences of quantity. Taylor.

[1] Compare the divisions of relation given in the Metaphys. lib. iv. c. 15.

[2] This must not be confounded with the *action* of habit alluded to in b. ii. c. 2, of the Ethics. Plotinus doubts whether habit in things related be other than a mere name. This chapter is a thorough specimen of Aristotelian prolixity, of which, by a slight change in the Horatian line, we may say,—

"Et facundia deseret hunc et lucidus ordo." Ars Poet. 41.

sort, are similarly spoken of, in relation to something. Reclining, station, sitting, are nevertheless certain positions, and position is a relative; but to recline, to stand, or to sit, are not themselves positions, but are paronymously denominated from the above-named positions.

2. Some relatives admit contrariety.

Yet there is contrariety in relatives, as virtue is contrary to vice, each of them being relative, and knowledge to ignorance;[1] but contrariety is not inherent in all relatives, since there is nothing contrary to double, nor to triple, nor to any thing of the sort.

3. Also degree.

Relatives appear, notwithstanding, to receive the more and the less, for the like and the unlike are said to be so, more and less, and the equal and the unequal are so called, more and less, each of them being a relative, for the similar is said to be similar to something, and the unequal, unequal to something.

4. Exceptions.

Not that all relatives admit of the more and less, for double is not called more and less double, nor any such thing, but all relatives are styled so by reciprocity,

5. Relatives reciprocally convertible.

as the servant is said to be servant of the master, and the master, master of the servant; and the double, double of the half, also the half, half of the double, and the greater, greater than the less, and the less, less than the greater. In like manner it happens as to other things, except that sometimes they differ in diction by case, as knowledge is said to be the knowledge of something knowable, and what is knowable is knowable by knowledge: sense also is the sense of the sensible, and the sensible is sensible by sense.

6. Except where the attribution of the relation is erroneous.

Sometimes indeed they appear not to reciprocate, if that be not appropriately attributed to which relation is made, but here he who attributes errs; for instance, a wing of a bird, if it be attributed to the bird, does not reciprocate, for the first is not appropriately

[1] These are relatives, according to their genus, which is habit in this case. It may, however, be inquired how Aristotle afterwards ranks science, virtue, and their opposites, amongst qualities? Because the same thing, as he shows throughout, according to its connexion with different relations, occupies often a different predicament. Hence, also, contrariety is only partly inherent in relatives, since they derive their contrariety *from* the contrariety of their predicaments: thus in habit or in quality they receive contrariety, but not in the double or triple, because quantity does not receive it. To admit contraries therefore, is not the peculiarity of relatives, since contrariety is not in all relatives, nor in them alone.

attributed, namely "wing" to "bird," since "wing" is not predicated of it so far as it is "bird," but so far as it is "winged," as there are wings of many other things which are not birds, so that if it were appropriately attributed, it would also reciprocate; as "wing" is the wing of "a winged creature," and "the winged creature" is "winged" by the "wing." It is sometimes necessary perhaps even to invent a name,[1] if there be none at hand, for that to which it may be properly applied: e. g. if a rudder be attributed to a ship, it is not properly so attributed, for a rudder is not predicated of a ship so far as it is "ship," since there are ships without rudders; hence they do not reciprocate, inasmuch as a ship is not said to be the ship of a rudder. The attribution will perhaps be more appropriate, if it were attributed thus, a rudder is the rudder of something ruddered, or in some other way, since a name is not assigned; a reciprocity also occurs, if it is appropriately attributed, for what is ruddered is ruddered by a rudder. So also in other things; the head, for example, will be more appropriately attributed to something headed, than to animal, for a thing has not a head, so far as it is an animal, since there are many animals which have not a head.

7. Necessity of sometimes inventing a name for the relata.

Thus any one may easily assume those things to which names are not given, if from those which are first, he assigns names to those others also, with which they reciprocate,[2] as in the cases adduced, "winged" from "wing," and "ruddered" from "rudder."

8. Rule for nomination of reciprocals.

All relatives therefore, if they be properly attributed, are referred to reciprocals, since if they are referred to something casual, and not to that to which they relate, they will not reciprocate. I mean, that neither will any one of those things which are admitted to be referrible to reciprocals, reciprocate, even though names be assigned to them, if the thing be attributed to something accidental, and not to that to which it has relation: for ex-

9. All proper relatives reciprocate.

[1] Conf. Top. i. 5, 1, also Anal. Post, ii. 7, 2. Definable objects are of two classes, producing a corresponding variety in the form of definition. 1st, Attributes, which include things belonging to every other category but that of substance. 2nd, Substances, which not existing in a subject, but per se, must be *assumed* before their attributes or relatives can be demonstrated. The definition of an attribute is to be found in its cause.

[2] See Blair's Lectures on Rhetoric, under Figurative Language.

ample, a servant, if he be not attributed as the servant of a master, but of a man, of a biped, or any thing else of the kind, will not reciprocate, for the attribution is not appropriate. If however that, to which something is referred, be appropriately attributed, every thing else accidental being taken away, and this thing alone being left, to which it is appropriately attributed, it may always be referred to it, as "a servant," if he is referred to "a master," every thing else accidental to the master being left out of the question, (as the being "a biped," and "capable of knowledge," and that he is "a man,") and his being "a master" alone, left, here the "servant" will always be referred to him, for a "servant" is said to be the servant of a "master." If again, on the other hand, that to which it is at any time referred is not appropriately attributed, other things being taken away, and that alone left, to which it is attributed, in this case it will not be referred to it. For let a "servant" be referred to "man," and a "wing" to "bird," and let the being "a master" be taken away from "man," the servant will no longer refer to man, since "master" not existing, neither does "servant" exist. So also let "being winged" be taken away from "bird," and "wing" will no longer be amongst relatives, for what is "winged" not existing, neither will "wing" be the wing of any thing. Hence it is necessary to attribute that, to which a thing is appropriately referred, and if indeed a name be already given to it, the application is easy; but if no name be assigned, it is perhaps necessary to invent one; but being thus attributed, it is clear that all relatives are referred to reciprocals.

10. So that the existence of one depends upon the other. Vide infra, 13.

Naturally, relatives appear simultaneous, and this is true of the generality of them, for "double" and "half" are simultaneous, and "half" existing, "double" exists, and "a master" existing, the "servant" is, and the "servant" existing, the "master" is, and other things are also like these. These also are mutually subversive, for if there is no "double" there is no "half," and no "half" there is no "double"; likewise as to other things of the same kind. It does not however appear to be true of all relatives, that they are by nature simultaneous, for the object of "science" may appear to be prior to "science," since for the most part we derive

11. Relatives by nature simultaneous, with some exceptions.

12. As science and its object, apparently.

science from things pre-existing, as in few things, if even in any, do we see science and its object originating together. Moreover, the object of science being subverted, co-subverts the science, but science being subverted, does not co-subvert the object of science, for there being no object of science, science itself becomes non-existent, (since there will be no longer a science of any thing);[1] but on the contrary, though science does not exist, there is nothing to prevent the object of science existing. Thus the quadrature of the circle, if it be an object of scientific knowledge, the science of it does not yet exist, though it is itself an object of science:[2] again, "animal" being taken away, there will not be "science," but still it is possible for many objects of science to be. Likewise also do things pertaining to sense subsist, since the sensible seems to be prior to the sense, as the sensible being subverted co-subverts sense, but sense does not co-subvert the sensible. For the senses are conversant with body, and are in body, but the sensible being subverted, body also is subverted, (since body is of the number of sensibles,) and body not existing, sense also is subverted, so that the sensible co-subverts sense. Sense on the other hand does not co-subvert the sensible, since if animal were subverted, sense indeed would be subverted, but yet

13. Sometimes, but not always, co-subversive.

14. Instance of things pertaining to sense.

[1] This is self-evident, as also that there are some few things in which science is the same as its object, e. g. things without matter are certainly present at the same time as the intellectual science which abides in energy. On the contrary, in the other case, as Simplicius observes, if indolence reject the knowledge of things, yet the things themselves remain, as music, etc. Vide also Brewer's Introduction to the Ethics, book v., as to the position occupied by ἐπιστήμη in the scheme of the five habits. It will thence appear second, and correspond to deduction from certain principles, the latter being a subdivision of abstract truth, thus:

Abstract truth

Principles νοῦς	Deductions from Principles ἐπιστήμη

together | σοφία.

[2] Aristotle selects this instance, as the quadrature of the circle does not appear from this, to have been known in his time, but Iamblichus asserts that it was known to the Pythagoreans, and Sextus Pythagoricus received it by succession. Archimedes is stated to have discovered the quadrature of the circle by a line called the line of Nicomedes: he himself styled it the quadratrix.

relative seems to apply to every category.

the sensible will remain; such for instance as "body," "warm," "sweet," "bitter," and every thing else which is sensible. Besides, "sense" is produced simultaneously with what is "sensitive," for at one and the same time "animal" and "sense" are produced, but the "sensible" is prior in existence to "animal" or "sense," for fire and water, and such things as animal consists of, are altogether prior to the existence of animal or sense, so that the sensible will appear to be antecedent to sense.

15. Primary substance has no relation.

It is doubtful however whether no substance is among the number of relatives, as seems to be the case, or whether this happens in certain second substances; for it is true in first substances, since neither the wholes, nor the parts, of first substances are relative. "A certain man" is not said to be a certain man of something, nor "a certain ox" said to be a certain ox of something; and so also with respect to the parts, for a "certain hand" is not said to be *a certain* hand of some one, but *the* hand of some one; and some head is not said to be *a certain* head of some one, but *the* head of some one, and in most secondary substances the like occurs. Thus man is not said to be the man of some one, nor an ox the ox of some one, nor the wood the wood of some one, but they are said to be the possession of some one; in such things therefore, it is evident, that they are not included amongst relatives.

16. But some secondary substances seem to possess relation, but the question is solved by an analysis of the definition of τῶν πρός τι.

In the case of some secondary substances there is a doubt, as "head," is said to be the head of some one, and "hand," the hand of some one, and in like manner, every such thing, so that these may appear amongst the number of relatives. If then the definition of relatives has been sufficiently framed, it is either a matter of difficulty, or of impossibility, to show that no substance is relative;[1] but if

[1] Plato's favourite method of definition, which however was rejected by Speusippus, was to take a wide genus, and by the addition of successive differentiæ, to arrive at a complex notion, co-extensive with the desired definition. Aristotle, on the other hand, to discover definition, employed the inductive method, (he does not name this however,) which consisted in examining the several individuals, of which the term to be defined is predicable, and observing what they had in common. This will apply to relatives and co-relatives equally, and hence we perceive that, properly speaking, all definition is an inquiry into attributes. Every substance definable must be a species, every attribute a property. Vide Scholia. Edinburgh Review, No. cxv. p. 236. Pacius on Anal. Post, 11, 13, 21.

the definition has not been sufficiently framed, but those things are relatives, whose substance is the same, as consists with a relation, after a certain manner, to a certain thing; somewhat, perhaps, in reply to this, may be stated. The former definition, however, concurs with all relatives, yet it is not the same thing, that their being, consists in relation, and that being what they are, they are predicated of other things. Hence it is clear, that he who knows any one relative, definitely, will also know what it is referred to, definitely. Wherefore also from this it is apparent, that if one knows this particular thing to be among relatives, and if the substance of relatives is the same, as subsisting in a certain manner, with reference to something, he will also know that, with reference to which, this particular thing, after a certain manner, subsists; for if, in short, he were ignorant of that, with reference to which, this particular thing, after a certain manner, subsists, neither would he know, whether it subsists, after a certain manner, with reference to something.

17. One relative being known, the correlative can be known.

18. Singulars.

And in singulars, indeed, this is evident; for if any one knows definitely, that this thing is "double," he will also forthwith know that, definitely, of which it is the double, since if he knows not that it is the double, of something definite, neither will he know that it is "double," at all. So again, if a man knows this thing, to be more beautiful than something else, he must straightway and definitely know that, than which, it is more beautiful. Wherefore, he will not indefinitely know, that this, is better, than that which is worse, for such is opinion and not science, since he will not accurately know that it is better than something worse, as it may so happen that there is nothing worse than it, whence it is necessarily evident, that whoever definitely knows any relative, also definitely knows that, to which it is referred.

19. The converse true of secondary substances.

It is possible, notwithstanding, to know definitely what the head, and the hand, and every thing of the sort are, which are substances; but it is not necessary to know that to which they are referred, since it is not necessary definitely to know whose, is the head, or whose, is the hand; thus these will not be relatives, but if these be not relatives, we may truly affirm no substance to be among relatives. It is, perhaps, difficult for a man to assert assuredly any thing of such matters, who has not frequently considered them, yet to have submitted each of them to inquiry, is not without its use.[1]

CHAP. VIII.—*Of the Quale and of Quality.*[2]

1. Quality and its species; the latter of four kinds. 1st, Habit and disposition—these explained.

By quality, I mean that, according to which, certain things, are said to be, what they are. Quality, however, is among those things which are predicated multifariously; hence one species of quality is called "habit" and "disposition," but habit, differs from disposition, in that it is a thing more lasting and stable.[3] Of this kind too, are both the sciences and the virtues,[4] for science appears to rank among those things, which continue more stable, and are hardly removed, even when science is but moderately attained, unless some great change should occur from disease, or from something of the sort; so also virtue, as justice, temperance, and so forth, does not appear capable of being moved or changed with facility. But those are termed dispositions, which are easily moved and quickly changed, as heat, cold, disease, health, and such things; or a man is disposed, after a manner, according to these, but is rapidly changed, from hot becoming cold, and from health passing to disease, and in like manner as to other things, unless some one of these qualities has, from

[1] Cf. Metaph. lib. iv. c. 15.

[2] Ποιότης. Def. "That which imparts what is apparent in matter, and what is the object of sense." Taylor's Explanation of Aristotelian Terms. See also Metaphys. lib. iv. c. 14, 19, and 20, Leip. The distinction in the text has been remarked upon, as exemplifying Aristotle's passion for definition, but it would be more correct to remember that it was perhaps less his inclination than his judgment, which induced him to lay down strict notions of verbal definition primarily, knowing that the thing signified, or idea, could never hold its proper position in the mind, if any doubt existed as to the meaning of the term or verbal symbol of it, ab origine. It is a great pity that modern controversialists so frequently neglect this.

[3] Cf. Ethics, book ii. ch. 5, and book ii. ch. 1. In the latter place, Aristotle shows that moral virtue arises from habit, in opposition to Plato, who taught that the virtues were not produced by learning or nature, but were divinely bestowed. Aristotle's opinion resembled Locke's, in the denial of innate ideas, the soul having nothing within it but inclination, τὸ πεφυκὸς. The student will profitably refer here to Bishop Butler's Analogy, on the growth of mental habits. Anal. part i. ch. 5. Bohn's Stand. Lib.

[4] So Cicero, de Off. lib. iii., connects these two, "temperantia est scientia." See also Montaigne's Essays, ch. xl. b. i., and ch. ii. b. iii.

length of time, become natural, immovable, or at least difficult to be moved, in which case we may term it a habit. But it is evident that those ought to be called habits, which are more lasting, and are with greater difficulty removed, for those persons who do not very much retain the dogmas of science, but are easily moved, are said not to possess a scientific habit, although they are in some manner disposed as to science, either worse or better ; so that habit differs from disposition in the one being easily removed, but the former is more lasting, and less easily removed. Habits are dispositions also,[1] but dispositions not necessarily habits, for those who have habits are also, after a manner, disposed according to them, but those who are disposed are not altogether possessed of the habit.

2nd species of quality, that which comprehends the faculties.

Another kind of quality is, that, according to which, we say that men are prone to pugilism, or to the course, or to health, or to disease, in short, whatever things are spoken of according to natural power, or weakness ; for each of these is not denominated from being disposed after a certain manner, but from having a natural power or inability of doing something easily, or of not suffering ; thus, men are called pugilistic, or fitted for the course, not from being disposed after a certain manner, but from possessing a natural power of doing something easily. Again, they are said to be healthy, from possessing a natural power of not suffering easily from accidents, but to be diseased, from possessing a natural incapacity to resist suffering easily from accidents : similarly to these, do hard and soft subsist, for that is called "hard" which possesses the power of not being easily divided, but "soft," that which has an impotence as to this same thing.

3rd, Passive qualities.

The third kind of quality consists of passive qualities and passions, and such are sweetness, bitter-

[1] The Ἦθος signifies the habitual disposition or "humour," as in Every Man out of his Humour, by Ben Jonson.

"When some one peculiar quality
Doth so possess a man, that it doth draw
All his affects, his spirits, and his powers,
In their conflictions, all to run one way—
This may be truly said to be a humour."

Vide Aristotle's Rhetoric, (Bohn's Class. Lib.). And again, Coriolanus, act iii. scene 2, —Away my disposition, and possess me
Some harlot's spirit!

Or, act iii. sc. 1, "Men: His *nature*, is too noble for the world," etc.

ness, sourness, and all their affinities, besides warmth, and coldness, and whiteness, and blackness. Now that these are qualities, is evident from their recipients being called from them, "qualia,"[1] as honey from receiving sweetness, is said to be sweet, and the body white, from receiving whiteness; in like manner in other things. They are called passive qualities,[2] not from the recipients of the qualities suffering any thing, for neither is honey said to be sweet from suffering any thing, nor any thing else of such a kind. In like manner to these are heat and cold called passive qualities, not from the recipients themselves suffering any thing, but because each of the above-mentioned qualities produces passion in the senses, they are denominated passive qualities; for as sweetness, produces a certain passion in the taste, and warmth, in the touch, so also do the rest. Whiteness, and blackness, and other colours are, on the contrary, not called passive qualities in the same manner with the above-mentioned, but from themselves being produced from passion; for that many changes of colours spring from passion is evident, since when a man blushes he becomes red, and when frightened, pale, and so every thing of this sort. Whence also if a man naturally suffers a passion of this nature, he will probably have a similar colour, since the disposition which is now produced about the body when he blushes, may also be produced in the natural constitution, so as that a similar colour should naturally arise. Whatever such symptoms then originate from certain passions diffi-

1. Exception in the case of colours.

[1] Simplicius doubts whether the same thing is signified by quale, and quality: probably the latter signifies the peculiarity itself, but quale that which participates in the peculiarity, as in the examples given above. As to the term "quality," Plato in his Theætetus insinuates that he was the author of it, and indeed some ancient philosophers, as Antisthenes, subverted certain qualities, and allowed only the subsistence of qualia, which they deemed incorporeal. The Stoics, on the contrary, thought the qualities of incorporeal natures incorporeal, and of bodies, corporeal. Simplicius defines qualities—"powers, active, yet not so, primarily, nor alone."

[2] It may perhaps seem strange that Aristotle distinguishes passions and passive qualities by the same characteristics as he has before used about habit and disposition; but it may be replied, that here he considers the passions and passive qualities which by nature are easily or hardly removed. Heat, so far as it disposes a subject, is a disposition; so far as that disposition is permanent, is a habit; if it be superficially effected by an agent, it is called a passion, and so far as the passion is produced permanently and intrinsically, it is called passive quality. Taylor.

cult to be removed and permanent are called passive qualities. For whether in the natural constitution, paleness, or blackness, be produced, they are called qualities, (for according to them we are called "quales;") or whether through long disease or heat, or any such thing, paleness or blackness happens, neither are easily removed, or even remain through life, these are called qualities, for in like manner, we are called "quales" in respect of them. Notwithstanding, such as are produced from things easily dissolved, and quickly restored, are called passions,[1] and not qualities, for men are not called "quales" in respect of them, since neither is he who blushes, in consequence of being ashamed, called red, nor he who turns pale, from fear, called pale, they are rather said to have suffered something, so that such things are called passions, but not qualities. Like these also are passive qualities, and passions denominated in the soul. For such things as supervene immediately upon birth from certain passions difficult of removal, are called qualities; as insanity, anger, and such things, for men according to these are said to be "quales," that is, wrathful and insane. So also as many other mutations as are not natural, but arise from certain other symptoms, and are with difficulty removed, or even altogether immovable, such are qualities, for men are called "quales" in respect of them. Those which, on the other hand, arise from things easily and rapidly restored, are called passions, as for instance, where one being vexed becomes more wrathful, for he is not called wrathful who is more wrathful in a passion of this kind, but rather he is said to have suffered something, whence such things are called passions, but not qualities.[2]

2. There may be πάθη.

3. Also affections of the soul.

The fourth kind of quality is figure and the form, which is about every thing, besides rectitude and curvature, and whatever is like them, for according to each of these a thing is called "quale." Thus a triangle or a square is said to be a thing of a certain quality, also a straight line or a curve, and every thing is said to be "quale" according to form. The rare and the dense, the rough and the smooth, may appear to signify a certain quality,

4th species of quality—form and figure.

Tupper 299

[1] Cf. Ethics, b. ii. ch. 5; also Metaphys. lib. iv. ch. 21; where the same examples of inanimate objects are given.

[2] Ethics, book ix. ch. 8. The being loved is like something passive.

but probably these are foreign from the division of quality, as each appears rather to denote a certain position of parts. For a thing is said to be "dense," from having its parts near each other, but "rare," from their being distant from each other, and "smooth," from its parts lying in some respect in a right line, but "rough," from this part, rising, and the other, falling.

5. Things called qualia paronymously from these qualities. There may perhaps appear to be some other mode of quality, but those we have enumerated are most commonly called so.

The above-named therefore are qualities, but "qualia" are things denominated paronymously according to them, or in some other manner from them; most indeed and nearly all of them are called paronymously,[1] as "a white man" from "whiteness," "a grammarian" from "grammar," a "just man" from "justice," and similarly of the rest. Still in some, from no names having been given to the qualities, it is impossible that they should be called paronymously from them; for instance, a "racer" or "pugilist," so called from natural power, is paronymously denominated from no quality, since names are not given to those powers after which these men are called "quales," as they are given to sciences, according to which men are said to be pugilists or wrestlers from disposition, for there is said to be a pugilistic and palæstric science, from which those disposed to them are paronymously denominated "quales." Sometimes however, the name being assigned, that which is called "quale" according to it, is not denominated paronymously, as from virtue, a man is called worthy, for he is called worthy, from possessing virtue, but not paronymously from virtue; this however does not often happen, wherefore those things are called "qualia," which are paronymously denominated from the above-mentioned qualities, or which are in some other manner termed from them.[2]

[1] Vide supra, Cat. i. Massinger's employment, of the very word, we are now discussing, presents a peculiar difficulty, in establishing the paronymous or denominative relation. In the Roman Actor, act i. scene 3, and also in the Picture, act ii. scene 1, the word quality is limited to actors and their profession. See Gifford's notes on Massinger. In fact, most of our ancient dramatists confined the word chiefly to histrionic performers.

[2] The name "conjugata" is more properly applied to derivatives from the same primitive, as sapiens, sapienter, sapientia; the σύστοιχα of Aristotle. Cf. Topics ii. 9, 1. Cic. Top. c. iii.

In quality, there is also contrariety,[1] as justice is contrary to injustice, and whiteness to blackness, and the like; also those things which subsist according to them are termed qualia, as the unjust to the just, and the white to the black. This however does not happen in all cases, for to the yellow, or the pale, or such like colours, though they are qualities, there is no contrary.[2] Besides, if one contrary be a quality, the other, will also be a quality, and this is evident to any one considering the other categories. For instance, if justice be contrary to injustice, and justice be a quality, then injustice will also be a quality, for none of the other categories accords with injustice, neither quantity, nor relation, nor where, nor in short any thing of the kind, except quality, and the like also happens as to quality in the other contraries.

6. Quality sometimes susceptible of contrariety.

7. If one contrary be a quale the other will be a quale.

Qualia also admit the more and the less,[3] as one thing is said to be more or less "white" than another, and one more and less "just" than another; the same thing also itself admits accession, for what is "white," can become more, "white." This however, does not happen with all, but with most things, for some one may doubt whether justice, can be said to be more or less justice, and so also in other dispositions, since some doubt about such, and assert that justice cannot altogether be called more and less, than justice, nor health than health, but they say, that one man has less health, than another, and one person less justice, than another, and so also of the grammatical and other dispositions. Still the things which are denominated according to these, do without question admit the more and the less, for one man is said

8. It can also admit degree, but not always.

[1] See below, Cat. xi. 5.

[2] *Repugnance* is not synonymous with *contrariety*, e. g. red and blue are repugnant, but not opposed. Archytas says, "Certain contraries are conjoined to quality, as if it received a certain contrariety and privation."

[3] Here he evidently means qualities by qualia, as the examples indicate. There were four opinions entertained, upon the admission by qualia, of degree. Plotinus, and the Platonists, asserted that all qualia, and qualities alike, received the greater and the less; others, limited intension, and remission, to the participants; the Stoics avowed that the virtues are incapable of either; and the fourth opinion, which Porphyry opposes, allows degree, to material, but denies it, to immaterial, and self-subsistent, qualities. Vide Simp. in Catego. Iamb. Opera. Aristotle, below, seems to refer to the second, of these opinions.

to be more grammatical, than another, and more healthy, and more just, and similarly in other things. Triangle and square appear nevertheless incapable of the more, as also every other figure, since those things which receive the definition of a triangle, and of a circle, are all alike triangles or circles, but of things which do not receive the same definition, none can be said to be more such, than another, as a square, is not more a circle, than an oblong, for neither of them admits the definition of the circle. In a word, unless both receive the definition of the thing propounded, one cannot be said to be more so and so than another, wherefore all qualities do not admit the more and the less.

Form incapable of degree. (Cf. Whately, b. ii. c. 5, sec. 6.)

9. It is the property of quality that similitude is predicated in respect of it.

Of the above-mentioned particulars then, no one is peculiar to quality, but things are said to be similar, and dissimilar, in respect of qualities alone, for one thing is not like another in respect of any thing else, than so far as it is quale, so that it will be peculiar to quality, that the like and the unlike should be termed so in respect of it.[1]

10. Reply to objection—that habit and disposition are reckoned amongst relatives as well as amongst qualities.

Yet we need not be disturbed lest any one should say that proposing to speak of quality, we co-enumerate many things which are relatives, for we said that habits and dispositions are among the number of relatives, and nearly in all such things the genera are called relatives, but not one of the singulars. Science, for example, although it is a genus, is said to be what it is, with respect to something else, for it is said to be the science of a certain thing, but of singulars no one is said to be what it is, with reference to something else as neither grammar is said to be the grammar of something nor music the music of something. But even perhaps these are called relatives, according to genus, as grammar is said to be the science of something, not the grammar of something and music the science of something, not the music of some-

[1] If impression and character produce similitude, and quality consist in character, it will justly have its peculiarity according to the similar and dissimilar. Archytas observes, "The peculiarity of quality is the similar and the dissimilar; for we say that all those things are similar in colour which have the same colour, and the same idea of character but those are dissimilar which subsist in a contrary manner."

thing; so that singulars are not of the number of relatives. Still, we are called quales from singulars,[1] for these we possess, as we are called scientific from possessing certain singular sciences; so that these may be singular qualities, according to which we are sometimes denominated quales, but they are not relatives; besides, if the same thing should happen to be both a particular quality and a relative, there is no absurdity in its enumeration under both genera.

11. Singulars not included amongst relatives. (Cf. Hill's Logic, de Divisione.)

CHAP. IX. *Of Action, Passion, and the other categories of Position: When: Where: and Possession.*

ACTION and Passion admit contrariety, and the more and the less, for to make warm, is contrary to making cold; to be warm, contrary to the being cold, to be pleased, contrary to being grieved; so that they admit contrariety. They are also capable of the more and the less, for it is possible to heat, more and less, to be heated, more and less, and to be grieved, more and less; wherefore, to act, and to suffer, admit the more and less, and so much may be said of these. But we have spoken of *the being situated* in our treatment of relatives,[2] to the effect that it is paronymously denominated, from positions: as regards the other categories, when, where, and to have, nothing else is said of them, than what was

1. Action and Passion admit contrariety and degree.

2. Recapitulation of the other categories.

[1] ταῖς καθ' ἕκαστα, etc. It may be useful here to give a general definition of the several meanings applied by Aristotle to peculiar uses of the preposition as regards relative action and relation. Δι' ὁ, on account of which, then signifies—the final cause; δι' οὗ through which—the instrumental cause; ἐξ οὗ or ἐν ᾧ, from or in which—the material cause; καθ' ὁ—according to which—form is thus denominated; πρὸς ὅ, with relation to which—or the paradeigmatic cause; and ὑφ' οὗ, by which—the demiurgic or fabricative cause. Cf. Top. lib. iv. c. 15, et seq. Taylor makes one continual mistake in the translation of καθ' ἕκαστα, by rendering it "particular," whereas the latter is "ἐν μερει." Buhle, on the contrary, is correct in this translation throughout.

[2] Aristotle here refers the reader to the category of relation, but as regards the opinion entertained of the remaining categories, Porphyry and Iamblichus consider them as accessorial relatives; e. g. "When" and "where" are not, per se, place and time, but when these two latter exist primarily, the former accede to them. Thus also "having" signifies something distinct from the existing thing, at the same time that it exists with it. Upon the reduction of the latter six categories to relation, see Hamilton on Reid, p. 688; also St. Hilaire's Translation, Preface, p. 68, et seq.

mentioned at first, because they are evident; e.g. that "to have," signifies to be shod, to be armed; "where," as in the Lycæum, in the Forum, and the rest which are spoken of these. Of the proposed genera therefore, sufficient has been stated.

CHAP. X.—*Of Opposites.*[1] 255

1. Opposites are of four kinds.

WE must now speak of opposites, in how many ways opposition takes place. One thing then is said to be opposed to another in four ways, either as relative, or as contrary, or as privation and habit, or as affirmation and negation. Thus speaking summarily, each thing of this kind is opposed, relatively, as "the double" to "the half," contrarily, as "evil" to "good," privatively and habitually, as "blindness" and "sight," affirmatively and negatively, as "he sits," "he does not sit."

1. Relative opposition.

Whatever things then are relatively opposed, are said to be what they are with reference to opposites, or are in some manner referred to them, as "the double of the half," is said to be what it is, with reference to something else, for it is said to be the double of something; and "knowledge" is opposed relatively to the object of knowledge, and is said, to be what it is, in reference to what may be known, and what may be known, is said to be what it is, in reference to an opposite, namely, "knowledge," for "the object of knowledge" is said to be so, to something, namely, to "knowledge."

[1] For a brief exposition of this chapter, the reader is referred to the nature and laws of logical opposition in necessary, impossible, and contingent matter, given in Aldrich, Huyshe, Whately, Hill, and Mansel. It will be remembered however that he here speaks of the opposition of *terms*, the rules for the opposition of *propositions* being more especially considered in the Interpretation: still a reference to that treatise, as well as to the authors cited above, will be useful, as elucidating the grounds on which *all* logical opposition is founded. Archytas (says Simplicius) does not omit, but seems to have more accurately explained the differences of contraries adduced by Aristotle. He says: Of contraries, some are in the genera of genera, as good and evil, the first being the genus of the virtues, the second of the vices: some again in the genera of species, as virtue to vice, the first being the genus of prudence, temperance, etc.; the other of imprudence, intemperance: lastly, some in species, as fortitude to timidity, etc.: but he adds, "there is nothing to prevent the contraries of genera being reduced under one genus, as good and evil under quality."

Things therefore relatively opposed are said to be, what they are, with reference to opposites, or in whatever manner, they are referrible to each other, but those which are opposed as contraries, are by no means, said to be what they are, with reference to each other, but are said to be contrary to each other, for neither is "good" said to be the "good" of "evil," but the contrary of evil, nor is "white," denominated the "white" of "black," but its contrary, so that these oppositions differ from each other. Such contraries however, as are of that kind, that one of them must necessarily be in those things, in which it can naturally be, or of which it is predicated, these have nothing intermediate; but in the case of those, in which it is not necessary, that one should be inherent, there is something intermediate. For instance, health and disease may naturally subsist in the body of an animal, and it is necessary that one, should be therein, either disease, or health; the odd and even are also predicated of number, and one of the two, either the odd or the even, must necessarily be in number, yet there is nothing intermediate between these, neither between disease and health, nor between the odd and the even. Those contraries, again, have something intermediate, in which one of them need not be inherent, as black and white are naturally in body, but it is not necessary, that one of these, should be inherent in body, for every body, is not white or black. Vileness, also and worth, are predicated of man, and of many others, yet one of these, need not be in those things of which it is predicated, for not all things are either vile or worthy; at least, there is something intermediate, as between white and black, there is dark brown, and pale, and many other colours, but between vileness and worth, that, is intermediate, which is neither vile, nor worthy. In some instances, the intermediates have names, thus, the dark brown, and the pale, and such colours are media between white and black, but in other cases, it is not easy to assign a name to the intermediate, but the latter is defined, by the negation of either extreme, as, for example, whatever is neither good nor bad, nor just nor unjust.[1]

2. Contrary opposition.

Privation, however,[2] and habit are predicated

3. Opposition

[1] Vide Whately, book ii. ch. 5, sect. 1; also book ii. ch. 3, sect. 4; also Metaph. lib. iv. c. 10.

[2] Cf. Metaph. lib. iv. c. 22 and 23. Examples of Positive, Privative,

of habit and privation.

of something identical, as sight and blindness of the eye, and universally, in whatever the habit is naturally adapted to be produced, of such is either predicated. We say then, that each of the things capable of receiving habit is deprived of it, when it is not in that, wherein it might naturally be, and when it is adapted naturally to possess it; thus we say that a man is toothless, not because he has no teeth, and blind, not because he has no sight, but because he has them not, when he might naturally have them, for some persons from their birth, have neither sight nor teeth, yet they are neither called toothless nor blind. To be deprived of, and to possess habit, then, are not privation and habit, for the sight is habit, but the privation is blindness, but to possess sight is not sight, nor to be blind, blindness, for blindness is a certain privation, but the being blind is to be deprived, and is not privation, for if blindness were the same as being blind, both might be predicated of the same person, but a man is said to be blind, yet he is never called blindness. To be deprived also, and to possess habit, appear to be similarly opposed, as privation and habit, since the mode of opposition is the same, for as blindness is opposed to sight, so likewise is the being blind, opposed to the possession of sight.[1]

1. Distinction in the meaning of habitual and privative opposition.

4. Opposition of affirmative and negative.

Neither is that, which falls under affirmation and negation, affirmation and negation; for affirmation is an affirmative sentence, and negation a negative

and Negative words are given in Hill's Logic, p. 27. Aldrich's definition of the three will be remembered here, namely, that the first signifies the presence of an attribute; the second, its absence from a subject capable of it; the last, its absence from a subject incapable of it. A definite noun and its corresponding indefinite noun together, constitute a perfect division.

[1] This opposition between propositions is said to be as to their quality; to this may be appended that contrariety of quality which exists between two particulars, properly called the opposition of sub-contraries. It may here be observed, that though this last-named form of contrariety is admitted by Aristotle, (Int. ch. 7,) he does not use the term ὑπεναντιως as expressive of it, but calls it, in Anal. Prior, ii. 15, an opposition κατὰ τὴν λέξιν. The term is used by the Greek commentators, (Ammonius Schol. p. 115, a. 15,) Boethius Int. ad Syll. p. 564. A poetical example of the mutual subversion of some relative opposites may be found in Shakspeare's King John, act iii. scene 1:

> "Indirection thereby grows direct,
> And falsehood falsehood cures: as fire cools fire
> Within the scorched veins of one new burn'd."

sentence, but nothing which falls under affirmation and negation is a sentence (but a thing). Still these are said to be mutually opposed, as affirmation and negation, since in them the mode of opposition is the same, for as affirmation is sometimes opposed to negation, for example, "he sits" to "he does not sit," so that thing which is under each is opposed, as "sitting" to "not sitting."

5. Privation and habit not relatively opposed.

But that privation and habit, are not opposed as relatives, is evident, since what a thing is, is not asserted of its opposite, for sight is not the sight of blindness, nor in any other way spoken in reference to it, so also blindness, cannot be called the blindness of sight, but blindness indeed is said to be the privation of sight, not the blindness of sight. Moreover, all relatives are referred to reciprocals, so that if blindness were relative, it would reciprocate with that to which it is referred, but it does not reciprocate, for sight is not said to be the sight of blindness.

(2.) Nor contrarily.

From these things, also, it is manifest that those which are predicated, according to privation and habit, are not contrarily opposed, for of contraries which have no intermediate, one must always necessarily be inherent, wherein it is naturally adapted to be inherent, or of which it is predicated, but between these, there is no intermediate thing wherein it was necessary that the one should be in what was capable of receiving it, as in the case, of disease and health, in odd and the even number. Of those however between which there is an intermediate, it is never necessary that one should be inherent in every thing; for neither is it necessary that every thing capable of receiving it, should be white or black, or hot or cold, since there is no prevention to an intermediate being between them. Again, of these also there was a certain medium, of which it was not requisite that one should be in its recipient, unless where one is naturally inherent, as in fire to be hot, and in snow to be white: still in these, one, must of necessity be definitely inherent, and not in whatever way it may happen, for neither does it happen that fire is cold, nor that snow is black.[1] Wherefore it is not necessary that one of them should be in every thing capable of receiving it, but

[1] Vide Whately and Hill's Logic, De terminorum distributione: also the former upon Fallacies, book i. sections 1 and 13.

only in those wherein the one is naturally inherent, and in these, that which is definitely and not casually, one. In privation however, and habit, neither of the above-mentioned particulars is true, since it is not always necessary that one should be inherent in what is capable of receiving it, as what is not yet naturally adapted to have sight, is neither said to be blind nor to have sight; wherefore these things will not be of such contraries as have nothing intermediate. But neither, on the other hand, will they be amongst those which have something intermediate, since it is necessary that at some time, one of them, should be inherent in every thing capable of receiving it: thus when a man is naturally fitted to have sight, then he will be said to be blind, or to have sight, and one of these, not definitely, but whichever may happen, since he need not necessarily be blind, nor see, but either, as it may happen. In respect nevertheless of contraries, which have an intermediate, it is by no means necessary that one, should be inherent in every thing, but in some things, and in these, one of them definitely, and neither casually, so that things which are opposed according to privation and habit, are evidently not in either of these ways opposed, as contraries.

6. Nature of intermediates in respect to opposition.

Again, in contraries, when the recipient exists, a change into each other may happen, unless one is naturally inherent in something, as for instance, in fire to be hot. It is possible also for the healthy to be sick, the white to become black, cold to become hot, (and the hot to become cold); from good it is possible to become bad, and from bad good, for he who is depraved, being led to better pursuits and discourses, advances, though but a little, to be better, and if he once makes an advancement ever so little, he will evidently become either altogether changed, or have made a very great proficiency,[1]

[1] Vide Ethics, book ii. ch. 1; also Magna Moralia, and Metaph. lib. viii. It will be observed that here, as elsewhere, he speaks of moral, not intellectual advancement: Truth, however, he considers the work of both the intellectual parts of the soul. Ethics, book vi. ch. 2. See Merchant of Venice, act iv. scene 1; and Massinger's beautiful lines on the progress of moral habit in the 5th act, 2nd scene, of the Virgin Martyr: also the duty of increasing the mental powers, Hamlet, act iv. sc. 4:

"Sure he that made us with such large discourse,
Looking before and after, gave us not
That capability and godlike reason
To fast in us unused."

since he ever becomes more disposed to virtue, even if he has obtained the smallest, increase, from the beginning. Wherefore he will probably acquire greater increase, and this perpetually occurring, he will at last be transformed entirely to a contrary habit, unless he be prevented by time ; but in privation and habit, it is impossible for a mutual change to occur, since it may take place from habit to privation, but from privation to habit is impossible, as neither can he who has become blind, again see, the bald again have hair, nor has the toothless ever yet again got teeth.

7. The peculiarity of affirmative, and negative opposition, that one should be true and the other false.

Whatever things are opposed, as affirmation and negation, are evidently opposed according to none of the above-mentioned modes, since in these alone it is always necessary that one should be true, but the other false;[1] as neither, is it always necessary in contraries that one should be true but the other false, nor in relatives, nor in habit and privation. For instance, health and disease, are contrary, yet neither of them is either true or false; so also the double and the half are relatively opposed, and neither of them is either true or false; nor in things which are predicated as to privation and habit, as sight and blindness. In short, nothing predicated without any conjunction, is either true or false, and all the above-named are predicated without conjunction. Not but that a thing of this kind may appear, to happen in contraries, which are predicated conjunctively, for "Socrates is well" is opposed to "Socrates is sick,"[2] yet neither in these is it always necessary, that one should be true and the other false, for while Socrates lives, one will be true and the other false, but when he is not alive, both will be false, since neither is it true that Socrates is sick, nor that he is well, when he is not

[1] Vide rules of natural opposition in the common Logical Treatises.

[2] These are properly contradictories, one being true and the other false, but the definition of contradictories does not include them as being given by Aldrich only of universals; the definition however given in Anal. Post, i. 2, 6, will include them—*ἀντίφασις δὲ ἀντίθεσις ἧς οὐκ ἔστι μεταξὺ καθ' αὑτην.* Some logicians call the opposition of singulars secondary contradiction. Boethius, p. 613, regards such instances as contradictories; also Wallis, lib. ii. ch. 5. Compare Aldrich's Logic upon rules of contradiction: it is remarkable that he does not mention the opposition of singulars until he comes to the causes of opposition of propositions. Cf. Interpretation 7, Anal. Prior, xi. 15.

in existence at all. In privation and habit, then when the subject is non-existent, neither is true, but when the subject exists, the one is not always true, nor the other false. "Socrates sees" is opposed to "Socrates is blind," as privation and habit, and whilst he exists, one need not be true or false, for when he is not naturally fitted to possess them, both are false, but when Socrates does not exist at all, both will thus be false, that he sees, and that he is blind. In affirmation and negation always, if Socrates be or be not, one will always be false and the other true; for it is evident with respect to these two, "Socrates is sick," and "Socrates is not sick," that when he exists one of them is true and the other false; and in like manner when he does not exist, for in the latter case that he is ill is false, but that he is not ill is true; so that in those things alone which are affirmatively and negatively opposed will it be the peculiarity that one of them is either true or false.

CHAP. XI.—*Opposites continued, especially as to the contrariety between the Evil and the Good.*

1. Opposition of good and evil.

"EVIL" is of necessity opposed to good, and this is evident from an induction of singulars, as disease to health, and cowardice to courage, and similarly of the rest. But to evil, at one time, good, is contrary, and at another, evil, for to indigence being an evil, excess is contrary, which is also an evil; in like manner, mediocrity, which is a good, is opposed to each of them. A man may perceive this in respect of a few instances, but in the majority the contrary to evil is always good.[1]

Rhet. b. i. c. 7, and Eth. b. ii. c. 2.

2. Where one contrary exists

Again, of contraries it is not required, if one is, that the remainder should be; for when every

[1] Compare note in the preceding chapter relative to the observation of Archytas as to generic and specific contrariety, whence it will be seen that this chapter is nothing else than an elaboration of the principle he lays down. He adds in his treatise on Opposites, "There are three differences of contraries; for some things are opposed as good to evil, as for instance health to sickness, some as evil to evil, as avarice to prodigality, and some as neither to neither, as the white to the black, and the heavy to the light." What he calls "neither," and Aristotle "the negation of extremes," subsequent philosophers called "indifferent," ἀδιάφορα. Comp. Cic. ad Atticum, also Sanct. Chrys. in Ep. ad Ephes. c. 5.

man is well, there will indeed be health, and not disease, and so also when all things are white, there will be whiteness, but not blackness. Besides, if "Socrates is well" be the contrary of "Socrates is ill," and both cannot possibly be inherent in the same subject, it follows, that when one of the contraries exists, the other cannot possibly exist, for "Socrates is well" existing, "Socrates is ill" cannot exist.[1]

It is not necessary that the other should exist—but sometimes one destroys the other.

Contraries, however, evidently are, by their nature, adapted to subsist about the same thing, either in species or genus, since disease and health naturally subsist in the body of an animal, but whiteness and blackness simply in body, and justice and injustice in the soul of man.

3. Contraries generally inherent in similar genera or species.

Notwithstanding, it is requisite that all contraries be either in the same genus, or in contrary genera, or be genera themselves; for white and black are in the same genus, as "colour" is the genus of them; but justice and injustice in contrary genera, for "virtue" is the genus of one, but "vice" of the other; lastly, "good" and "bad" are not in a genus, but are themselves the genera of certain things.

4. They must be either in the same genus, or in contrary genera, or be genera themselves.

CHAP. XII.—*Of Priority.*[2]

A THING is said to be prior to another in four respects: first and most properly, in respect of time, according to which, one is said to be older and more ancient than another, since it is called older and more ancient, because the time is longer. Next, when it does not reciprocate, according to the consequence of existence: thus one is prior to two, for two existing, it follows directly that one exists; but when one is, it is not necessary that two should be, hence the consequence of the remainder's existence does not reciprocate from the existence of the one; but such a thing appears to be prior, from which the consequence of existence does not reciprocate.

1. Priority fourfold.

1st, In respect of time.

2nd, When there is no reciprocity as to the consequence of existence.

[1] Logic taking no cognizance of understood matter, the necessary, impossible, and contingent should be omitted from the table of opposition.—Mansel. Compare also Whately de Oppositione, cited above.

[2] Cf. Metaph. lib. iv. c. 11.

3rd, In respect of order.

Thirdly, the prior is that predicated according to a certain order, as in the instance of sciences and discourses, for in demonstrative sciences, the prior and the posterior, subsist in order, since the elements are prior in order, to the diagrams, and in grammar, letters are before syllables; so also of discourses, as the proem is prior, in order, to the narration.

4th, In excellence.

Moreover, besides what we have mentioned, the better and more excellent appear to be prior by nature. The common people are accustomed to say, that those whom they chiefly honour and especially regard, are prior in their esteem;[1] but this is nearly the most foreign of all the modes, wherefore such are (nearly) the modes of priority which have been enumerated.

2. Another mode of priority may be added, where one thing is the cause of another's existing.

Besides the above-mentioned, there may yet appear to be another mode of the prior; as of things reciprocating, according to the consequence of existence, that which in any respect is the cause of the existence of the one, may justly be said to be by nature prior, and that there are, certain things of this kind, is manifest. For that man exists, reciprocates, according to the consequence of existence, with the true sentence respecting him, since if man is, the sentence is true, by which we say, that man is, and it reciprocates, since if the sentence be true, by which we say that man is, then man is. Notwithstanding, a true sentence, is by no means the cause of a thing's existence, but in some way, the thing appears the cause of the sentence being true, for in consequence of a thing existing, or not existing, is a sentence said to be true or false. Wherefore one thing may be called prior to another, according to five modes.[2]

[1] In the text, *τοὺς ἐντιμωτέρους*. The adverbial construction represented in Greek by the neuter plural, was frequently the form of employing *πρῶτος* in this sense: thus Herod. vi. 100, *Αἰσχίνης ὁ Νόθωνος ἐὼν τῶν Ἐρετριέων τὰ πρῶτα.* In Latin the same expression occurs for great men, primates equivalent to optimates, and sometimes primores; thus Liv. Primoribus patrum; Hor. Populi primores, etc. An odd instance of "first" for "noblest" occurs in Coriolanus, act iv. scene 1,

"My first son,
Whither wilt thou go?" where see note, Knight's ed.

[2] The tautological baldness of this whole chapter, it is hopeless to remedy, its arrangement also is slovenly: for the latter portion, the next

CHAP. XIII.—*Of things simultaneous.*

THINGS are called simultaneous simply and most properly, whose generation occurs at the same time, for neither is prior or posterior; these, therefore, are said to be simultaneous as to time. But by nature those are simultaneous, which reciprocate according to the consequence of existence, although one, is by no means the cause of the existence of the other, as in the double and the half, for these reciprocate; thus the double existing, the half also exists, and the half existing, the double exists, but neither is the cause of existence to the other.

1. Those things are simultaneous which at the same time are produced, and which reciprocate, but do not either cause the other's existence.

Those, also, which being derived from the same genus, are by division mutually opposed, are said to be naturally simultaneous;[1] but they, are said to have a division opposite to each other, which subsist according to the same division; thus the winged is opposed to pedestrian and aquatic, as these being derived from the same genus, are by division mutually opposed, for animal is divided into these, viz. into the winged, the pedestrian, and aquatic, and none of these is prior or posterior, but things of this kind appear naturally simultaneous. Each of these again, may be divided into species, for instance, the winged, the pedestrian, and the aquatic; wherefore, those will be naturally simultaneous which, derived from the same genus, subsist according to the same division. But genera are always prior to species, since they do not reciprocate according to the consequence of existence;[2] for the aquatic existing, animal exists, but though animal exists, it is not necessary that the aquatic should.

2. Or which as species of the same genus, are opposed in the same relation of division.

Hence those are called naturally simultaneous, which indeed reciprocate, according to the consequence of existence; but the one is by no means the cause of existence to the other, which is also the case with things that, derived from the same

chapter will appear elucidatory, and, in fact, is the same statement of the whole, in reverse.

[1] Porphyry recognises only a relative difference between two given species. See Introduction; also Hill's Logic.

[2] See Whately, book ii. ch. 5.

genus, have by division a mutual opposition; those, however, are simply simultaneous whose generation is at the same time.[1]

CHAP. XIV.—*Of Motion.*[2]

1. Motion of six kinds.

OF motion, there are six species, generation, corruption, increase, diminution, alteration, and change of place.

The other motions then evidently differ from each other, for neither is generation, corruption, nor increase, diminution, nor alteration, change of place, and so of the rest. In the case of alteration however, there is some doubt, whether it be not sometimes necessary that what is altered, be so, in respect to some one, of the other motions, but this is not true, for it happens that we are altered, as to nearly all the passions, or at least the greater part of them, without any participation of the other motions, for it is not necessary that what is passively moved should be either increased or diminished. Wherefore, alteration will differ from the other motions, since if it were the same, it would be necessary that what is altered, be forthwith increased or diminished, or follow some of the other motions, but this is not necessary. Similarly, also, what is increased or moved with any other motion, ought to be altered (in quality); but some things are increased which are not so altered, as a square is increased when a gnomon[3] is placed about it, but it has

2. Alteration questionably relative to the rest, this disproved.

1st, By no increase or diminution necessarily occurring in what is altered.

2nd, By no change taking place in quality.

[1] The office of Logic being to guard against ambiguity in the use of terms; it is clear that by nominal division alone, species from the same genus will often have a subordinate opposition, as antagonistic in its nature, as opposite genera; for example, purple, yellow, etc., under colour. Boethius uses division in three senses: 1. Of a genus into species. 2. Of a whole into its parts. 3. Of an equivocal term into its several significations. Cicero, Top. vi. ch., calls the first, divisio, the second, partitio. Aristotle approves division by contraries. See Top. vi. 6, 3, de part. Anim. i. 3.

[2] Compare the Physics, books iii. v. vi. vii. viii., also Metaph. lib. x. ch. 9, 11, 12. In the 11th ch. of the 10th book, Meta., he defines motion; Ἥ κίνησις ἐνέργεια μὲν εἶναι δοκεῖ τις ἀτελὴς δὲ. Vide also the Scholia Marc. ed. Waitz, Ἡ κινησίς ἐστιν ἐξάλλαξις καὶ ἔκστασὶς.

[3] The following figure will illustrate this comparison: the use of the γνώμον being the ascertainment of right angles.

not become altered (in quality); and in like manner with other things of this kind, so that these motions will differ from each other.

3. Generic and specific contrariety to motion.

Nevertheless simply, rest is contrary to motion, the several rests to the several motions, corruption to generation, diminution to increase, rest in place to change in place; but change to a contrary place seems especially opposed, as ascent to descent, downwards to upwards. Still it is not easy, to define the contrary to the remainder of these specified motions, but it seems to have no contrary, unless some one should oppose to this, rest according to quality, or change of quality into its contrary, just as in change of place, rest according to place, or change to a contrary place. For alteration is the mutation of quality, so that to motion according to quality, will rest according to quality, or change to the contrary of the quality, be opposed; thus becoming white is opposed to becoming black, since a change in quality occurs, there being an alteration of quality into contraries.

CHAP. XV.—*Of the verb "to Have."*

1. Having predicated in many ways.
1. Quality.

To have, is predicated in many modes; either as habit and disposition or some other quality, for we are said to have knowledge and virtue;[1]

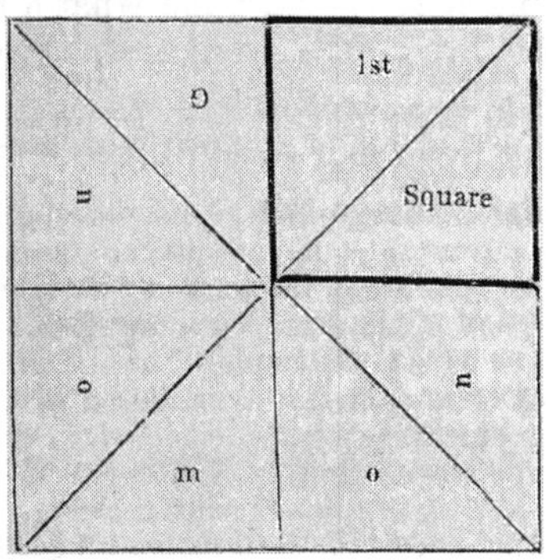

[1] This form is often cognate, and almost identical with the 7th, of possession, thus St. Paul's Ep. 2 Cor. iv. 7; as to the 2nd, the idiom of the English does not fully correspond with the Greek ἔχειν, our word in relation to quantity being "to hold." A rare use of the word "havings" occurs in the Lover's Complaint of Shakspeare; see Knight's edition: "Whose rarest *havings* made the blossoms dote."

2. Quantity — or as to quantity, as the size which any one has; thus he is said to have the size of three or four cubits; or 3. Investiture. — as things about the body, as a garment or a 4. In a part. — tunic;[1] or as in a part, as a ring in the hand; 5. As to a part. — or as a part, as the hand or the foot; or as in a 6. In measure. — vessel, as a bushel has wheat, or a flagon, wine, for the flagon is said to have[2] the wine, and the bushel the wheat; all these therefore are said to have, as in a vessel; or 7. Possession. — as a possession, for we are said to have a house or land.

A man is also said to have a wife, and the wife a husband, but the mode now mentioned, of "to have," seems the most 8. Also indirectly or by analogy. — foreign, for we mean nothing else by having a wife, than that she cohabits with a man; there may perhaps appear to be some other modes of having, but those usually mentioned have nearly all been enumerated.

ON INTERPRETATION.[3]

CHAP. I.—*What Interpretation is, which is here discussed: of the Symbols or Exponents of the Passions by the voice—of Nouns and Verbs.*

1. Things enunciated by the voice are symbols of the passions in the soul. — WE must first determine what a noun, and what a verb, are; next, what are negation, affirmation, enunciation, and a sentence.

Those things therefore which are in the voice,

[1] This is Shakspearian usage also. Sometimes this form is applied generally to condition or estate, and even attire, and manner. See Winter's Tale, iv. 3. The next are in the sense of "holding," again.

[2] More properly χωρεῖν. It is evident throughout this chapter, that the elliptical modes in which we employ "have" as an auxiliary verb are endless, and in the use of it, the assimilation of the English to the Greek is peculiar. Sometimes a very decided verb is omitted, and the auxiliary made to stand alone; thus, in K. Henry VIII. act ii. sc. 2,

——"All the clerks,
I mean the learned ones, in Christian kingdoms,
Have their free voices"——for "have *sent*" their free voices.

For the Aristotelian usages of the word, compare Metaph. lib. iv. c. 23.

[3] Having discussed in the Categories the doctrine of simple terms, Aristotle, in the following treatise, proceeds to the discussion of Proposi-

are symbols of the passions of the soul, and when written, are symbols of the (passions) in the voice, and as there are not the same letters among all men, so neither have all the same voices, yet those passions of the soul, of which these are primarily the signs, are the same among all, the things also, of which these are the similitudes, are the same. About these latter, we have spoken in the treatise "Of the Soul,"[1] for they are parts belonging to another discussion, but as in the soul, there is sometimes a conception, without truth or falsehood, and at another time, it is such, as necessarily to have one of these, inherent in it, so also is it with the voice, for falsehood and truth are involved in composition and division.[2] Nouns therefore and verbs of them-

2. Truth and falsehood of enunciation dependent on

tion, which is the result of the conjunction of simple terms, and discarding the other species of sentence, confines himself to the categoric form of the enunciative sentence simply, preparatory to the systematic inquiry into the nature of syllogism, hereafter to be conducted in the Analytics. Indeed, for this reason, as occupying a middle place between simple terms and syllogism, this treatise is more properly introduced here, as Waitz, Buhle, Averrois, and Taylor place it, than after the Topics, as by Bekker. So highly is it esteemed by Ammonius, (in librum Aris. de Int., Venet. 1545,) that he states his gratitude to the god Hermes if he shall be able to add any thing to its elucidation, from what he recollects of the interpretations of Proclus, the Platonist, his preceptor.

As to the title, notwithstanding much difference of opinion, the fruit of primary misconception of the term (περὶ ἑρμηνείας), its application here seems well grounded, as descriptive of language in its construction, being enunciative of the gnostic powers of the soul; it may therefore, we think, (with the learned author of the Prolegomena Logica, Mansel,) be adequately Anglicized, "Of language as the interpretation of thought." Boethe defines it, "Interpretatio est vox significativa, per se ipsam, aliquid significans," to which Waitz adds the remark, "latius patet ἑρμηνεία quam λέξις." Isidore of Seville observes: "Omnis elocutio conceptæ rei interpres est: inde perihermeniam nominant quam interpretationem nos appellamus." For various interpretations of the word, see St. Hilaire, de la Logique d' Aristote, p. i. ch. 10. The treatise itself may be divided into four parts: First, concerning the principles of the enunciative sentence, including definitions of its component parts; the three others informing us of proposition: as, 1st, purely enunciative; 2nd, more complex, wherein something is added to the predicate, making in fact a fourth term; 3rd, modal: at the end he annexes an inquiry connected with a case of problematic contrariety.

[1] Vide de Anim. iii. 6; also Metaph.

[2] This is evident, since logic itself is psychological; but observe, he does not say *all* truth is conversant with composition and division, the last is indeed excluded from the *idealities* of Plato. Thought, per se, has no need of systematic language, the most accurate development of which does

composition and division of words, as symbols.

selves resemble conception, without composition and division, as "man," or "white," when something is not added, for as yet it is neither true nor false, an instance of which is that the word τραγέλαφος[1] signifies something indeed, but not yet any thing true or false, unless to be, or not to be, is added, either simply, or according to time.

CHAP. II.—*Of the Noun and its Case.*

1. Definition of the noun—its parts not separately significant—distinction between simple and composite.

A NOUN therefore is a sound significant[2] by compact without time, of which no part is separately significant; thus in the noun κάλλιππος, the ἵππος signifies nothing by itself, as it does in the sentence καλὸς ἵππος; neither does it happen with simple nouns as it does with composite, for in the former there is by no means the part significant, but in the latter a part would be, yet signifies nothing separately, as in the word ἐπακτροκέλης,[3] the κέλης signifies nothing by itself. But it is according to compact,[4] because naturally there is no noun; but when it

2. Ex instituto, conf. c. 4.

not touch, in all cases, its subtlety. On the distinction between σημεῖον and ὁμοιώμα, see Waitz, vol. i. 324. It will be remembered that the legitimate office of logic is not establishment of the truth or falsehood of the subject matter, except in so far as that truth or falsehood results from certain relations of original data according to fixed rules. (Vide Whately, Hill, Huyshe.) It is needless to quote the definition given by Aldrich of Proposition here.

[1] That is, an animal partly a goat and partly a stag. Compare with this and the following chapters, ch. xx. of the Poetics.

[2] Φωνὴ σημαντικὴ, called by Aldrich vox, by Boethius and Petrus Hispanus, vox, significativa ad placitum. Logical nouns are equivalent to simple terms, or categorems, in opposition to syncategorems, which are not, per se, significative. Here Aristotle mentions the noun and the verb: but (ch. xx. Poetics) he elsewhere adds the conjunction and article (φωναὶ ἄσημοι). Cf. Harris Hermes, ch. iii.; also Hill's Logic.

[3] A piratical ship. The word is a vox complexa—φωνὴ, συμπεπλεγμένη, a compound word, whereof each part has a meaning in composition; φωνὴ ἁπλῆ, where the parts have no meaning. Vide Sanderson's Logic.

[4] Primo quidem declarat conceptum deinde supponit pro re. Aldrich. When Aristotle makes the assertion in the text, he does not dissent from that of Socrates in the Cratylus; but whilst he denies the subsistence of names from nature, an opinion adopted by Heraclitus, he shows in his Physical Auscultation, and various other places, that names accord with things. In this very treatise the name of "an indefinite noun," or of "contradic-

becomes a symbol, since illiterate sounds also signify something, as the sounds of beasts, of which there is no noun.

3. The indefinite not a noun.

"Not man," however, is not a noun, neither is a name instituted by which we ought to call it, since it is neither a sentence, nor a negation;[1] but let it be an indefinite noun because it exists in respect of every thing alike, both of that which is, and of that which is not.[2]

4. Cases of the noun differ from the noun in that, being joined to the verb, or copula, they signify neither truth nor falsehood.

Φίλωνος indeed, or φίλωνι, and such like words are not nouns, but cases of a noun,[3] but the definition of it (that is, of the case) is the same as to other things (with the definition of a noun), but (it differs in) that, with (the verb) "is" or "was" or "will be," it does not signify what is true or false, but the noun always (signifies this), as "Philonus is," or "is not," for as yet, this neither signifies what is true, nor what is false.

CHAP. III.—*Of the Verb, its Case, and of those called Verbs generally.*[4]

1. Definition of the verb or ῥῆμα.

A VERB, is that which, besides something else, signifies time; of which no part is separately significant, and it is always indicative of those things which

tion," given by him, clearly shows his opinion about names. The suppositio of Aldrich is not found in Aristotle, but may be traced to the Greek Logic of Michael Psellus.

[1] Not a noun, that is, not a true and perfect noun, nor a sentence, since it is neither "verum vel falsum significans;" neither is it a negation, for it wants a verb, without which there is no negation.

[2] Signifies as well being as non-being: in the original ὁμοίως ἐφ' ὁτουοῦν ὑπάρχει. Waitz omits the rest of this sentence from "indefinite noun."

[3] Aristotle considers the oblique cases of a noun (πτώσεις), not the nominative, the Stoics regarded the nominative (εὐθεία) *also* a case. Oblique cases are syncategorematic, that is, can only form part of a term, the nominative may be a term by itself.

[4] Aristotle does not employ the term categorematic, but defines his simple terms, ὅροι εἰς οὓς διαλύεται ἡ πρότασις,—with him categorematic words are the noun as subject, and the verb as predicate. Vide Boeth. Introd. ad Syll. and Pet. Hisp. Tract i. Cf. Trendelenburg, Elementa, § 3. Waitz, vol. i. 267. The copula has been called the only logical verb, but is, properly speaking, no verb at all, and cannot correspond with the ῥῆμα of Aristotle, except by coalescing with the predicate. Vide Mansel's

are asserted of something else. But I say that it signifies time, besides something else, as for instance, "health" is a noun, but "is well" is a verb; for it signifies, besides being well, that such is the case now: it is always also significant of things asserted of something else, as of those which are predicated of a subject, or which are in a subject.

2. A verb joined with negation, or in its tenses out of the present, is not a proper logical verb.

Nevertheless I do not call, "is not well," and, "is not ill"—verbs; for indeed they signify time, besides something else, and are always (significant) of something, yet a name is not given to this difference, let either be therefore an indefinite verb, because it is similarly inherent both in whatever does, and does not exist.[1] So also "was well" or "will be well" are not *verbs*, but they are cases of a verb, and differ from a verb, because the latter, besides something else, signifies present time; but the others, that which is about the present time.

3. Infinitives properly nouns.

Verbs therefore so called, by themselves, are nouns, and have a certain signification, for the speaker establishes the conception,[2] and the hearer acquiesces, but they do not yet signify[3] whether a thing "is" or "is not," for neither is "to be" or "not to be" a sign of a thing,

Logic; also Pacius de Interp., c. 3. The *ονομα* is *ἄνευ χρόνου*, the verb *προσσημαῖνει χρονον*: this distinction is lost by those who, with Aldrich, resolve the verb into copula and predicate. Vide Ammonius Scholia, p. 105, b. 29. The infinitive is not included under "verb," for it is a noun-substantive, nor the participle, which is a noun-adjective, neither can the former ever be the predicate, except when another infinitive is the subject. Vide Whately, b. ii. c. i. § 3. For case as appertaining to verbs, see post, ch. 20. By Aristotle, number, tense, and mood, were all reckoned cases, *πτωσεις*, or fallings, of the noun and verb, so our English word "fall" in music.

[1] Boeth. translates *ἀόριστον*, infinitum. The translation is blamed by Vives de Caus. Corr. Art. lib. iii. Sir W. Hamilton uses the word indesignate.

[2] That is, in the mind of the hearer. The expression *ἵστησι τὴν διάνοιαν* is rendered by Taylor "stops the discursive power"—a meaning which is however equivalent to "establishes the conception," since *διάνοια* being properly the movement of the intellect towards investigating truth, is "arrested," when a conception is fixed upon it: thus Buhle, "constituit conceptionem." Taylor's translation is strictly exact, but besides being obscure, enforces the introduction of many words into the text. *Διάνοιά* is more nearly akin to logical discursus than to any other energy: see the note upon Anal. Post, lib. i. ch. 33.

[3] i. e. before they are enunciatively joined with nouns.

nor if you should say merely, "being," for that is nothing; they signify however, besides something else, a certain composition, which without the composing members it is impossible to understand.[1]

4. They are insignificant except in composition.

CHAP. IV.—*Of the Sentence.*[2]

A SENTENCE is voice significant by compact,* of which any part separately possesses signification, as indeed a word, yet not as affirmation or negation; now I say for example "man" is significant, but does not imply that it "is" or "is not;"[3] it will however be affirmation or negation, if any thing be added to it. One syllable of the word ἄνθρωπος, is not however (significant),[4] neither the "ῦς" in "μῦς," but it is now merely sound; still in compound words a part is significant, but not by itself, as we have observed.

1. Definition of the sentence —λόγος.

* κατὰ, συνθήκην omitted by Waitz.

Now every sentence is significant, not as an instrument, but, as we have said, by compact, still not every sentence is enunciative,[5] but that in which truth or falsehood is inherent, which things do not exist in all sentences, as prayer is a sentence, but it is neither true nor false. Let therefore the other sentences be dismissed, their consideration belongs more properly to Rhetoric or Poetry; but the enunciative sentence to our present theory.

2. Other kinds of sentence belong to Rhetoric—Logic conversant with the enunciative alone.

[1] Cf. Mansel's Prol. Log. p. 63. I follow Waitz and Buhle; Taylor's rendering is altogether erroneous.

[2] Compare Poetics, ch. 20; also this treatise, ch. 5; Analy. Post, lib. ii. cap. 10; Metap. vii. 4; also Aldrich, sub vocis speciebus.

[3] That is, it neither affirms nor denies something; a verb must be added to make it significant.

[4] In the Poetics, c. 20, he defines a syllable, a sound without signification, composed of a mute and an element which has sound, (i. e. a vowel or semi-vowel). An article, again, is a sound insignificant, showing the finals or distinctions of a word. Buckley has well called the description most obscure: Aristotle, the star of definition, is at last confused by his own ray!

[5] Ἀποφαντικὸς δὲ οὐ πᾶς. The quality of signifying either what is true or false is the logical property of proposition, and is the immediate consequence of its difference, namely, affirmation or negation. Hill's Logic, p. 90. Vide also Whately, Aldrich, and the other treatises on Logic.

CHAP. V.—*Of Enunciation.*[1]

1. Divisions of the enunciative sentence—λόγος ἀποφαντικός.

ONE first enunciative sentence[2] is affirmation; afterwards negation, and all the rest are one by conjunction. It is necessary however that every enunciative sentence should be from a verb, or from the case of a verb, for the definition of "man," unless "is," or "was," or "will be," or something of this kind, be added, is not yet an enunciative sentence. Why indeed is the sentence "a terrestrial biped animal" one thing, and not many things? for it will not be one, because it is consecutively pronounced: this however belongs to another discussion.[3] One enunciative sentence, moreover, is either that which signifies one thing,[4] or which is one by conjunction,[5] and many (such sentences) are either those which signify many things[6] and not one thing, or which are without conjunction.[7] Let therefore a noun or a verb be only a word, since we cannot say that he enunciates who thus

2. Simple or composite.

[1] Cum disseramus de oratione cujus variæ species sunt—est una inter has ad propositum potissima quæ pronuntiabilis appellatur, absolutam sententiam comprehendens, sola ex omnibus veritati at falsitati obnoxia, quam vocat Sergius, "*effatum*," Varro, "*proloquium*," Cicero, "*enunciatum*," Græce "*protasin*," tum "*axioma*;"—familiarius tamen dicetur "*propositio*."—Apuleius de Dogm. Platonis, lib. iii. As Mansel observes justly, he has not distinguished between ἀπόφανσις and πρότασις, the former of which is rendered by Boethius "enunciatio," the latter "propositio." Vide Elem. sect. 2, Trendelenburg; Aquinas, Opusc. 48, Tract. de Enunc. The distinction drawn by the latter is not implied by Aristotle either here or Anal. Pr. i. 1, 2.

[2] Λόγος ἀποφαντικος. Oratio indicativa, Pet. Hispanus. Boethius, "Oratio enunciativa." For καταφασίς, &c. see next chapter. Aldrich's definition errs against the third rule, and *hardly* presses on the second—for good definition.

[3] Definition is a sentence, but not as if one enunciation; its consideration belongs to the first philosophy, and the reader will find the question solved in lib. 6, of the Metaphysics.

[4] As "a man runs," the purely categorical.

[5] This may be disjunctive, which is a species of hypothetical or compound, as "it is either day or night." Vide Whately, book ii. ch. ii. sect. 1.

[6] These come under the class ambiguous, founded often on one equivocal term only, as the "dog is moved," where dog may signify many things.

[7] As "I congratulate you," &c. Compare Hill and Whately; in the former many examples are given.

expresses any thing by his voice whether he is interrogated by any one or not, but that he speaks from deliberate intention.[1] Now of these enunciations one is simple, for instance something of* something, or from† something, but another is composed of these,‡ as a certain sentence which is already a composite; simple enunciation, then, is voice significant about something being inherent, or non-inherent, according as times are divided.§ [2]

* i. e. simple affirmation.
† i. e. Simple negation.
‡ e. g. "it is day, not night."
3. Definition of simple enunciation, σημαντικὴ περὶ τοῦ ὑπάρχειν.
§ i. e. into past, present, and future.

CHAP. VI.—*Of Affirmation and Negation.*[3]

AFFIRMATION is the enunciation of something concerning something, but negation is the enunciation of something from something.[4] Since,

1. Distinctive definition of affirmation (κατάφασις) and

[1] This form arises from our usual elliptical method of expression, in regard to interrogatives, when the repeated verb is understood but not expressed; as, "Who reads? Socrates," i. e. "Socrates reads."

[2] These sentences are known by the barbarous name of propositions de inesse, that is, denoting the *inherency* or *inbeing* of the predicated quality in the class or thing expressed by the subject. The expression τοῦ ὑπαρχειν in Aristotle, has two meanings, one in which the predicate is said to be in the subject, which is equivalent to κατηγορεῖται, as all B is A, τὸ A κατηγορεῖται κατὰ παντὸς τοῦ B; and Εἶναι ἐν, whereby the subject is said to be in the predicate, as all A is B, A ἐστιν ἐν ὅλῳ τῷ B., which is exactly the reverse of κατηγορεῖται. See note 3, p. 80. On the different species of sentences alluded to in the above chapter, see also Petrus Hispanus, Sum. Log. Tract 1. "Vocum significativarum ad placitum, alia complexa ut *oratio*, alia incomplexa ut *nomen* et *verbum*. Orationum perfectarum, alia indicativa, ut 'Homo currit;' alia imperativa, ut 'Petre fac ignem;' alia optativa, ut "Utinam esset bonus clericus!" alia subjunctiva, ut "si veneris ad me dabo tibi equum;" alia deprecativa, ut "miserere mei Deus!" Harum autem orationum sola indicativa oratio dicitur esse propositio." Cf. Boeth. de Syll. Cat. p. 582, also Poet. c. 20.

[3] Upon the import of Propositions, see Mill's Logic, book i. ch. 5. Reid defines judgment after the above manner: "an act of the mind whereby one thing is affirmed or denied of another." Affirmative judgment is called by Aldrich, "compositio," negative, "divisio," σύνθεσις and διαίρεσις: comp. 1st ch. of this treatise. Apuleius calls the sentence either Propositio dedicativa or abdicativa.

[4] My translation is identical with that of Boethius: Aldrich's definition is applicable only to propositions "tertii adjacentis," and is in fact accidental. Vide Huyshe, p. 51.

negation (ἀπόφασις.) however, a man may enunciate what is inherent as though it were not,[1] and what is not [2] as though it were; that which is, as if it were, and that which is not, as if it were not, and in like manner about times external to the present; it is possible that whatever any one affirms may be denied, and that whatever any one denies may be affirmed, whence it is evident that to every affirmation there is an opposite negation, and to every negation an opposite affirmation.[3] Let this be contradiction, affirmation and negation being opposites,[4] but I call that opposition which is of the same respecting the same,[5] not equivocally, and such other particulars of the kind as we have concluded against sophistical importunities.[6]

2. Opposition between affirmative and negative constitutes contradiction (ἀντίφασις). Cf. Cat. x. 1.

CHAP. VII.—*Of Contraries and Contradictories.*

1. Distinction between the universal (τὰ καθόλου) and the singular (τὰ καθέκαστον).

OF things, since some are universal, but others singular,[7] (and by universal I mean whatever may naturally be predicated of many things, but by singular, that which may not: as "man" is universal, but "Callias" singular,) it is necessary to enunciate that something is, or is not, inherent, at one time, in

[1] A false negation, ([2]) a false affirmation: of the subsequent examples, the first is a true affirmation, and the second a true negation.

[3] This classification originates in the *logical* difference of propositions, see Hill's Logic, page 96.

[4] αἱ ἀντικείμεναι (προτάσεις), this term is sometimes by Aristotle limited to contradictories.

[5] "When having the same subject and predicate they differ in quantity, or quality, or both." Whately. Vide also some general remarks on this subject in Huyshe, p. 51, note.

[6] Vide "Sophistical Elenchi."

[7] Taylor has mistaken καθ' ἑκαστον, by translating it "particular," as usual: see note, page 33. Compare An. Pr. i. 1, 2. Omnis is the sign of an universal proposition taken distinctively, as Omnis homo est animal; when collectively, the proposition is singular. Individual names are distinguished as individua signata, as "Socrates:" individua demonstrativa, by a demonstrative pronoun, hic homo: individua vaga, by an indefinite pronoun, aliquis, quidam: this distinction is found in the Greek commentators. Cf. Albert de Predicab. Tract. iv. cap. 7. Aquinas. The two first form singular propositions; a doubt has been entertained as to the last, whether they form singulars or particulars. Mansel's Logic,

an universal, at another in a singular thing. Now, if any one universally enunciates of an universal, that something is or is not inherent, these enunciations will be contrary:[1] I mean universally enunciates of an universal, as that "every man is white," "no man is white." When on the other hand he enunciates of universals, not universally,[2] these are not contraries, though the things signified may sometimes be contrary; but I mean by not universally enunciating of universals, as that "man is white," "man is not white:" for man being universal, is not employed as an universal in the enunciation, since the word "every" does not signify the universal, but (shows that the subject is) universally (taken). Now to predicate universally of what is universally predicated is not true, for no affirmation will be true in which the universal is predicated of an universal predicate,[3] as for instance, "every man" is "every animal." Wherefore I say affirmation is opposed to negation contradictorily, the affirmation which signifies the universal to that which is not universal, as "every man is white," "not every man is white," "no man is white," "some man is white." But contrarily is between universal affirmative and universal negative, as "every man is white," "no man is white," "every man is just," "no man is just."[4] Wherefore it is impossi-

2. Nature of contrariety—ἐναντίαι αἱ ἀποφάνσεις.

3. Of contradiction; (ἀντιφατικῶς ἀντικεῖσθαι).

p. 46. When a singular term is the predicate, it must of course be coextensive with its subject. On the above chapter compare Whately, book ii. 2, 3, and Hill, 9, et seq.: in fact, a slight acquaintance even with Aldrich's Logic will suffice to place the principle of opposition, as copied here, clearly before the reader; for mere simplification we have annexed the usual scheme of opposition.

[1] That is, adds the universal mark, or sign, "every" or "none." It should be recollected also, as Taylor observes here, "that contraries may at one and the same time be absent from a subject, but they cannot at one and the same time be inherent in it;" this Aristotle indeed points out in this chapter. ([2]) "Not universally, i. e. does not add the universal mark"—he adds, "the things signified may be contraries, that is to say, the mental conceptions may be, whilst the enunciations are still indefinite. The extent of the indefinite is regulated by the *matter* of the proposition, and is universal in necessary and impossible matter."

[3] For example, to say, every man is every animal, is false, unless man is horse, ox, etc.; or to say every man is every visible thing will be false, because the predicate of every man may be also said of Socrates, hence Socrates would be every thing visible. Socrates would therefore be Plato, and Aristotle, and every thing visible, which is absurd.—Taylor.

[4] These contraries cannot be at one and the same time true, but they may be both false, or one true, and the other false. In necessary matter, af-

4. Contraries themselves cannot at the same time be true, though their opposites may.

ble that these should at one and the same time be true, but the opposites to these may sometimes possibly be co-verified about the same thing, as that "not every man is white," and "some man is white."[1] Of such contradictions then of universals, as are universally made, one must necessarily be true or false, and also such as are of singulars, as "Socrates is white," "Socrates is not white;" but of such contradictions as are indeed of universals, yet are not universally made, one is not always true, but the other false. For at one and the same time we may truly say that "man is white," and that "man is not white," and "man is handsome," and "man is not handsome," for if he is deformed he is not handsome, and if any thing is *becoming* to be, it *is*, not. This however may at once appear absurd, because the assertion "man is not white," seems at the same time to signify the same thing, as "no man is white," but it neither necessarily signifies the same thing, nor at the same time.[2]

5. One negation incident

Notwithstanding it is evident that of one affirmation there is one negation, for it is necessary

firmatives are true, negatives false, in impossible matter negatives true, affirmatives false, in contingent matter both false. Properly speaking, it is contrary to the very nature of logical inquiry to admit any reference whatever to the understood *matter* of proposition, of which Logic can take no cognizance, its province being, to establish argument when necessarily deducible from propositions placed in a certain connexion. From the truth of the universal or the falsehood of the singular we infer the accidental quality of all the opposed propositions; but from the falsehood of an universal or truth of a singular, we only know the quality of the contradictory.

[1] He means "singular sub-contraries," which contradict the universals mutually contrary to each other, hence are co-verified in the same thing, i. e. in contingent matter, as in the above instance. The expression subcontrary (ὑπεναντίως) is not used by Aristotle, though he admits the opposition above; he calls it in Anal. Prior, ii. 15, an opposition κατὰ τὴν λέξιν; but not κατ' ἀλήθειαν: subalterns (ὑπάλληλοι) are not noticed by Aristotle, the first who gave the laws of this species of opposition was Apuleius De Dogmate Platonis, lib. iii., who was followed by Marcianus Capella, and Boethius. The three kinds of opposition are called by the earlier writers, Alterutræ, Incongruæ, and Suppares.

[2] Viz. what he has said, that indefinites are at one and the same time true. Indefinite enunciation may seem to be universal, because it has an universal subject, but it is not universal, because it wants the universal mark, "every" or "no one." It is not requisite that the universal and indefinite should be at one and the same time true nor false, for one may be true and the other false.

that the negation should deny the same thing which the affirmation affirmed, and also from the same, (i. e.) either from some singular or some universal, universally or not universally; I say, for instance, that "Socrates is white," "Socrates is not white." If however there is something else from the same thing, or the same thing from something else, that (enunciation) will not be opposite, but different from it;[1] to the one, "every man is white," the other (is opposed) "not every man is white," and to the one, "a certain man is white," the other, "no man is white;" and to the one, "man is white," the other, "man is not white." to each affirmation.

That there is then one affirmation contradictorily opposed to one negation, and what these are, has been shown, also that there are other contraries, and what they are, and that not every contradiction is true or false, and why and when it is true or false.

[1] That is, if the negative differs from the affirmative in the predicate or the subject. The instance "Socrates is white," Socrates is not white, is contradictory, the one being true always, and the other false; which constitutes the essential feature of contradictories included in the definition given Anal. Post, i. 2, Ἀντίφασις δὲ ἀντίθεσις ἧς οὐκ ἔστι μεταξὺ καθ' αὑτήν. Some logicians call the opposition of singulars "secondary contradiction." Vide Boethius, p. 613. Wallis, lib. ii. c. 5. For the rules of contradiction, vide Aldrich, Whately, Huyshe. The following scheme from Aldrich gives the opposition of necessary, impossible, and contingent matter (n, i. c.) as to universal contraries A. E., and sub-contraries I. and O., with their verity (v.) or falsity (f.). See also scheme page 3.

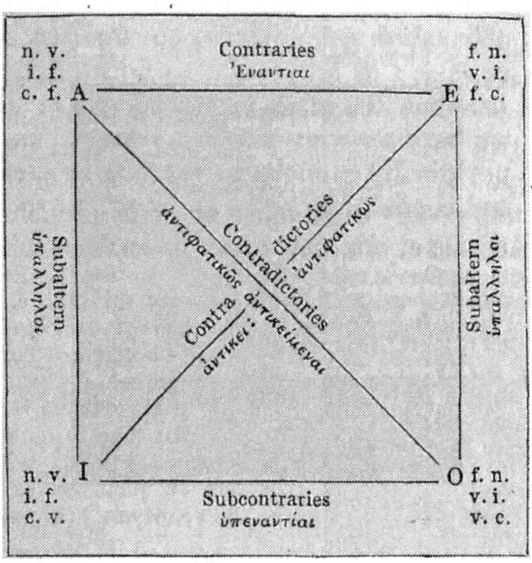

CHAP. VIII.—*Of Opposition when there is not one Affirmation, nor one Negation.*[1]

1. What constitutes single affirmation and negation, is the unity of the subject, and of the predicate, without equivocation.

THE affirmation and negation are one, which indicate one thing of one, either of an universal, being taken universally, or in like manner if it is not, as "every man is white," "not every man is white," "man is white," "man is not white," "no man is white," "some man is white," if that which is white signifies one thing. But if one name be given to two things, from which one thing does not arise, there is not one affirmation nor one negation;[2] as if any one gave the name "garment" to a "horse," and to "a man;" that "the garment is white," this will not be one affirmation, nor one negation, since it in no respect differs from saying "man" and "horse" are "white," and this is equivalent to "man is white," and "horse is white." If therefore these signify many things, and are many, it is evident that the first enunciation either signifies many things or nothing,[3] for "some man is not a horse," wherefore neither in these is it necessary that one should be a true, but the other a false contradiction.[4]

CHAP. IX.—*Of Opposition in contingent Futures.*

1. In things past affirmation and negation must necessarily be true or false, but otherwise in respect of the future.

IN those things which are, and have been,[5] the affirmation and negation must of necessity be true or false; in universals, as universals, always one true but the other false, and also in singulars, as we have shown; but in the case of universals not universally enunciated, there is no such necessity, and concerning these we have also spoken, but as

[1] Vide Whately, b. ii. c. 2, sect. 3.

[2] That is, enunciation is equivocal.

[3] "The garment is white" signifies many things, i. e. if the word "garment" be assumed for "man" and "horse;" or it signifies nothing, that is, if it is so assumed as to signify one thing, since being taken for man, horse, the latter is not one thing, but nothing.

[4] For both may be true, as every garment (i. e. man) is rational, not every garment (i. e. horse) is rational; or they may be both false.

[5] Taylor reads γινομένων, after the Laurentian MS. Waitz, Bekker, and Buhle γενομένων. In iis quæ sunt et quæ facta sunt. Averrois. Of course Aristotle does not mean by the assertion in the text, other than that one is true and the other false.

to singulars and futures, this is not the case. For if every affirmation or negation be true or false, it is also necessary that every thing should exist or should not exist, for if one man says that a thing will be, but another denies the same, one of them must evidently of necessity speak truth, if every affirmation or negation be true or false, for both will not subsist in such things at one and the same time. Thus if it is true to say that "a thing is white," or that "it is not white," it must of necessity be "white" or not "white," and if it is white or not white, it was true to affirm or to deny it: also if it *is not*, it is falsely said to be, and if it is falsely said to be, it is not; so that it is necessary that either the affirmation or the negation should be true or false. Indeed there is nothing which either is, or is generated fortuitously, nor casually, nor will be, or not be, but all things are from necessity, and not casually, for either he who affirms speaks truth, or he who denies, for in like manner it might either have been or not have been, for that which subsists casually neither does nor will subsist more in this way than in that.[1] Moreover if a thing is now "white," it

2. Whatever true affirmation or negation is made of futures excludes casual existence.

[1] Pluribus modis Aristoteles repetit et inculcat quod si aut affirmatio aut negatio necessario sit vera de rebus futuris item e veritate in dicendo colligi possit quomodo res ipsæ evenire debeant atque ex ipsis rebus judicetur quid sit verum, quid falsum: etenim si certum est et definitum utrum verum sit, utrum falsum in iis quæ de rebus futuris pronuntiantur, præstituta sunt omnia, et quæ eveniunt, necessario eveniunt. Waitz. It is well observed by Ammonius, that the observations here made by Aristotle "are conversant not only with logic, but with every part of philosophy." Not all things are assumed to exist from necessity, but some are supposed to be in our own power; this constitutes the doctrine of moral responsibility with the theologian, the scientific investigation of the philosopher, and the division into necessary and contingent of the logician: with respect to the last, the inquiry here seems to be whether all contradiction definitely or only indefinitely comprehends these. The fatalist looks to the doctrine of necessity as authorizing his "affections and antipathies" to become "the laws ruling his moral state," (Vide Shelley's Queen Mab,) forgetful of the moral faculty of self-approval and the contrary, (δοκιμαστικὴ) and (ἀποδοκιμαστικὴ), admitted by Epictetus, (Arr. Epict. lib. i. Capt. 1,) whilst others are led by it into the "visionary presumption of a peculiar destiny." Vide Foster's Essays on the Epithet Romantic. For the Ethical discussion of the subject, the reader is referred to Butler's Analogy, and so far as certain laws of thought form the basis of logical necessity, he will find an admirable paper in chap. vi. of Mansel's Prolegomena Logica. It is sufficient for our present purpose to state that

was true to say before that it will be "white," so that it was always true to say of any thing generated that it either is, or that it will be; but if it was always true to say that it is, or will be, it is impossible that this is not, nor should be; and whatever must of necessity be, it is impossible that it should not have been generated, and what it is impossible should not have been generated must of necessity have been generated; wherefore all things that will be, it is necessary should be generated, and hence there will be nothing casual nor fortuitous, for if it were fortuitous it would not be of necessity. Nor is it possible to say, that neither of them is true, as that it will neither be, nor will not be, for in the first place the affirmation being false, the negation will not be true, and this being false, it results that the affirmation is not true. And besides, if it were true to say that a thing is at the same time "white" and "great," both must of necessity be, but if it shall be to-morrow, it must necessarily be to-morrow, and if it will neither be nor will not be to-morrow, it will not be a casual thing, for example, a naval engagement, for it would be requisite that the engagement should neither occur nor not occur.

3. Result of denying the truth of both.

Example.

These and similar absurdities then will happen, if of every affirmation and negation, whether in respect of universals enunciated universally, or of singulars, it is necessary that one of the opposites be true and the other false, but that nothing happens casually in those things which subsist, but that all are, and are generated of necessity; so that it will neither be necessary to deliberate nor to trouble ourselves, as if we shall do this thing, something definite will occur, but if we do not, it will not occur. For there is nothing to prevent a person for ten thousand years asserting that this will happen, and another person denying it, so that of necessity it will have been then true to assert either of them. And it makes no difference whether any persons have uttered a contradiction or not, for

4. What absurdity follows from denying the casual.

Aristotle traces here the institution of a word to the primary concept of the thing, so that if affirmation is true, a thing is, if negation is true, a thing is not. If either be true or false, he who affirms or denies says truly or falsely, so that if affirmative be true or false, a thing must necessarily exist or not exist. He alleges two enthymematic proofs, terminating in a reductio ad absurdum.

it is evident that the things are so, although the one should not have affirmed any thing, or the other have denied it, since it is not, because it has been affirmed or denied, that therefore a thing will or will not be, neither will it be more so for ten thousand years than for any time whatever. Hence if a thing so subsisted in every time that one of these is truly asserted of it, it was necessary that this should take place; and each thing generated, always so subsisted, as to have been generated from necessity, for when any one truly said that it will be, it was not possible not to have been generated, and of that which is generated, it was always true to say that it will be.

* Vide Bekker, Waitz, Buhle, and the Leipsic edition. Taylor omits the εἰ.

But * if these things are impossible—(for we see that there is a beginning of future things, both from our deliberation and practice, and briefly in things which do not always energize, there is equally a power of being and of not being, in which both to be and not to be occurs, as well as to have been generated and not to have been generated; and, indeed, we have many things which evidently subsist in this manner, for example, it is possible for this garment to have been cut in pieces, and it may not be cut in pieces, but be worn out beforehand, so also it is possible that it may not be cut in pieces, for it would not have been worn out before, unless it had been possible that it might not be cut in pieces, and so also in respect of other productions, which are spoken of according to a power of this kind—) then it is evident that all things neither are, nor are generated of necessity, but that some things subsist casually, and that their affirmation is not more true than their negation, and that there are others in which one of these subsists more frequently, and for the most part,[1] yet so, that either might possibly have occurred, but the other not.[2]

5. Many things have a casual subsistence as to the nature of their affirmation or negation.

Wherefore, being, must of necessity be when it is,[3] and non-being, not be, when it is not; but it is not necessary that every being should be, nor that non-being should not be, since it is not the same thing for every being

[1] As for instance, finding a treasure; here the negation is oftener true than the affirmation: except recently in California and Australia.

[2] That is, the rarer may occur, but the more common may not.

[3] Hypothetically, i. e. a thing must be, if it is supposed to be, because being and non-being cannot concur in eodem, eodem tempore.

In the same place at same time

to be from necessity, when it is, and simply to be from necessity, and in like manner as to non-being. There is the same reasoning also in the case of contradiction; to be or not to be is necessary for every thing, also that it shall, or shall not be, yet it is not requisite to speak of each separately, but I say, for instance, that it is necessary for a naval action to occur or not occur to-morrow, yet it is not necessary that there should be a naval action to-morrow, nor that there should not be; it is necessary, however, that it should either be or not be. Wherefore, since assertions and things are similarly true, it is evident that things which so subsist, as that whatever have happened, the contraries also were possible, it is necessary that contradiction should subsist in the same manner, which happens to those things which are not always, or which not always, are not. For of these, one part of the contradiction must necessarily be true or false, not indeed this or that, but just as it may happen, and one must be the rather true, yet not already true nor false;[1] so that it is evidently not necessary that of every affirmation and negation of opposites, one should be true, but the other false;[2] for it does not happen in the same manner with things which are not, but which either may or may not be, as with things which are, but it happens as we have said.[3]

6. Parallel reasoning as to contradiction, and a difficulty as to the necessary truth or falsehood of contingent futures, solved.

[1] When the contingents of course are unequal.

[2] That is, definitely.

[3] Quæ ex casu pendent et esse possunt et non esse; quare in his affirmatio et negatio (ἡ ἀντίφασις) quum nihil præstitutum sit, eodem jure veræ vel falsæ pronuntiantur (ὁ μοίως ἔχει) altera utra enim admittenda erit neque tamen, altera alteri præferenda, tanquam sit destinatum, et certum quod eventurum sit; quamvis enim alteram veram fore magis sit probabile quam alteram (μᾶλλον ἀληθῆ) nondum vera est donec eventus eam comprobaverit. Waitz. Aristotle's object, whilst he admits the contingent, is to reduce it, for all logical purposes, to a necessary certainty of consequence. The whole of this chapter proves at once the practical turn of his mind, opposed alike to the ideal of Plato, the merely probable (as a *result*) of the Academics, and the versatile scepticism of Pyrrho, against whom Montaigne ushers in his own Philippic (Essay 12, book ii.) by the famous quotation from Sextus Empiricus.

"Nil sciri si quis putat, id quoque nescit
An sciri possit quo se, nil sciri fatetur."

Compare the philosophical principle of *formal* necessity in this chapter with Bp. Butler's distinction between, "by necessity," and acting "necessarily," Analogy, ch. 6, also his Introduction, and part ii. ch. 2, upon the nature of the contingent and proof.

An indefinite Verb 2

CHAP. X.—*Of Opposition with the addition of the Copula.*[1]

SINCE affirmation signifies something of something, and this is either a noun, or anonymous,[2] (i. e. indefinite,) but what is in affirmation must be one and of one thing,[3] all affirmation and negation will be either from a noun and a verb, or from an indefinite noun and verb. (But what a noun is, and what the anonymous, has been shown before, for I do not reckon "not man" a noun, but an indefinite noun, for an indefinite noun signifies in a certain respect one thing, just as "is not well" is not a verb, but an indefinite verb.) Still without a verb there is neither an affirmation nor negation, for "is," or "will be," or "was," or "is going to be," and so forth, are verbs, from what has been already laid down, since in addition to something else they signify time. Hence the first affirmation and negation (will be), "man is," "man is not," afterwards "non-man is," "non-man is not." Again, "every man is," "every man is not," "every non-man is," "every non-man is not," and the same reasoning holds in times beyond (the present).[4] But when "is," is additionally

1. The parts of enunciation.

Cf. ch. 2, and 3.

[1] This is called oppositio tertii adjacentis, and a proposition is so denominated where the copula is separated from the predicate; otherwise where the two form one word, as "He walks," the proposition is called secundi adjacentis; hitherto the latter has been treated of, and the copula and predicate considered equivalent to a single verb, as λευκον (De Int. ch. 2) to λευκόν ἐστι. I have followed Taylor in finishing the sentence before the bracket.

[2] Ἀνώνυμον vocat τὸ ἀόριστον ὄνομα quod ex sequentibus apparet, quamquam τὸ ἀνώνυμον alium sensum habere solet apud Arist. Waitz. Vide supra. "Something of something," means of which something is asserted.

[3] This is true also of negation. The statement has already been made, ch. 8, that there must be one subject, and one predicate. Vide Whately, b. ii. c. 2.

[4] Literally, "external times," τῶν ἐκτὸς δὲ χρόνων. On the distinction between the copula and the third per. sing. of εἴμι, as predicating existence, see Pacius de Int. c. 3, and Biese, vol. i. p. 95.—Upon the predicate having the negation added to it for the sake of obtaining a particular affirmative premise, see Whately, b. ii. ch. 2: where of course it is added to the subject, as in the text, it becomes an indefinite subject, to which the finite is stated prior, as being of an incomplex nature, and by this means the character of the proposition is sometimes changed, and the

predicated as the third thing, then the oppositions are enunciated doubly;[1] I say for instance, "a man is just;" here the word "is," I say, is placed as a third thing, whether noun or verb, in the affirmation, so that on this account, these will be four, of which two will subsist with respect to affirmation and negation, according to the order of consequence, as privations, but two will not.[2] But I say that the word "is," will be added to "just" or to "not just,"* so that also negation is added, wherefore there will be four. We shall understand, however, what is said from the under-written examples:[3] "A man is just," the negation of this is, "a man is not just;" "he is not a just man," the negative of this is, "he is not not a just man," for here the word "is," and "is not," will be added to the "just" and the "not just," wherefore these things, as we have shown in the Analytics, are thus arranged. The same thing will happen if the affirmation be of a noun taken universally,[4] as for instance, "every man is just;" of this the negation is, "not every man is just," "every man is not just," "not every man is not just," except that it does not similarly happen that those which are diametrically opposed are co-verified;[5] sometimes, however, this does hap-

2. If the copula be added, there will be four enunciations—their subsistence exemplified.

* Man or non-man, Waitz.

An. Pr. 46.

3. Four others, with their peculiarity, universals.

subject admits an affirmative. Vide Huyshe, 51, and the translator's note, Aldrich's Log., Oxford, 1843.

[1] That is, besides the two terms, (man) subject, and (just) predicate.

[2] The enunciations will be four which have the same predicate, and in a certain respect the same subject. Two of these, he says, will subsist with respect to affirmation and negation according to the order of consequence, because "man is not just," man not is not just, are referred to "man is just," "man not is just," as privations are referred to habits. By the word negation here, he does not mean the whole proposition, but the words "not is." Farther on he calls "not" negative.

[3] Ἐκ τῶν ὑπογεγραμμενων. Tabula hoc modo disponenda erit

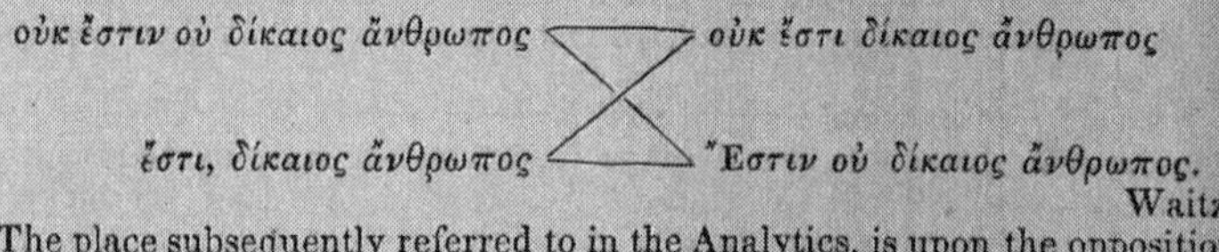

Waitz.

The place subsequently referred to in the Analytics, is upon the opposition of indefinites.

[4] That is, of a distributed subject, which is the case in universal proposition. Vide Whately, book ii. ch. 2, sect. 2.

[5] Since indefinites are compared to particulars, in contingent matter

pen, these two therefore are opposed to each other. But the other two (are opposed) in respect to "non-man," as to a certain added subject, as "non-man is just," "non-man is not just," "the non-just is not man," "the not non-just is not man:" there are not, however, more oppositions than these, but these without those, will be by themselves, as using the noun, "non-man." In those, however, wherein, "is," is not adapted,—as in "he enjoys health," and "he walks,"—here it produces the same when thus placed, as if "is" were added; as "every man enjoys health," "every man does not enjoy health," "every non-man enjoys health," "every non-man does not enjoy health." For it must not be said, "not every man," but the negation, "not," must be added to "man;" for "every" does not signify universal, but that (the thing is taken) universally.[1] This is however evident, from "a man enjoys health," "a man does not enjoy health," "non-man is well," "non-man is not well," these differ from those, in not being universally (taken).[2] Hence "every," or "no one," signifies nothing else, than that affirmation or negation is of a noun universally (assumed); wherefore it is necessary to add other things of the same kind.[3]

4. Others with an indefinite subject.

But because the contrary negation to this, "every animal is just," is that which signifies that "no animal is just," it is evident that these will never be either true at the same time, nor in respect to the same subject, but the opposites to these will sometimes be so, as "not every animal is just," and "some animal is just."[4] But these follow; the one, "no man is just," follows "every man

5. Consequence of the negative

opposite enunciations may be true. Contraries are both false in contingent matter, never both true; subcontraries both true in contingent matter, never both false; contradictories always one true, another false. Vide scheme of opposition.

[1] "Every," "all," "no," etc., are called universal signs, and show that the subject is distributed; but when the common term has no sign at all, the indefinite is decided by the propositional matter, i. e. is universal in impossible, aud particular in contingent matter. Vide the common Logics.

[2] The enunciations, "man is well," "man is not well," differ from "every man is well," "every man is not well."

[3] That is, as the indefinite is made indefinite by the addition of negation to the subject, the same should be done in a definite enunciation, as "every man is well," every non-man is well. τὰ οὖν ἄλλα τὰ αὐτὰ δεῖ προστιθέναι, "reliqua ergo eadem oportet (dicentem) apponere." Buhle.

[4] These are the particulars, or subcontraries.

upon the affirmative, and vice versâ.

is not just," but the opposite, "some man is just," follows "not every man is not just," for it is necessary that some man should be just. In the case also of singulars, it is evident that if a man being questioned denies truly, he asserts also truly, as, "Is Socrates wise? No!" Socrates therefore is not a wise man. But in the case of universals, what is similarly asserted is not true, but the negation is true, as, "Is every man wise? No!" Every man therefore is not wise; for this is false, but this, "not every man then is wise," is true, and this is opposite, but that is contrary.

ἀντικειμενη— ἐναντια.

Opposites, however, as to indefinite nouns and verbs, as "non-man" and "non-just," may seem to be negations without a noun and verb, but they are not so, for the negation must always of necessity be either true or false, but he who says "non-man" does not speak more truly or falsely, but rather less, than he who says "man," except something be added. Still the assertion, "every non-man is just," does not signify the same as any one of those (propositions), nor the opposite to this, namely, "not every non-man is just;" but the assertion, "every one not just is not a man," means the same with, "no one is just who is not a man."

6. An indefinite not a legitimate enunciation.

Nouns and verbs indeed, when transposed, have the same signification, as, "he is a white man," "he is a man white," for unless it be so, there will be many negations of the same thing, but it has been shown that there is one of one; of this, "he is a white man," there is the negation "he is not a white man," and of the other, "he is a man white," (except this be the same with "he is a white man,") the negation will either be "he is not, not a man white," or "he is not a man white." But the one is a negation of this, "he is not a man white," and the other of this, "he is a white man" (so[1] that there will be two negations of one

7. No difference in affirmation or negation produced

[1] This parenthetical sentence is omitted by Taylor, but given by Bekker, Waitz, Buhle, and Averrois; the last gives the following scheme of

Enunciationum indefinitarum dispositio.

A	Affirmativa simplex Homo est justus	Negativa simplex Homo non est justus	B
C	Negativa infinita Homo non est non justus	Affirmativa infinita Homo est non justus	D
E	Negativa privatoria Homo non est injustus	Affirmativa privatoria Homo est injustus	F

affirmation); wherefore it is evident that when a noun and verb are transposed, the same affirmation and negation result.

by transposition.

CHAP. XI.—*Of the Composition and Division of Propositions.*

1. One thing cannot be said of many, nor many of one, by one affirmation or negation.—Exception.

To affirm, and deny, one thing of many, or many of one, is not one affirmation nor one negation, except that is some one thing which is manifested from the many; I mean by one, not if one name be given to many things, nor if one thing result from them, as "man" is perhaps "animal," and "biped," and "mild," yet one thing results from these; but from "white" and "man," and "to walk," one thing does not result, so that neither if a person affirm one certain thing of these is it one affirmation, but there is one articulate sound indeed,[1] yet many affirmations, nor if he affirmed these things of one, (would there be one affirmation,) but in like manner, many. If, then, dialectic interrogation be the seeking of an answer, either of a proposition, or of either part of a contradiction, (but a proposition is a part of one contradiction,) there would not be one answer to these, for neither is there one interrogation, not even if it be true: we have, however, spoken of these in the Topics, at the same time it is evident that, What is it? is not a dialectic interrogation,[2] for a choice should be given from the interrogation to

Topics, viii. 7. Soph. El. c. 6. Cf. Prior An. i. 1.

He divides also "universals" and "particulars" after the same manner. The whole treatise he distinguishes into two books, the 2nd commencing with this chapter, and treating of indefinite enunciations generally. The Greeks resolved it into five sections; Boethius, sometimes into two, and at others into six books; the Latin translators generally, into two books. These differences, in the earlier commentators, have given rise to much confusion in quotation, amongst their successors.

[1] Or φωνὴ μία—una vox. Aristotle's doctrine in the Topics differs from that of Porphyry, as the latter does from Aldrich. The word κατηγόρημα, occurrent lower down, signifies a predicable—the expressions categorematic and syncategorematic are not Aristotelian, but are met with in Michael Psellus. Cf. Trendelenburg, Elem. sect. 9. Waitz, vol. i. p. 267.

[2] On the nature of the interrogation, see Whately ii. 2, 1, and upon interrogational fallacy, book iii. sect. 9. Si quis vero quærit ita ut quod responderi debeat unum quidem sit, sed definitione datâ exponendum, unum quidem est quod quæritur et quod respondetur, quæstio vero dia-

προδιορίσασθαι. Taylor.

enunciate this or that part of the contradiction; but the interrogator must besides define, whether this particular thing, or not this, be a man.

Κατηγόρημα.

As, however, there are some things predicated as composites, so that there is one whole predicable, of those which are predicated separately, but others are not so, what is the difference? For in respect of "man," we may truly and separately predicate "animal" and "biped," and these as one thing; also "man" and "white," and these as one thing; but not if he is "a shoemaker" and "a good man," is he therefore also a good shoemaker. For if, because each of these is true, both, conjointly, should be of necessity true, many absurdities would follow, for "man" and "white" are truly predicated of a man, so that the whole together may be;[1] again, if the thing "is white," the whole conjointly "is white," wherefore, it will be "a man white, white," even to infinity; again, "a musician white walking," and these frequently involved to infinity. Once more, if "Socrates" is "Socrates" and "man," "Socrates" is also "Socrates man," and if he is "man" and "biped," he is also "man biped;" wherefore it is evident, if a man says conjunctions are simply produced,[2] the result will be that he will utter many absurdities.

3. Disjunctions not to be assumed, as conjunctively true.

Let us now show how they are to be placed. Of things predicated, and of those of which it happens to be predicated, whatever are accidentally enunciated, either in respect of the same, or the one of the other, these will not be one; as "man is white," and "a musician;" but "whiteness" and

lectica, quoniam quæstione dialecticâ non interrogatur quæ sit hominis definitio, sed utrum hæc sit hominis definitio, an non sit. Waitz.

[1] Since "man" and "white" are predicated at the same time, and the subject may be said to be "a white man." The rule is, that we cannot use a separate predicate when there is in the subject any thing so opposed to a portion of the predicate, as to cause any contradiction, as if a dead man were called a man. If there is any contradiction between the predicate and subject, the proposition will be false, yet if there be no such contradiction, it does not follow that the latter is always true. In most cases, however, of this sort, we find a fourth term surreptitiously introduced, by the ambiguity of the copula.

[2] Τὰς συμπλοκὰς ἁπλῶς γίνεσθαι, si quis simpliciter dicat complexiones fieri. Averrois. Compare Whately, book i. and ii. ch. 5; also book iii. sect. 9; also Hill's Logic, 108, et seq., and observations upon logical division.

"music" are not one thing, for both are accidents to the same thing. Neither if it be true to call what is white musical, yet at the same time will "musical" "white" be one thing, for what is "white" is "musical" per accidens, so that "white musical" will not be one thing, wherefore neither is a man said to be "a good shoemaker" singly, but also "a biped animal," because these are not predicated of him per accidens. Moreover, neither are such things which are inherent in another (to be added), hence, neither is "whiteness" (to be predicated) repeatedly, nor is "a man" "a man animal," nor (a man) "biped," since both animal and biped are inherent in man; still it is true to assert it singly of some one, as that "a certain man is a man," or that "a certain white man is a white man," but this is not the case always. But when some opposition is in the adjunct which a contradiction follows, it is not true, but false, as to call a dead man a man, but when such is not inherent, it is true. Or when something (contradictory) is inherent, it is always not true; but when it is not inherent, it is not always true, as "Homer" is something, "a poet," for instance, "*is*" he therefore, or "*is*" he not? for "is" is predicated of Homer accidentally, since "*is*" is predicated of Homer because he is a poet, but not per se (or essentially). Wherefore, in whatever categories, contrariety is not inherent, if definitions are asserted instead of nouns, and are essentially predicated, and not accidentally, of these a particular thing may be truly and singly asserted; but non-being, because it is a matter of opinion, cannot truly be called a certain being, for the opinion of it is, not that it is, but that it is not.

4. Rules for simple and composite predication.

CHAP. XII.—*On Modal Proposition.*[1]

THESE things then being determined, let us consider how the affirmations, and negations of the possible and impossible to be, subsist with reference to each other, also of the contingent and the

1. Of the negations τοῦ δυνατὸν εἶναι, ἐνδεχόμενον εἶναι, and the like.

[1] Aristotle here enumerates four modes, but in Anal. Prior, i. 2, they are reduced to two, the necessary and contingent. See St. Hilaire's Translation. The Greek commentators have multiplied the modes, by allowing any adverb, added to the predicate, or adjective qualifying the subject to constitute a modal. The word τρόπος, as applied to the modes

non-contingent, and of the impossible and necessary, since this has some doubtful points. For if among the complex, those contradictions are mutually opposed, which are arranged according to the verb "to be," and "not to be," (as for instance the negation "to be a man," is "not to be man," not this, "to be not a man," and the negation of "to be a white man" is "not to be a white man," and not this "to be not a white man," since if affirmation or negation be true of every thing, it will be true to say "that wood is not a white man,")—if this be so, in those things to which the verb "to be" is not added, that which is asserted instead of the verb "to be," will produce the same thing. For example, the negation of "a man walks," will not be "non-man walks," but, "a man does not walk," for there is no difference in saying that "a man walks," or that "a man is walking," so that if this is every where the case, the negation of "it is possible to be," will be "it is possible not to be," and not "it is not possible to be." But it appears that it is possible for the same thing both to be, and not to be, for every thing which may possibly be cut, or may possibly walk, may also possibly not be cut, and not walk, and the reason is that every thing which is thus possible, does not always energize,[1] so that negation will also belong to it, for that which is capable of walking, may not walk, and the visible may not be seen. Still however it is impossible that opposite affirmations and negations should be true of the same thing, wherefore the ne-

2. The possible—οὐκ ἀεὶ ἐνεργεῖ.

of propositions and of syllogisms, comes from the Greek commentators, but is not Aristotelian. (Ammonius Schol. p. 130, a. 16.) The admission of modals into Logic, has been strongly advocated and opposed; the determination of the *implied* matter of a *pure* proposition is extralogical of course, but respecting the *expressed* matter of a modal, the reader will find some valuable remarks in Mansel's Logic. The authorities are, on one side of the question Sir W. Hamilton, on the other Kant and St. Hilaire. A modal is reducible to a pure categorical, by uniting the modal word to the predicate, or to the subject when the mode only expresses the nature of the matter of the proposition, e. g. a fish necessarily lives in the water, i. e. all fish live in the water. Though the manner of connexion between the extremes is expressed in a modal, yet it does not thereby test the quantity of the proposition, as there are universals and particulars in each mode. On the distinction of propositional matter, see Sir. W. Hamilton, Ed. Rev. No. 115, p. 217. Also the commentary of Ammonius, de Int. 7, (Scholia, p. 115, a. 14).

[1] "Non semper in actu est." Averrois. Cf. Metap. lib. ii. 4, and books 7 and 8; also Physics, lib. ii.

gation of "it is possible to be," is not "it is possible not to be." Now it results from this that we either at the same time affirm and deny the same thing of the same, or that the affirmations and negations are not made according to the additions, "to be" or "not to be;[1]" if therefore, that, be impossible, this, will be to be taken, wherefore the negation of "it is possible to be," is "it is not possible to be," (but* not it is possible not to be). Now there is the same reasoning also about the being contingent, for the negation of this is, not to be contingent, and in like manner as to the rest, for example the necessary and impossible, since as in those it happens that, "to be," and, "not to be," are additions, but "whiteness" and "man" are subjects, so here "to be" and "not to be," become as subjects, but "to be possible," and "to be contingent," are additions which determine the true and false in the (enunciations) "to be possible" and "to be not possible," similarly as in those, "to be," and "not to be."[2] But of "it is possible not to be," the negation is not, "it is not possible to be," but "it is not possible not to be," and of "it is possible to be," the negation is not, "it is possible not to be," but, "it is not possible to be;" wherefore, "it is possible to be," and, "it is possible not to be," will appear to follow each other; for it is the same thing, "to be possible to be," and "not to be," since such things are not contradictories of each other, namely, "it is possible to be," and, "it is possible not to be." But "it is pos-

* Omitted by Bekker.

[1] Sequitur enim hinc aut idem vere simul affirmari et negari de eodem aut non secundum apposita quatenus ea, *sunt et non sunt*, fieri affirmationes et negationes. Si ergo illud fieri nequit (*ut negatio propositionis modalem negativam efficiat*) hoc (*ut negatio modi efficiat modalem negativam*) eligendum fuerit. Buhle.

[2] Vide Huyshe's Logic, p. 50. As regards modality, judgments according to Kant are problematical, assertorial, and apodeictical. The first are accompanied by a consciousness of the bare possibility of the judgment; the second by a consciousness of its reality; the third by a consciousness of its necessity. Modality is thus dependent on the manner in which a certain relation between two concepts is maintained, and may vary according to the state of different minds, the given concepts, and consequently the matter of the judgment, remaining unaltered. Mansel's Prol. Log., and Appendix, note G. The real state of the case appears to be that, in the endeavour to combine psychological variation with logical distinctness, philosophers have sacrificed the proper office of the latter. As far as proposition is concerned, modals may be turned at once into pure categoricals, in fact, they affect not the *relation* between the terms, but simply the subject or predicate, in other words, the terms themselves alone.

sible to be," and "it is not possible to be," are never true of the same thing at the same time, for they are opposed, neither at least are, "it is possible not to be," and "it is not possible not to be," ever true at the same time of the same thing. Likewise of, "it is necessary to be," the negation is not, "it is necessary not to be," but this, "it is not necessary to be," and of, "it is necessary not to be," (the negation) is this, "it is not necessary not to be." Again, of, "it is impossible to be," the negation is not "it is impossible not to be," but "it is not impossible to be," and of, "it is impossible not to be," (the negation) is, "it is not impossible not to be." In fact, universally, as we have said, "to be" and "not to be," we must necessarily regard as subjects, but those things which produce affirmation and negation we must connect with "to be" and "not to be:" we ought also to consider these as opposite affirmations and negations; possible, impossible, contingent, non-contingent, impossible, not impossible, necessary, not necessary, true, not true.

2. The εἶναι and μὴ εἶναι to be considered as subjects, with which the affirmation and negation is to be connected.

CHAP. XIII. *Of the Sequences of Modal Propositions.*

1. Proper method of disposing relative consequences.

THE consequences are rightly placed thus: "it happens to be," follows, "it is possible to be," and this reciprocates with that; also, "it is not impossible to be" and "it is not necessary to be." But, "it is not necessary not to be," and, "it[1] is not impossible not to be;" follow, "it is possible not to be," and, "it may happen not to be;" and, "it is necessary not to be," and, "it is impossible to be," follow, "it is not possible to be," and, "it does not happen to be;" but, "it is necessary to be," and also, "it is impossible not to be," follow, "it is not possible not to be," and, "it is not contingent not to be:" what we say however may be seen from the following description:

1	3
It is possible to be	It is not possible to be
It may happen to be	It may not happen to be

[1] Bekker, Buhle, and Waitz read this clause differently: as all are, however, agreed in the scheme given, I have reconciled their variation by a reference to that. Taylor appears to have done the same.

It is not impossible to be	It is impossible to be
It is not necessary to be.	It is necessary not to be.
2	4
It is possible not to be	It is not possible not to be
It may happen not to be	It may happen not to be
It is not impossible not to be	It is impossible not to be
It is not necessary not to be.	It is necessary to be.

Therefore the impossible, and the not impossible, follow contradictorily the contingent, and the possible, and the non-contingent, and the not possible, and vice versâ;* for the negation of the impossible, namely, "it is not impossible to be," follows, "it is possible to be," but affirmation follows negation, for, "it is impossible to be" follows "it is not possible to be," since "it is impossible to be," is affirmation, but, "it is not impossible to be," is negation.

1. τὸ ἀδύνατον. καὶ οὐκ ἀ: * ἀντεστραμμένως, reciproce. Buhle.

Let us next see how it is with necessary matter, now it is evident that it does not subsist thus, but contraries follow, and contradictories (are placed) separately,[1] for, "it is not necessary to be," is not the negation of "it is necessary not to be," since both, may possibly be true of the same thing, as that which necessarily, is not, need not of necessity, be. But the reason why the necessary follows not, in like manner, other propositions, is that the impossible being enunciated contrarily to the necessary, signifies the same thing; for what it is impossible should exist, must not of necessity *be*, but *not be*, and what is impossible should *not be*, this must of necessity *be;* so that if these similarly follow the possible and the not possible, these (do so) in a contrary mode,[2] since the necessary and the impossible do not signify the same thing, but, as we have said,

2. τὸ ἀναγκαῖον, its peculiarity, with the reason and proof.

[1] Contrarias eas appellat, quum propterea quod non est aliud nomen, quod iis melius conveniat, tum maxime propter locos, quos occupant in tabulâ quam adscripsit: nam in hâc ἐξ ἐναντίας collocatæ sunt *οὐκ ἀναγκαῖον εἶναι* et *ἀναγ. μὴ εἶναι.* Waitz. In the table given above the two former in each column are contraries to the two former in the opposite; and the two latter in each are contrary sequences from the two former. Necessity, according to Aristotle, (Ethics, ch. iii.,) was either absolute (ἁπλῶς), or hypothetical (ἐξ ὑποθέσεως), the former immutable, the latter only conditional. See also Metap. lib. iv.

[2] Namely, "it is necessary and it is not necessary."

Buhle and Averrois omit the question.

vice versâ. Or is it impossible that the contradictories of the necessary should be thus disposed? for, what, "is necessary to be" is "possible to be," since if not, negation would follow, as it is necessary either to affirm or deny, so that, if it is not possible to be, it is impossible to be, wherefore it would be impossible for that to be, which necessarily is, which is absurd, but the enunciation, "it is not impossible to be" follows the other, "it is possible to be," which again is followed by, "it is not necessary to be," whence it happens that what necessarily exists does not necessarily exist, which is absurd. But again neither does, "it is necessary to be" follow "it is possible to be," nor does the proposition, "it is necessary not to be," for to that, both, may occur, but whichever of these is true,[1] those[2] will be no longer true, for at one and the same time, it is possible to be, and not to be, but if it is necessary either to be or not to be, both, will not be possible. It remains therefore, that "it is not necessary not to be," follows "it is possible to be;" for this[3] is also true in respect of what is necessary to be, since this becomes the contradiction of that proposition which follows, viz. "it is not possible to be;" as "it is impossible to be," and "it is necessary not to be," follow that, of which the negation is, "it is not necessary not to be." Wherefore these contradictions follow according to the above-mentioned mode, and nothing absurd results, when they are thus disposed.[4]

2. Solution of a difficulty as to the above, by the distinction between rational and irrational potentiality.

Still it may be doubted whether "it is possible to be," follows "it is necessary to be," for if it does not follow, the contradiction will be consequent, namely, "it is not possible to be," and if a man should deny this to be a contradiction, it will be necessary to call, "it is possible not to be," a contradiction, both which are false in respect of necessary matter. Nay, on the contrary, it appears to be possible that the same thing should "be cut" and "not be cut," should "be" and "not be," so that what necessarily "is," may happen "not to be," which is false. Nevertheless it is evident that not every thing which *can* "be," and *can* "walk," is capable also of the opposites, for in some cases this is not true. In the first place,

[1] That is, it is necessary to be, and it is necessary not to be.
[2] It is possible to be, and it is possible not to be.
[3] It is not necessary not to be.
[4] As above.

in those things which are potent irrationally,[1] as fire is calorific, and has irrational power; rational powers then are those of many things, and of the contraries; but not all irrational powers, for, as we have said, fire cannot heat, and not heat, nor such other things as always energize. Yet even some irrational powers can at the same time receive opposites; but this has been stated by us, because not every power is susceptible of contraries, not even such as are predicated, according to the same species. Moreover, some powers are equivocal, for the possible is not predicated, simply; but one thing is (called so), because it is true, as being in an energy, as it is possible for a man to walk, because he walks, and in short, a thing is possible to be, because that is already in energy which is said to be possible; on the other hand, another thing (is said to be possible), because it may be in energy; as it is possible to walk, because a man may walk. Now *this* power exists in movable natures only, but *that* in immovable; but with respect to both, it is true to say, that it is not impossible to walk or to be, and that a man is now walking and energizing, and has the power to walk, hence it is not true[2] to predicate that which is thus possible, in respect of necessary matter, simply, but the other is true. Wherefore since the universal follows the particular, to be able to be, but not all ability, follows that which is of necessity, and indeed the necessary and the non-necessary may perhaps be

αἱ μετὰ λόγον δυνάμεις.

3. The ἀναγκαῖον καὶ μὴ ἀν,

[1] Non secundum rationem possibilia. Buhle. "Non secundum rationem possunt." Averrois. Compare Metaph. lib. ii. and iv. and viii. In the last place, the same distinction between rational and irrational powers is maintained; the reader will find also that the whole of the 8th chapter turns on the difference between δυνάμις and ἐνεργεια. Briefly, the former is (as here) simple potentiality; the latter, that active state, in which potentiality may be. Aristotle places the ἐνεργεια, and properly, antecedent to the δῦναμις. Vide also Ethics, book i. ch. 2. Δυνάμεις considered as faculties were five, of which vegetables possessed one, brutes four, and man all. Compare Aristot. de Animâ. The resistance given, has respect to the potentiality of the *will*, which of course is excluded from irrational subjects, hence they are, in a sense, unsusceptible of contraries; man's will, being potential, has power to restrict his δυνάμεις, or place them in ἐνεργειᾷ, but irrational subjects have no potential will, hence the difference.

[2] It is only truly asserted of what is hypothetically necessary, because a thing must of necessity be, when it will be, though it will not necessarily be.

are the ἀρχὴ πάντων εἶναι, ἢ μὴ εἶναι?

the principle of the existence, or of the non-existence of all things, and we should consider other things as consequent upon these.[1] Hence from what we have stated, it is clear that whatever exists of necessity, is in energy, so that if eternal natures are prior in existence, energy also is prior to power, and some things, as the first substances, are energies without power, but others with power, namely, those which are prior by nature, but posterior in time: lastly, there are some which are never energies, but are capacities only.

4. The τὸ ἐξ ἀνάγκης ὄν, κατ' ἐνεργειάν ἐστιν. Priority.

CHAP. XIV. *Of Contrary Propositions.*[2]

1. Those opinions are con-

BUT whether is affirmation contrary to negation, or affirmation to affirmation? and is the sentence

[1] The following order will explain:

1	3
It is necessary to be	It is not necessary to be
It is not possible not to be	It is possible not to be
It may not happen not to be	It may happen not to be
It is impossible not to be.	It is impossible not to be.
2	**4**
It is necessary not to be	It is not necessary not to be
It is not possible to be	It is possible to be
It may not happen to be	It may happen to be
It is impossible to be.	It is not impossible to be.

Waitz observes that he does not consider the πρώτη οὐσια here as in the Categories, but as in the Metaphysics. Vide Metap. b. iii. 4, 6, etc., also Physics, lib. ii. and De Anima, i. 1, 2, and ii. 1, 2. Ed. Trendelenburg. The learned note of Ammonius, too long to insert, tends to show no more than what can be gleaned by the student from a reference to the places quoted, namely, that with Aristotle, energy is prior to capacity, and that the necessary being invariably the same in subsistence, can only be predicated of things which are always in energy: this conclusion being syllogistically educed, he proceeds to evolve the contingents and consequences, placing form in energy, matter in capacity. In the Meta. 12th book, he calls the gods—essences in energy. Composites are those which participate of matter, and either may or may not retain form: thus beings are, first, energies simple and immutable, next, those which are mutable, yet connected with energy, others, which precede energy as to time, but do not always obtain it, lastly, others which subsist as to capacity alone, and are not naturally adapted to energy. Vide Ammonius in librum de Interpretatione.

[2] This chapter is not given separately in the text, by Waitz: with Ammonius it forms the fifth section of the treatise. He considers it either

which says, "every man is just," contrary to the one, "no man is just," or the sentence "every man is just," to, "every man is unjust," as "Callias is just," "Callias is not just," "Callias is unjust,"—which of these are contraries? For if things in the voice, follow those which exist in the intellect,[1] but there the opinion of a contrary is contrary, as for instance, that "every man is just," is contrary to, "every man is unjust," it is necessary that affirmations also in the voice should subsist in the same manner, but if there, the opinion of a contrary be not contrary, neither will affirmation be contrary to affirmation, but the before-named negation. Hence it must be considered what false opinion is contrary to the true opinion, whether that of negation or that which opines it to be the contrary. I mean in this way, there is a certain true opinion of good that it is good, but another false opinion that it is not good, lastly, a third, that it is evil, which of these therefore is contrary to the true opinion? and if there is one, according to which is it contrary? If then a man should fancy contrary opinions to be defined by this, that they are of contraries, it would be erroneous, for of good that it is good, and of evil that it is evil, there is perhaps the same opinion, and it is true whether there be many (opinions) or one: but these are contraries, yet not from their being of contraries are they contraries, but rather from their subsisting in a contrary manner.[2] If then there is an opinion of good that it is good, but another that it is not good, and there is also something else, which is neither inherent, nor can be, in good, we cannot admit any contrary of the rest, neither

trary which are of contrary matter, and the propositional contrariety corresponds with the contrariety of opinion.

as spuriously introduced by some one posterior to Aristotle, or written by him to exercise the reader's judgment upon what has been said, as in the Categories he contends that what is sensible is prior to sense, explaining the system of relation generally in his Physical Auscultation.

[1] Vide supra, ch. i.; also Ethics, book vi. ch. 1 and 2. As Waitz observes, he seems to refer to the same subject in the Metaphysics, where he takes for granted that ἐναντία ἐστὶ δόξα δοξῇ ἡ τῆς ἀντιφάσεως, and again in the Topics. Waitz, 363. Vide also Whately, book ii. ch. 2, 3, and Huyshe, sect. 4: whose remarks will fully explain this chapter. The example, Callias is just—is unjust, is in fact a contradiction. (Vide De Interpretatione, ch. 7.)

[2] μαλλον τῷ ἐναντίως, in a form of logical contrariety. On the threefold division of good, by the Pythagoreans and Peripatetics, see Cic. Acad. i. 5; Tusc. v. 85. Ethics, book i. 8.

such opinions as imagine the non-inherent to be inherent, nor the inherent to be non-inherent, (for both are infinite,[1] both as many as imagine the non-inherent to be inherent, and the inherent to be non-inherent); but in those things in which there is deception, (therein we admit contraries,) and these are from which there are generations; generations however are from opposites, wherefore deceptions also. If then good is good and not evil, and the one is essential, but the other accidental —(for it is accidental to it not to be evil) and of every thing the opinion is more true and false which is essential, if the true (be assumed)—the opinion that good is not good, is false in respect of that which is essentially inherent, but the opinion that it is evil is false of that which is from accident, so that the opinion of the negation of good would be more false than the opinion of the contrary. He is however especially deceived about every thing who holds a contrary opinion, for contraries belong to things which are the most diverse about the same thing. If then one of these is contrary, but the opinion of the negation is more contrary, it is evident that this itself will be (truly) contrary; but the opinion that the good is evil is complex, for it is necessary perhaps, that the same man should suppose (good) not good. Once more, if it is requisite for the like to occur in other things, it may seem to have been well said in this case also; for the (opposition) of negation is either every where or no where; but whatever things have no contraries, of these, the opposite to the true opinion is false, as he is mistaken who fancies "a man" "not a man," if then these (negations) are contrary the other (opinions) also, of negation, are. Besides, it is the same as to the opinion of good that it is good, and of what is not good, that it is not good; and also the opinion of good, that it is not good, and of what is not good that it is good; to the opinion then of the not good that it is not good, which is true, what will be the contrary? Certainly not that which says that it is evil, since it may at one and the same time be true; but truth is never contrary to truth, for whatever is not good is evil, so that it will happen that these opinions, shall be at one and the same time, true. Nor again will that (opinion) that it is not

2. Nature of contrariety between affirmation and negation.

[1] This parenthesis is omitted by Taylor. I follow the reading of Buhle and Waitz.

evil, be (the contrary), for that is also true, and these may exist at the same time, wherefore (the opinion) of what is not good, that it is good, remains as a contrary to the opinion of what is not good, that it is not good, and this will be false, so that the opinion of good that it is not good, will be the contrary to that of what is good, that it is good. That there will be no difference though we should propose universal affirmation is evident, for universal negation will be the contrary; as for instance, to the opinion which supposes every thing good to be good, that nothing of good things is good (will be the contrary opinion), for the opinion of good that it is good, if good be universal, is the same with that which opines that whatever is good is good, and this differs in no respect from the opinion that every thing which is good is good, and the like takes place as to that which is not good. So that if this be the case in opinion, and affirmations and negations in the voice are symbols of (conceptions) in the soul, it is clear that the universal negation which is about the same thing, is contrary to affirmation. For instance, to "every thing good is good," or that "every man is good," (the negation is contrary,) that "nothing or no man is good;" but this, that "not every thing, or not every man," (is good, is opposed) contradictorily. It is however evident, that true opinion can neither possibly be contrary to true opinion, nor true negation (to true negation), for those are contraries which subsist about opposites; but about the same things the same may be verified, but contraries cannot possibly be inherent in the same thing, at one and the same time.[1]

8. Contraries cannot co-exist ἅμα ἐν τῷ αὐτῷ.

[1] Vide the canones oppositarum. Aldrich. Also notes upon the 7th chap. de Interpret.

"...Prior Analytics placed first in the Organon, as it contains the theory of the Syllogism." Enc. Brit. 492
See P. 244

THE PRIOR ANALYTICS.[1]

BOOK I.

CHAP. I.—*Of Proposition, Term, Syllogism, and its Elements.*

1. Purport of this treatise—the attainment of demonstrative science.

IT is first requisite to say what is the subject, concerning which, and why, the present treatise is undertaken, namely, that it is concerning demonstration, and for the sake of demonstrative science; we must afterwards define, what is a proposition, what a term, and what a syllogism, also what kind of syllogism is perfect, and what imperfect; lastly, what it is for a thing to be, or not to be, in a certain whole, and what we say it is to be predicated of every thing, or of nothing (of a class).

2. Definition of (πρότασις) proposition. It is either,
1. καθόλου, universal,
2. ἐν μέρει, particular,
3. or ἀδιόριστον, indefinite.

A proposition then is a sentence which affirms or denies something of something,[2] and this is universal, or particular, or indefinite; I denominate universal, the being present[3] with all or none; particular, the being present with something, or not with something, or not with every thing; but the indefinite the being present or not being present, without the universal or particular (sign); as for example, that there is the same science of contraries, or that

[1] Aristotle herein analyzes syllogism and demonstration into their principles; the names Prior and Posterior were given to these treatises in the time of Galen, but it is remarkable, that when Aristotle cites them, he denominates the former, "Concerning Syllogism," and the latter "Concerning Demonstration." Upon the subject of title, compare St. Hilaire, Mémoire, vol. i. p. 42, with Waitz, vol. i. p. 367; and for general elucidation of the treatise itself, much information has been derived from the valuable commentary of Pacius.

[2] Oratio indicativa, etc., Aldrich, "Oratio enunciativa," Boethius. The latter's definition is the better.

[3] The word ὑπάρχειν, inesse, has given ample scope for the exercise of logical contention: Taylor objects to translating it, the being inherent, and points out an anomaly arising from Pacius' use of it in this way, in the next chapter. He asserts that the real Aristotelian sense is "being present with." For the account of the word, see note, p. 53.

3. Difference between the demonstrative (ἀποδεικτικὴ) and the διαλεκτικὴ πρότασις.

pleasure is not good. But a demonstrative proposition differs from a dialectic in this, that the demonstrative is an assumption of one part of the contradiction, for a demonstrator does not interrogate, but assume, but the dialectic is an interrogation of contradiction.[1] As regards however forming a syllogism from either proposition, there will be no difference between one and the other, since he who demonstrates and he who interrogates syllogize, assuming that something is or is not present with something.

4. The syllogistic proposition.

Wherefore a syllogistic proposition will be simply an affirmation or negation of something concerning something, after the above-mentioned mode: it is however demonstrative if it be true, and assumed through hypotheses from the beginning,[2] and the dialectic proposition is to him who inquires an interrogation of contradiction, but to him who syllogizes, an assumption of what is seen and probable, as we have shown in the Topics. What therefore a proposition is, and wherein the syllogistic demonstrative and dialectic differ, will be shown accurately

5. The demonstrative.

[1] The oldest Greek commentator, Alexander Aphrodisiensis, speaks of the λογικὴ καὶ συλλογιστικὴ πραγματεία as containing under it, ἀποδεικτική, διαλεκτική, πειραστική, and σοφιστική. Schol. p. 149, a. 19.

[2] These are ἀξιώματα, the truth of which are self-evident. Waitz. They correspond to the κοιναὶ ἔννοιαι of the mathematicians. The place referred to is the 1st book of the Topics. As assumption by the name of hypothesis forms one of the Aristotelian ἀρχαί, or principles of science, we annex the following table of the latter from Mansel's Appendix.

'Αρχαὶ

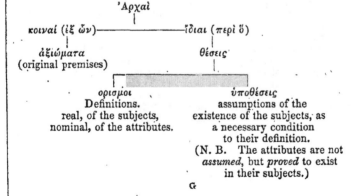

κοιναί (ἐξ ὧν) — ἴδιαι (περὶ ὅ)

ἀξιώματα (original premises) | θέσεις

θέσεις:

ορισμοι
Definitions.
real, of the subjects,
nominal, of the attributes.

ὑποθέσεις
assumptions of the existence of the subjects, as a necessary condition to their definition.
(N. B. The attributes are not *assumed*, but *proved* to exist in their subjects.)

in the following treatises, but for our present requirements what has now been determined by us may perhaps suffice. Again, I call that a "term," into which a proposition is resolved, as for instance, the predicate and that of which it is predicated, whether to be or not to be is added or separated. Lastly, a syllogism is a sentence in which certain things being laid down, something else different from the premises necessarily results, in consequence of their existence.[1] I say that, "in consequence of their existence," something results through them, but though something happens through them, there is no need of any external term in order to the existence of the necessary (consequence). Wherefore I call a perfect syllogism that which requires nothing else, beyond (the premises) assumed, for the necessary (consequence) to appear: but an imperfect syllogism, that which requires besides, one or more things, which are necessary, through the supposed terms, but have not been assumed through propositions.[2] But for one thing to be in the whole of another, and for one thing to be predicated of the whole of another, are the same thing, and we say it is predicated of the whole, when nothing can be assumed of the subject, of which the other may not be asserted, and as regards being predicated of nothing, in like manner.[3]

6. Definition of a term—ὅρος.

7. And of a syllogism.

1. The latter either perfect, τέλειος, or, 2. ἀτελής.

8. Definition of predication de omni et nullo.

[1] Vide Aldrich. Aristotle's definition is translated by Aulus Gellius, xv. 26. Oratio in quâ, consensis quibusdam et concessis aliud quid, quam quæ concessa sunt, per ea, quæ concessa sunt necessario conficitur. On the subject of the syllogism being a petitio principii, vide Mansel's Logic, Appendix D.

[2] Cf. Aquinas Opusc. 47. de Syll. cap. viii. Scotus, lib. i. Anal. Prior, Quæst. xxii. seqq. Occam, Log. p. 3, cap. 6. The direct and indirect syllogisms of the Schoolmen must not be confounded with the perfect and imperfect of Aristotle: an indirect syllogism has the minor term the predicate, and the major the subject, of the conclusion.

[3] That is, when nothing can be assumed of the subject of which the other can be predicated. With Aristotle the "dictum de omni et nullo," is the principle of all syllogism. Vide Whately, b. i. sect. 4. See also the same principle, Categor. 3.

CHAP. II.—*On the Conversion of Propositions.*

SINCE every proposition is either of that which is present (simply), or is present necessarily or contingently, and of these some are affirmative, but others negative, according to each appellation; again, since of affirmative and negative propositions some are universal, others particular, and others indefinite, it is necessary that the universal negative proposition of what is present should be converted in its terms; for instance, if "no pleasure is good," "neither will any good be pleasure." But an affirmative proposition we must of necessity convert not universally, but particularly,[1] as if "all pleasure is good," it is also necessary that "a certain good should be pleasure;" but of particular propositions, we must convert the affirmative proposition particularly, since if "a certain pleasure is good," so also "will a certain good be pleasure;" a negative proposition however need not be thus converted, since it does not follow, if "man" is not present with "a certain animal," that animal also is not present with a certain man.

1. Doctrine of conversion, with example of conversion in E, universally.

2. A and I to be converted particularly.

3. Conversion of O unnecessary.

Let then first the proposition A B be an universal negative; if A is present with no B, neither will B be present with any A, for if it should be present with some A, for example with C, it will not be true, that A is present with no B, since C is something of B. If, again, A is present with every B, B will be also present with some A, for if with no A, neither will A be present with any B, but it was supposed to be present with every B. In a similar manner also if the proposition be particular, for if A

4. Examples.

[1] Aristotle's account of conversion differs from that of Aldrich, since he divides conversion into universal and particular, having respect to the quality of the proposition *after conversion*. Ἁπλῆ ἀντιστροφη is mentioned by Philoponus Scholia. On the conversion per accidens, of the logicians, see Whately, b. ii. sect. 4. Boethius uses the expressions generalis and per accidens. Whately's term, conversion by limitation, is far better. The example in the text is worked out more shortly by Theophrastus and Eudemus. It is to be noticed that, having in Inter. ch. 12, spoken of four modes, he here reduces them to two Vide St. Hilaire's Translation, Preface, p. 66.

be present with some B, B must also necessarily be present with some A, for if it were present with none, neither would A be present with any B, but if A is not present with some B, B need not be present with some A, for example, if B is "animal," but A, "man," for man is not present with "every animal," but "animal" is present with "every man."

CHAP. III.—*On the Conversion of Modal Propositions.*[1]

1. Rule for modal conversion the same as for pure propositions. Example of the necessary modal.

THE same system will hold good in necessary propositions, for an universal negative is universally convertible, but either affirmative proposition particularly; for if it is necessary that A should be present with no B, it is also necessary that B should be present with no A, for if it should happen to be present with any, A also might happen to be present with some B. But if A is of necessity present with every or with some certain B, B is also necessarily present with some certain A; for if it were not necessarily, neither would A of necessity be present with some certain B: a particular negative however is not converted, for the reason we have before assigned.

In contingent propositions, (since contingency is multifariously predicated, for we call the necessary, and the not necessary, and the possible, contingent,) in all affirmatives, conversion will occur in a similar manner, for if A is contingent to every or to some certain B, B may also be contingent to some A; for if it were to none, neither would A be to any B; for this has been shown before.

(Vide ch. 2.)

The like however does not occur in negative propositions, but such things as are called contingent either from their being necessarily not present, or from their being not necessarily present, (are converted) similarly (with the

[1] Modality is not altogether excluded from Logic; but is admitted by Aristotle, only when, being expressed in a proposition, it necessitates under certain conditions a corresponding modification of consequence. Logic has nothing to do with deciding the truth or falsity of proposition, *per se*, necessarily or contingently; it only ascertains the necessary inference of conclusion from premises according to certain canons. Vide some admirable remarks by Sir W. Hamilton on this subject. Psellus and Petrus Hispanus are both extra-logical in their consideration of matter.

former); e. g. if a man should say, that it is contingent, for "a man," not to be "a horse," or for "whiteness" to be present with no "garment." For of these, the one, is necessarily not present, but the other, is not necessarily, present; and the proposition is similarly convertible, for if it be contingent to no "man" to be "a horse," it also concurs with no "horse" to be "a man," and if "whiteness" happens to no "garment," a "garment" also happens to no "whiteness;" for if it did happen to any, "whiteness" will also necessarily happen to "a certain garment," and this has been shown before, and in like manner with respect to the particular negative proposition. But whatever things are called contingent as being for the most part and from their nature, (after which manner we define the contingent,) will not subsist similarly in negative conversions, for an universal negative proposition is not converted, but a particular one is, this however will be evident when we speak of the contingent. At present, in addition to what we have said, let thus much be manifest, that to happen to nothing, or not to be present with any thing, has an affirmative figure,* for "it is contingent," is similarly arranged with "it is," and "it is" always and entirely produces affirmation in whatever it is attributed to, e. g. "it is not good," or, "it is not white," or in short, "it is not this thing." This will however be shown in what follows, but as regards conversions, these will coincide with the rest.

2. Of the contingent, with example.

(Ch. 2.)

3. Of things called contingent, with the differences in conversion between E and O.

* Cf. ch. 12, de Interpretatione.

CHAP. IV.—*Of Syllogism, and of the first Figure.*

THESE things being determined, let us now describe by what, when, and how, every syllogism is produced, and let us afterwards speak of demonstration, for we must speak of syllogism prior to demonstration, because syllogism is more universal, since, indeed, demonstration is a certain syllogism, but not every syllogism is demonstration.

1. Syllogism being more universal than demonstration is first discussed—its nature and construction.

When, then, three terms so subsist, with reference to each other, as that the last is in the whole of the middle, and the middle either is, or is not, in the whole of the first, then it is necessary that there should be a perfect syllogism of the extremes.

2. Definition of ὁ μέσος, and of ἄκρα—example of syllogism.

But I call that the middle,[1] which is itself in another, whilst another is in it,[2] and which also becomes the middle by position,[3] but the extreme[4] that which is itself in another, and in which another also is.[5] For if A is predicated of every B, and B of every C, A must necessarily be predicated of every C, for it has been before shown, how we predicate "of every;" so also if A is predicated of no B, but B is predicated of every C, A will not be predicated of any C. But if the first is in every

[1] That is, in the first figure, because the middle is placed otherwise in the second and third figures.

[2] That is, in the first figure; the middle is the subject of the major premise, and predicate of the minor.

[3] That is, the middle is placed between the extremes. Aristotle, in his figures, regards rather the extension of the middle, than its position in the two premises. Vide Trendelenburg, Elem. sect. 28. Waitz, Anal. Pr. 23.

[4] The majus extremum, τὸ μεῖζον ἄκρον, is called also τὸ πρωτὸν. An. Pr. book i. ch. 31; the minus, τὸ ἔλαττον, also τὸ ἔσχατον. An. Pr. book ii. ch. 8. Cf. Aldrich, cap. iii. sect. 3.

[5] The minor extreme is the subject of the middle in the minor premise; and the major extreme is the predicate of the middle in the major premise.

Ex. 1.	Every man is an animal No horse is a man Every horse is an animal.	Every man is an animal No stone is a man No stone is an animal.
Ex. 2.	No line is science No medicine is a line Every medicine is science.	No line is science No unity is a line No unity is science.
Ex. 3.	Some habit {is / is not} good All prudence is a habit All prudence is good.	Some habit {is / is not} good All ignorance is a habit No ignorance is good.
Ex. 4.	Some horse {is / is not} white No swan is a horse Every swan is white.	Some horse {is / is not} white No crow is a horse No crow is white.
Ex. 5.	Every man is an animal Something white (i. e. a swan) is not a man Every swan is an animal.	Every man is an animal Something white (i. e. snow) is not a man No snow is an animal.
Ex. 6.	No man is inanimate Something white (i. e. snow) is not a man All snow is inanimate.	No man is inanimate Something white (i. e. a swan) is not a man No swan is inanimate.

middle, but the middle is in no last, there is not a syllogism of the extremes, for nothing necessarily results from the existence of these, since the first happens to be present with every, and with no extreme; so that neither a particular nor universal (conclusion) necessarily results, and nothing necessary resulting, there will not be through these a syllogism. Let the terms of being present universally, be "animal," "man," "horse," and let the terms of being present with no one be "animal," "man," "stone."* Since, then, neither the first term is present with the middle, nor the middle with any extreme, there will not thus be a syllogism. Let the terms of being present, be "science," "line," "medicine," but of not being present, "science," "line," "unity;"† the terms then being universal, it is manifest in this figure, when there will and when there will not be a syllogism, also that when there is a syllogism, it is necessary that the terms should subsist, as we have said, and that if they do thus subsist there will evidently be a syllogism.

* Example (1.)

† Example (2.)

But if one of the terms be universal and the other particular, in relation to the other, when the universal is joined to the major extreme, whether affirmative or negative, but the particular to the minor affirmative, there must necessarily be a perfect syllogism, but when the (universal) is joined to the minor, or the terms are arranged in some other way, a (syllogism) is impossible. I call the major extreme that in which the middle is, and the minor that which is under the middle. For let A be present with every B, but B with some C, if then to be predicated "of every" is what has been asserted from the first, A must necessarily be present with some C, and if A is present with no B, but B with some C, A must necessarily not be present with some C, for what we mean by the being predicated of no one has been defined, so that there will be a perfect syllogism. In like manner, if B, C, being affirmative, be indefinite, for there will be the same syllogism, both of the indefinite, and of that which is assumed as a particular.

3. Definition of τὸ μεῖζον, and τὸ ἔλαττον ἄκρον.

4. Syllogistic ratio the same for indefinite as for the particular.

If indeed to the minor extreme an universal affirmative or negative be added, there will not be a syllogism, whether the indefinite, or particular, affirms or denies, e. g. if A is or is not present

5. No syllogism if the minor be universal, but the major particular, or indefinite.

with some B, but B is present to every C; let the terms of affirmation be "good," "habit," "prudence," and those of negation, "good," "habit," "ignorance."* Again, if B is present with no C, but A is present or is not present with some B, or not with every B; neither thus will there be a syllogism; let the terms of being present with every (individual) be "white,"† "horse," "swan;" but those of being present with no one, be "white," "horse," "crow." The same also may be taken if A, B be indefinite. Neither will there be a syllogism, when to the major extreme the universal affirmative or negative is added; but to the minor, a particular negative, whether it be indefinitely or particularly taken, e. g. if A is present with every B; but B is not present with some, or not with every C, for to what the middle is not present, to this, both to every, and to none, the first will be consequent. For let the terms, "animal," "man," "white," be supposed, afterwards from among those white things, of which man is not predicated, let "swan" and "snow" be taken; hence "animal" is predicated of every individual of the one, but of no individual of the other, wherefore there will not be a syllogism.‡ Again, let A be present with no B, but B not be present with some C, let the terms also be "inanimate," "man," "white," then let "swan" and "snow" be taken from those white things, of which man is not predicated, for inanimate is predicated of every individual of the one, but of no individual of the other.§ Once more, since it is indefinite for B not to be present with some C, (for it is truly asserted, that it is not present with some C, whether it is present with none, or not with every C,) such terms being taken, so as to be present with none, there will be no syllogism (and this has been declared before). Wherefore it is evident, that when the terms are thus, there will not be a syllogism, since if one could be, there could be also one in these, and in like manner it may be shown, if even an universal negative be taken. Nor will there by any means be a syllogism, if both particular intervals[1] be predicated either as affirmative or nega-

* Example (3.)

† Example (4.)

6. Nor when the major is A or E, but the minor O.

‡ Example (5.)

§ Example (6.)

7. Nor when both are particular, etc.

[1] Propositions. "Propositio ipsa vocatur passim ab Aristotele, 'inter-

tive, or the one affirmative and the other negative, or the one indefinite, or the other definite, or both indefinite; but let the common terms of all be "animal," "white," "man," "animal," "white," "stone."* *Example (7.)

From what has been said, then, it is evident, that if there be a particular syllogism in this figure, the terms must necessarily be as we have said, and that if the terms be thus, there will necessarily be a syllogism, but by no means if they are otherwise. It is also clear, that all the syllogisms in this figure are perfect,[1] for all are perfected through the first assumptions; and that all problems are demonstrated by this figure, for by this, to be present with all, and with none, and with some, and not with some, (are proved,) and such I call the first figure.[2]

8. Σχῆμα πρῶτον. The first figure complete, and comprehends all classes of affirmation and negation.

Chap. V.—*Of the second Figure.*

When the same (middle term) is present with every individual, (of the one,) but with none, (of the other,) or is present to every or to none of each,

1. Σχῆμα, Β., its denomination, with the position of the

vallum,' 'διάστημα,' quoniam duobus extremis terminis includitur, eorumque intervallum efficit." Buhle.

Ex. 7. Something white {is / is not} an animal	Something white {is / is not} an animal
Some man {is / is not} white	Some stone {is / is not} white
Every man is an animal.	No stone is an animal.

[1] For the special and general rules of syllogism, see the common Logics. It is sufficient to observe here, that the Aristotelian dictum is directly applicable only to the first figure, which is therefore the type of all syllogisms, and that the special rules, as laid down by Petrus Hispanus, may all be found in this and the following chapters.

[2] On the term προβλήματα, compare Alexander Schol. p. 150, b. xl. with this place, and also with Topics, i. 4. Schol. p. 256, a. 14, here, it is used as ζητούμενα, or "quæstiones," upon which vide Aldrich, cap. 3. The term σχήματα, is employed, as Pacius thinks, by Aristotle, because of his illustration of syllogisms by geometrical figures. Vide Waitz, vol. i. 384. The invention of the fourth figure (disowned by Aristotle) is attributed by Averrois to Galen. Τρόπος, or mood, is not used in Aldrich's sense by Aristotle, except, perhaps, in the 28th chapter of this book. In the same meaning, Aristotle uses πτῶσις in An. i. 26. Upon the perfect and imperfect moods, vide Whately and Aldrich, (Mansel's Ed.)

terms—no perfect syllogism in this figure—its connexion with both universal and particular quantity.

a figure of this kind I call the second figure. The middle term[1] also in it, I call that which is predicated of both extremes, and the extremes I denominate those of which this middle is predicated, the greater extreme being that which is placed near the middle, but the less, that which is farther from the middle. Now the middle is placed beyond the extremes, and is first in position; wherefore by no means will there be a perfect syllogism in this figure. There may however be one,* both when the terms are, and are not, universal,[2] and if they be universal there will be a syllogism when the middle is present with all and with none, to which ever extreme the negation is added,[3] but by no means in any other way. For let M be predicated of no N, but of every O; since then a negative proposition is convertible, N will be present with no M; but M was supposed to be present with every O, wherefore N will be present with no O, for this has been proved before. Again, if M be present with every N, but with no O, neither will O be present with any N, for if M be present with no O, neither will O be present with any M; but M was present with every N, hence also O will be present with no N; for again the first figure is produced; since however a negative proposition is converted, neither will N be present with any O; hence there will be the same syllogism. We may also demonstrate the same things, by a deduction to the impossible; it is evident therefore, that when the terms are thus, a syllogism, though not a perfect one, is produced, for the necessary is not only perfected from first assumptions, but from other things also.[4] If also M is predicated of every N and of every O, there

* i. e. a syllogism.

2. From universal affirm-

[1] Aristotle gives a separate definition of the three terms in each figure. Cicero and others call the middle "argumentum."

[2] There is in this expression an ellipse of πρὸς τὸν ἕτερον, the phrase means strictly that one term is predicated universally, i. e. of the whole of—the other; ὅρος, is not properly a premise in Aristotle.

[3] Whichever denies, if the other only affirms.

[4] i. e. a necessary conclusion. Syllogism is, in its strictest sense, a logical deduction or inference, and often appears used in this way by Aristotle, as in this same chapter.

Ex. 1. Every animal is a substance	Every animal is a substance
Every man is a substance	Every stone is a substance
Every man is an animal.	No stone is an animal.

will not be a syllogism, let the terms of being present be "substance," "animal," "man," and of not being present "substance," "animal," "stone," the middle term "substance."* Nor will there then be a syllogism, when M is neither predicated of any N, nor of any O, let the terms of being present be "line," "animal," "man;" but of not being present, "line," "animal," "stone."†

atives there is no consequence.

* Example (1.)

† Example (2.)

Hence it is evident, that if there is a syllogism when the terms are universal, the latter must necessarily be, as we said at the beginning,[1] for if they are otherwise, no necessary (conclusion) follows. But if the middle be universal in respect to either extreme, when universal belongs to the major either affirmatively or negatively, but to the minor particularly, and in a manner opposite to the universal, (I mean by opposition, if the universal be negative, but the particular affirmative, or if the universal is affirmative, but the particular negative,) it is necessary that a particular negative syllogism should result. For if M is present with no N, but with a certain O, N must necessarily not be present with a certain O, for since a negative proposition is convertible, N will be present with no M, but M was by hypothesis present with a certain O, wherefore N will not be present with a certain O, for a syllogism is produced in the first figure.

3. When the major is A or E, and the minor I or O, the conclusion is O.

Again, if M is present with every N, but not with a certain O, N must of necessity not be present with a certain O, for if it is present with every O, and M is predicated of every N,

Ex. 2.	No animal is a line	No animal is a line
	No man is a line	No stone is a line
	Every man is an animal.	No stone is an animal.

[1] One affirmative and the other negative. Taylor uses categoric and privative, for the usual expressions affirmative and negative, whereas in Aristotle κατηγορικὸς always signifies affirmative, and is opposed to στερητικός. Vide Sir W. Hamilton, Ed. Rev. No. 115.

Ex. 3.	Not every substance is an animal	Not every thing white is an animal
	Every crow is an animal	Every crow is an animal
	Every crow is a substance.	No crow is white.
Ex. 4.	Some substance is an animal	Some substance is an animal
	No stone is an animal	No science is an animal
	Every stone is substance.	No science is substance.

M must necessarily be present with every O, but it was supposed not to be present with a certain O, and if M is present with every N, and not with every O, there will be a syllogism, that N is not present with every O, and the demonstration will be the same. But if M is predicated of every O, but not of every N, there will not be a syllogism; let the terms of presence be "animal," "substance," "crow," and of absence "animal," "white," "crow;"* neither will there be a syllogism when M is predicated of no O, but of a certain N, let the terms of presence be "animal," "substance," "stone," but of absence, "animal," "substance," "science."†

* Example (3.)

† Example (4.)

When therefore universal is opposed to particular, we have declared when there will, and when there will not, be a syllogism; but when the propositions are of the same quality,[1] as both being negative or affirmative, there will not by any means be a syllogism. For first, let them be negative, and let the universal belong to the major extreme, as let M be present with no N, and not be present with a certain O, it may happen therefore that N shall be present with every and with no O; let the terms of universal absence be "black," "snow," "animal;"‡ but we cannot take the terms of universal presence, if M is present with a certain O, and with a certain O not present. For if N is present with every O, but M with no N, M will be present with no O, but by hypothesis, it was present with some O, wherefore it is not possible thus to assume the terms. We may prove it nevertheless from the indefinite,[2]

ὁμοιοσχήμονες. 4. If both premises be of the same *quality*, no syllogism results.

‡ Example (5.)

[1] Taylor forgets that the affirmation and negation of proposition constitute its quality, so construes ὁμοιοσχήμονες, "of the same figure,"—a classical exactitude procured by an illogical ambiguity. Buhle, "eâdem formâ."

Ex. 5. No snow is black
Some animal is not black
No animal is snow.

[2] Called ἀδιόριστος, or indefinite, because it does not explain whether the attribution is true, alone in a part, or universally. Taylor.

Ex. 6. Every swan is white
Some stone is white
No stone is a swan.

Ex. 7. Every swan is white
Some bird is not white
Every bird is a swan.

Every swan is white
Every bird is a swan
Every bird is white.

for since M was truly asserted not to be with some certain O, even if it is present with no O; yet being present with no O, there was not a syllogism, it is evident, that neither now will there be one. Again, let them* be affirmative, and let the universal be similarly assumed, e. g. let M be present with every N, and with a certain O, N may happen therefore to be present, both with every and with no O, let the terms of being present with none, be "white," "swan," "snow;"† but we cannot assume the terms of being present with every, for the reason which we have before stated, but it may be shown from the indefinite.‡ But if the universal be joined to the minor extreme, and M is present with no O, and is not present with some certain N, it is possible for N to be present with every and with no O; let the terms of presence be "white," "animal," "crow," but of absence, "white," "stone," "crow."§ But if the propositions are affirmative, let the terms of absence be "white," "animal," "snow," of presence, "white," "animal," "swan."‖ Therefore it is evident, when the propositions are of the same quality, and the one universal, but the other particular, that there is by no means a syllogism. Neither, however, will there be one, if a thing be present to some one of each term, or not present, or to the one, but not to the other, or to neither universally, or indefinitely; let the common terms of all be "white," "animal," "man;" "white," "animal," "inanimate."¶

* i. e. both propositions.

† Example (6.)

‡ Example (7.)

§ Example (8.)

‖ Example (9.)

¶ Example (10.)

Wherefore it is evident, from what we have stated, that if the terms subsist towards each other, as has been said, there is necessarily a syllogism, and if there be a syllogism, the terms must thus subsist. It is also clear that all syllogisms

Ex. 8.	Some animal is not white	Some stone is not white
	No crow is white	No crow is white
	Every crow is an animal.	No crow is a stone.
Ex. 9.	Some animal is white	Some animal is white
	All snow is white	Every swan is white
	No snow is an animal.	Every swan is an animal.
Ex. 10.	Some animal {is / is not} white	Some animal {is / is not} white.
	Some man {is / is not} white	Something inanim. {is / is not} white
	Every man is an animal.	Nothing inanimate is an animal.

in this figure are imperfect, for all of them are produced from certain assumptions, which are either of necessity in the terms, or are admitted as hypotheses, as when we demonstrate by the impossible. Lastly, it appears that an affirmative syllogism is not produced in this figure, but all are negative, both the universal and also the particular.[1]

5. No affirmative conclusion in this figure.

Chap. VI.—*Of Syllogisms in the third Figure.*

1. Σχῆμα Γ, the third figure, its characteristic—the middle is the subject of both premises—no perfect syllogism in this figure.

When with the same thing one is present with every, but the other with no individual, or both with every, or with none, such I call the third figure; and the middle in it, I call that of which we predicate both, but the predicates the extremes, the greater extreme being the one more remote from the middle, and the less, that which is nearer to the middle. But the middle is placed beyond the extremes, and is last in position; now neither will there be a perfect syllogism, even in this figure, but there may be one,* when the terms are joined to the middle, both universally, and not universally. Now when the terms are universally so, when, for instance, P and R are present with every S, there will be a syllogism, so that P will necessarily be present with some certain R, for since an affirmative is convertible, S will be present to a certain R. Wherefore since P is present to every S, but S to some certain R, P must necessarily be present with some R, for a syllogism arises in the first figure. We may also make the demonstration through the impossible, and by exposition.[2] For if both are present with every S, if some S is assumed, (e. g.) N, both P and R

* i. e. a syllogism.

διὰ τοῦ ἐκθέσθαι.

[1] For the special rules and necessary negative conclusion in this figure, vide Whately and Aldrich; and for the principles of the several figures, compare Hill's Logic. The enumeration of distinct axioms for the second and third figures, occurs in Lambert Nues Organon, part i. ch. 4, sect. 232. According to him, the use of the second figure is for the discovery and proof of differences in things; and of the third, for those of examples and exceptions.

[2] The method called ἔκθεσις signifies by exhibiting an individual case, "exponere sensui," hence a syllogism with singular premises is called "syllogismus expositorius." It is doubtful whether Aristotle regarded

will be present with this, wherefore P will be present with a certain R, and if R is present with every S, but P is present with no S, there will be a syllogism, so that P will be necessarily inferred as not present with a certain R; for the same mode of demonstration will take place, the proposition R S being converted; this may also be demonstrated by the impossible, as in the former syllogisms. But if R is present with no S, but P with every S, there will not be a syllogism; let the terms of presence be "animal," "horse," "man," but of absence "animal," "inanimate," "man."* Neither when both are predicated of no S, will there be a syllogism, let the terms of presence be "animal," "horse," "inanimate," but of absence "man," "horse," inanimate," the middle "inanimate."† Wherefore also in this figure it is evident, when there will, and when there will not, be a syllogism, the terms being universal, for when both terms are affirmative, there will be a syllogism, in which it will be concluded that extreme is with a certain extreme,[1] but when both terms are negative there will not be. When however one is negative and the other affirmative, and the major is negative but the other affirmative, there will be a syllogism, that the extreme is not present with a certain extreme, but if the contrary there will not be.

* Example (1.)

† Example (2.)

2. When both premises are affirmative there will be a syllogism, but not when both are negative—the major moreover may be negative, and the minor, affirmative.

If indeed one be universal in respect to the middle,[2] and the other particular, both being affirmative, syllogism is necessarily produced, whichever term be universal. For if R is present

the ἔκθεσις as a syllogism at all. Vide Aquinas, Opusc. 47. Zabarella, cap. 7.

Ex. 1. Every man is an animal	Every man is an animal
No man is a horse	No man is inanimate
Every horse is an animal.	Nothing inanimate is a horse.
Ex. 2. Nothing inanimate is an animal	Nothing inanimate is a man
Nothing inanimate is a horse	Nothing inanimate is a horse
Every horse is an animal.	No horse is a man.

[1] i. e. the major with the minor.

[2] i. e. Universally predicated of the middle.

Ex. 3. Every animal is animate
Some animal is not a man
Every man is animate.

with every S, but P with a certain S, P must necessarily be present with a certain R, for since the affirmative is convertible, S will be present with a certain P, so that since R is present to every S, and S with a certain P, R will also be present with a certain P, wherefore also P will be present with a certain R. Again, if R is present with a certain S, but P is present with every S, P must necessarily be present with a certain R, for the mode of demonstration is the same, and these things may be demonstrated like the former, both by the impossible, and by exposition. If however one be affirmative, and the other negative, and the affirmative be universal, when the minor is affirmative there will be a syllogism; for if R is present with every S, and P not present with a certain S, P must also necessarily not be present with a certain R, since if P is present with every R, and R with every S, P will also be present with every S, but it is not present, and this may also be shown without deduction, if some S be taken with which P is not present. But when the major is affirmative there will not be a syllogism, e. g. if P is present with every S, but R is not present with a certain S; let the terms of being universally present with be "animate," "man," "animal."* But it is not possible to take the terms of universal negative, if R is present with a certain S, and with a certain S is not present, since if P is present with every S, and R with a certain S, P will also be present with a certain R, but it was supposed to be present with no R, therefore we must assume the same as in the former syllogisms. As to declare something not present with a certain thing is indefinite, so that also which is not present with any individual, it is true to say, is not present with a certain individual, but not being present with any, there was no syllogism, (therefore it is evident there will be no syllogism).[1]

* Example (3.)

[1] i. e. when it is assumed not to be present with a certain individual.

Ex. 4.	Something wild is an animal Nothing wild is a man Every man is an animal.	Something wild is an animal Nothing wild is science No science is an animal.
Ex. 5.	Something wild is not an animal Nothing wild is science No science is an animal.	Something wild is not an animal Nothing wild is a man Every man is an animal.

But if the negative term be universal, (yet the particular affirmative,) when the major is negative, but the minor affirmative, there will be a syllogism, for if P is present with no S, but R is present with a certain S, P will not be present with a certain R, and again there will be the first figure, the proposition R S being converted. But when the minor is negative, there will not be a syllogism; let the terms of presence be "animal," "man," "wild," but of absence, "animal," "science," "wild," the middle of both, "wild."* Nor will there be a syllogism when both are negative, the one universal, the other particular: let the terms of absence when the minor is universal as to the middle, be "animal," "science," "wild," (of presence, "animal," "man," "wild)."† When however the major is universal, but the minor particular, let the terms of absence be "crow," "snow," "white;"‡ but of presence we cannot take the terms, if R is present with some S, and with some is not present, since if P is present with every R, but R with some S, P will also be present with some S, but it was supposed to be present with no S, indeed it may be proved from the indefinite. Neither if each extreme be present or not present with a certain middle, will there be a syllogism; or if one be present and the other not; or if one be with some individual and the other with not every or indefinitely. But let the common terms of all be, "animal," "man," "white," "animal," "inanimate," "white."§ Wherefore it is clear in this figure also, when there will and when there will not be a syllogism, and that when the terms are disposed as we have stated, a syllogism of necessity subsists, and that there should be a syllogism, it is necessary that the terms should be thus. It is also clear that all syllogisms in this figure are imperfect, for

* Example (4.)

† Example (5.)

‡ Example (6.)

§ Example (7.)

3. No universal conclusion de-

Ex. 6. Nothing white is a crow
Not every thing white is snow
No snow is a crow.

Ex. 7. Something white {is / is not} an animal — Something white {is / is not} an animal

Something white {is / is not} a man — Something white {is / is not} inanimate.

Every man is an animal. — Nothing inanimate is an animal.

rived from this figure.

they are all perfected by certain assumptions, and that an universal conclusion either negative or affirmative, cannot be drawn from this figure.[1]

CHAP. VII.—*Of the three first Figures, and of the Completion of Incomplete Syllogisms.*

IN all the figures it appears that when a syllogism is not produced, both terms being affirmative, or negative, (and particular,[2]) nothing, in short, results of a necessary character; but if the one be affirmative and the other negative, the negative being universally taken, there is always a syllogism of the minor extreme with the major. For example, if A is present with every or with some B, but B is present with no C, the propositions being converted, C must necessarily not be present with some A; so also in the other figures, for a syllogism is always produced by conversion: again, it is clear that an indefinite taken for a particular affirmative, will produce the same syllogism in all the figures.

1. If one premise be A or I, and the other E, there will be a conclusion in which the minor is predicated of the major.

Moreover it is evident that all incomplete syllogisms are completed by means of the first figure, for all of them are concluded, either ostensively or per impossibile, but in both ways the first figure is produced: being ostensively*[3] completed, (the first figure is produced,) because all of them were concluded by conversion, but conversion produces the first figure: but if they are de-

* δεικτικῶς.

[1] Vide Hill, p. 196; also Whately, pp. 60 and 61. For the uses of the three figures also Aldrich, iii. 8.

[2] The words "and particular" are omitted by Waitz.

[3] Taylor translates this "demonstratively." "Simplici et rectâ demonstratione." Buhle. Reduction is expressed by the verb ἀνάγεσθαι, never ἀπαγεσθαι. Mansel. He is also right in drawing attention to the incorrectness of the phrase, "reductio ad impossibile;" it ought to be "per deductionem ad impossibile, or elliptically, per impossibile." The general phrase is a palpable absurdity. Vide An. ii. 11, C. Upon the nature of the ἀπαγὼγη εἰς τὸ ἀδυνατον, wherein, after all, the word does not mean reduction, see Mansel's Logic, Appendix, note G. The antithesis to δεικτικὸς, is ἐξ ὑποθέσεως. Cf. ch. 23 of this 1st book of Analytics: also Whately, book ii. ch. 3, sect. 5 and 6. Although the indirect moods have been attributed to the invention of Theophrastus, by Alexander, (Schol. p. 153,) we find two of them recognised here by Aristotle, and the other three in Anal. Prior, ii. 1.

monstrated per impossibile, (there will be still the first figure,) because the false being assumed, a syllogism arises in the first figure. For example, in the last figure, if A and B are present with every C, it can be shown that A is present with some B, for if A is present with no B, but B is present with every C, A will be present with no C; but it was supposed that A was present with every C, and in like manner it will happen in other instances.

2. All syllogisms may be reduced to universals in the first figure (ἀναγαγεῖν)—the various methods.

It is also possible to reduce all syllogisms to universal syllogisms in the first figure. For those in the second, it is evident, are completed through these, yet not all in like manner, but the universal by conversion of the negative, and each of the particular, by deduction per impossibile. Now, particular syllogisms in the first figure are completed through themselves, but may in the second figure be demonstrated by deduction to the impossible. For example, if A is present with every B, but B with a certain C, it can be shown that A will be present with a certain C, for if A is present with no C, but is present with every B, B will be present with no C, for we know this by the second figure. So also will the demonstration be in the case of a negative, for if A is present with no B, but B is present with a certain C, A will not be present with a certain C, since if A is present with every C, and with no B, B will be present with no C, and this was the middle figure. Wherefore, as all syllogisms in the middle figure are reduced to universal syllogisms in the first figure, but particular in the first are reduced to those in the middle figure, it is clear that particular will be reduced to universal syllogisms in the first figure. Those, however, in the third, when the terms are universal, are immediately completed through those syllogisms;*[1] but when particular (terms) are assumed (they are completed) through particular syllogisms in the first figure; but these† have been reduced to those,‡ so that also particular syllogisms in the third figure (are reducible to the same). Wherefore, it is evident that all can be reduced to universal syllogisms in the first figure; and we have therefore shown how syllogisms de inesse and de non inesse

* i. e. universals of the first figure.
† i. e. particulars.
‡ Universals.

[1] By a deduction to an absurdity.

subsist, both those which are of the same figure, with reference to themselves, and those which are of different figures, also with reference to each other.

CHAP. VIII.—*Of Syllogisms derived from two necessary Propositions.*

1. Variety of syllogisms, viz. those τοῦ ὑπάρχειν—and those τοῦ ἀναγκαῖον εἶναι, and τοῦ ἐνδέχεσθαι. Cf. Whately, b. 2. ch. 4.

SINCE however to exist, to exist necessarily, and to exist contingently are different, (for many things exist, but not from necessity, and others neither necessarily, nor in short exist, yet may happen to exist,) it is evident that there will be a different syllogism from each of these, and from the terms not being alike; but one syllogism will consist of those which are necessary, another of absolute, and a third of contingent. In necessary syllogisms it will almost always be the same, as in the case of absolute subsistences,[1] for the terms being similarly placed in both absolute existence, and in existing, or not of necessity, there will and there will not be a syllogism, except that there will be a difference in necessary or non-necessary subsistence being added to the terms. For a negative is in like manner convertible, and we assign similarly to be in the whole of a thing, and to be (predicated) of every. In the rest then it will be shown by the same manner, through conversion, that the conclusion is necessary, as in the case of being present; but in the middle figure, when the universal is affirmative, and the particular negative, and again, in the third figure, when the universal is affirmative, but the particular negative, the demonstration will not be in the like manner; but it is necessary that proposing something with which either extreme is not present, we make a syllogism of this, for in respect of these there will be a necessary (conclusion). If, on the other hand, in respect to the proposed term, there is a necessary conclusion, there will be also one (a necessary conclusion) of some individual of that term, for what is proposed is part of it, and each syllogism is formed under its own appropriate figure.

2. Necessary syllogisms resemble generally those which are absolute.

[1] i. e. Pure categoricals.

CHAP. IX.—*Of Syllogisms, whereof one Proposition is necessary, and the other pure in the first Figure.*

1. Conclusion of a syllogism with one premise necessary often follows the major premise,—example and proof,—universals and particulars.

IT sometimes happens also that when one proposition is necessary, a necessary syllogism arises,[1] not however from either proposition indifferently, but from the one that contains the greater extreme.[2] For example, if A is assumed to be necessarily present or not present with B, but B to be alone present with C, for the premises being thus assumed, A will necessarily be present or not with C; for since A is or is not necessarily present with every B, but C is something belonging to B, C will evidently of necessity be one of these.* If, again, A B (the major) is not necessary, but B C (the minor) is necessary, there will not be a necessary conclusion, for if there be, it will happen that A is necessarily present with a certain B, both by the first and the third figure, but this is false, for B may happen to be a thing of that kind, that A may not be present with any thing of it. Besides, it is evident from the terms, that there will not be a necessary conclusion, as if A were "motion," B "animal," and C "man," for "man" is necessarily "an animal," but neither are "animal" nor "man" necessarily "moved;" so also if A B is negative, for there is the same demonstration. In particular syllogisms, however, if the universal is necessary, the conclusion will also be necessary, but if the particular be, there will not be a necessary conclusion, neither if the universal premise be negative nor affirmative. Let then, in the first place, the universal be necessary, and let A be necessarily present with every B,

* i. e. will or will not be A.

2. Case of I necessary.

[1] Theophrastus and Eudemus allowed a necessary conclusion to follow from two necessary premises only. Vide Alex. Aphr.

[2] Majori necessaria, necessario aliquid inesse concluditur. Buhle.

Ex. 1. Every animal is moved	No animal is moved
It is necessary that something white should be an animal	It is necessary that something white should not be an animal
Therefore something white is moved.	Therefore something white is not moved.
This is not necessary, for it might possibly not be moved.]	[This is not necessary, because it may be moved.]

but B only be present with a certain C; it is necessary therefore that A should of necessity be present with a certain C, for C is under* B, and A was of necessity present with every B. The same will occur if the syllogism be negative, for the demonstration will be the same, but if the particular be necessary, the conclusion will not be necessary, for nothing impossible results,† as neither in universal syllogisms. A similar consequence will result also in negatives; (let the terms be) "motion," "animal," "white."‡

* i. e. is joined to B.

† i. e. though a non-necessary conclusion be admitted.

‡ Example (1.)

CHAP. X.—*Of the same in the second Figure.*

1. In the second figure, when a necessary is joined with a pure premise, the conclusion follows the negative necessary premise.—Example and proof.

IN the second figure, if the negative premise be necessary, the conclusion will also be necessary, but if the affirmative (be necessary, the conclusion) will not be necessary. For first, let the negative be necessary, and let it not be possible for A to be in any B, but let it be present with C alone; as then a negative proposition may be converted, B cannot be present with any A, but A is with every C, hence B cannot be present with any C, for C is under§ A. In like manner also, if the negative be added to C,‖ for if A cannot be with any C, neither can C be present with any A, but A is with every B, so neither can C be present with any B, as the first figure will again be produced; wherefore, neither can B be present with C, since it is similarly converted.

§ i. e. belongs to A.

‖ The conclusion will be necessary.

2. If the affirmative be necessary, the conclusion will not be.

If, however, the affirmative premise be necessary, the conclusion will not be necessary; for let A necessarily be present with every B, and alone not be present with any C, then the negative being converted, we have the first figure; but it was shown in the first, that when the major negative (proposition) is not necessary, neither will the conclusion be necessary, so that neither in these will there be a necessary conclusion.¶ Once more, if the conclusion is necessary, it results that C is not necessarily present with a certain A, for if B is necessarily present with no C, neither will C be necessarily present with any B, but B is present necessarily with

¶ i. e. in syllogisms of the second figure with a necessary affirmative.

a certain A, if A is necessarily present with every B. Hence, it is necessary that C should not be present with a certain A; there is, however, nothing to prevent such an A being assumed, with which universally C may be present. Moreover, it can be shown by exposition of the terms, that the conclusion is not simply necessary, but necessary from the assumption of these, e. g. let A be "animal," B "man," C "white," and let the propositions be similarly assumed: for it is possible for an animal to be with nothing "white," then neither will "man" be present with any thing white, yet not from necessity, for it may happen for "man" to be "white," yet not so long as "animal" is present with nothing "white," so that from these assumptions there will be a necessary conclusion, but not simply necessary.

3. Case the same with particulars.

The same will happen in particular syllogisms, for when the negative proposition is universal and necessary, the conclusion also will be necessary, but when the affirmative is universal and necessary, and the negative particular,* the conclusion will not be necessary. First, then, let there be an universal and necessary negative, and let A not possibly be present with any B, but with a certain C. Since, therefore, a negative proposition is convertible, B can neither be possibly present with any A, but A is with a certain C, so that of necessity B is not present with a certain C. Again, let there be an universal and necessary affirmative, and let the affirmative be attached to B, if then A is necessarily present with every B, but is not with a certain C, B is not with a certain C it is clear, yet not from necessity, since there will be the same terms for the demonstration, as were taken in the case of universal syllogisms. Neither, moreover, will the conclusion be necessary, if a particular necessary negative be taken as the demonstration is through the same terms.

* Taylor inserts "and not necessary," which words are omitted by Bekker and Waitz.

CHAP. XI.—*Of the same in the third Figure.*

1. In this figure if either premise be necessary, and both

IN the last figure, when the terms are universally joined to the middle,[1] and both premises are affirmative, if either of them be necessary, the

[1] That is, are predicated of it.

be A, the conclusion will be necessary. conclusion will also be necessary; and if one be negative, but the other affirmative, when the negative is necessary, the conclusion will be also necessary, but when the affirmative (is so, the conclusion) will not be necessary. For first, let both propositions be[1] affirmative, and let A and B be present with every C, and let A C be a necessary (proposition). Since then B is present with every C, C will also be present with a certain B, because an universal is converted into a particular: so that if A is necessarily present with every C, and C with a certain B, A must also be necessarily present with a certain B, for B is under C,* hence the first figure again arises. In like manner, it can be also demonstrated if B C is a necessary (proposition), for C is converted with a certain A, so that if B is necessarily present with every C, (but C with a certain A,) B will also of necessity be present with a certain A. Again let A C be a negative (proposition), but B C affirmative, and let the negative be necessary; as therefore an affirmative proposition is convertible, C will be present with some certain B, but A of necessity with no C, neither will A necessarily be present with some B, for B is under C. But if the affirmative is necessary, there will not be a necessary conclusion; for let B C be affirmative and necessary, but A C negative and not necessary; since then the affirmative is converted C will also be with a certain B of necessity; wherefore if A is with no C, but C with a certain B, A will also not be present with a certain B, but not from necessity, for it has been shown by the first figure,† that when the negative proposition is not necessary, neither will the conclusion be necessary. Moreover this will also be evident from the terms, for let A

1st case.

* i. e. belongs to it.

2nd case.

3rd case an exception.

† Vide ch. 9.

[1] Taylor, by mistake, reads "necessary."

Ex. 1. No horse is good
It is necessary that every horse should be an animal
Therefore some animal is not good.

Ex. 2. No horse {wakes / sleeps}
It is necessary that every horse should be an animal
∴ Some animal does not {wake / sleep.}

be "good," B "animal," and C "horse," it happens therefore that "good" is with no "horse," but "animal" is necessarily present with every "horse," but it is not however necessary that a certain "animal" should not be "good," for every "animal" may possibly be "good."* Or if this is not possible, (viz. that every animal is good,) we must assume another term, as "to wake," or "to sleep," for every "animal" is capable of these.† If then the terms are universal in respect to the middle, it has been shown when there will be a necessary conclusion.

* Example (1.)

† Example (2.)

2. If one proposition be A or I, when A is necessary the conclusion is necessary, but not when I is necessary.

But if one term is universally but the other particularly (predicated of the middle), and both propositions are affirmative, when the universal is necessary the conclusion will also be necessary, for the demonstration is the same as before, since the particular affirmative is convertible. If therefore B is necessarily present with every C, but A is under C, B must also necessarily be present with a certain A,[1] and if B is with a certain A, A must also be present necessarily with a certain B, for it is convertible; the same will also occur if A C be a necessary universal proposition, for B is under C. But if the particular be necessary, there will not be a necessary conclusion, for let B C be particular and necessary, and A present with every C, yet not of necessity, B C then being converted we have the first figure, and the universal proposition is not necessary, but the particular is necessary, but when the propositions are thus there was not a necessary conclusion,‡ so that neither will there be one in the case of these.§ Moreover this is evident from the terms, for let A be "wakefulness," B "biped," but C, "animal;" B then must necessarily be present with a certain

‡ Vide ch. 6.

§ Example (3.)

[1] This succeeding clause is omitted by Taylor, though read by Buhle and Waitz.

Ex. 3. Every C is A.
It is necessary that some { C should be B / B should be C }
∴ Some B is A.

Ex. 4. Every animal wakes
It is necessary that some animal should be biped
∴ Some biped wakes.

tain C, but A may happen to be present with every C, and yet A is not necessarily so with B, for a certain "biped" need not "sleep" or "wake."* So also we may demonstrate it by the same terms if A be particular and necessary.† But if one term be affirmative and the other negative, when the universal proposition is negative and necessary, the conclusion will also be necessary, for if A happens to no C, but B is present with a certain C, A must necessarily not be present with a certain B. But when the affirmative is assumed as necessary, whether it be universal or particular, or particular negative, there will not be a necessary conclusion, for we may allege the other same (reasons against it), as in the former cases.[1] But let the terms when the universal affirmative is necessary be "wakefulness," "animal," "man," the middle "man."‡ But when the particular affirmative is necessary, let the terms be "wakefulness," "animal," "white," for "animal" must necessarily be with something "white," but "wakefulness" happens to be with nothing "white," and it is not necessary that wakefulness should not be with a certain animal.§ But when the negative particular is necessary, let the terms be "biped," "motion," "animal," and the middle term, "animal."‖

* Example (4.)
† Example (5.)

3. When the affirmative is necessary either A or I, or when O is assumed, there will not be a necessary conclusion.

‡ Example (6.)

§ Example (7.)

‖ Example (8.)

Ex. 5. It is necessary that some animal should be a biped	Every animal wakes
Every animal wakes	It is necessary that some biped should be an animal
∴ Something that wakes is a biped.	∴ Some biped wakes.

[1] Because by reduction to the first figure the minor will be necessary, but the major pure; hence no necessary conclusion can be inferred. (Vide supra.)

Ex. 6. Some man does not wake
It is necessary that every man should be an animal
∴ Some animal does not wake.

Ex. 7. Nothing white wakes
It is necessary that something white should be an animal
∴ Some animal does not wake.

Ex. 8. It is necessary that some animal should not be a biped
Every animal is moved
∴ Something which is moved is not a biped.

CHAP. XII.—*A comparison of pure with necessary Syllogisms.*[1]

IT appears then, that there is not a syllogism de inesse unless both propositions signify the being present with,[2] but that a necessary conclusion follows, even if one alone is necessary. But in both,* the syllogisms being affirmative, or negative, one of the propositions must necessarily be similar to the conclusion; I mean by similar, that if (the conclusion) be (simply) that a thing is present with, (one of the propositions also signifies simply) the being present with, but if necessarily, (that is, in the conclusion, one of the propositions is also) necessary. Wherefore this also is evident, that there will neither be a conclusion necessary nor simple de inesse, unless one proposition be assumed as necessary, or purely categorical, and concerning the necessary, how it arises, and what difference it has in regard to the de inesse, we have almost said enough.

* i.e. pure and modal.

1. Distinction between an absolute and necessary conclusion as regards the latter's dependence upon the premises; their connexion also with it.

CHAP. XIII.—*Of the Contingent, and its concomitant Propositions.*

1. Definition of the contingent (τοῦ ἐνδεχομένου) given and confirmed. (Vide Metaph. lib. v. 2,) also Interpret. 13.

LET us next speak of the contingent, when, and how, and through what (propositions) there will be a syllogism; and to be contingent, and the contingent, I define to be that which, not being necessary, but being assumed to exist, nothing impossible will on this account arise, for we say that the necessary is contingent equivocally. But, that such

[1] Vide the previous notes on the subject of modals. The reader who wishes to ascertain how far logic is conversant with the *expressed* matter of modal proposition, will find arguments "ad rem," and "ad nauseam" both, in relation to the various views of the question, in Ed. Review, No. 118; Kant, Logik, sec. 30; St. Hilaire's preface. In both modals and pure categoricals, the formal consequence alone is really the legitimate object of consideration to the logician, with the material he has strictly nothing to do. Whately has shown that a modal may be stated as a pure proposition, by attaching the mode to one of the terms; this being done, the rule of consequence applies to both equally.

[2] i. e. in categoricals both premises must be affirmative for the conclusion to be so.

is the contingent, is evident from opposite negatives and affirmatives, for the assertions—"it does not happen to be," and, "it is impossible to be," and, "it is necessary not to be," are either the same, or follow each other; wherefore also the contraries to these, "it happens to be," "it is not impossible to be," and, "it is not necessary not to be," will either be the same, or follow each other; for of every thing, there is either affirmation or negation, hence the contingent will be not necessary, and the not-necessary will be contingent. It happens, indeed, that all contingent propositions are convertible with each other. I do not mean the affirmative into the negative, but as many as have an affirmative figure, as to opposition; e. g. "it happens to exist," (is convertible into) "it happens not to exist," and, "it happens to every," into "it happens to none," or, "not to every," and, "it happens to some," into "it happens not to some." In the same manner also with the rest,* for since the contingent is non-necessary, and the non-necessary may happen not to exist, it is clear that if A happens to be with any B, it may also happen not to be present, and if it happens to be present with every B, it may also happen not to be present with every B. There is the same reasoning also in particular affirmatives, for the demonstration is the same, but such propositions are affirmative and not negative, for the verb "to be contingent," is arranged similarly to the verb "to be," as we have said before.†

2. Contingent προτάσεις capable of conversion.

* i. e. is conversion effected.

† Vide c. 3.

3. The contingent predicated in two ways—the one general, the other indefinite—the method of conversion not the same to each.

These things then being defined, let us next remark, that to be contingent is predicated in two ways, one that which happens for the most part and yet falls short of the necessary—(for instance, for a man to become hoary, or to grow, or to waste, or in short whatever may naturally be, for this has not a continued necessity, for the man may not always exist, but while he does exist it is either of necessity or for the most part)[1]—the other way (the contingent is) indefinite, and is that which may be possibly thus and not thus; as for an animal to walk, or while it is walking for an earthquake to happen, or in short whatever occurs casually, for

[1] i. e. that he is subject to these things.

nothing is more naturally produced thus, or in a contrary way. Each kind of contingent however is convertible according to opposite propositions, yet not in the same manner, but what may naturally subsist is convertible into that which does not subsist of necessity; thus it is possible for a man not to become hoary, but the indefinite is converted into what cannot more subsist in this than in that way. Science however and demonstrative syllogism do not belong to indefinites, because the middle is irregular, but to those things which may naturally exist; and arguments and speculations are generally conversant with such contingencies, but of the indefinite contingent we may make a syllogism, though it is not generally investigated. These things however will be more defined in what follows,[1] at present let us show when and how and what will be a syllogism from contingent propositions.

4. The indefinite contingent of less use in syllogism.

Since then that *this* happens to be present with *that* may be assumed in a twofold respect,—(for it either signifies that with which this is present, or that with which it may be present, thus the assertion, A is contingent to that of which B is predicated, signifies one of these things, either that of which B is predicated, or that of which it may be predicated; but the assertion that A is contingent to that of which there is B, and that A may be present with every B, do not differ from each other, whence it is evident that A may happen to be present with every B in two ways,)—let us first show if B is contingent to that of which there is C, and if A is contingent to that of which there is B, what and what kind of syllogism there will be, for thus both propositions are contingently assumed. When however A is contingent to that with which B is present, one proposition is de inesse, but the other of that which is contingent, so that we must begin from those of similar character, as we began elsewhere.[2]

5. An inquiry into the construction of contingent syllogisms prepared.

[1] In the Post Analytics, i. c. 8. In Rhetoric, b. ii. c. 24, he admits accident to be an element of apparent argument, but in Metap. lib. v. c. 3, denies that there is any science of it, and regards it as a σημεῖον.

[2] That is, from syllogisms, each of whose propositions is contingent.

CHAP. XIV.—*Of Syllogisms with two contingent Propositions in the first Figure.*

1. With the contingent premises both universal there will be a perfect syllogism.

WHEN A is contingent to every B, and B to every C, there will be a perfect syllogism, so that A is contingent to every C, which is evident from the definition, for thus we stated the universal contingent (to imply). So also if A is contingent to no B, but B to every C, (it may be concluded) that A is contingent to no C, for to affirm that A is contingent in respect of nothing to which B is contingent, this were to leave none of the contingents which are under B. But when A is contingent to every B, but B contingent to no C, no syllogism arises from the assumed propositions, but B C[1] being converted according to the contingent, the same syllogism arises as existed before, as since it happens that B is present with no C, it may also happen to be present with every C, which was shown before,* wherefore if B may happen to every C, and A to every B, the same syllogism will again arise. The like will occur also if negation be added with the contingent (mode) to both propositions, I mean, as if A is contingent to no B, and B to no C, no syllogism arises through the assumed propositions, but when they are converted there will be the same as before. It is evident then that when negation is added to the minor extreme, or to both the propositions, there is either no syllogism, or an incomplete one, for the necessity (of consequence) is completed by conversion. If however one of the propositions be universal, and the other be assumed as particular, the universal belonging to the major extreme there will be a perfect syllogism, for if A is contingent to every B, but B to a certain C, A is also contingent to a certain C, and this is clear from the definition of universal contingent. Again, if A is contingent to no B, but B happens to be present with some C, it is necessary that A should happen not to be present with some C, since the de-

2nd case. 3rd case. * Vide ch. 13. 4th case.

2. When the premises are both negative or the minor negative, there is either no syllogism or an incomplete one—case of the major universal with the minor particular, different.

[1] That is, the minor negative being made affirmative.

monstration is the same; but if the particular proposition be assumed as negative, and the universal affirmative, and retain the same position as if A happens to be present to every B, but B happens not to be present with some C, no evident syllogism arises from the assumed propositions, but the particular being converted and B being assumed to be contingently present with some C, there will be the same conclusion as before in the first syllogisms.[1] Still if the major proposition be taken as particular, but the minor as universal, and if both be assumed affirmative or negative, or of different figure, or both indefinite or particular, there will never be a syllogism; for there is nothing to prevent B from being more widely extended than A, and from not being equally predicated. Now let that by which B exceeds A, be assumed to be C, to this it will happen[2] that A is present neither to every, nor to none, nor to a certain one, nor not to a certain one, since contingent propositions are convertible, and B may happen to be present to more things than A. Besides, this is evident from the terms, for when the propositions are thus, the first is contingent to the last, and to none, and necessarily present with every individual, and let the common terms of all be these; of being present necessarily[3] "animal," "white," "man," but of not being contingent, "animal," "white," "garment."* Therefore it is clear that when the terms are thus there is no syllo-

2. Vice versâ.

* Example (1.).

[1] In the universal imperfect syllogisms mentioned towards the beginning of this chapter.

[2] Because C is necessarily not present, and the necessary is distinguished from the contingent.

[3] That is, of the major being with the minor.

Ex. 1. It happens that something white {is / is not} an animal

It happens that {every / no / some / not every} man is white

It is necessary that every man should be an animal.

It happens that something white {is / is not} an animal

It happens that {every / no / some / not every} garment is white

It is necessary that no garment should be an animal.

gism, for every syllogism is either de inesse, or of that which exists necessarily or contingently, but that this is neither de inesse, nor of that which necessarily exists, is clear, since the affirmative is subverted by the negative, and the negative by the affirmative, wherefore it remains that it is of the contingent, but this is impossible, for it has been shown that when the terms are thus, the first is necessarily inherent in all the last, and contingently is present with none, so that there cannot be a syllogism of the contingent, for the necessary is not contingent. Thus it is evident that when universal terms are assumed in contingent propositions, there arises always a syllogism in the first figure, both when they are affirmative and negative, except that being affirmative it is complete, but if negative incomplete, we must nevertheless assume the contingent not in necessary propositions, but according to the before-named definition, and sometimes a thing of this kind escapes notice.

3. When the premises are universal, A or E, there is always a syllogism in the first figure—the former (A) complete—the latter (E) incomplete. (Vide last chapter.)

Chap. XV.—*Of Syllogisms with one simple and another contingent Proposition in the first Figure.*

1. No syllogism with mixed premises, pure and modal—if the major is contingent the syllogism will be perfect, not otherwise.

If one proposition be assumed to exist, but the other to be contingent, when that which contains the major extreme signifies the contingent, all the syllogisms will be perfect and of the contingent, according to the above definition. But when the minor (is contingent) they will all be imperfect, and the negative syllogisms will not be of the contingent, according to the definition, but of that which is necessarily present with no one or not with every; for if it is necessarily present with no one, or not with every, we say that "it happens" to be present with no one and not with every. Now let A be contingent to every B, and let B be assumed to be present with every C, since then C is (included) under B, and A is contingent to every B, A is also clearly contingent to every C, and there is a perfect syllogism. So also if the proposition A B is negative, but B C affirmative, and A B is assumed as contingent, but B C to be present with (simply), there will be a perfect syllogism, so that A will happen to be present with no C.

1. Case of a perfect syllogism, when the minor is pure.

It appears then that when a pure minor is assumed the syllogisms are perfect, but that when it is of a contrary character it may be shown per impossibile that there would be also syllogisms, though at the same time it would be evident that they are imperfect, since the demonstration will not arise from the assumed propositions. First, however, we must show that if A exists, B must necessarily exist, and that if A is possible, B will necessarily be possible; let then under these circumstances A be possible but B impossible, if therefore the possible, since it is possible to be, may be produced, yet the impossible, because it is impossible, cannot be produced. But if at the same time A is possible and B impossible, it may happen that A may be produced without B; if it is produced also, that it may exist, for that which has been generated, when it has been so generated, exists. We must however assume the possible and impossible,[1] not only in generation, but also in true assertion, and in the inesse, and in as many other ways as the possible is predicated, for the case will be the same in all of them. Moreover (when it is said) if A exists B is, we must not understand as if A being a certain thing B will be, for no necessary consequence follows from one thing existing; but from there being two at least, as in the case of propositions subsisting in the manner we have stated in syllogism. For if C is predicated of D, but D of F, C will also necessarily be predicated of F; and if each be possible, the conclusion will be possible, just as if one should take A as the premises, but B the conclusion; it will not only happen that A being necessary, B is also necessary, but that when the former is possible, the latter also will be possible.

2. Digression to prove the nature of true consequence in respect of the possible and impossible, and necessary.

This being proved, it is manifest that when there is a false and not impossible hypothesis, the consequence of the hypothesis will also be false and not impossible, e. g. if A is false yet not impossible, but when A is, B also is,—here B will also be false yet not impossible. For since it has been shown that A ex-

3. From a false hypothesis, not impossible, a similar conclusion follows.

[1] The possible is either that which may be when it is not, or that which is simply, or that which necessarily is; and to all these the above rule applies, and the formal consequence follows as directly from the premises, as to its character, as in the case of categoricals. Cf. Metap. 13. The nature of the possible is fully discussed, Rhetoric, b. ii. ch. 19.

isting, B also exists, when A is possible, B will be also possible, but A is supposed to be possible, wherefore B will be also possible, for if it were impossible the same thing would be possible and impossible at the same time. These things then being established, let A be present with every B, and B contingent to every C, therefore A must necessarily happen to be present with every C; for let it not happen, but let B be supposed to be present with every C, this is indeed false yet not impossible; if then A is not contingent to C, but B is present with every C, A is not contingent to every B, for a syllogism arises in the third figure. But it was supposed (that A was) contingently present with every (B), therefore A must necessarily be contingent to every C, for the false being assumed, and not the impossible,[1] the consequence is impossible.* We may also make a deduction to the impossible in the first figure by assuming B to be present with every C, for if B is with every C, but A contingent to every B, A will also be contingent to every C, but it was supposed not to be present with every C.† Still we must assume the being present with every, not distinguishing it by time, as "now," or "at this time," but simply; for by propositions of this kind, we also produce syllogisms,[2]

* Example (1.)

† Example (2.)

4 Universal predication has

[1] i. e. that A is not contingent to every C.

Ex. 1.	Every B is A	It is necessary that some C should not be A
	It happens that every C is B	Every C is B
. ˙ .	It happens that every C is A.	. ˙ . Not every B is A.
Ex. 2.	Every B is A	It happens that every B is A
	It happens that every C is B	Every C is B
. ˙ .	It happens that every C is A.	. ˙ . It happens that every C is A.

[2] Vide note to chap. 13, also Post Anal. Book i. He takes only propositions which are universally and immutably true for the elements of the sciences.

Ex. 3.	Whatever is moved is a man	Whatever is moved is an animal
	It happens that every horse is moved	It happens that every man is moved
	It is necessary that no horse should be a man.	It is necessary that every man should be an animal.
Ex. 4.	No B is A	It is necessary that some C should be A
	It happens that every C is B	Every C is B
. ˙ .	It happens that no C is A.	. ˙ . Some B is A.

since when a proposition is taken as to the present it will not be syllogism, since perhaps there is nothing to hinder "man" from being present some time or other with every thing moved, viz. if nothing else is moved, but what is moved is contingent to every "horse," yet "man" is contingent to no "horse." Moreover, let the first term be "animal," the middle, "that which is moved," and the last, "man;" the propositions will then be alike, but the conclusion necessary, and not contingent, for "man" is necessarily "an animal," so that it is evident that the universal must be taken simply and not deprived by time.*

no reference to time. (Cf. Aldrich and Hill's Logic.)

* Example (3.)

Again, let the proposition A B be universal negative, and let A be assumed to be present with no B, but let B contingently be present with every C; now from these positions A must necessarily happen to be present with no C, for let it not so happen, but let B be supposed to be present with C, as before; then A must necessarily be present with some B, for there is a syllogism in the third figure, but this is impossible, wherefore A can be contingent to no C, for the false and not the impossible being assumed, the impossible results.† Now this syllogism is not of the contingent according to the definition, but of what is necessarily present with none, for this is a contradiction of the given hypothesis, because A was supposed necessarily present with some C, but the syllogism per impossibile is of an opposite[1] contradiction. Besides, from the terms it appears clearly that there is no contingent conclusion, for let "crow" stand for A, "that which is intelligent" for B, and "man" for C; A is therefore present with no B, for nothing intelligent is a "crow;" but B is contingent to every C, since it happens to every "man" to be "intelligent," but A is necessarily present with no C, wherefore the conclusion is not contingent.‡ But neither is the conclusion always necessary, for let A be "what is moved," B "science," and C "man," A will then be present with no B, but B is contingent to every C, and the conclusion

2. E pure. A contingent.

† Example (4.) (Vide supra.)

‡ Example (5.)

[1] Vide Whately's Logic, b. ii. c. 3, sect. 7.

Ex. 5. Nothing intelligent is a crow
It happens that every man is intelligent
It is necessary that no man should be a crow.

will not be necessary, for it is not necessary that no "man" should be "moved," but also it is not necessary that a certain man should be moved; therefore it is clear that the conclusion is of that which is necessarily present with no one, hence the terms must be assumed in a better manner.[1] But if the

3. Minor negative contingent. negative be joined to the minor extreme, signifying to be contingent, from the assumed propositions there will be no syllogism, but there will be as in the former

[1] That is, instead of science, or an abstract term, we must assume one which may concur with man, e. g. "scientific," since a man may be "scientific," though he cannot be "science."

Ex. 6. It happens that $\left\{\begin{array}{l}\text{every}\\ \text{no}\end{array}\right\}$ animal is white
No snow is an animal
It is necessary that all snow should be white.

It happens that $\left\{\begin{array}{l}\text{every}\\ \text{no}\end{array}\right\}$ animal is white
No pitch is an animal
It is necessary that no pitch should be white.

Ex. 7. It happens that $\left\{\begin{array}{l}\text{every}\\ \text{no}\end{array}\right\}$ animal is white
Some snow is not an animal
It is necessary that all snow should be white.

It happens that $\left\{\begin{array}{l}\text{every}\\ \text{no}\end{array}\right\}$ animal is white
Some pitch is not an animal
It is necessary that no pitch should be white.

Ex. 8. It happens that $\left\{\begin{array}{l}\text{something}\\ \text{not every thing}\end{array}\right\}$ white is an animal
$\left\{\begin{array}{l}\text{Every}\\ \text{No}\\ \text{Some}\\ \text{Not every}\end{array}\right\}$ man is white
It is necessary that every man should be an animal.

It happens that $\left\{\begin{array}{l}\text{something}\\ \text{not every thing}\end{array}\right\}$ white is an animal
$\left\{\begin{array}{l}\text{Every}\\ \text{No}\\ \text{Some}\\ \text{Not every}\end{array}\right\}$ garment is white
It is necessary that no garment should be an animal.

$\left.\begin{array}{l}\text{Something}\\ \text{Not every thing}\end{array}\right\}$ white is an animal
It happens that $\left\{\begin{array}{l}\text{every}\\ \text{no}\\ \text{some}\\ \text{not every}\end{array}\right\}$ man is white
It is necessary that every man should be an animal.

instances, when the contingent proposition is converted. For let A be present with every B, but B contingent to no C, now when the terms are thus, there will be nothing necessary inferred, but if B C be converted, and B be assumed to be contingent to every C, a syllogism arises as before, since the terms have a similar position. In the same manner, when both the propositions are negative, if A B signifies not being present, but B C to be contingent to no individual, through these assumptions no necessity arises, but the contingent proposition being converted, there will be a syllogism. Let A be assumed present to no B, and B contingent to no C, nothing necessary is inferred from these; but if it is assumed that B is contingent to every C, which is true, and the proposition A B subsists similarly, there will be again the same syllogism. If however B is assumed as not present with C, and not that it happens not to be present, there will by no means be a syllogism, neither if the proposition A B be negative nor affirmative; but let the common terms of necessary presence be "white," "animal," "snow," and of non-contingency "white," "animal," "pitch."* It is evident, therefore, that when terms are universal, and one of the propositions is assumed, as simply de inesse, but the other contingent, when the minor premise is assumed contingent, a syllogism always arises, except that sometimes it will be produced from the propositions themselves, and at other times from the (contingent) proposition being converted; when, however, each of these occurs, and for what reason, we have shown. But if one proposition be assumed as universal, and the other particular, when the universal contingent is joined to the major extreme, whether it be affirmative or negative, but the particular is a simple affirmative de inesse, there will be a perfect

4. Both premises negative.

* Example (6.)

5. General law of mixed syllogisms; when minor premise is contingent, a syllogism is constructed, either directly or by conversion.

6. Of particulars with an universal major.

Something / Not every thing } white is an animal

It happens that { every / no / some / not every } garment is white

It is necessary that no garment should be an animal.

syllogism, just as when the terms are universal, but the demonstration is the same as before. Now when the major is universal, simple, and not contingent, but the other (the minor) particular and contingent, if both propositions be assumed affirmative or negative, or if one be affirmative and the other negative, there will always be an incomplete syllogism, except that some will be demonstrated per impossibile, but others by conversion of the contingent proposition, as in the former cases. There will also be a syllogism, through conversion, when the universal major signifies simply inesse, or non-inesse, but the particular being negative, assumes the contingent, as if A is present, or not present, with every B, that B happens not to be present with a certain C; for the contingent proposition B C being converted, there is a syllogism. Still when the particular proposition assumes the not being present with, there will not be a syllogism. Now let the terms of presence be "white," "animal," "snow," but of not being present "white," "animal," "pitch," for the demonstration must be assumed through the indefinite.* Yet if the universal be joined to the less extreme, but particular to the greater, whether negative or affirmative, contingent or pure, there will by no means be a syllogism, nor if particular or indefinite propositions be assumed, whether they take the contingent, or simply the being present with, or vice versâ, will there thus be a syllogism, and the demonstration is the same as before; let however the common terms of being present with from necessity be "animal," "white," "man;" and of not being contingent "animal," "white," "garment."† Hence it is evident, that if the major be universal, there is always a syllogism, but if the minor be so, (if the major be particular,) there will never be.

2. Major A or E pure.

3.

4.

7. If the major is particular there will be no syllogism, nor if both premises be particular or indefinite.

* Example (7.)

† Example (8.)

Chap. XVI.—*Of Syllogisms with one Premise necessary, and the other contingent in the first Figure.*

1. The law relative to syllogisms of this character.

When one is a necessary proposition simple, de inesse, or non-inesse, and the other signifies being contingent, there will be a syllogism, the terms subsisting similarly, and it will be perfect when the minor premise[1] is necessary; the conclusion however, when the terms are affirmative, will be contingent, and not simple, whether they are universal or not universal. Nevertheless, if one proposition be affirmative, and the other negative, when the affirmative is necessary, the conclusion will in like manner signify the being contingent, and not the not-existing or being present with; and when the negative is necessary, the conclusion will be of the contingent non-inesse, and of the simple non-inesse, whether the terms are universal or not. The contingent also in the conclusion, is to be assumed in the same way as in the former syllogisms, but there will not be a syllogism wherein the non-inesse will be necessarily inferred, for it is one thing "inesse" not necessarily, and another "non-inesse" necessarily. Wherefore, it is evident that when the terms are affirmative, there will not be a necessary conclusion. For let A necessarily be present with every B, but let B be contingent to every C, there will then be an incomplete syllogism, whence it may be inferred that A happens to be present with every C; but that it is incomplete, is evident from de-

2. When both premises are A, there will not be a necessary conclusion.

[1] Major premise ἡ πρὸς τῷ μείζονι ἄκρῳ πρότασις—minor ἡ πρὸς τῷ ἐλάττονι ἄκρῳ πρότασις. Conclusion συμπέρασμα. In Anal. Pr. ii. 14, this last signifies also the minor term.

Ex. 1.	It is necessary that no B should be A It happens that every C is B ∴ No C is A.	It is necessary that no A should be B Some C is A ∴ It is necessary that some C should not be B.
Ex. 2.	It happens that {every / no} animal is white It is necessary that no snow should be an animal It is necessary that all snow should be white.	It happens that {every / no} animal is white It is necessary that no pitch should be an animal It is necessary that no pitch should be white.
Ex. 3.	It is necessary that something white should {be / not be} an animal It happens that {every / no} man is white It is necessary that every man should be an animal.	It is necessary that something white should {be / not be} an animal It happens that {every / no} garment is white It is necessary that no garment should be an animal.

monstration, for this may be shown after the same manner as in the former syllogisms. Again, let A be contingent to every B, but let B be necessarily present with every C, there will then be a syllogism wherein A *happens* to be present with every C, but not (simply) is it present with every C, also it will be complete, and not incomplete, for it is completed by the first propositions. Notwithstanding, if the propositions are not of similar form, first, let the negative one be necessary, and let A necessarily be contingent to no B, but let B be contingent to every C; therefore, it is necessary that A should be present with no C; for let it be assumed present, either with every or with some one, yet it was supposed to be contingent to no B. Since then a negative proposition is convertible, neither will B be contingent to any A, but A is supposed to be present with every or with some C, hence B will happen to be present with no, or not with every C, it was however supposed, from the first, to be present with every C.* Still it is evident, that there may also be a syllogism of the contingent non-inesse, as there is one of the simple non-inesse. Moreover, let the affirmative proposition be necessary, and let A be contingently present with no B, but B necessarily present with every C: this syllogism then will be perfect, yet not of the simple, but of the contingent non-inesse, for the proposition (viz. the contingent non-inesse) was assumed from the major extreme, and there cannot be a deduction to the impossible, for if A is supposed to be present with a certain C, and it is admitted that A is contingently present with no B, nothing impossible will arise therefrom. But if the minor premise be negative when it is contingent, there will be a syllogism by conversion, as in the former cases, but when it is not contingent, there will not be; nor when both premises are negative, but the minor not contingent: let the terms be the same of the simple inesse "white," "animal," "snow," and of the non-inesse "white," "animal," "pitch."†

1. Negative necessary.

* Example (1.)

2. Affirmative necessary.

3. Minor negative contingent.

† Example (2.)

The same will also happen in particular syllogisms, for when the negative is necessary, the conclusion will be of the simple non-inesse. Thus if A is contingently present with no B, but B contingently present with a certain C, it is necessary that A should not be

3. Case of particular syllogisms. 1.

present with a certain C, since if it is present with every C, but is contingent to no B, neither will B be contingently present with any A. So that if A is present with every C, B is contingent with no C, but it was supposed contingent to a certain C. When however in a negative syllogism the particular affirmative is necessary, as for example B C, or the universal in an affirmative syllogism, e. g. A B, there will not be a syllogism de inesse, the demonstration however is the same as in the former cases. But if the minor premise be universal, whether affirmative or negative and contingent, but the major particular necessary, there will not be a syllogism, let the terms of necessary presence be "animal," "white," "man," and of the non-contingent "animal," "white," "garment."* But when the universal is necessary, and the particular contingent, the universal being negative, let the terms of presence[1] be "animal," "white," "crow," and of non-inesse "animal," "white," "pitch."†

2.

3.

* Example (3.)

† Example (4.)

But when (the universal) affirms let the terms of presence be "animal," "white," "swan," but of the non-contingent be "animal," "white," "snow."‡ Nor will there be a syllogism when indefinite propositions are assumed or both particular, let the common terms, de inesse, be "animal," "white," "man," de non-inesse "animal," "white," "inanimate;" for "animal" is necessarily and not contingently

4.

‡ Example (5.)

4. Case of both premises indefinite or particular.

[1] That is, of the major being with the minor.

Ex. 4.

It happens that something white $\left\{\begin{matrix}\text{is}\\ \text{is not}\end{matrix}\right\}$ an animal	It happens that something white $\left\{\begin{matrix}\text{is}\\ \text{is not}\end{matrix}\right\}$ an animal
It is necessary that no crow should be white	It is necessary that no pitch should be white
It is necessary that every crow should be an animal.	It is necessary that no pitch should be an animal.

Ex. 5.

It happens that something white $\left\{\begin{matrix}\text{is}\\ \text{is not}\end{matrix}\right\}$ an animal	It happens that something white $\left\{\begin{matrix}\text{is}\\ \text{is not}\end{matrix}\right\}$ an animal
It is necessary that every swan should be white	It is necessary that all snow should be white
It is necessary that every swan should be an animal.	It is necessary that no snow should be an animal.

present with something "white," and "white" is also necessarily and not contingently present with something "inanimate;" the like also occurs in the contingent, so that these terms are useful for all.*

* Example (6.)

From what has been said then it appears that when the terms are alike both in simple and in necessary propositions, a syllogism does and does not occur, except that if the negative proposition be assumed de inesse there will be a syllogism with a contingent (conclusion), but when the negative is necessary there will be one of the character of the contingent and of the non-inesse, but it is clear also that all the syllogisms are incomplete,[1] and that they are completed through the above-named figures.

5. Conclusion from the above. (Compare c.15.)

CHAP. XVII.—*Of Syllogisms with two contingent Premises in the second Figure.*

1. Rule for contingent syllogisms in this figure.

In the second figure, when both premises are assumed contingent, there will be no syllogism, neither when they are taken as affirmative, nor negative, nor universal, nor particular; but when one signifies the simple inesse, and the other the contingent, if the affirmative signifies the inesse, there will never be a syllogism, but if the universal negative (be pure, there will) always (be a

Ex. 6.

It happens that something white {is / is not} an animal	It happens that something white {is / is not} an animal
It is necessary that some man should {be / not be} white	It is necessary that something inanimate should {be / not be} white
It is necessary that every man should be an animal.	It is necessary that nothing inanimate should be an animal.
It is necessary that something white should {be / not be} an animal	It is necessary that something white should {be / not be} an animal
It happens that some man {is / is not} white	It happens that every thing inanimate is white
It is necessary that every man should be an animal.	It is necessary that nothing inanimate should be an animal.

[1] Those are syllogisms with a contingent minor, but a necessary or pure major.

syllogism). In the same manner, when one premise is assumed as necessary, but the other contingent; still in these syllogisms we must consider the contingent in the conclusions, as we did in the former ones. Now in the first place, we must show that a contingent negative is not convertible, e. g. if A is contingent to no B, it is not necessary that B should also be contingent to no A. For let this be assumed, and let B be contingently present with no A, therefore since contingent affirmatives, both contrary and contradictory, are convertible into negatives, and B is contingently present with no A, it is clear that B may be contingently present with every A; but this is false, for if this is contingent to all of that, it is not necessary 1.
that that should be contingent to this, wherefore a negative (contingent) is not convertible. Moreover, there is nothing to prevent A being contingent to no B, but B not necessarily present with a certain A, e. g. "whiteness" may happen not to be present with every "man," (for it may also happen) to be present; but it is not true to say, that man is *contingently* present with nothing "white," for he is *necessarily* not present with many things (white), and the necessary is not the contingent. Neither can it be shown convertible per impossibile, as if a man should think, since it is false that B is contingently present with no A, that it is true that it 2.
(A) is not contingent to no one (B), for these are affirmation and negation; but if this be true B is necessarily present with a certain A, therefore A is also with a certain B, but this is impossible, since it does not follow if B is not contingent to no A, that it is necessarily present with a certain A. For not to be contingent to no individual, is predicated two ways, the one if a thing is necessarily present with something, and the other if it is necessarily not present with something. For what necessarily is not present with a certain A, cannot be truly said to be contingently not present with every A; as neither can what is necessarily present with a certain thing, be truly said to be contingently present with every thing; if, then, any one thinks that because C is not contingently present with every D, it is necessarily not present with a certain D, he would infer falsely, for, perchance, it is present with every D; still because a thing is

2. Terms of a contingent negative not convertible.

3. Contingency predicated negatively in two ways—the character of the consequent opposition.

necessarily present with certain things, on this account, we say that it is not contingent to every individual. Wherefore the being present necessarily with a certain thing, and the not being present with a certain thing necessarily, are opposed to the being contingently present with every individual, and in like manner, there is a similar opposition to the being contingent to no individual. Hence it is evident, that when the contingent and non-contingent are taken, in the manner we first defined, not only the necessarily being present with a certain thing, but also the necessarily not being present with it, ought to be assumed; but when this is assumed, there is no impossibility to a syllogism being produced, whence it is evident, from what we have stated, that a negative contingent is not convertible.

4. From two premises universal (A) or (E) contingent in the 2nd figure, no syllogism is constructed.

This then being demonstrated, let A be assumed contingent to no B, but contingent to every C; by conversion, therefore, there will not be a syllogism, for it has been said that a proposition of this kind is inconvertible, neither, however, will there be by a deduction per impossibile. For B being assumed contingently present with every C, nothing false will happen, for A may contingently be present with every, and with no C.*[1] In short, if there is a syllogism, it is clear that it will be of the contingent, (because neither proposition is assumed as de inesse,) and this either affirmative, or negative; it is possible, however, in neither way, since, if the affirmative be assumed, it can be shown by the terms, that it is not contingently present; but if the negative, that the conclusion is not contingent, but necessary. For let A be "white," B "man," and C "horse," A therefore, i. e. "whiteness," is contingently present with every individual of the one, though with no individual of the other,

* Example (1.)

[1] Ex. 1. It happens that no B is A
It happens that every C is A
∴ It happens that no C is B.

It happens that no B is A
It is necessary that every or some C should be B
∴ It happens that every or some C is not A.

I have followed Waitz here. Buhle reads the letters and statement of premises differently.

Ex. 2. It happens that no man is white
It happens that every horse is white
It is necessary that no horse should be a man.

but B is neither contingently present, nor yet contingently not present, with C. It is evident that it is not contingently present, for no "horse" is "a man," but neither does it *happen* not to be present, for it is *necessary* that no "horse" should be "a man," and the necessary is not the contingent, wherefore there is no syllogism.* This may be also similarly shown, if the negative be transposed,[1] and if both propositions be assumed affirmative, or negative, for the demonstration will be by the same terms.† When one proposition also is universal, but the other particular, or both particular or indefinite, or in whatever other way it is possible to change the propositions, for the demonstration will always be through the same terms.‡ Hence it is clear that if both propositions are assumed contingent there is no syllogism.[2]

* Example (2.)

† Example (3.)

5. Nor from one univ. and the other par., or both par. or indef.

‡ Example (4.)

CHAP. XVIII.—*Of Syllogisms with one Proposition simple, and the other contingent, in the second Figure.*

IF one proposition signifies inesse, but the other the contingent, the affirmative proposition being simple, but the negative contingent, there will never be a syllogism, neither if the terms be as-

1. Rule for universals in this figure, with one pure premise, and

[1] i. e. If the major affirm, and the minor deny.

Ex. 3. It happens that $\left\{\begin{matrix}\text{every}\\ \text{no}\end{matrix}\right\}$ man is white
It happens that $\left\{\begin{matrix}\text{every}\\ \text{no}\end{matrix}\right\}$ horse is white
It is necessary that no horse should be a man.

Ex. 4. It happens that $\left\{\begin{matrix}\text{every}\\ \text{no}\end{matrix}\right\}$ man is white
It happens that some horse $\left\{\begin{matrix}\text{is}\\ \text{is not}\end{matrix}\right\}$ white
It is necessary that no horse should be a man.

It happens that some man $\left\{\begin{matrix}\text{is}\\ \text{is not}\end{matrix}\right\}$ white
It happens that $\left\{\begin{matrix}\text{every}\\ \text{no}\end{matrix}\right\}$ horse is white
It is necessary that no horse should be a man.

It happens that some man $\left\{\begin{matrix}\text{is}\\ \text{is not}\end{matrix}\right\}$ white
It happens that some horse $\left\{\begin{matrix}\text{is}\\ \text{is not}\end{matrix}\right\}$ white
It is necessary that no horse should be a man.

[2] The last sentence is omitted by Taylor.

the other contingent. sumed universally, or partially, still the demonstration will be the same, and by the same terms, yet when the affirmative is contingent, but the negative simple, there will be a syllogism. For let A be assumed present
1. with no B, but contingent with every C, then by conversion of the negative, B will be present with no A, but A is contingent to every C, therefore there is a syllogism in the first figure, that B is contingent to no C. So also if the negative be added to C; but if both propositions be negative, and one signifies the simple, but the other the contingent non-inesse, from these assumed propositions nothing necessary is inferred, but the contingent proposition being converted,[1] there is a syllogism, wherein B is contingently present with no C, as in the former, for again there will be the first figure. If, however, both propositions be assumed

[1] If the contingent negative proposition be changed into an affirmative.

Ex. 1.	It happens that every animal is well	It happens that every horse is well
	Every man is well	Every man is well
	It is necessary that every man should be an animal.	It is necessary that no man should be a horse.
	Every animal is well	Every horse is well
	It happens that every man is well	It happens that every man is well
	It is necessary that every man should be an animal.	It is necessary that no man should be a horse.
Ex. 2.	It happens that no animal is well	It happens that no horse is well
	Some man is well	Some man is well
	It is necessary that every man should be an animal.	It is necessary that no man should be a horse.
	Every animal is well	Every horse is well
	It happens that some man is not well	It happens that some man is not well
	It is necessary that every man should be an animal.	It is necessary that no man should be a horse.
Ex. 3.	Some animal {is / is not} well	Some horse {is / is not} well
	It happens that some man {is / is not} well	It happens that some man {is / is not} well
	It is necessary that every man should be an animal.	It is necessary that no man should be a horse.

affirmative, there will not be a syllogism: let the terms of presence be "health," "animal," "man," but of not being present with "health," "horse," "man."* The same will happen in the case of particular syllogisms, for when the affirmative is pure, taken either universally, or particularly, there will be no syllogism, and this is shown in like manner through the same terms as before.† But when the negative is simple, there will be a syllogism by conversion, as in the former cases. Again, if both premises be taken negative, and that which signifies simply the non-inesse be universal; from these propositions no necessity will result, but the contingent being converted as before there will be a syllogism. If however the negative be pure but particular, there will not be a syllogism, whether the other premise be affirmative or negative. Neither will there be one, when both propositions are assumed indefinite, whether affirmative, negative, or particular, and the demonstration is the same and by the same terms.‡

2.

* Example (1.)

2. Particular syllogisms.

† Example (2.)

‡ Example (3.)

CHAP. XIX.—*Of Syllogisms with one Premise necessary and the other contingent, in the second Figure.*

IF however one premise signifies the being present necessarily, but the other contingently, when the negative is necessary there will be a syllogism, wherein not only the contingent but also the simple non-inesse (may be inferred), but when the affirmative (is necessary) there will be no syllogism. For let A be assumed necessarily present with no B, but contingent to every C, then by conversion of the negative neither will B be present with any A, but A was contingent to every C, wherefore there is again a syllogism in the first figure, so that B is contingently present with no C. At the same time it is shown that neither is B present with any C, for let it be assumed to be

1. Rule, in these when the negative premise is necessary, a syllogism may be constructed.
1. Case.

It happens that some animal {is / is not} well	It happens that some horse {is / is not} well
Some man {is / is not} well	Some man {is / is not} well
It is necessary that every man should be an animal	It is necessary that no man should be a horse.

present, therefore if A is contingent to no B, but B is present with a certain C, A is not contingent to a certain C, but it was supposed contingent to every C, and it may be shown after the same manner, if the negative be added to C. Again, let the affirmative proposition be necessary, but the other negative and contingent, and let A be contingent to no B, but necessarily present with every C; now when the terms are thus, there will be no syllogism, for it may happen that B is necessarily not present with C. Let A be "white," B "man," C "a swan;" "whiteness," then, is necessarily present with "a swan," but is contingent to no "man," and "man" is necessarily present with no "swan;" therefore that there will be no syllogism of the contingent is palpable, for what is necessary is not contingent.*[1] Yet neither will there be a syllogism of the necessary, for the latter is either inferred from two necessary premises, or from a negative (necessary premise); besides, from these data it follows that B may be present with C, for there is nothing to prevent C from being under B, and A from being contingent to every B, and necessarily present with C, as if C is "awake," B "animal," and A "motion;" for "motion" is necessarily present with whatever is "awake," but contingent to every "animal," and every thing which is "awake" is "an animal."† Hence it appears that neither the non-inesse is inferred, since if the terms are thus the inesse is necessary, nor when the enunciations are opposite,[2] so that there will be no syllogism. There

2. Case of a necessary affirmative.

* Example (1.)

† Example (2.)

[1] Ex. 1. It happens that no man is white
It is necessary that every swan should be white
It is necessary that no swan should be a man.

Ex. 2. It happens that no animal is moved
It is necessary that every thing awake should be moved
Every thing awake is an animal.

Alexander Aphrodisiensis observes that the example would be clearer, if "walking" were assumed instead of "awake," because it is more obviously necessary that a thing which walks should be "moved," than a thing which is awake.

[2] "Will there be a syllogism from such propositions"—there is an ellipse of these words here. The case is that neither a contingent nor necessary affirmation is to be inferred, since sometimes the non-inesse is necessary.

will be also a similar demonstration if the affirmative premise be transposed, but if the propositions are of the same character, when they are negative, a syllogism is always formed, the contingent proposition being converted, as in the former cases. For let A be assumed necessarily not present with B, and contingently not present with C, then the propositions being converted, B

3. Case of both negative.

Ex. 3. It is necessary that every swan should be white
It happens that every man is white
It is necessary that no man should be a swan.

Ex. 4.	It happens that no man is white	It happens that no animal is moved
	It is necessary that some swan should be white	It is necessary that something awake should be moved
	It is necessary that no swan should be a man.	It is necessary that every thing awake should be an animal.

It is necessary that every swan should be white
It happens that some man is not white
It is necessary that no man should be a swan.

Ex. 5.	It is necessary that every swan should be white	It happens that every man is white
	It happens that some man is a swan	It is necessary that some swan should be white
	It is necessary that no man should be a swan.	It is necessary that no swan should be a man.
	It is necessary that some swan should be white	It happens that some man is white
	It happens that every man is white	It is necessary that every swan should be white
	It is necessary that no man should be a swan.	It is necessary that no swan should be a man.

Ex. 6.	It happens that some animal {is / is not} white	It happens that some animal {is / is not} white
	It is necessary that some man should {be / not be} white	It is necessary that something inanimate should {be / not be} white
	It is necessary that every man should be an animal	It is necessary that nothing inanimate should be an animal.
	It is necessary that some animal should {be / not be} white	It is necessary that some animal should {be / not be} white
	It happens that some man {is / is not} white	It happens that something inanimate {is / is not} white
	It is necessary that every man should be an animal	It is necessary that nothing inanimate should be an animal.

is present with no A, and A is contingent with every C, and the first figure is produced; the same would also occur if the negation belongs to C. But if both propositions be affirmative, there will not be a syllogism, clearly not of the non-inesse, nor of the necessary non-inesse, because a negative premise is not assumed, neither in the simple, nor in the necessary inesse. Neither, again, will there be a syllogism of the contingent non-inesse, for necessary terms being assumed, B will not be present with C, e. g. if A be assumed "white," B "a swan," and C "man;" nor will there be from opposite affirmations, since B has been shown necessarily not present with C, in short, therefore, a syllogism will not be produced.* It will happen the same in particular syllogisms, for when the negative is universal and necessary, there will always be a syllogism of the contingent, and of the non-inesse, but the demonstration will be by conversion; still, when the affirmative (is necessary), there will never be a syllogism, and this may be shown in the same way as in the universals, and by the same terms.† Nor when both premises are assumed affirmative, for of this there is the same demonstration as before,‡ but when both are negative, and that which signifies the non-inesse is universal, and necessary; the necessary will not be concluded through the propositions, but the contingent being converted, there will be a syllogism as before. If however both propositions are laid down indefinite, or particular, there will not be a syllogism, and the demonstration is the same, and by the same terms.§

4. Case of both affirmative.

* Example (3.)

2. Particular syllogisms.

† Example (4.)

‡ Example (5.)

§ Example (6.)

It appears then, from what we have said, that an universal, and necessary negative being assumed, there is always a syllogism, not only of the contingent, but also of the simple non-inesse; but with a necessary affirmative, there will never be a syllogism; also that when the terms subsist in the same manner, in necessary, as in simple propositions, there is, and is not, a syllogism; lastly, that all these syllogisms are incomplete, and that they are completed through the above-mentioned figures.[1]

3. Conclusion. (Cf. cap. 18.)

[1] Although all incomplete syllogisms are completed through the first figure, yet some are, after a manner, rendered more useful through another

Chap. XX.—*Of Syllogisms with both Propositions contingent in the third Figure.*

In the last figure, when both premises are contingent, and when only one is contingent, there will be a syllogism, therefore when the premises signify the contingent, the conclusion will also be contingent; also if one premise signifies the contingent, but the other, the simple inesse. Still when one premise is assumed necessary, if it be affirmative, there will not be a conclusion either necessary or simple, if on the contrary it is negative, there will be a syllogism of the simple non-inesse as before; in these however the contingent must be similarly taken in the conclusions. First then let the premises be contingent, and let A and B be contingently present with every C; since therefore a particular affirmative is convertible, but B is contingent to every C, C will also be contingent to a certain B, therefore if A is contingent to every C, but C is contingent to a certain B, it is necessary also that A should be contingent to a certain B, for the first figure is produced. If again A is contingently present with no C, but B with every C, A must also of necessity be contingently not present with a certain B, for again there will be the first figure by conversion;[1] but if both propositions be assumed negative from these the necessary will not result, but the propositions being converted there will be a syllogism as before. For if A and B are contingently not present with C,

1. Review—rule for propositions of this class.

1. Both premises contingent.

2.

3.

figure, as by changing the contingent affirmative proposition into the negative.

[1] That is, by conversion of the minor.

Ex. 1. It happens that something white {is / is not} an animal
It happens that something white {is / is not} a man
It is necessary that every man should be an animal

It happens that something white {is / is not} a horse
It happens that something white {is / is not} a man
∴ It is necessary that no man should be a horse.

if the contingently not present be changed, there will again be the first figure by conversion. If however one term be universal but the other particular, when they are so, as in the case of simple inesse, there will, and will not, be a syllogism; for let A be contingently present with every C, and B present with a certain C, there will again be the first figure by conversion of the particular proposition, since if A is contingent to every C, and C to a certain B, A is also contingent to a certain B, and in like manner if the universal be joined to B C. This also will be produced in a similar way if A C be negative, but B C affirmative, for again we shall have the first figure by conversion, if however both are negative, the one universal and the other particular, by the assumed propositions there will not be a syllogism, but there will be when they are converted as before. Lastly, when both are indefinite or particular, there will not be a syllogism, for A must necessarily be present with every and with no B, let the terms de inesse be "animal," "man," "white," and de non-inesse "horse," "man," "white," the middle term "white."*

4. One premise universal and the other particular.

5.

6. Both particular or indefinite.

* Example (1.)

CHAP. XXI.—*Of Syllogisms with one Proposition contingent and the other simple in the third Figure.*

IF however one premise signifies the inesse, but the other the contingent, the conclusion will be that a thing is contingent to, and not that it is present with (another), and there will be a syllogism, the terms subsisting in the same manner as the previous ones. For, first, let them be affirmative,[1] and let A be in every C, but B contingent with every C; B C then being converted there will be the first figure, and the conclusion will be that A is contingently present with a certain B, for when one premise in the first figure signifies the contingent, the conclusion also was contingent. In like manner if the proposition B C[2] be of the simple inesse, but the proposition

1. Rule of consequence—a contingent is inferred from one absolute and another contingent premise. (Vide supra.)

1st case, Both affirmative.

2nd, Minor simple affirmative, major contin-

[1] "Predicative."—Averrois. [2] That is, the minor.

A C be contingent, and if A C[1] be negative, but B C affirmative, and either of them be pure; in both ways the conclusion will be contingent, since again there arises the first figure. Now it has been shown that where one premise in that figure signifies the contingent, the conclusion also will be contingent; if however the negative be annexed to the minor premise, or both be assumed as negative, through the propositions laid down themselves, there will not indeed be a syllogism, but by their conversion[2] there will be, as in the former cases.

gent and negative.

3rd, From a negative minor or from two negatives, no syllogism results.

Nevertheless if one premise be universal and the other particular, yet both affirmative, or the universal negative but the particular affirmative, there will be the same mode of syllogisms; for all are completed by the first figure, so that it is evident there will be a syllogism of the contingent and not of the inesse. If however the affirmative be universal and the negative particular, the demonstration will be per impossibile; for let B be with every C and A happen not to be with a certain C, it is necessary then that A should happen not to be with a certain B, since if A is necessarily with every B, but B is assumed to be with every C, A will necessarily be with every C, which was demonstrated before, but by hypothesis A happens not to be with a certain C.

4. Cases of particulars.

1.

2.

When both premises are assumed indefinite, or particular, there will not be a syllogism, and the demonstration is the same as in universals,[3] and by the same terms.*

* Example (1)

[1] Major. [2] i. e. the negative contingent being changed into affirmative.

[3] Alexander Aphrodis. thinks we should read ἢ καὶ επὶ τῶν ἐξ ἀμφοτέρων ἐνδεχομένων, (instead of ἢ καὶ ἐντοῖς καθόλου,) i. e. which was in syllogisms, both the propositions of which are contingent.—Taylor, Julius Pacius, and Zell approve of this emendation, but I agree with Waitz in thinking it unnecessary. Cf. cap. 20, and 21.

Ex. 1. Something white {is / is not} an animal

It happens that something white {is / is not} a man

It is necessary that every man should be an animal.

Something white {is / is not} a horse

It happens that something white {is / is not} a man

It is necessary that no man should be a horse.

CHAP. XXII.—*Of Syllogisms with one Premise necessary, and the other contingent in the third Figure.*

1. Rules for universals in the third figure, with one necessary, and the other contingent premise.

IF one premise be necessary, but the other contingent, the terms being affirmative there will be always a syllogism of the contingent; but when one is affirmative but the other negative, if the affirmative be necessary there will be a syllogism of the contingent non-inesse; if however it be negative, there will be one both of the contingent and of the absolute non-inesse. There will not however be a syllogism of the necessary non-inesse, as neither in the other figures. Let then, first, the terms be affirmative, and let A be necessarily with every C, but B happen to be with every C; therefore since A is necessarily with every C, but C is contingent to a certain B, A will also be contingently, and not necessarily, with some certain B; for thus it is concluded in the first figure. It can be similarly proved if B C be assumed as necessary, but A C contingent.*

1. Each proposition, affirmative.

* Example (1.)

2. Major negative, minor affirmative.

Again, let one premise be affirmative, but the other negative, and let the affirmative be necessary; let also A happen to be with no C, but let B necessarily be with every C; again there will be the first figure;[1]

It happens that something white $\left\{\begin{matrix}\text{is}\\ \text{is not}\end{matrix}\right\}$ an animal
Something white $\left\{\begin{matrix}\text{is}\\ \text{is not}\end{matrix}\right\}$ a man
It is necessary that every man should be an animal.

It happens that some animal $\left\{\begin{matrix}\text{is}\\ \text{is not}\end{matrix}\right\}$ a horse
Something white $\left\{\begin{matrix}\text{is}\\ \text{is not}\end{matrix}\right\}$ a man
It is necessary that no man should be a horse.

Ex. 1. It happens that every man is white	It happens that every man is white
It is necessary that every man should be an animal	It is necessary that some animal should be a man
∴ It happens that some animal is white	∴ It happens that some animal is white.

[1] Taylor inserts here — "and the conclusion will be contingent, but not pure"—which is omitted by Waitz.

for the negative premise signifies the being contingent, it is evident therefore that the conclusion will be contingent, for when the premises were thus in the first figure, the conclusion was also contingent. But if the negative premise be necessary, the conclusion will be that it is contingent, not to be with something, and that it is not with it; for let A be supposed necessarily not with C, but contingent to every B, then the affirmative proposition B C being converted, there will be the first figure, and the negative premise will be necessary. But when the premises are thus, it results that A happens not to be with a certain C, and that it is not with it; wherefore it is necessary also that A should not be with a certain B. When however the minor premise is assumed negative there will be a syllogism, if that be contingent by the premise being converted as in the former cases, but if it be necessary there will not be, for it is necessary to be with every, and happens to be with none; let the terms of being with every individual, be "sleep," a "sleeping horse," "man;" of being with none "sleep," a "waking horse," "man."*

3. Vice versâ.

* Example (2.)

It will happen in the same way, if one term be joined to the middle universally, but the other partially, for both being affirmative there will be a syllogism of the contingent, and not of the absolute, also when the one is assumed as negative but the other affirmative, and the affirmative is necessary. But when the negative is necessary, the conclusion will also be of the not being present with; for there will be the same mode of demonstration, whether the terms are universal or not universal, since it is necessary that the syllogisms be completed by the first figure, so that it is requisite that the same should result, in these,[1]

4. Case of particulars.

Ex. 2.	It happens that every man sleeps	It happens that every man sleeps
	It is necessary that no man should be a sleeping horse	It is necessary that no man should be a waking horse
	It is necessary that every sleeping horse should sleep.	It is necessary that no waking horse should sleep.
Ex. 3.	It happens that some man sleeps	It happens that some man sleeps
	It is necessary that no man should be a sleeping horse	It is necessary that no man should be a waking horse
	It is necessary that every sleeping horse should sleep.	It is necessary that no waking horse should be asleep.

[1] i. e. in syllogisms of the first figure.

as in those.[1] When however the negative, universally assumed, is joined to the less extreme, if it be contingent, there will be a syllogism by conversion, but if it be necessary there will not be, and this may be shown in the same mode as in universals, and by the same terms.† Wherefore in this figure it it is evident, when and how there will be a syllogism,[2] and when of the contingent, and when of the absolute, all also it is clear are imperfect, and are perfected by the first figure.

† Example (3.)

CHAP. XXIII.—*It is demonstrated that every Syllogism is completed by the first Figure.*

1. Observations preliminary to proving that every syllogism results from universals of the first figure.

THAT the syllogisms then in these figures are completed by the universal syllogisms in the first figure, and are reduced to these, is evident from what has been said; but that in short every syllogism is thus, will now be evident, when it shall be shown that every syllogism is produced by some one of these figures.

2 Syllogism must demonstrate the absolute universally or particularly. Of the ostensive.

It is then necessary that every demonstration, and every syllogism, should show either something inesse or non-inesse, and this either universally or partially, moreover either ostensively or by hypothesis. A part however of that which is by hypothesis is produced per impossibile, therefore let us first speak of the ostensive (syllogisms), and when these are shown, it will be evident also in the case of those leading to the impossibile, and generally of those by hypothesis.

3. For a simple conclusion we must have two propositions.

If then it is necessary to syllogize A of B either as being with or as not being with, we must assume something of something, if then A be assumed of B, that which was from the first (proposed) will be assumed (to be proved), but if A be assumed of C, but C of nothing, nor any thing else of it, nor of A, there will be no syllogism, for there is no necessary result from assuming one thing of one, so that we must take another premise. If then A be assumed of something else, or something

[1] In syllogisms of the third.

[2] i. e. there will be a syllogism from both propositions being contingent, or from one being pure and the other contingent, or from one necessary and the other contingent.

else of A, or of C, there is nothing to hinder a syllogism, it will not however appertain to B[1] from the assumptions. Nor when C is predicated of something else, and that of another, and this last of a third,[2] if none of these belong to B, neither thus will there be a syllogism with reference to B, since in short we say that there never will be a syllogism of one thing in respect of another unless a certain middle is assumed, which refers in some way to each extreme in predication. For a syllogism is simply from premises, but that which pertains to this in relation to that, is from premises belonging to this in relation to that,[3] but it is impossible to assume a premise relating to B, if we neither affirm nor deny any thing of it, or again of A in relation to B, if we assume nothing common, but affirm or deny certain peculiarities of each.

4. These connected by a middle term; which connexion is three-fold. (Vide Aldrich.)

Hence a certain middle of both must be taken, which unites the predications, if there shall be a syllogism of one in relation to the other; now if it is necessary to assume something common to both, this happens in a three-fold manner, (since we either predicate A of C, and C of B,[4] or C[5] of both or both of C,[6]) but these are the before-mentioned figures—it is evident that every syllogism is necessarily produced by some one of these figures, for there is the same reasoning, if A be connected with B, even through many media, for the figure in many media will be the same.

2. Of syllogisms per impossibile there is the same method.

Wherefore that all ostensive syllogisms are perfected by the above-named figures is clear, also that those per impossibile (are so perfected) will appear from these, for all syllogisms concluding per impossibile collect the false, but they prove by hypothesis the original proposition, when contradiction being admitted some impossibility results,[7] as for instance that the diameter of a square is incommensurate with the side, because, a common measure being given, the odd would be equal to the even.

[1] A will not be concluded of B—but something else.
[2] i. e. C of D, D of E, E of F.
[3] i. e. in which the middle is connected with each extreme.
[4] The first figure. [5] The second figure. [6] The third figure.
[7] This, as Dr. Hessey remarks, in his valuable tables upon the nature of Enthymem, corresponds very closely to the definition of ἐλεγκτικὸν ἐνθύμημα in the Rhetoric ii. 2, 15, and to the instance given Rhetoric ii. 24, 3. He thus exhibits the operation, which the reader will find applied to the instance in the text, in table 4 of Schemata Rhetorica.

They collect then that the odd would be equal to the even, but show from hypothesis that the diameter is incommensurate, since a falsity occurs by contradiction. This then it is, to syllogize per impossibile, namely, to show an impossibility from the original hypothesis, so that as by reasonings leading to the impossible, an ostensive syllogism of the false arises, but the original proposition is proved by hypothesis; and we have before said about ostensive syllogisms, that they are perfected by these figures—it is evident that syllogisms also per impossibile will be formed through these figures. Likewise all others which are by hypothesis, for in all there is a syllogism of that which is assumed,[1] but the original proposition is proved by confession, or some other hypothesis. Now if this is true, it is necessary that every demonstration and syllogism should arise through the three figures before named, and this being shown, it is manifest that every syllogism is completed in the first figure, and is reduced to universal syllogisms in it.

1. What this kind of syllogism is.

3. Also of syllogisms, ἐξ ὑποθέσεως—recapitulation.

CHAP. XXIV.—*Of the Quality and Quantity of the Premises in Syllogism.—Of the Conclusion.*

1. One affirmative and one universal term necessary, in all syllogisms. (Proof.)

MOREOVER it is necessary in every syllogism, that one term should be affirmative and one universal, for without the universal there will not be a syllogism, or one not pertaining to the thing proposed, or the original (question) will be the subject of petition.[2] For let it be proposed that pleasure from music is

If A is B, then P is Q,
But that P is Q is absurd.
∴ If it is absurd to say that P is Q, it is absurd to say that A is B.
∴ A is not B. Q. E. D.

[1] πρὸς τὸ μεταλαμβανόμενον.—For example, in the hypothetical syllogism—If the soul is moved by itself it is immortal: but it is moved by itself, ∴ it is immortal: the assumption is, the soul is moved by itself. The disjunctive syllogism owes its origin to the ἀπαγωγὴ εἰς τὸ ἀδύνατον, one of the principal kinds of hypotheticals mentioned by Aristotle, whose use of the latter expression, it is necessary to remember, is not opposed to categorical, but to ostensive (δεικτικὸς) syllogism, as in this very chapter. The reader is referred for some valuable observations upon this subject to note G, Appendix, Mansel's Logic. Hypothetical syllogisms, as we employ the term, are not discussed by Aristotle; vide Aldrich de Syllogismis Hypotheticis.

[2] αἰτήσεται. Distinction is not an Aristotelian term, but the rules

commendable, if then any one should require it to be granted that pleasure is commendable, and did not add all pleasure, there would not be a syllogism, but if that a certain pleasure is so, if indeed it is a different pleasure, it is nothing to the purpose, but if it is the same it is a petitio principii, this will however be more evident in diagrams, for instance, let it be required to show that the angles at the base of an isosceles triangle are equal.[1] Let the lines A B be drawn to the centre of a circle, if then he assumes the angle A C to be equal to the angle B D, not in short requiring it to be granted that the angles of semicircles are equal, and again that C is equal to D, not assuming the whole (angle) of the section, if besides he assumes that equal parts being taken from equal whole angles, the remaining angles E F are equal, he will beg the original (question), unless he assume that if equals are taken from equals the remainders are equal. Wherefore in all syllogism we must have an universal; universal is also shown from all universal terms, but the particular in this or that way, so that if the conclusion be universal, the terms must of necessity be universal, but if the terms be universal, the conclusion may happen not to be universal. It appears also that in every syllogism either both premises or one of them must be similar to the conclusion, I mean not only in its being affirmative or negative, but in that it is either necessary, or absolute, or contingent; we must also have regard to other modes of predication.[2]

2. An universal conclusion follows from universal premises but sometimes only a particular results.

3. One premise must resemble the conclusion in character and quality.

In a word then it is shown when there will and will not be a syllogism, also when it is possible,[3] and when perfect, and that when there is a syllogism it must have its terms according to some one of the above modes.

4. Recapitulation.

belonging thereto are implied in his account of the figures. The several directions given by Aldrich, on the construction of syllogistic inquiry, occur successively in this and the succeeding chapters, as comprised in the old memorial—"Distribuas Medium," etc.

[1] This is demonstrated in one way by Euclid, and in another by Pappus. See also Proclus Commen. lib. i. Euclid. Elem. One of the five modes of the "petitio principii," is not in form distinguishable from the legitimate syllogism. Conf. Top. viii. 13; Anal. Pr. ii. 16.

[2] As the impossible, probable, etc.

[3] By possible here he means an imperfect, which may be brought into a perfect syllogism. For the elucidation of this chapter and the follow-

CHAP. XXV.—*Every Syllogism consists of only three Terms, and of two Premises.*

1. Demonstration is conveyed by three terms only—proof.

IT appears that every demonstration will be by three terms and no more, unless the same conclusion should result through different[1] arguments, as E[2] through A B,[3] and through C D,[4] or through A B, A C, and B C, for there is nothing to prevent many media subsisting of the same (conclusions). But these being (many), there is not one syllogism, but many syllogisms; or again, when each of the propositions A B is assumed by syllogism, as A through D E,[5] and again B through F G,* or when the one is by induction,[6] but the other by syllogism. Thus in this manner indeed there are many syllogisms, for there are many conclusions, as A and B and C, and if there are not many but one, it is thus possible, that the same conclusion may arise through many syllogisms, but in order that C may be proved through A B, it is impossible.† For let the conclusion be E, collected from A B C D, it is then necessary that some one of these should be assumed with reference to something else, as a whole, but another as a part, for this has been shown before, that when there is a syllogism, some of the terms should necessarily thus subsist; let then A be thus with reference to B, from these there is a certain conclusion, which is either E or C or D, or some other different from these.

* F the major, G the minor.

2. The same conclusion may arise from many syllogisms.

† i. e. that there should be more than three terms.

ing more particularly, the reader is referred to Mansel's, Whately's, and Hill's Logic.

[1] The Leipsic copy omits the example, and Taylor's reading is somewhat different to that of Averrois, Buhle, and Waitz. By demonstration Aristotle here means syllogism generally.

[2] The conclusion. [3] A the major, B the minor.

[4] C the major, D the minor.

[5] A the major of the prosyllogism in which the major of the principal syllogism is proved—E the minor of the same. Though in the first part E signifies the conclusion of the principal syllogism, yet the conclusion is at present called C.—Taylor.

[6] As far as induction is logical at all, in its process it is equally formal with, though it proceeds in an inverse order to, syllogism. It is defined by Aristotle, proving the major term of the middle by means of the minor. Anal. Pr. ii. 23. The Sorites is not recognised distinctively by Aristotle, though, as Melancthon observes, it is implied in Cat. 3, and is alluded to in this chapter; its distinct exposition is attributed to the Stoics.

Now if E is concluded, the syllogism would be from A B alone, but if C D are so as that the one is universal, and the other particular, something also will result from these which will either be E or A or B, or something else different from these, and if E is collected, or A or B, there will be either many syllogisms, or, as it was shown possible, the same thing will happen to be collected through many terms. If, however, any thing else different from these is collected, there will be many syllogisms unconnected with each other; but if C is not so with respect to D, as to produce a syllogism, they will be assumed to no purpose, except for the sake of induction or concealment, or something of the sort. Still if from A B, not E, but some other conclusion is produced, and from C D, either one of these, or something different from these, many syllogisms arise, yet not of the subject, for it was supposed that the syllogism is of E. If, again, there is no conclusion from C D, it will happen that they are assumed in vain, and the syllogism is not of the primary problem, so that it is evident that every demonstration and every syllogism will be through three terms only.[1]

3. These three terms are included in two propositions. Vide Aldrich and Whately.

This then being apparent, it is also clear that a syllogism consists of two premises and no more; for three terms are two premises, unless something is assumed over and above, as we observed at first, for the perfection of the syllogisms. Hence it appears, that in the syllogistic discourse, in which the premises, through which the principal conclusion is collected, are not even,—(for it is requisite that some of the former conclusions should be premises,)—this discourse is either not syllogistically constructed,[2] or has required more than is necessary to the thesis.

When then the syllogisms are taken according to the principal propositions, every syllogism will consist of propositions

[1] The prosyllogism, or antecedent syllogism of Aristotle, is a syllogism used to prove one of the premises of another syllogism. Vide Pacius Anal. Pr. i. 35. Biese, vol. i. p. 157.

[2] Taylor erroneously uses the active here, contrary to Waitz and Averrois, the latter translates (συλλελόγισται) similarly to the rendering above—"est ratiocinatu." Aristotle calls a thesis, the consequent "extra syllogismum spectata," as Aldrich says, that is, the "problem," "question," τὸ ζητούμενον—the last, however, is used more extensively in signification. Vid. An. Post, i. 1, and ii. 3.

which are even, but of terms which are odd, for the terms exceed the premises by one, and the conclusions will be half part of the premises.[1] When, however, the conclusion results through pro-syllogisms, or through many continued middles,[2] as A B through C D, the multitude of terms, in like manner, will exceed the premises by one, (for the term interpolated will be added either externally or in the middle; but in both ways it will happen that the intervals are fewer than the terms by one,) but the propositions are equal to the intervals, the former, indeed, will not always be even, but the latter odd, but alternately, when the propositions are even the terms are odd, but when the terms are even the propositions are odd; for together with the term, one proposition is added wherever the term is added.[3] Hence, since the propositions were even, but the terms odd, it is necessary they should change when the same addition is made; but the conclusions will no longer have the same order, neither with respect to the terms, nor to the propositions, for one term being added, conclusions will be added less than the pre-existent terms by one, because to the last term alone* there is no conclusion made; but to all the rest, e. g. if D is added to A B C, two conclusions are immediately added, the one to A and the other to B. The same occurs in the other cases also, if the term be inserted in the middle after the same manner, for it will not make a syllogism to one term alone, so that the conclusions will be many more than the terms, and than the propositions.

ὁ παρεμπίπτων ὅρος—incidens terminus. Buhle.

4. Of the number of terms, propositions, and conclusions in composite syllogisms.

* The minor.

CHAP. XXVI.—*On the comparative Difficulty of certain Problems, and by what Figures they are proved.*[4]

1. The conclusion by more figures constitutes the rela-

SINCE we have those particulars with which syllogisms are conversant, and what is their quality in each figure, and in how many ways demon-

[1] For there is one conclusion to two propositions.
[2] As in Sorites. Vide Mansel's Logic, p. 83.
[3] At the beginning, middle, or end. See Waitz, vol. i. p. 440, and 441.
[4] Edocemur hoc capite et seq., quomodo ars dialectica cohæreat cum demonstrandi arte, Topica cum Analyticis. Waitz.

tive facility of demonstration. Enumeration of the conclusion in the second figures.

tration takes place, it is also manifest to us, what kind of problem is difficult, and what easy of proof, for that which is concluded in many figures, and through many cases, is more easy, but that is in fewer figures, and by fewer cases, is more difficult. An universal affirmative then is proved through the first figure alone, and by this in one way only; but a negative, both through the first and through the middle, through the first in one way, but through the middle in two ways; the particular affirmative again through the first and through the last, in one way through the first figure, but in three ways through the last; lastly, the particular negative is proved in all the figures, but in the first in one way, in the middle in two ways, and in the last in three ways. Hence it appears most difficult to construct an universal affirmative, but most easy to subvert it, in short, universals are easier to subvert than particulars, because the former are subverted, whether a thing is present with nothing, or is not with a certain thing, of which the one, namely, the not being with a certain thing, is proved in all the figures, and the other, the being with nothing, is proved in two. The same mode also prevails in the case of negatives, for the original proposition is subverted, whether a thing is with every, or with a certain individual,[1] now this was in two figures. In particular problems there is one way (of confutation), either by showing a thing to be with every, or with no individnal, and particular problems are easier of construction, for they are in more figures, and through more modes.[2] In short, we ought not to forget that it is possible to confute universal mutually through particular problems, and these through universal, yet we cannot construct universal through particular, but the latter may be through the former, at the same time that it is easier to subvert than to construct is plain.

2. Universals easier of subversion than particulars.

3. Particulars easier of construction.

In what manner then every syllogism arises, through how

[1] This clause is omitted by Taylor.

[2] Aristotle employs πτῶσις here in the sense of τρόπος, which latter is not an Aristotelian expression, except, as some think, in cap. 28 of this book. He shows in each figure what propositional combinations are admissible. In Apuleius there is a distinction between modi, or moduli, and conjugationes, the former referring to combinations of three propositions, the latter to those of two.

4. Recapitulation.

many terms and premises, how they subsist with reference to each other, also what sort of problem may be proved in each figure, and what in many and in fewer modes, may be gathered from what has been said.[1]

CHAP. XXVII.—*Of the Invention and Construction of Syllogisms.*[2]

1. How to provide syllogisms, from certain principles.

We must now describe how we may always obtain a provision of syllogisms for a proposed question, and in what way we may assume principles about each, for perhaps it is not only requisite to consider the production of syllogisms, but also to possess the power of forming them.

2. The several sorts of predicates. Some cannot be truly predicated universally, of other than individuals, etc.

Of all beings then, some are of such a nature as not to be truly predicated universally of any thing else, as "Cleon," and "Callias," that which is singular,[3] and that which is sensible, but others are predicated of these, (for each of these is man and animal); some again are predicated of others, but others not previously of these; lastly, there are some which are themselves predicated of others, and others of them, as "man" is predicated of Callias, and "animal" of man. That some things therefore are naturally adapted to be predicated of nothing is clear, for of sensibles each is almost of such a sort, as not to be predicated of any thing except accidentally, for we sometimes say that that white thing is Socrates, and that the object approaching is Callias. But that we must stop somewhere in our upward progression we will again show, for the present let this be admitted. Of these things then we cannot point out another predicate,

Vide b. i. ch. 19, Post Anal., et seq.

[1] As a digest of the method of proof, we may state that

A is proved in one figure and one mood				
E	— —	two figures and three moods		
I	— —	two	— —	four
O	— —	three	— —	six.

Thus A is the easiest to overthrow, and the nearest to establish: O the reverse.

[2] Averrois, following the old divisions, commences his 2nd section here, "De abundantiâ Propositionum."

[3] The employment of singulars as predicates, is open to much objection, in connexion with singular propositions. See the Thesis appended to Wallis's Logic.

except according to opinion, but these may be predicated of others, nor can singulars[1] be predicated of others, but others of them. It appears however that those which are intermediate, are capable in both ways (of demonstration), for they may be predicated of others, and others of them, and arguments and speculations are almost all conversant with these.

2. How to assume propositions as to these, in order to inference.

Still it is requisite to assume the propositions about each thing thus:—In the first place, the subject, (by hypothesis,) the definitions, and such peculiarities as exist of the thing; next, whatever things are consequent to the thing, and which the thing follows;[2] lastly, such as cannot be in it; those however which it cannot be in are not to be assumed, because of the conversion of the negative. We must also distinguish in the consequents what things belong to "what a thing is," what are predicated as properties,[3] and what as accidents; also of these, those which are (predicated) according to opinion, and those, according to truth; for the greater number any one has of these, the quicker will he light upon a conclusion, and the more true they are, the more will he demonstrate. We must too select not those which are consequent to a certain one, but those which follow the whole thing, e. g. not what follows a certain man, but what follows every man, for a syllogism consists of universal propositions. If therefore a proposition is indefinite, it is doubtful whether it is universal, but when it is definite, this is manifest. So also we must select those things the whole of which a thing follows, for the reason given above, but the whole consequent itself need not be assumed to follow; I say for instance, (it must not be assumed) that every "animal" is consequent to "man," or every science to music, but only that they are simply consequent, as we set forth,[4] for the other is useless and impossible,[5] as that "every man" is "every animal," or that "justice is every thing good." To whatever (subject) a consequent is attached, the sign "every" is added; when however the sub-

1. Distinctions to be drawn.

[1] Taylor here falls into his common mistake of translating καθ' ἕκαστα—"particular." Averrois, "singularia"—which is right.

[2] Omitted by Taylor.

[3] The ἴδιον, both by Porphyry and Aristotle, is considered as co-extensive and convertible with its subject, and answers to the fourth predicable.

[4] i. e. as we form propositions.

[5] That is, a predicate with the universal sign.

ject is comprehended by a certain thing,[1] the consequents of which we must assume, those which follow or which do not follow the universal, we are not to select in these—for they were assumed in those, since whatever are consequent to "animal," are also consequent to "man," and as to whatever things are not absolutely present with in like manner; but the properties of each thing must be taken, for there are certain properties in species not common to genus, since it is necessary that certain properties should be in different species. Nor are we to select those in regard to the universal, which the thing comprehended follows, as those which "man" follows ought not to be assumed to "animal," for it is necessary if animal follows man that it follows all these,[2] but these more properly belong to the selection of the antecedents of "man."[3] We must also assume those which are generally consequent and antecedent, for of general problems the syllogism also is from propositions, all or some of which are general, as the conclusion of each syllogism resembles its principles. Lastly, we are not to select things consequent to all, since there will not be composed a syllogism from them, on account of a reason which will appear from what follows.

2. ἴδια to be assumed. Vide Aldrich and Hill.

CHAP. XXVIII.—*Special Rules upon the same Subject.*

1. What should be the inspection of terms that an universal or particular affirmative or negative may be demonstrated.

THOSE therefore who desire to confirm any thing of a certain universal, should look to the subject matter of what is confirmed, in respect of which it happens to be predicated; but of whatever ought to be predicated, of this, he should examine the consequents; for if one of these happens to be the same, one must necessarily be in the other. But if (it is to be proved) that a thing is not present universally, but particularly, he must examine those which each follows,[4] for if any of these is the same, to be particularly present is

[1] i. e. by an universal predicate.

[2] Of which man is predicated.

[3] That is, the subjects to man ought to be chosen and assumed per se. The reader is referred for the rules specified here to the common Logics, especially Whately, b. ii. c. 111.

[4] The antecedent of both predicate and subject.

necessary; but when the presence with nothing is necessary,[1] as to what it need not be present with,[2] we must look to those which cannot be present with it;[3] or on the contrary, (as regards that) with which[4] it is necessary not to be present, we must look to those which cannot be with it, but as to what ought not to be present, to the consequents. For whichever of these are identical, it will happen that the one is in no other, since sometimes a syllogism arises in the first and at other times in the middle figure. If however the particular non-inesse (is to be proved), that with which it ought not to be present, and those which it follows, are to be looked to; but of that which ought not to be present, those must be considered, which it is impossible can be in it, for if any of these be identical the particular non-inesse is necessary. What has been said however will perhaps be more clear thus. Let the consequents to A be B, but let those to which it is consequent be C; those again which cannot be in it, D; again, let the things present with E be F, and those to which it is consequent, G; lastly, those which cannot be in it, H. Now if a certain C and a certain F are identical, it is necessary that A should be with every E, for F is present with every E, and A with every C, so that A is with every E; but if C and G are identical, A must necessarily be with a certain E, for A follows every C, and E every G. If however F and D are identical, A will be with no E from a pro-syllogism,[5] for since a negative is convertible and F is identical with D, A will be with no F, but F is with every E; again, if B and H are the same, A will be with no E, for B is with every A, but with no E, for it was the same as H, and H was with no E. If D and G are identical, A will not be with a certain E, for A will not be with G, since it is not present with D, but G is under E, so that neither will it be with a certain E. Moreover if B is identical with G there will be an inverse syllogism, for G will be with every A, (since B is with A,) and E with B (for B is the same as G); still it is not necessary that A should be with every E, but it is neces-

[1] When E was to be proved.
[2] i. e. the subject of the question.
[3] Taylor inserts with Buhle here εἰς τὰ ἑπομένα, which alters the sense. I follow Waitz.
[4] The predicate. The confusion of the various readings here is endless.
[5] In which the major premise of the principal syllogism is proved.

sary that it be with a certain E, because an universal predication may be converted into a particular one.

2. Every portion of the problem to be examined.

Wherefore we must evidently regard what has been mentioned as to each part of every problem,[1] since all syllogisms are from these; but in consequents, and the antecedents of each thing, we must look to first elements, and to those which are for the most part universal, as in the case of E we must look more to K F than only to F,[2] but in the case of A more to K C than to C only. For if A is present with K C it is also present with F and with E,[3] but if it is not consequent to this, yet it may be consequent to F; in like manner we must examine those which the thing itself is consequent to, for if it follows the primary, it also does those which are included under them, and if it does not follow these, yet it may those which are arranged under them.[4]

3. Speculation consists of three terms and two propositions.

Speculation then, plainly, consists of three terms and two propositions, and all syllogisms are through the above-mentioned figures; for A is shown present with every E, when of C and F something identical may be assumed. Now this will be the middle term,[5] and A and E the extremes, and there is the first figure, but (presence with) a certain thing is shown when C and G are assumed identical, and this is the last figure, for G becomes the middle. Again, (presence with) none, when D and F are identical, but thus also the first figure and the middle are produced; the first, because A is with no F, (since a negative is converted,) but F is with every E; and the middle because D is with no A, but with every E. Not to be present also with a certain one, (is shown) when D and G are the same, and this is the last figure, for A will be with no G, and E with every G. Wherefore all syllogisms are evidently through the above-named figures, and we must not select those which are consequent to all, because no syllogism arises from them; as, in short, we cannot construct from con-

[1] As to both subject and predicate.

[2] K F is the genus of both K and F, and K C stands in the same relation to K and C. [3] F is contained under K, and E under F.

[4] Thus if "living" follows "animal," it also follows "man," and though it does not follow "body," it follows that which is under "body."—Taylor.

[5] viz. C F—A the major—E the minor.

sequents, nor deduce a negative through an universal consequent, for it must be in one, and not in the other.[1]

That other modes of speculation[2] also, as regards selection, are useless for the construction of syllogism is apparent; for instance, if the consequents to each are identical, or if those which A (the predicate) follows, and which cannot be with E (the subject), or again those which cannot concur to be with either, for no syllogism arises through these. If then the consequents are identical, as B and F, the middle figure is produced, having both premises affirmative; but if those which A follows, and which cannot be with E, as C and H, there will be the first figure having the minor premise negative; again, if those are identical which cannot be with either, as D and H,[3] both propositions will be negative, either in the first or in the middle figure: thus, however, there will by no means be a syllogism.

4. Other modes than the first useless, as regards selection of the middle.

We see moreover that we must assume in speculation things identical, and not what are different, or contrary; first, because our inspection is for the sake of the middle, and we must take as a middle, not what is different, but what is identical. Next, in whatever a syllogism happens to be produced, from the assumption of contraries, or of those things which cannot be with the same, all are reduced to the before-named modes, as if B and F are contraries, or cannot be with the same thing; if these are assumed there will be a syllogism that A is with no E: this however does not result from them, but from the above-named mode; for B is with every A, and with no E, so that B must necessarily be identical with a certain H. Again, if B and G do not concur to be with the same thing, (it will follow) that A will not be with a certain E, and so there will be the middle figure, for B is

5. We must select in investigation, not that wherein the terms differ, but in which they agree.

[1] That is, he who wishes to conclude a negative must take a middle, which concurs with one extreme, and not with the other, but in the case cited both propositions would be affirmative—here *κατασκευάζειν*, "affirmative colligere," is opposed to *ἀποστερειν*, "negative colligere." Confer. Waitz, vol. i. page 450.

[2] *σκέψεις τῶν κατὰ τὰς ἐκλογὰς ἀχρεῖοι.*—Vide Waitz, vol. i. 451, and Biese, i. p. 166, also Mansel's Logic, page 79. See also the definition of *τόπος* given by Cicero (Top. ch. ii.); the name originally alluded to the *place* in which we look for middle terms. Vide Rhet. ii. 26, 1; also note on Top. i. 1.

[3] Taylor reads G, erroneously.

with every A, and with no G,[1] so that B must necessarily be identical with some H. For the impossibility of B and G being in the same thing, does not differ from B being the same as a certain H, since every thing is assumed which cannot be with E.

6. Recapitulation.

From these observations, then, it is shown that no syllogism arises; but if B and F are contraries, B must necessarily be identical with a certain H, and a syllogism arises through these. Nevertheless it occurs to persons thus inspecting, that they look to a different way than the necessary, from the identity of B and H escaping them.

CHAP. XXIX.—*The same Method applied to other than categorical Syllogisms.*

1. The same method to be observed for selecting a middle term in syllogisms of "the impossible," as in the others.

SYLLOGISMS which lead to the impossible subsist in the same manner as ostensive, for these also arise through consequents, and those (antecedents) which each follows,[2] and the inspection is the same in both, for what is ostensively demonstrated may be also syllogistically inferred per impossibile, and through the same terms, and what is demonstrated per impossibile, may be also proved ostensively, as that A is with no E. For let it be supposed to be with a certain E, therefore since B is with every A, and A with a certain E, B also will be with a certain E, but it was present with none; again, it may be shown that A is with a certain E, for if A is with no E, but E is with every H, A will be with no H, but it was supposed to be with every H. It will happen the same in other problems, for always and in all things demonstration per impossibile will be from consequents, and from those which each follows. In every problem also there is the same consideration, whether a man wishes to syllogize ostensively, or to lead to the impossible, since both demonstrations are from the same terms, as for example, if A were shown to be with no E, because B happens to be with a certain E, which is impossible, if it is assumed that B is with no E, but with every A, it is evident that A will be with no E. Again, if it is ostensively collected that A

[1] Waitz incorrectly reads E.
[2] i. e. the predicate and subject of the question.

is with no E, to those who suppose that it is with a certain E, it may be shown per impossibile to be with no E. The like will also occur in other cases, for in all we must assume some common term different from the subject terms to which there will appertain a syllogism of the false, so that this proposition being converted,[1] but the other remaining the same, there will be an ostensive syllogism through the same terms. But an ostensive syllogism differs from that per impossibile, because in the ostensive both premises are laid down according to truth,[2] but in that which leads to the impossible one is laid down falsely.[3]

2. Wherein the ostensive and per impossibile syllogisms differ.

These things however will more fully appear by what follows, when we come to speak of the impossible, for the present let so much be manifest to us, that both he who wishes to syllogize ostensively, and per impossibile, must observe these things. In other syllogisms indeed which are hypothetical, such as those which are according to transumption, or according to quality, the consideration will be in the subject terms, not in the original ones, but in those taken afterwards, but the mode of inspection will be the same; but it is necessary also to consider, and distinguish, in how many ways hypothetical syllogisms arise.

3. The mode of investigation the same in hypotheticals.

Each problem then is demonstrated thus, and some of them we may infer syllogistically after another method, for example, universals by an hypothetical inspection of particulars, for if C and H are the same, and if E is assumed to be with H alone,

[1] That is, the proposition being assumed contradicting the conclusion of the syllogism leading to the impossible.—Taylor.

[2] They are assumed as true, though sometimes false.

[3] As if false—to be confuted by a conclusive absurdity. Compare the 23rd chap. of this book of the Analytics. In the place just quoted the *τὸ μεταλαμβανόμενον* is explained by Alexander as applying to the conclusive expression of the syllogism, because it is taken differently to the manner in which it was originally enunciated, being at first part of a conditional agreement, and afterwards a categorical conclusion. For this reason the syllogism is here said to be *κατὰ μετάληψιν*. Were it not for this authority it would seem simpler to interpret *μετάληψις*, "change of question." As to the hypotheticals called *κατὰ ποιότητα*, mentioned here, we have no data for even a plausible conjecture —Mansel. Philoponus (Scholia, p. 178, b. 9) says it is a syllogism, *ἐκ τοῦ μαλλον ἢ ἐκ τοῦ ἧττον, ἢ ἐκ τοῦ ὁμοίου*. Vide Whately's and Hill's Logic. Waitz identifies both terms. See vol. i. 456.

A will be with every E; and again, if D and H are the same, and E is predicated of H alone, (it may be shown) that A is with no E. Wherefore the inspection must clearly be in this way after the same manner both in the necessary and contingent, for the consideration is the same, and the syllogism both of the contingent and the absolute will be through terms the same in order; in the contingent however we may assume things which are not with, but which may be, for it has been shown that by these a contingent syllogism is produced, and the reasoning is similar in the case of the other predications. From what has been said then it appears not only that it is allowable for all syllogisms to be formed in this, but that they cannot be formed in any other way, for every syllogism has been shown to originate through some one of the before-named figures, and these may not be constituted through any other than the consequents and antecedents of a thing, for from these are the premises and assumption of the middle, so that it is not admissible that a syllogism should be produced through other things.

4. Conclusion.

CHAP. XXX.—*The preceding method of Demonstration applicable to all Problems.*

1. The method of demonstration laid down previously, is applicable to all objects of philosophical inquiry.

THE way then of proceeding in all (problems), both in philosophy and in every art and discipline, is the same, for we must collect about each of them those things which are with, and the subjects which they are with, and be provided with as many as possible of these, considering them also through three terms in one way subverting, but in another constructing according to truth (we reason) from those which are truly described to be inherent, but as regards dialectic syllogisms (we must reason) from probable propositions. Now the principles of universal syllogisms have been mentioned, how they subsist, and how we must investigate them, that we may not direct our attention to every thing which is said, nor to constructing and subverting the same things, nor both constructing universally or particularly, nor subverting wholly or partially, but look to things fewer and definite; as to each however we must make a selection, as of good or of science. The peculiar principles indeed in every science are many, hence it is the province of experience to deliver the principles of every thing, for instance, I say that astrological experience gives the principles of astrological science, for from phenomena being sufficiently assumed, astrological demonstrations have thus been invented, so also is it in every other art and science. Wherefore if things are assumed which exist in individuals, it is now our duty readily to exhibit demonstrations, for if as regards history nothing is omitted of what is truly present with things, we shall be able about every thing of which there is demonstration to discover and demonstrate this, and to make that clear which is naturally incapable of demonstration.

2. Experience is to supply the principles of demonstration in every science.

Universally then we have nearly shown how propositions ought to be selected, but we have discussed this accurately in the treatise on Dialectic.[1]

3. The end of analytical investigation to elucidate subjects naturally abstruse.

CHAP. XXXI.—*Upon Division; and its Imperfection as to Demonstration.*[2]

THAT the division through genera[3] is but a certain small portion of the method specified, it is easy to perceive, for division is, as it were, a weak syllogism, since it begs what it ought to demonstrate,

Διαίρεσις. 1. Division, its use and abuse in argument. It is a species of

[1] In the Topics. The dialectic however of Aristotle, as enunciated here, differs from that art as exhibited in the Topics, in that he discusses it in the Analytics as a mere formal method of reasoning, but in the Topics he gives it an entirely material character. The dialectic of Plato corresponds more nearly with the metaphysics of Aristotle: again, the dialectic of Aristotle is an art, but his analytic a science; see note on Top. i. 1.

[2] Vide Whately, b. iii. sect. 11.

[3] i. e. by which genera are divided into species by the addition of differences. Plato used division as a means of demonstrating definitions, and the utility of them, according to Aristotle, consists in employing them as tests of definitions when obtained. Amongst the later Peripatetics, division rose in estimation, and Andronicus Rhodius composed a treatise on the subject. Modern logicians have chiefly drawn from Boethius' work de Divisione. Compare Top. vi. 2. Dichotomy, or the division alluded to above of genus, is approved by Aristotle when effected by contraries, but not by contradictories. Compare Eth. Nic. vii. 6; Kant, Logic, sect. 113; Trend. Elem. sect. 58; also Categor. 10.

weak syllogism.

and always infers something of prior matter.[1] Now this has first escaped the notice of all those who use it, and they endeavour to show that demonstration about essence and the very nature of a thing is possible, so that they neither perceive that those who divide happen to syllogize, nor that it is possible in the manner we have said. In demonstrations therefore, when it is requisite to infer absolute presence, the middle term by which the syllogism is produced must always be less, and must not be universally predicated of the first extreme, but on the contrary, division takes the universal for the middle term. For let animal be A, mortal B, immortal C, and man of whom we ought to assume the definition D, every animal then comprehends either mortal or immortal, but this is that the whole of whatever may be A is either B or C. Again, he who divides man, admits that he is animal, so that he assumes A to be predicated of D, hence the syllogism is that every D is either B or C, wherefore it is necessary for man to be either mortal or immortal, yet it is not necessary that animal should be mortal, but this is desired to be granted, which was the very thing which ought to have been syllogistically inferred.* Again, taking A for mortal animal, B for pedestrian, C without feet, and D for man, in the same manner it assumes A to be either with B or C, for every mortal animal is either pedestrian or without feet, and that A is predicated of D, for it has assumed that man is a mortal animal, so that it is necessary that man should be either a pedestrian

2. In demonstration of the absolute, the middle must be less, and not universal in respect of the first extreme.

* Example (1.)

[1] i. e. of universals, or of things more nearly approaching to these.

Ex. 1. Every animal is either mortal or immortal
Every man is an animal
∴ Every man is either mortal or immortal.

The conclusion here was to have been, that every man is mortal; but he who divides does not prove this, but desires it to be granted.

Ex. 2. Every mortal animal is pedestrian or without feet
Every man is a mortal animal
∴ Every man is pedestrian or without feet.

Ex. 3. Every length is or is not commensurable
Every diameter is a length
∴ Every diameter is or is not commensurable.

animal or without feet, but that he is pedestrian is not necessary, but they assume it, and this again is what they ought to have proved.* After this manner it always happens to those who divide, namely, that they assume an universal middle, and what they ought to show, and the differences as extremes. In the last place, they assert nothing clearly, as that it is necessary that this be a man, or that the† question necessarily is whatever it may be, but they pursue every other way, not apprehending the available supplies. It is clear however, that by this method we can neither subvert nor syllogistically infer any thing of accident or property or genus, or of those things of which we are a priori ignorant as to how they subsist, as whether the diameter of a square be incommensurable, for if it assumes every length to be either commensurable or incommensurable, but the diameter of a square is a length, it will infer that the diameter is either incommensurable or commensurable, and if it assumes that it is incommensurate, it will assume what it ought to prove, wherefore that we cannot show, for this is the way, and by this we cannot do it; let however the incommensurable or commensurable be A, length B, and diameter C.‡ It is clear then that this mode of inquiry does not suit every speculation, neither is useful in those to which it especially appears appropriate, wherefore from what sources, and how demonstrations arise, and what we must regard in every problem, appear from what has been said.

* Example (2.)

† τὸ ζητούμενον. (Vide supra.)

3. Division not suitable for refutation, nor for various kinds of question.

‡ Example (3.)

CHAP. XXXII.—*Reduction of Syllogisms to the above Figures.*[1]

How then we may reduce syllogisms to the above-named figures must next be told, for this is the remainder of the speculation, since if we have noticed the production of syllogisms, and have the power of inventing them, if moreover we analyze them when formed into the before-named figures,

1. Method of reducing every syllogism to one of the three figures to be considered. (Compare ch. 28.)

[1] Averrois commences his third section here, "de syllogismorum resolutione." The word ἀνάγειν, and not ἀπαγειν, as significative of reduction, has been already commented upon; it is employed in its strict meaning at this place.

our original design will have been completed. At the same time, what has before been said will happen to be confirmed, and be more evident that they are thus from what shall now be said, for every truth must necessarily agree with itself in every respect.

Rule 1st. Propositions to be investigated as to quantity, &c.

First then we must endeavour to select the two propositions of a syllogism, for it is easier to divide into greater than into less parts,[1] and composites are greater than the things of which they are composed; next we must consider whether it is in a whole or in a part, and if both propositions should not be assumed, oneself placing one of them. For those who propose the universal[2] do not receive the other which is contained in it,[3] neither when they write, nor when they interrogate, or propose these,[4] but omit those[5] by which these are concluded, and question other things to no purpose. Therefore we must consider whether any thing superfluous has been assumed, and any thing necessary omitted, and one thing is to be laid down, and another to be removed, until we arrive at two propositions, for without these we cannot reduce the sentences which are thus the subjects of question. Now in some it is easy to see what is deficient, but others escape us, and seem to be syllogisms,[6] because something necessarily happens from the things laid down, as if it should be assumed that essence not being subverted, essence is not subverted,[7] but those things being subverted, of which a thing consists, what is composed of these is subverted also; for from these

2nd rule. Examine their superfluities and deficiencies as to the proper construction of syllogism.

[1] i. e. into propositions than into terms.

[2] i. e. the major proposition, which is always universal in the first figure.

[3] i. e. the minor, which stands towards the major in the relation of particular to universal.

[4] i. e. the propositions of the principal syllogism.

[5] i. e. the propositions of the pro-syllogism. This last is the antecedent in a minor premise, which makes it enthymematic. Vide Whately, book ii. ch. 4, sect. 7, note.

[6] Vide Whately's table of Fallacies, book iii.

[7] In the propositions adduced, the syllogistic form is not present, but syllogistic inferences may be derived from them. In the place of the major, we have an equivalent proposition expressed, and in place of the minor—the major of the pro-syllogism proving that minor is added; this major, however, is changed so far, as it is made more universal.

positions it is necessary that a part of essence should be essence, yet this is not concluded through the assumptions, but the propositions are wanting. Again, if because man exists, it is necessary that animal should be, and animal existing, that there should be essence; then, because man exists, essence must necessarily be; but this is not yet syllogistically inferred,[1] for the propositions do not subsist as we have said they should;[2] but we are deceived in such, because something necessary happens from the things laid down, and because also a syllogism is something necessary. The necessary, however, is more extensive than the syllogism, for every syllogism is necessary, but not every thing necessary is a syllogism; so that if any thing occurs from certain positions, we must not immediately endeavour to reduce, but first assume two propositions, then we must divide them into terms, in this manner, that term we must place as the middle which is said to be in both propositions, for the middle must necessarily exist in both, in all the figures. If then the middle predicates, and is predicated of, or if it indeed predicates, but another thing is denied of it, there will be the first figure, but if it predicates, and is denied by something, there will be the middle figure, and if other things are predicated of it, and one thing is denied, but another is predicated, there will be the last figure; thus the middle subsists in each figure. In a similar manner also, if the propositions should not be universal, for the determination of the middle is the same,[3] wherefore it is evident, that in discourse, where the same thing is not asserted more than once, a syllogism does not subsist, since the middle is not assumed. As, however, we know what kind of problem is deduced in each figure,[4] in what the universal, and in what the particular, it is clear that we must not regard all the figures, but that one which is appropriate to each problem, and whatever things are deduced in many figures, we may ascertain the figure of by the position of the middle.

3rd rule. Consider the reality of inference.

4th rule. Ascertain the figure to which properly the problem belongs, by the middle.

[1] i. e. it is not categorical, but hypothetical.

[2] They neither affirm nor deny.

[3] For an universal does not differ from a particular, by reason of the middle term, but by the circumscription and determination of the verbal sign, "every," "none," called προσδιορισμος. See Hill's Logic, and Whately.

[4] From chapter 26.

CHAP. XXXIII.—*On Error, arising from the quantity of Propositions.*

1. Cause of deception about syllogisms—our inattention to the relative quantity of propositions.

It frequently happens then, that we are deceived about syllogisms, on account of the necessary (conclusion), as we have before observed, and sometimes by the resemblance[1] in the position of the terms, which ought not to have escaped us.

Thus if A is predicated of B, and B of C, there would appear a syllogism from such terms, yet neither is any thing necessary produced, nor a syllogism. For let A be that which always is; B, Aristomenes the object of intellect; and C, Aristomenes; it is true then that A is with B, for Aristomenes is always the object of intellect; but B is also with C, for Aristomenes is Aristomenes the object of intellect, but A is not with C, for Aristomenes is corruptible, neither would a syllogism be formed from terms thus placed, but the universal proposition[2] A B must be assumed, but this is false,[3] to think that every Aristomenes who is the object of intellect always exists, when Aristomenes is corruptible. Again, let C be Miccalus, B Miccalus the musician, A to die to-morrow; B therefore is truly predicated of C, since Miccalus is Miccalus the musician, and A is truly predicated of B, for Miccalus the musician may die to-morrow, but A is falsely predicated of C. This case therefore is the same with the preceding, for it is not universally true that Miccalus the musician will die to-morrow, and if this is not assumed, there would be no syllogism.[4]

This deception arises therefore from a small (matter), since we concede, as if there were no difference between saying that *this* thing is present with *that*, and *this* present *with every individual of that.*

[1] In indefinites, which are mistaken for universals.

[2] i. e. the major.

[3] Because the distributive particle "every" shows that any particular is assumed.

[4] Here the fallacy arises from the major not being universal, for it is not said that every Miccalus, a musician, will die to-morrow. Vide Appendix to Hill's Logic.

CHAP. XXXIV.—*Error arising from inaccurate exposition of Terms.*[1]

1. Nature of deception shown as arising from terms inaccurately set out.

DECEPTION will frequently occur from the terms of the proposition being improperly expounded,[2] as if A should be health, B disease, and C man, for it is true to say that A cannot be with any B, for health is with no disease, and again that B is with every C, for every man is susceptible of disease, whence it would appear to result that health can be with no man. Now the reason of this is, that the terms are not rightly set out in expression, since those words which are significant of habits being changed, there will not be a syllogism, as if the word "well" were taken instead of "health," and the word "ill" instead of "disease," since it is not true to say, that to be well cannot be present with him that is ill. Now this not being assumed, there is no syllogism except of the contingent,[3] which indeed is not impossible, for health may happen to be with no man. Again, in the middle figure there will likewise be a falsity, for health happens to be with no disease, but may happen to be with every man, so that disease shall be with no man.[4] In the third figure however falsity occurs by the contingent, for it is possible that health and disease, science and ignorance, in short, contraries, shall be with the same individual, but it is impossible that they should be present with each other: this, however, differs from the preceding observations,* since when many things happen to be present with the same individual they also happen to be so with each other.

* Vide ch. 20.

Evidently then in all these cases deception arises from the setting forth of the terms, as if those are changed which relate to the habits, there is no falsity, and it is therefore apparent

[1] Vide Hill, on verbal and material fallacy; also Whately, who refers the Aristotelian division of fallacies (οἱ παρὰ τὴν λέξιν and οἱ ἔξω τῆς λέξεως) to logical and material, upon a species of conjecture. Confer. Waitz, vol. ii. p. 532.

[2] Because an abstract term, "health," is assumed for a concrete, as "sane."

[3] For a man now ill, may not hereafter be well; that to be ill is present with every man, therefore to be well present with no man.

[4] This is against the rule laid down in ch. 2, of the next book, wherein he shows that the false cannot be collected from the true.

that in such propositions, what relates to habit[1] must always be exchanged and placed for a term instead of habit.[2]

CHAP. XXXV.—*Middle not always to be assumed as a particular definite thing, ὡς τόδε τι.*

1. One word cannot always be used for some terms, inasmuch as they are sentences.

IT is not always necessary to seek to expound the terms by a name,[3] since there will oftentimes be sentences to which no name is attached, wherefore it is difficult to reduce syllogisms of this kind, but we shall sometimes happen to be deceived by such a search, for example, because a syllogism is of things immediate.[4] For let A[5] be two right angles, B a triangle, C an isosceles triangle. A then is with C through B, but no longer with B through any thing else, for a triangle has of itself two right angles, so that there will not be a middle of the proposition A B,[6] which is demonstrable. The middle then must clearly not thus be always assumed, as if it were a particular definite thing,[7] but sometimes a sentence, which happens to be the case in the instance adduced.

CHAP. XXXVI.—*On the arrangement of Terms, according to nominal appellation; and of Propositions according to case.*[8]

1. For the construction of a syllogism, it is not always requisite that one term should be

FOR the first to be in the middle, and the latter in the extreme, it is unnecessary to assume as if they were always predicated of each other, or in like manner,[9] the first of the middle, and this in

[1] The concrete word "well."
[2] The abstract, "health." [3] One word.
[4] Between which there is no middle—they may be proved, however, by a definition of the subject, as in the Post Ana. Vide Pacius and Biese, vol. i. p. 157; also Aquinas, Op. 48. cap. 1. The word ἄμεσος is used by Aristotle, either to express a proposition not proved by any higher middle term, (vide An. Post, i. 2, and ii. 19,) or a premise immediate, as regards its conclusion, i. e. not requiring the insertion of lower middle terms, for connexion of its terms with those of the conclusion.
[5] i. e. three angles, equal to two right.
[6] A certain middle thing, signified by one word.
[7] As one thing expressed by one word.
[8] Aristotle distinguishes κλήσεις and πτώσεις, (which last word he uses for τρόπος,) the first as being nouns in the nominative case, the other the oblique cases. See Hermen. c. 2. [9] i. e. in the same case.

predicated of the other "casu recto." Since either major or minor premise, or both, may have an oblique case.

the last, and also likewise in the case of non-inesse. Still in so many ways as to be is predicated, and any thing is truly asserted, it is requisite to consider that we signify the inesse, as that of contraries there is one science.

For let A be, there is one science, and B, things contrary to each other, A then is present with B, not as if contraries are one science,[1] but because it is true in respect of them, to say that there is one science of them. It sometimes occurs indeed, that the first is predicated of the middle, but the middle not of the third, as if wisdom is science, but wisdom is of[2] good, the conclusion is that science is of good: hence good' is not wisdom, but wisdom is science. Sometimes, again, the middle is predicated of the third, but the first not of the middle, e. g. if there is a science of every quality or contrary, but good is a contrary and a quality, the conclusion then is, that there is a science of good, yet neither good, nor quality, nor contrary is science, but good is these.[3] Sometimes, again, neither the first is predicated of the middle, nor this of the third, the first indeed being sometimes predicated of the third, and sometimes not,[4] for instance, of whatever there is science, there is genus, but there is science of good, the conclusion is that there is a genus of good, yet none of these is predicated of any. If, nevertheless, of what there is science, this is genus, but there is a science of good, the conclusion is that good is genus, hence the first is predicated of the extreme, but there is no predication of each other.[5]

2. Method the same with negatives.

In the case of the non-inesse there must be the same manner of assumption, for this thing not being present with this, does not always signify that this is not this, but sometimes that this is not of this, or that this is not with this, as there is not a motion of motion or generation of generation, but there is (a motion and generation) of pleasure: pleasure therefore is not generation. Again, there is of laughter a sign, but there is not a sign of a

[1] Waitz inserts αὔτων. [2] Here he also inserts ἐπιστήμη. Aristotle means, that in the major proposition the greater extreme is in a direct, but in the minor proposition the middle is in an oblique case.

[3] i. e. good is a quality, and is contrary, hence the minor is direct.

[4] i. e. "rectâ predicatione." Buhle.

[5] The conclusion is direct, but the propositions are oblique.

sign, so that laughter is not a sign, and similarly in other cases, wherein the problem is subverted from the genus being in some way referred to it.[1] Moreover, occasion is not opportune time, for to the divinity there is occasion, but not opportune time, because there is nothing useful to divinity,[2] we must take as terms, occasion, opportune time, and divinity, but the proposition must be assumed according to the case of the noun, since, in short, we assert this universally, that we must always place the terms according to the appellations of the nouns, e. g. man, or good, or contraries, not *of* man, nor *of* good, nor *of* contraries, but we must take propositions according to the cases of each word, since they are either to this as the equal, or of this as the double, or this thing as striking, or seeing, or this one as man, animal, or if the noun falls in any other way, according to the proposition.

3. Method of assuming propositions and terms.

CHAP. XXXVII.—*Rules of Reference to the forms of Predication.*

1. For true and absolute predication we must accept the several varieties of categorical division.

FOR this thing to be with that, and for one thing to be truly predicated of another, must be assumed in as many ways as the categories are divided; the latter must also be taken either in a certain respect,[3] or simply, moreover either as simple [4] or connected,[5] in a similar manner also with regard to the non-inesse; these however must be better considered and defined.

[1] Either directly or obliquely. Aristotle calls the middle term in the second figure, genus, because as the latter is predicated, the middle term in the second figure is also predicated; otherwise they differ greatly, since genus is predicated of species affirmatively, but the middle in the second figure is partly predicated affirmatively, and partly negatively, since one premise ought to affirm, and the other deny.

[2] This syllogism is in the third figure; the middle term being "divinity."

[3] As, an Ethiopian has white teeth.

[4] As, a swan is an animal.

[5] As, a swan is a white animal.

CHAP. XXXVIII.—*Of Propositional Iteration and the Addition to a Predicate.*

WHATEVER is reiterated*[1] in propositions must be annexed to the major and not to the middle term; I mean for instance, if there should be a syllogism, that there is a science of justice "because it is good," the expression "because it is good," or "in that it is good," must be joined to the major. For let A be "science, that it is good;" B, "good;" and C, "justice;" A then is truly predicated of B, since of good there is science that it is good: but B is also true of C; for justice is what is good, thus therefore the solution is made.† But if, "that it is good" be added to B,[2] it will not be true; for A will indeed be truly predicated of B, but it will not be true that B is predicated of C, since to predicate of justice, good that it is good, is false, and not intelligible. So also it may be shown that the healthy is an object of science in that it is good, or that hircocervus is an object of opinion, quoad its nonentity,[3] or that man is corruptible, so far as he is sensible, for in all super-predications, we must annex the repetition to the (major) term.

* ἐπαναδιπλούμενον.

1. Whatever is reiterated must be annexed to the major, not to the middle term.

† Example (1.)

ἐπικατηγορούμενα.

[1] ἐπαν. dicitur in oratione, quod accedit, præsertim si ita accedit ut sensûs aut leviter, aut omnino non mutetur. Waitz. A syllogism is however said to be produced μετὰ προσθήκης, when something is added to the predicate, τὸ ἐπικατηγορούμενον.

Ex. 1. Of good there is science that it is good
Justice is good
.·. Of justice there is science that it is good.

[2] That is, to the middle.

[3] An animal formed from the union of a goat and a stag. The syllogism may be thus constructed.

Non-being is an object of opinion quoad nonentity
An hircocervus is a nonentity
.·. An hircocervus is an object of opinion quoad nonentity.

Ex. 2. Every being is an object of science
Good is being
.·. Good is an object of science.

Ex. 3. Of being there is science, that it is being
Good is being
.·. Of good there is science, that it is being.

2. The terms not the same as to assumption whether the inference is simple or with a certain qualification.

The position of the terms is nevertheless not the same when a thing is syllogistically inferred simply, and when this particular thing, or in a certain respect, or in a certain way. For instance, I mean, as when good is shown to be an object of science, and when it is shown to be so because it is good; but if it is shown to be an object of science simply, we must take "being" as the middle term;* if (it is proved that it may be scientifically known) to be good, a certain being (must be taken as the middle). For let A be "science, that it is a certain being," B "a certain being," and C "good;" to predicate then A of B is true, for there is science of a certain being, that it is a certain being; but B is also predicated of C, because C is a certain being;† therefore A will be predicated of C, hence there will be science of good that it is good, for the expression "a certain being" is the sign of peculiar or proper essence. If, on the other hand, "being" is set as the middle, and being simply and not a certain being is added to the extreme, there will not be a syllogism that there is a science of good, that it is good, but that it is being: for example, let A be science that it is being; B, being; and C, good.‡ In such syllogisms then as are from a part,[1] we must clearly take the terms after this manner.

* Example (2.)

† i. e. good.

‡ Example (3.)

CHAP. XXXIX.—*The Simplification of Terms in the Solution of Syllogism.*

1. In syllogistic analysis terminal simplicity and perspicuity to be studied.

WE must also exchange those which have the same import; nouns for nouns, and sentences for sentences, and a noun and a sentence,[2] and always take the noun for the sentence, for thus the exposition of the terms will be easier. For example, if there is no difference in saying that what is supposed is not the genus of what is opined, or that what is opined is not any thing which may be supposed, (for the signification is the same,) instead of the sentence already expressed we must

[1] Ἐν μέρει vocat eos qui non ἁπλῶς τι sed τόδε τι concludunt. Waitz. Vide Biese, i. p. 179, not. 2.

[2] Either for either. This is omitted by Taylor, though read by Averroïs, Buhle, Waitz. This direction, except carefully done, gives rise to frequent fallacies. Quando pro termino repetendo, substituitur vox illi æquipollens. Aldrich. Whately on Fallacies.

take what may be supposed and what may be opined, as terms.

CHAP. XL.—*The definite Article to be added according to the nature of the Conclusion.*

1. Effect of the addition of the article, and rule.

SINCE however it is not the same, for pleasure to be *good*, and for pleasure to be *the good*, we must not set the terms alike; but if there is a syllogism that pleasure is *the good, the good* (must be taken as a term) if that it is *good, good* (must be taken), and so of the rest.

CHAP. XLI.—*On the Distinction of certain forms of Universal Predication.*

1. The expression καθ' οὗ τὸ B κατὰ παντὸς τὸ A λεγεσθαι, though not per se identical with καθ' οὗ παντὸς τὸ B κατὰ τοῦτου παντὸς καὶ το A, is equivalent to A being predicated of every thing of which B is predicated.

IT is neither in fact nor in word the same thing to assert that A is present with every individual with which B is present, and to say that A is present with every individual of what B is present with, since there is nothing to prevent B from being with C, yet not with every C.[1] For instance, let B be beautiful, but C white, if then beautiful is with something white, it is true to say that beauty is present with what is white, yet not perhaps with every thing white. If then A is with B, but not with every thing of which B is predicated, neither if B is present with every C, nor if it is alone present, it is necessary that A should not only not be present with every C, but that it should not be present (at all), but if that of which B is truly predicated, with every individual of this A is present, it will happen that A will be predicated of every individual of which B is predicated of every individual. But if A is predicated of that of which B is universally predicated, there is nothing to prevent B from being present with C with not every or with no individual of which A is present, therefore in (three terms it is evident that) the assertion that A is predicated of every individual of which B is predicated, signifies that of whatever B is predi-

[1] Therefore "that with which B is present," and "that with every individual of which B is present," do not mean the same thing.

cated of all these A is predicated also, and if B is predicated of every, A will also thus be predicated, but if it is not predicated of every individual it is not necessary that A should be predicated of every individual.

Still we need not imagine that any absurdity will occur from this exposition, for we do not use the expression that this is a particular definite thing,[1] but as a geometrician says that this is a foot in length, is a straight line, and is without breadth though it is not so, he does not however so use them, as if he inferred[2] from these. In a word, that which is not as a whole to a part, and something else in reference to this as a part to a whole, from nothing of these can a demonstrator demonstrate, wherefore neither is there a syllogism, but we use exposition as we do sense[3] when we address a learner, since we do not (use it) so as if it were impossible to be demonstrated without these, as (we use propositions) from which a syllogism is constructed.

2. Certain expressions used for illustration.

CHAP. XLII.—*That not all Conclusions in the same Syllogism are produced through one Figure.*

1. The conclusion an evidence in what figure the inquiry is to be made.

LET us not forget that all conclusions in the same syllogism are not produced by one figure, but one through this figure, and another through that, so that clearly we must make the[4] resolutions in the same manner, but since not every problem is proved in every[5] figure, but arranged in each, it is evident from the conclusion in what figure the inquiry must be made.[6]

[1] Examples are not adduced to prove, but to illustrate.

[2] Tanquam ex his ratiocinans. Averrois.

[3] *Τῷ δ' ἐκτίθεσθαι* (exhibere sensui) *ὄυτω χρώμεθα ὥσπερ καὶ τῷ αἴσθάνεσθαι.* Cf. Aquinas Opusc. 47. Zabarella, cap. vii. *αἴσθησις*, sensation, signifies the perception of the external senses. Vide Ethics, b. vi. chap. 2, and 11; Phys. b. iii. and vii.

[4] i. e. the several syllogisms to their proper figures.

[5] As no affirmative in the second nor universal in the third.

[6] In quâ figurâ quærendum sit problema aliquod. Buhle.

CHAP. XLIII.—*Of Arguments against Definition, simplified.*

1. For brevity's sake the thing impugned in the definition, and not the whole definition itself, is to be laid down.

WITH regard, however, to arguments against definition, and by which a particular thing in the definition is attacked, that term must be laid down which is attacked, and not the whole definition, for it will result that we shall be less disturbed by prolixity, e. g. if we are to show that water is humid potable, we must place potable and water as terms.[1]

CHAP. XLIV.—*Of the Reduction of Hypotheticals and of Syllogisms ad impossibile.*

1. Reason for our not reducing hypotheticals.

WE must not endeavour, moreover, to reduce hypothetical syllogisms, for we cannot reduce them, from the things laid down,[2] since they are not proved syllogistically, but are all of them admitted by consent. Thus if a man supposing that except there is one certain power of contraries, there will neither exist one science of them, it should afterwards be dialectically proved that there is not one* power of contraries; for instance, of the wholesome and of the unwholesome, for the same thing will be wholesome and unwholesome at the same time—here it will be shown that there is not one power of all contraries, but that is not a science, has not been shown. We must yet acknowledge that there is, not however by syllogism, but by hypothesis, wherefore we cannot reduce this, but that, we may, viz. that there is not one power, for this perhaps was a syllogism, but that an hypothesis. The same thing happens in the case of syllogisms, which infer a consequence per impossibile, since neither can we analyze these, though we may a

* πασα. Waitz.

2. Nor syllogisms per impossibile.

[1] Waitz states that Pacius has misapprehended this place, by following Philoponus, and avers that διαλέγεσθαι here is not "disserere contra aliquid," sed "disputare de aliquâ re." Pacius thinks that the chapter refers to such syllogisms as impugn the definition.

[2] ἐκ τῶν κειμένων. Vide Whately, book ii. ch. 4; also Mansel's Logic, Appendix, note G. It has been questioned whether hypothetical can be reduced to categorical; the reader will find the subject well and fully treated in Mansel, p. 88.

deduction to the impossible, (for it is demonstrated by syllogism,) but the other we cannot, for it is concluded from hypothesis. They differ nevertheless from the before-named,[1] because we must in them indeed have admitted some thing previously, if we are about to consent, as if, for example, one power of contraries should have been shown, and that there was the same science of them, now here they admit, what they had not allowed previously on account of the evident falsity, as if the diameter of a square having been admitted commensurable with the side, odd things should be equal to even.

3. Further consideration of hypotheticals deferred.

Many others also are concluded from hypothesis, which it is requisite to consider, and clearly explain; what then are the differences of these, and in how many ways an hypothetical syllogism is produced, we will show hereafter;[2] at present, let only so much be evident to us, that we cannot resolve such syllogisms into figures; for what reason we have shown.

CHAP. XLV.—*The Reduction of Syllogisms from one Figure to another.*

* Anal. i. 4 and 26; Topics, i. 4 and 11.

As many problems* as are demonstrated in many figures, if they are proved in one syllogism, may be referred[3] to another, e. g. a negative in the first may be referred to the second, and one in the middle to the first, still not all, but some only.[4] This will appear from the following: if A is with no B, but B with every C, A is with no C, thus the first figure arises; but if the negative is converted, there will be the middle, for B will be with no A, and with every C. In the same manner, if the syllogism be not universal, but particular, as if A is with no B, but B is with a certain C, for the negative being converted there will be the middle figure.

1. Whatever syllogisms are proved in many figures, may be reduced from one figure to another—case of universal and particular in the first and second figures.

[1] i. e. from syllogisms, by hypothesis.

[2] No work is extant of Aristotle's upon this subject; with St. Hilaire, however, we think that though the subject is not worked out by Aristotle, we have ample data from which to elucidate it.

[3] ἀναγαγεῖν—vide Mansel's Appendix.

[4] i. e. may be reduced, or referred.

Of syllogisms, however, in the middle figure, the universal will be reduced to the first, but only one of the particular,[1] for let A be with no B, but with every C, then by conversion of the negative there will be the first figure, since B will be with no A, but A with every C. Now if the affirmative be added to B, and the negative to C, we must take C as the first term, since this is with no A, but A is with every B, wherefore C is with no B, neither will B be with any C, for the negative is converted. If however the syllogism be particular, when the negative is added to the major extreme, it will be reduced to the first figure, as if A is with no B, but with a certain C, for by conversion of the negative there will be the first figure, since B is with no A, but A with a certain C. When however the affirmative (is joined to the greater extreme), it will not be resolved, as if A is with every B, but not with every C, for the proposition A B does not admit conversion,[2] nor if it were made would there be a syllogism.

2. Universals in the second are reducible to the first, but only one particular.

Again, not all in the third figure will be resolvable into the first,[3] but all in the first[4] will be into the third, for let A be with every B, but B with a certain C, since then a particular affirmative is convertible, C will be with a certain B, but A was with every B, so that there is the third figure. Also if the syllogism be negative, there will be the same result, for the particular affirmative is convertible, wherefore A will be with no B, but with a certain C. Of the syllogisms in the last figure, one alone is not resolvable into the first,[5] when the negative is not placed universal, all the rest however are resolved. For let A and B be predicated of every C, C therefore is convertible partially to each extreme, wherefore it is present with a certain B, so that there will be the first figure, if A is with every C, but C with a certain B. And if A is with every C, but B with a certain C, the reasoning is the same,

3. Of those in the third figure, one only, when the negative is not universal, is not reducible to the first.

[1] Viz. Festino and not Baroko. Of these reductions it may be generally observed, that only negative syllogisms are reducible to the second, and only particular to the third figure. Barbara, Baroko, and Bokardo cannot be ostensively reduced to any other figure.

[2] Being A it does not admit simple conversion.

[3] For Bokardo is excepted.

[4] Darii and Ferio—because universals cannot be reduced to the third figure, in which the conclusion is particular.

[5] i. e. Bokardo.

for B reciprocates with C. But if B is with every C, and A with a certain C, B must be taken as the first term, for B is with every C, but C with a certain A, so that B is with a certain A; since however the particular is convertible, A will also be with a certain B. If the syllogism be negative, when the terms are universal, we must assume in like manner, for let B be with every C, but A with no C, wherefore C will be with a certain B, but A with no C, so that C will be the middle term. Likewise, if the negative is universal, but the affirmative particular, for A will be with no C, but C with a certain B; if however the negative be taken as particular, there will not be a resolution,* e. g. if B is with every C, but A not with a certain C, for by conversion of the proposition B C, both propositions will be partial.

* ἀνάλυσις.

4. The conversion of the minor premise necessary for reduction.

It is clear then, that in order mutually to convert these figures,[1] the minor premise must be converted in either figure, for this being transposed a transition[2] is effected; of syllogisms in the middle figure,[3] one is resolved,[4] and the other is not[5] resolved into the third, for when the universal is negative there is a resolution, for if A is with no B, but with a certain C, both similarly reciprocate with A, wherefore B is with no A, but C with a certain A, the middle then is A. When however A is with every B, and is not with a certain C, there will not be resolution, since neither proposition after conversion is universal.

Syllogisms also of the third figure may be resolved into the middle, when the negative is universal, as if A is with no C, but B is with some or with every C, for C will be with no A, but will be with a certain B, but if the negative be particular, there will not be a resolution, since a particular negative does not admit conversion.

5. Those syllogisms not mutually reducible into the other figures which are not into the first.

We see then that the same syllogisms[6] are not resolved in these figures,[7] which were not resolved into the first figures, and that when syllogisms are reduced to the first figure, these only are concluded per impossibile.

How therefore we must reduce syllogisms, and

[1] Viz. the first and third.

[2] Μετάβασις—transitus fit ex unâ in aliam figuram.—Buhle.

[3] Those are particular, because there is no universal conclusion in the third. [4] Festino. [5] Baroko.

[6] Baroko and Bokardo. [7] In the second and third figures.

that the figures are mutually resolvable, appears from what has been said.

CHAP. XLVI.—*Of the Quality and Signification of the Definite, and Indefinite, and Privative.*

1. Difference in statement arising from "not to be" and "to be not,"—with the reason. (Cf. Herm. 6.)

THERE is some difference in the construction or subversion of a problem, whether we suppose the expressions "not to be this particular thing," and "to be not this particular thing," have the same, or different signification, e. g. "not to be white," and "to be not white." Now they do not signify the same thing, neither of the expression "to be white," is the negation "to be not white," but, "not to be white;" and the reason of this is as follows. The expression "he is able to walk," is similar to "he is able not to walk," the expression "it is white" to, "it is not white," and "he knows good," to "he knows what is not good." For these, "he knows good," or "he has a knowledge of good," does not at all differ, neither "he is able to walk," and "he has the power of walking;" wherefore also the opposites, "he is not able to walk," and "he has not the power of walking," (do not differ from each other). If then "he has not the power of walking," signifies the same as "he has the power of not walking," these will be at one and the same time present with the same, for the same person is able to walk, and not to walk, and is cognizant of good, and of what is not good, but affirmation and negation being opposites, are not at the same time present with the same thing.[1] Since therefore it is not the same thing "not to know good," and "to know what is not good," neither is it the same thing to be "not good" and "not to be good," since of things having analogy,[2] if the one is different the other also differs. Neither is it the same to be "not equal," and "not to be equal,"[3] for to the one, namely, "to that which

[1] Aristotle demonstrates the difference between infinite affirmation and finite negation by an hypothetical syllogism leading to an absurdity. The reader may find the principle of proper logical affirmation and negation discussed in Whately, b. ii. ch. 2, and Hill, p. 96, et seq.

[2] Eandem rationem.—Buhle. Similitude or identity of relation.

[3] For "to be not equal" implies at all events that a thing exists, which is affirmation, but "not to be equal" may be nothing, which is pure negation. Hence, as Taylor remarks, Aristotle infers that "not every

is not equal," something is subjected, and this is the unequal, but to the other there is nothing subjected, wherefore "not every thing is equal or unequal," but "every thing is equal or not equal." Besides this expression, "it is not white wood," and this, "not is white wood," are not present together at the same time, for if it is "wood not white," it will be wood; but "what is not white wood" is not of necessity "wood," so that it is clear that of "it is good" the negation is not "it is not good." If then of every one thing either the affirmation or negation is true, if there is not negation, it is evident that there will in some way be affirmation, but of every affirmation there is negation, and hence of this[1] the negation is, "it is not not good." They have this order indeed with respect to each other: let to be good be A, not to be good B, to be not good C under B, not to be not good D under A. With every individual then either A or B will be present, and (each) with nothing which is the same and C or D with every individual,[2] and with nothing which is the same, and with whatever C is present, B must necessarily be present with every individual, for if it is true to say that "a thing *is* not white," it is also true to say that "*not it* is white," for a thing cannot at one and the same time be white and not white, or be wood not white and be white wood, so that unless there is affirmation, negation will be present.—C however is not always (consequent) to B, for in short, what is not wood will not be white wood, on the contrary, with whatever A is present D also is present with every individual, for either C or D will be present. As however "to be not white"* and "to be white,"† cannot possibly co-subsist, D will be present, for of what is white we may truly say, that it is not not white, yet A is not predicated of every D, for, in short, we cannot truly predicate A of what is not wood, namely, to assert that it is white wood, so that D will be true, and A will not be true, namely, that it is white wood. It appears also, that A and C are present with nothing identical, though B and D may be present with the same.

2. Order of affirmation and negation.

* C.

† A.

thing" is equal or unequal, because that which is not is neither equal nor unequal; but that "every thing" is equal or is not equal," because this is contradiction.

[1] "It is not good:"—affirmative. [2] Taylor omits this clause.

3. Relation between (ἀι στηρήσεις) privatives and attributes (κατηγορίαι).

Privatives also subsist similarly to this position with respect to attributes,[1] for let equal be A, not equal B, unequal C, not unequal D. In many things also, with some of which the same thing is present and not with others, the negative may be similarly true, that, "not all things are white," or "that not each thing is white;" but, "that each thing is not white," or, "that all things are not white," is false. So also of this affirmation, "every animal is white," the negation is not, "every animal is not white," for both are false, but this, "not every animal is white." Since however it is clear that "is not white," signifies something different from "not is white," and that one is affirmation and the other negation, it is also clear that there is not the same mode of demonstrating each, for example,[2] "whatever is an animal is not white," or "happens not to be white;" and that we may truly say, "it is not white," for this is "to be not white." Still there is the same mode as to it is true to say it is white or not white, for both are demonstrated constructively* through the first figure, since the word "true" is similarly arranged with "is," for of the assertion "it is true to say it is white," the negation is not, "it is true to say it is not white," but "it is not true to say it is white." But if it is true to say, "whatever is a man is a[3] musician, or is not[4] a musician," we must assume that "whatever is an animal is either a musician or is not a musician,"[5] and it will be demonstrated, but that "whatever is a man is not a musician," is shown negatively† according to the three modes[6] stated.

* κατασκευαστικῶς, "constructive," Averr. "confirmative," Buhle.

4. The difference of the character of assertion shown by the difference in the mode of demonstration.

† ἀνασκευαστικως, "destructive." Averrois.

5. Relative consequence proved in certain cases.

In short, when A and B are so, as that they cannot be simultaneously in the same thing, but one of them is necessarily present to every indi-

[1] κάτηγοριαι—predicamenta. Averrois. The word must here be understood as opposed to privation in the sense of "habits," not as a species of quality, as it is considered in the Categor. ch. 8.

[2] We cannot demonstrate the two assertions given, in the same way.

[3] An universal finite affirmative.

[4] An universal indefinite affirmative.

[5] This is the major premise, to which if the minor, "every man is an animal," is added, the syllogism will be in Barbara.

[6] Viz. Celarent, Cesare, Camestres.

vidual, and again C and D likewise, but A follows C and does not reciprocate, D will also follow B, and will not reciprocate, and A and D may be with the same thing, but B and C cannot. In the first place then, it appears from this that D is consequent to B, for since one of C D is necessarily present with every individual, but with what B is present C cannot be, because it introduces with itself A, but A and B cannot consist with the same, D is evidently a consequent. Again, since C does not reciprocate with A, but C or D is present with every, it happens that A and D will be with the same thing, but B and C cannot, because A is consequent to C, for an impossibility results,[1] wherefore it appears plain that neither does B reciprocate with D, because it would happen that A is present together with D.[2]

6. Fallacy arising from not assuming opposites properly.

Sometimes also it occurs that we are deceived by such an arrangement of terms, because of our not taking opposites rightly, one of which must necessarily be with every individual, as if A and B cannot be simultaneously with the same, but it is necessary that the one should be with what the other is not, and again C and D in like manner, but A is consequent to every C; for B will happen necessarily to be with that with which D is, which is false. For let the negative of A B which is F be assumed, and again the negative of C D, and let it be H, it is necessary then, that either A or F should be with every individual, since either affirmation or negation must be present. Again also, either C or H, for they are affirmation and negation, and A is by hypothesis present with every thing with which C is, so that H will also be present with whatever F is. Again, since of F B, one is with every individual, and so also one of H D, and H is consequent to F, B will also be consequent to D, for this we know. If then A is consequent to C, B will also follow D, but this is false, since the sequence was the reverse in things so subsisting, for it is not perhaps necessary that either A or F should be with every individual, neither F nor B, for F is not the negative of A, since of "good" the negation is "not good," and "it is not good" is not the same with "it is neither good nor not good." It is the same also of C D, for the assumed negatives are two.

[1] i. e. A and B would co-subsist.
[2] Because A cannot be present with B.

BOOK II.

CHAP. I.—*Recapitulation.—Of the Conclusions of certain Syllogisms.*

1. Reference to the previous observations. Universal syllogisms infer many conclusions.

IN how many figures, through what kind and number of propositions, also when and how a syllogism is produced, we have therefore now explained; moreover, what points both the constructor and subverter of a syllogism should regard, as well as how we should investigate a proposed subject after every method; further, in what manner we should assume the principles of each question. Since, however, some syllogisms are universal, but others particular, all the universal always conclude a greater number of things, yet of the particular, those which are affirmative many things, but the negative one conclusion only. For other propositions are converted, but the negative is not converted, but the conclusion is something of somewhat; hence other syllogisms conclude a majority of things, for example, if A is shown to be with every or with a certain B, B must also necessarily be with a certain A, and if A is shown to be with no B, B will also be with no A, and this is different from the former. If however A is not with a certain B, B need not be not present with a certain A, for it possibly may be with every A.[1] This then is the common cause of all syllogisms, both universal and particular; we may however speak differently of universals, for as to whatever things are under the middle, or under the conclusion, of all there will be the same syllogism, if some are placed in the middle, but others in the conclusion,[2] as, if A B is a conclusion through C, it is necessary that A should be predicated of whatever is

2. So also do particular affirmative, but not the negative particular.

3. Difference between universals of the first and those of the second figure.

[1] As if A were "man;" a "certain animal," a certain B; and animal, B; therefore though "man" is not present with "a certain animal," (e. g. "a lion,") yet "animal" is with every "man."

[2] Hence three conclusions, he means, may be drawn from the same syllogism, one of the minor extreme, another of what is under the minor and the third of what is the subject of the middle.

under B or C, for if D is in the whole of B, but B in the whole of A, D will also be in the whole of A. Again, if E is in the whole of C, and C is in A, E will also be in the whole of A, and in like manner if the syllogism be negative; but in the second figure it will be only possible to form a syllogism of that which is under the conclusion. As, if A is with no B, but is with every C, the conclusion will be that B is with no C; if therefore D is under C, it is clear that B is not with it, but that it is not with things under A, does not appear by the syllogism, though it will not be with E, if it is under A. But it has been shown by the syllogism that B is with no C, but it was assumed without demonstration[1] that it is not with A, wherefore it does not result by the syllogisms that B is not with E. Nevertheless in particular syllogisms of things under the conclusion, there is no necessity incident, for a syllogism is not produced,[2] when this* is assumed as particular, but there will be of all things under the middle, yet not by that syllogism, e. g. if A is with every B, but B with a certain C, there will be no syllogism of what is placed under C, but there will be of what is under B, yet not through the antecedent syllogism. Similarly also in the case of the other figures, for there will be no conclusion of what is under the conclusion, but there will be of the other, yet not through that syllogism; in the same manner, as in universals, from an undemonstrated proposition, things under the middle were shown, wherefore either there will not be a conclusion there,[3] or there will be in these also.[4]

* (πρότασις.) major in 1st figure.

CHAP. II.—*On a true Conclusion deduced from false Premises in the first Figure.*

1. Material truth or falsity of propositions, is not shared by the conclusion.

It is therefore possible that the propositions may be true, through which a syllogism arises, also that they may be false, also that one may be true and the other false; but the conclusion must of

[1] A being assumed of no B, B is in a manner assumed of no A, because a proposition universal negative reciprocates.

[2] Because in the 2nd figure both propositions affirm; hence nothing is concluded.

[3] In universal syllogisms.

[4] In particular. For the recognition of the indirect modes, in this chapter, by Aristotle, see Mansel, p. 66, and 74, note.

necessity be either true or false. From true propositions then we cannot infer a falsity, but from false premises we may infer the truth, except that not *the why*,* but the mere *that* (is inferred), since there is not a syllogism of the why from false premises, and for what reason shall be told hereafter.[1]

* οὐ διότι ἀλλ' ὅτι, "non propter quid sed quia."—Averr. (Hill's Logic, p. 287.)

First then, that we cannot infer the false from true premises, appears from this: if when A is, it is necessary that B should be, when B is not it is necessary that A is not, if therefore A is true, B is necessarily true, or the same thing (A) would at one and the same time be and not be,[2] which is impossible. Neither must it be thought, because one term, A, is taken, that from one certain thing existing, it will happen that something will result from necessity, since this is not possible, for what results from necessity is the conclusion, and the fewest 1.
things through which this arises are three terms, but two intervals and propositions. If then it is true that with whatever B is A also is, and that with whatever C is B is, it is necessary that with whatever C is A also is, and this cannot be false, for else the same thing would exist and not exist at the same time. Wherefore A is laid down as one thing, the two propositions being co-assumed. 2.
It is the same also in negatives, for we cannot show the false from what are true; but from false propositions we may collect the truth,[3] either when both premises are false, or one only, and this not indifferently, but the minor, if it comprehend the whole false,[4] but if the whole is not assumed to be false, the true may be collected from either.† Now let A be with the whole of C, but with no B, nor B with C,

2. We may infer the true from false premises, but not the false from true premises. Proof—(Vide Aldrich, general rules of syllogism.)

† being assumed false.

[1] In ch. 2 of 1st book, Post Anal.

[2] Because it is true by hypothesis, but B being denied true, A cannot be true.

[3] See the general rules of syllogism in Aldrich, and Hill's Logic. Hereafter Aristotle expounds this more fully; he means that a true conclusion may always be inferred in the first figure, unless the major is wholly false, and the minor true.

[4] By this expression he means, as he explains further on, an universal proposition, contrary to the true, as "no man is an animal." An universal contradictory to the true is of course a particular false proposition, (vide table of opposition,) and a proposition is said to be false in part, when what is partly true and partly false, is affirmed, or denied, universally.

and this may happen to be the case, as animal is with no stone, nor stone present with any man, if then A is assumed present with every B, and B with every C, A will be with every C, so that from propositions both false, the conclusion will be true, since every man is an animal.*

* Example (1.)

So also a negative conclusion (is attained), for neither A
3. may be assumed, nor B present with any C, but let A be with every B, for example, as if, the same terms being taken, man was placed in the middle, for neither animal nor man is with any stone, but animal is with every man. Wherefore if with what† it ‡is present universally, it is assumed to be present with none,§ but with what it is not present, we assume that it is present with every individual,|| from both these false premises, there will be a true conclusion.¶
4. The same may be shown if each premise is assumed partly false, but if only one is admitted false, if the major is wholly false, as A B, there will not be a true conclusion, but if B C, (the minor is wholly false,) there will be (a true conclusion).
3. Instance of a false proposition. Now I mean by a proposition wholly false that which is contrary (to the true), as if that was assumed present with every, which is present with none, or that present with none, which is present with every. For let A be with no B, but B with every C, if then we take the proposition B

† Man.
‡ Animal.
§ In the major.
|| In the minor.
¶ Example (2.)

Ex. 1. Every stone is an animal
Every man is a stone
∴ Every man is an animal.

Ex. 2. No man is an animal
Every stone is a man
∴ No stone is an animal.

Ex. 3. Every animal (B) is a stone (A)
Every man (C) is an animal (B)
∴ Every man (C) is a stone (A).

Ex. 4. Every thing white (B) is an animal (A)
Every swan (C) is white (B)
∴ Every swan (C) is an animal (A).

Ex. 5. Nothing white (B) is an animal (A)
All snow (C) is white (B)
∴ No snow (C) is an animal (A).

C as true, but the whole of A B as false, and that A is with every B, it is impossible for the conclusion to be true, for it was present with no C, since A was present with none of what B was present with, but B was with every C.*

* Example (3.)

5.

In like manner also the conclusion will be false, if A is with every B, and B with every C, and the proposition B C is assumed true, but A B wholly false, and that A is present with no individual with which B is, for A will be with every C, since with whatever B is, A also is, but B is with every C. It is clear then, that, the major premise being assumed wholly false, whether it be affirmative or negative, but the other premise being true, there is not a true conclusion; if however the whole is not assumed false, there will be. For if A is with every C, but with a certain B, and B is with every C; e. g. animal with every swan, but with a certain whiteness, and whiteness with every swan, if A is assumed present with every B, and B with every C, A will also be truly present with every C, since every swan is an animal.†

4. When the major is wholly false, but the minor is true, the conclusion is false; but when the whole is not false, the conclusion is true. Affirmative.

† Example (4.)

2. Negative.

So also if A B be negative, for A concurs with a certain B, but with no C, and B with every C, as animal with something white, but with no snow, and whiteness with all snow; if then A is assumed present with no B, but B with every C, A will be present with no C.‡

‡ Example (5.)

5. If the major is true wholly, but the minor wholly false, the conclusion is true.

If however the proposition A B were assumed wholly true, but B C wholly false, there will be a true syllogism,[1] as nothing prevents A from being with every B and every C, and yet B with no C, as is the case with species of the same genus, which

[1] Here is another instance of "syllogism" being employed in its pure sense, equivalent to "conclusion," frequently it signifies the propositional arrangement necessarily inferring the conclusion.

Ex. 6. Every horse (B) is an animal (A)
Every man (C) is a horse (B)
∴ Every man (C) is an animal (A).

Ex. 7. No music (B) is an animal (A)
All medicine (C) is music (B)
∴ No medicine (C) is an animal (A).

are not subaltern, for animal concurs both with horse and man, but horse with no man; if therefore A is assumed present with every B, and B with every C, the conclusion will be true, though the whole proposition B C is false.* It will be the same, if the proposition A B is negative. For it will happen that A will be neither with any B, nor with any C, and that B is with no C, as genus to those species which are from another genus, for animal neither concurs with music nor with medicine, nor music with medicine: if then A is assumed present with no B, but B with every C, the conclusion will be true.† Now if the proposition B C is not wholly but partially false, even thus the conclusion will be true. For nothing prevents A from concurring with the whole of B, and the whole of C, and B with a certain C, as genus with species and difference, thus animal is with every man and with every pedestrian, but man concurs with something, and not with every thing pedestrian: if then A is assumed present with every B, and B with every C, A will also be present with every C,‡ which will be true.

1. Affirmative.

* Example (6.)

† Example (7.)

‡ Example (8.)

Ex. 8. Every man (B) is an animal (A)
Every pedestrian thing (C) is a man (B)
∴ Every pedestrian thing (B) is an animal (A).

Ex. 9. No prudence (B) is an animal (A)
All contemplative knowledge (C) is prudence (B)
∴ No contemplative knowledge (C) is an animal (A).

Ex. 10. All snow (B) is an animal (A)
Something white (C) is snow (B)
∴ Something white (C) is an animal (A).

Ex. 11. No man (B) is an animal (A)
Something white (C) is a man (B)
∴ Something white (C) is not an animal (A).

The same will occur if the proposition A B be negative. For A may happen to be neither with any B, nor with any C, yet B with a certain C, as genus with the species and difference which are from another genus. Thus animal is neither present with any prudence nor with any thing contemplative, but prudence is with something contemplative; if then A is assumed present with no B, but B with every C, A will be with no C, which will be true.*

2. Negative.

* Example (9.)

In particular syllogisms however, when the whole of the major premise is false, but the other true, the conclusion may be true; also when the major A B is partly false, but B C (the minor) wholly true; and when A B the major is true, but the particular false, also when both are false. For there is nothing to prevent A from concurring with no B, but with a certain C, and also to prevent B from being present with a certain C, as animal is with no snow, but is with something white, and snow with something white. If then snow is taken as the middle, and animal as the first term, and if A is assumed present with the whole of B, but B with a certain C, the whole proposition A B will be false, but B C true, also the conclusion will be true.†

6. In particulars with a major false, but a minor true, there may be a true conclusion.

1. Affirmative.

† Example (10.)

It will happen also the same, if the proposition A B is negative, since A may possibly be with the whole of B, and not with a certain C, but B may be with a certain C. Thus animal is with every man, but is not consequent to something white, but man is present with something white; hence if man be placed as the middle term, and A is assumed present with no B, but B with a certain C, the conclusion will be true, though the whole proposition A B is false.‡

2. Negative.

‡ Example (11.)

If again the proposition A B be partly false,[1]

7. If the major

[1] Taylor and Buhle insert, "when B C is true," which is omitted by Waitz and Averrois.

Ex. 12. Every thing beautiful (B) is an animal (A)
Something great (C) is beautiful (B)
∴ Something great (C) is an animal (A).

is partly false, the conclusion will be true.

the conclusion will be true. For nothing hinders A from concurring with B, and with a certain C, and B from being with a certain C; thus animal may be with something beautiful, and with something great,[1] and beauty also may be with something great. If then A is taken as present with every B, and B with a certain C, the proposition A B will be partly false; but B C will be true, and the conclusion will be true.*

1. Affirmative.

* Example (12.)

2. Negative.

Likewise if the proposition A B is negative, for there will be the same terms, and placed in the same manner for demonstration.†

† Example (13.)

3. Major true, minor false.

Again, if A B be true, but B C false, the conclusion will be true, since nothing prevents A from being with the whole of B, and with a certain C, and B from being with no C. Thus animal is with every swan, and with something black, but a swan with nothing black; hence, if A is assumed present with every B, and B with a certain C, the conclusion will be true, though B C is false.‡

‡ Example (14.)

Ex. 13. Nothing beautiful (B) is an animal (A)
Something great (C) is beautiful (B)
∴ Something great (C) is not an animal (A).

[1] i. e. to prove a true conclusion from premises, one partly false, and the other true.

Ex. 14. Every swan (B) is an animal (A)
Something black (C) is a swan (B)
∴ Something black (C) is an animal (A).

Ex. 15. No number (B) is an animal (A)
Something white (C) is number (B)
∴ Something white (C) is not an animal (A).

Ex. 16. Every thing white (B) is an animal (A)
Something black (C) is white (B)
∴ Something black (B) is an animal (A).

Likewise if the proposition A B be taken as negative, for A may be with no B, and may not be with a certain C, yet B may be with no C. Thus genus may be present with species, which belongs to another genus, and with an accident, to its own species, for animal indeed concurs with no number, and is with something white, but number is with nothing white. If then number be placed as the middle, and A is assumed present with no B, but B with a certain C, A will not be with a certain C, which would be true, and the proposition A B is true, but B C false.* 4. Major negative.

* Example (15.)

Also if A B is partly false, and the proposition B C is also false, the conclusion will be true, for nothing prevents A from being present with a certain B, and also a certain C, but B with no C, as if B should be contrary to C, and both accidents of the same genus, for animal is with a certain white thing, and with a certain black thing, but white is with nothing black. If then A is assumed present with every B, and B with a certain C, the conclusion will be true.† 5. Major partly, minor wholly, false.

† Example (16.)

Likewise if the proposition A B is taken negatively, for there are the same terms, and they will be similarly placed for demonstration.‡[1] 6. Negative.

‡ Example (17.)

If also both are false, the conclusion will be true, since A may be with no B, but yet with a 7. Both false.

[1] To prove a true conclusion may be drawn from false premises.

B A
Ex. 17. Nothing white is an animal
C B
Something black is white
C A
∴ Something black is not an animal.

B A
Ex. 18. Every number is an animal
C B
Something white is number
C A
∴ Something white is an animal.

B A
Ex. 19. No swan is an animal
C B
Something black is a swan
C A
∴ Something black is not an animal.

certain C, but B with no C, as genus with species of another genus, and with an accident of its own species, for animal is with no number, but with something white, and number with nothing white. If then A is assumed present with every B, and B with a certain C, the conclusion indeed will be true, while both the premises will be false.*

* Example (18.)

8. Major negative.

Likewise if A B is negative, for nothing prevents A from being with the whole of B, and from not being with a certain C, and B from being with no C, thus animal is with every swan, but is not with something black, swan however is with nothing black. Wherefore, if A is assumed present with no B, but B with a certain C, A is not with a certain C, and the conclusion will be true, but the premises false.†[1]

† Example (19.)

CHAP. III.—*The same in the middle Figure.*

1. In this figure we may infer the true from premises, either one or both wholly or partially false.

IN the middle figure it is altogether possible to infer truth from false premises, whether both are assumed wholly false, or one partly, or one true, but the other wholly false, whichever of them is placed false, or whether both are partly false, or one is simply true, but the other partly false, or one is wholly false, but the other partly true, and as well in universal as in particular syllogisms.

1. Universals.

For if A is with no B but with every C, as animal is with no stone but with every horse, if the propositions are placed contrariwise, and A is assumed present with every B, but with no C, from premises wholly false, the conclusion will be true.‡ Likewise if A is with every B but with no C, for the syllogism will be the same.§[1]

‡ Example (1.)

§ Example (2.)

[1] Vide Waitz, vol. i. pp. 483 and 487.

B A	B A
Ex. 1. Every stone is an animal	Ex. 2. No horse is an animal
C A	C A
No horse is an animal	Every stone is an animal
C B	C B
∴ No horse is a stone.	∴ No stone is a horse.

[2] One of these syllogisms is in Cesare, but the other in Camestres: yet both are similar in respect of being produced by the same terms; proving the truth from false premises, and deducing almost the same conclusion.

2. One wholly false, the other wholly true.

Again, if the one is wholly false, but the other wholly true, since nothing prevents A from being with every B and with every C, but B with no C, as genus with species not subaltern, for animal is with every horse and with every man, and no man is a horse. If then it is assumed to be with every individual of the one, but with none of the other, the one proposition will be wholly false, but the other wholly true, and the conclusion will be true to whichever proposition the negative is added.[1] * Also if the one is partly false, but the other wholly true, for A may possibly be with a certain B and with every C, but B with no C, as animal is with something white, but with every crow, and whiteness with no crow. If then A is assumed to be present with no B, but with the whole of C, the proposition A B will be partly false; but A C wholly true, and the conclusion will be true.† Likewise when the negative is transposed,[2] since the demonstration is by the

* Example (3.)

3. One partly false.

† Example (4.)

4. Minor or negative.

[1] i. e. whether the major or minor premise is negative.

Ex. 3.
B A
Every horse is an animal
C A
No man is an animal
C B
∴ No man is a horse.

B A
No horse is an animal
C A
Every man is an animal
C B
∴ No man is a horse.

Ex. 4.
B A
Nothing white is an animal
C A
Every crow is an animal
C B
∴ No crow is white.

[2] If the minor premise denies.

Ex. 5.
B A
Every crow is an animal
C A
Nothing white is an animal
C B
∴ Nothing white is a crow.

Ex. 6.
B A
Every thing white is an animal
C A
No pitch is an animal
C B
∴ No pitch is white.

Ex. 7.
B A
Every thing white is an animal
C A
Nothing black is an animal
C B
∴ Nothing black is white.

* Example (5).

5. Affirmative partly false.

same terms.* Also if the affirmative premise is partly false, but the negative wholly true, for nothing prevents A being present with a certain B, but not present with the whole of C, and B being present with no C, as animal is with something white, but with no pitch, and whiteness with no pitch. Hence if A is assumed present with the whole of B, but with no C, A B is partly false, but A C wholly true, also the conclusion will be true.†

† Example (6.)

6. Both partly false.

Also if both propositions are partly false, the conclusion will be true, since A may concur with a cer-

B A
Ex. 8. Nothing white is an animal
C A
Every thing black is an animal
C B
∴ Nothing black is white.

B A
Ex. 9. No man is an animal
C A
Something white is an animal
C B
∴ Something white is not a man.

B A
Ex. 10. Every thing inanimate is an animal
C A
Something white is not an animal
C B
∴ Something white is not inanimate.

B A
Ex. 11. No number is an animal
C A
Something inanimate is an animal
C B
∴ Something inanimate is not number.

B A
Ex. 12. Every man is an animal
C A
Something pedestrian is not an animal
C B
∴ Something pedestrian is not a man.

B A
Ex. 13. Every science is an animal
C A
A certain man is not an animal
C B
∴ A certain man is not science.

tain B, and with a certain C, but B with no C, as animal may be with something white, and with something black, but whiteness with nothing black. If then A is assumed present with every B, but with no C, both premises are partly false, but the conclusion will be true.* Likewise when the negative is transposed by the same terms.†

* Example (7.)

† Example (8.)

2. Particulars.

This is evident also as to particular syllogisms, since nothing hinders A from being with every B, but with a certain C, and B from not being with a certain C, as animal is with every man, and with something white, yet man may not concur with something white. If then A is assumed present with no B, but with a certain C, the universal premise will be wholly false, but the particular true, and the conclusion true.‡ Likewise if the proposition A B is taken affirmative, for A may be with no B, and may not be with a certain C,§ and B not present with a certain C; thus animal is with nothing inanimate, but with something white, and the inanimate will not be present with something white. If then A is assumed present with every B, but not present with a certain C, the universal premise A B will be wholly false, but A C true, and the conclusion true.‖ Also if the universal be taken true, but the particular false, since nothing prevents A from being neither consequent to any B nor to any C, and B from not being with a certain C, as animal is consequent to no number, and to nothing inanimate, and number is not consequent to a certain inanimate thing. If then A is assumed present with no B, but with a certain C, the conclusion will be true, also the universal proposition, but the particular will be false.¶ Likewise if the universal proposition be taken affirmatively, since A may be with the whole of B and with the whole of C, yet B not be consequent to a certain C, as genus to species and difference, for animal is consequent to every man, and to the whole of what is pedestrian, but man is not (consequent) to every pedestrian. Hence if A is assumed present with the whole of B, but not with a certain C, the universal proposition will be true, but the particular false, and the conclusion true.*

1. Major negative.

‡ Example (9.)

2. Major affirmative.

§ This clause omitted by Taylor.

‖ Example (10.)

3. Univ. true, part. false.

¶ Example (11.)

4. Univ. affirm.

* Example (12.)

5. Case of both premises false.

Moreover it is evident that from premises both false there will be a true conclusion, if A happens to be present with the whole of B and of C, but B to be not consequent to a certain C, for if A is assumed present with no B, but with a certain C, both propositions are false, but the conclusion will be true. In like manner when the universal premise is affirmative, but the particular negative, since A may follow no B, but every C, and B may not be present with a certain C, as animal is consequent to no science, but to every man, but science to no man. If then A is assumed present with the whole of B, and not consequent to a certain C, the premises will be false, but the conclusion will be true.*

* Example (13.)

CHAP. IV.—*Similar Observations upon a true Conclusion from false Premises in the third Figure.*

1. The case the same as with the preceding figures.

THERE will also be a conclusion from false premises in the last figure, as well when both are false and either partly false or one wholly true, but the other false, or when one is partly false, and the other wholly true, or vice versâ, in fact in as many ways as it is possible to change the propositions. For there is nothing to prevent either A or B being present with any C, but yet A may be with a certain B;[1] thus neither man, nor pedestrian, is consequent to any thing in-

1. Both univ. affirm.

[1] Taylor has made a mistake here both in the letters and in this and the succeeding syllogistic example. I have followed Waitz, Buhle, Averrois, and Bekker; for the general rules to which these chapters refer, the reader may find the subject fully treated in Whately and Hill.

```
               C         A
Ex. 1. Every thing inanimate is a man.
               C         B
       Every thing inanimate is pedestrian
               B      A
   ∴ Something pedestrian is a man.

         C     A
Ex. 2. No swan is an animal
         C       B
       Every swan is black
               B       A
   ∴ Something black is not an animal.
```

animate, yet man consists with something pedestrian. If then A and B are assumed present with every C, the propositions indeed will be wholly false, but the conclusion true.* Likewise also if one premise is negative, but the other affirmative, for B possibly is present with no C but A with every C, and A may not be with a certain B. Thus blackness consists with no swan, but animal with every swan, and animal is not present with every thing black. Hence, if B is assumed present with every C, but A with no C, A will not be present with a certain B, and the conclusion will be true, but the premises false.† If, however, each is partly false, there will be a true conclusion, for nothing prevents A and B being present with a certain C, and A with a certain B, as whiteness and beauty are consistent with a certain animal, and whiteness is with something beautiful, if then it is laid down that A and B are with every C, the premises will indeed be partly false, but the conclusion true.‡ Likewise if A C is taken as negative, for nothing prevents A not consisting with a certain C, but B consisting with

* Example (1.)

2. One negative.

† Example (2.)

3. One partly false.

‡ Example (3.)

4. Negatives.

Ex. 3. Every animal (C) is white (A)
Every animal (C) is beautiful (B)
∴ Something beautiful (B) is white (A).

Ex. 4. No animal (C) is white (A)
No animal (C) is beautiful (B)
∴ Something beautiful (B) is not white (A).

Ex. 5. No swan (C) is an animal (A)
Every swan (C) is white (B)
∴ Something white (B) is not an animal (A).

Ex. 6. No swan (C) is black (A)
Every swan (C) is inanimate (B)
∴ Something inanimate (B) is not black (A).

a certain C, and A not consisting with every B, as whiteness is not present with a certain animal, but beauty is with some one, and whiteness is not with every thing beautiful, so that if A is assumed present with no C, but B with every C, both premises will be partly false, but the conclusion will be true.* Likewise, if one premise be assumed wholly false, but the other wholly true, for both A and B may follow every C, but A not be with a certain B, as animal and whiteness follow every swan, yet animal is not with every thing white. These terms therefore being laid down, if B be assumed present with the whole of C, but A not with the whole of it, B C will be wholly true, and A C wholly false, and the conclusion will be true.† So also if B C is false, but A C true, for there are the same terms for demonstration, black, swan, inanimate.[1]‡ Also even if both premises are assumed affirmative, since nothing prevents B following every C, but A not wholly being present with it, also A may be with a certain B, as animal is

* Example (4.)

5. One wholly false, the other true.

† Example (5.)

6.

‡ Example (6.)

7. Both affirm.

[1] i. e. to deduce a true conclusion from false premises.

Ex. 7. Every swan (C) is black (A)
Every swan (C) is an animal (B)
.·. Some animal (B) is black (A).

Ex. 8. Every swan (C) is an animal (A)
Every swan (C) is black (B)
.·. Something black (B) is an animal (A).

Ex. 9. Every man (C) is beautiful (A)
Every man (C) is a biped (B)
.·. Some biped (B) is beautiful (A).

Ex. 10. Every man (C) is a biped (A)
Every man (C) is beautiful (B)
Something beautiful (B) is a biped (A).

with every swan, black with no swan, and black with a certain animal. Hence if A and B are assumed present with every C, B C will be wholly true, but A C wholly false, and the conclusion will be true.* Similarly, again, if A C is assumed true, for the demonstration will be through the same terms.† Again, if one is wholly true, but the other partly false, since B may be with every C, but A with a certain C, also A with a certain B, as biped is with every man, but beauty not with every man, and beauty with a certain biped. If then A and B are assumed present with the whole of C, the proposition B C is wholly true, but A C partly false, the conclusion will also be true.‡ Likewise, if A C is assumed true, and B
C partly false, for by transposition of the same 8.
terms,[1] there will be a demonstration.§ Again, if one is negative and the other affirmative, for since B may possibly be with the whole of C, but A with a certain C, when the terms are thus, A will not be with every B. If B is assumed present with the whole of C, but A with none, the negative is partly false, but the other wholly true, the conclusion will also be true. Moreover, since it has been shown that A being present with no C, but B with a certain C, it is possible that A may not be with a certain B, it is clear that when A C is wholly true, but B C partly false, 9.
the conclusion may be true, for if A is assumed present with no C, but B with every C, A C is wholly true, but B C partly false.

* Example (7.)
† Example (8.)
‡ Example (9.)
§ Example (10.)

2. Particulars follow the same rule, i. e. those with one universal and one particular premise.

Nevertheless, it appears that there will be altogether a true conclusion by false premises, in the case also of particular syllogisms. For the same terms must be taken, as when the premises were universal, namely, in affirmative propositions, affirmative terms, but in negative propositions, negative terms, for there is no difference[2] whether when a thing consists with no individual, we assume it present with every,[3] or being present with a certain one, we assume it present uni-

[1] In these two last examples, the greater and less extremes change places, yet a true conclusion is deduced.

[2] i. e. things assumed in particular, do not differ from the same things assumed in universal syllogisms.

[3] i. e. entirely false.

3. Also negatives.
4. If the conclusion is false there must be falsity in one or more of the premises—but this does not hold good vice versâ. Reason of this.

versally,[1] as far as regards the setting out of the terms;[2] the like also happens in negatives. We see then that if the conclusion is false, those things from which the reasoning proceeds, must either all or some of them be false; but when it (the conclusion) is true, that there is no necessity, either that a certain thing, or that all things, should be true; but that it is possible, when nothing in the syllogism is true, the conclusion should, nevertheless, be true, yet not of necessity. The reason of this however is, that when two things[3] so subsist with relation to each other, that the existence of the one necessarily follows from that of the other, if the one[4] does not exist, neither will the other be,[5] but if it[6] exists that it is not necessary that the other[7] should be. If however the same thing[8] exists, and does not exist, it is impossible that there should of necessity be the same (consequent);[9] I mean, as if A being white, B should necessarily be great, and A not being white, that B is necessarily great, for when this thing A being white, it is necessary that this thing B should be great, but B being great, C is not white, if A is white, it is necessary that C should not be white. Also when there are two things,[10] if one is,[11] the other[12] must necessarily be, but this not

[1] i. e. partly false.

[2] That is, the terms being proposed, it may be shown, that we can deduce a true inference from false premises.

[3] i. e. antecedent and consequent.

[4] The consequent.

[5] The antecedent. It is valid to argue from the subversion of the consequent, the subversion of the antecedent; thus if man is, animal is, but animal is not, therefore man is not.

[6] The consequent.

[7] The antecedent. It is not necessary that this should exist, because an inference of the existence of the antecedent from that of the consequent is invalid.

[8] The antecedent.

[9] Because we cannot collect the consequent from the affirmation or negation of the antecedent; as, if man is, animal is; and if man is not, animal is.

[10] That is, two subject terms, as A and B. He now enunciates that an argument from the negative of the consequent to the negative of the antecedent is valid. Buhle and Waitz read this passage differently to Taylor, by the insertion of the letter merely.

[11] That is, the antecedent.

[12] The consequent.

existing, it is necessary that A* should not be, thus B not being great, it is impossible that A should be white.

* (Illud.) Buhle. i. e. the first.

But if when A is not white, it is necessary that B should be great, it will necessarily happen that B not being great, B itself is great, which is impossible. For if B is not great, A will not be necessarily white, and if A not being white, B should be great, it results, as through three (terms), that if B is not great, it is great.†

† Example (11.)

CHAP. V.—*Of Demonstration in a Circle, in the first Figure.*[1]

1. Definition of this kind of demonstration—and example.

THE demonstration of things in a circle, and from each other, is by the conclusion, and by taking one proposition converse in predication, to conclude the other, which we had taken in a former syllogism. As if it were required to show that A is with every C, we should have proved it through B;[2] again,[3] if a person should show that A is with B, assuming A present with C, but C with B, and A with B; first, on the contrary, he assumed B present with C. Or if it is necessary to demonstrate that B is with C,[4] if he should have taken A (as predicated) of C, which was the conclusion,[5] but B to be present with A, for it was first assumed[6] conversely, that A was with B. It is not however possible in any other manner to demonstrate them from each other, for whether another middle[7] is taken, there will not be (a demonstration) in a circle, since nothing is assumed of the same,[8] or whether something of these (is assumed), it is necessary that one alone[9] should (be taken), for

Ex. 11. If A is not white B is great
If B is not great A is not white
∴ If B is not great it is great.

[1] Vide Mansel's Logic, on this kind of demonstration, pp. 103—105.
[2] The first syllogism, A B C.
[3] The second, A C B, in which the major of the first proposition is proved.
[4] i. e. the minor proposition of the first syllogism.
[5] In the first syllogism. [6] In the first syllogism.
[7] i. e. different from A B C, the original terms.
[8] Of the premises in the former syllogism.
[9] Of the premises of the first syllogism.

2. A demonstration of this kind not truly made, except through converted terms, and then by assumption "pro concesso," only.

if both[1] there will be the same conclusion, when we need another. In those terms then which are not converted, a syllogism is produced from one undemonstrated proposition, for we cannot demonstrate by this term, that the third is with the middle, or the middle with the first, but in those which are converted we may demonstrate all by each other, as if A B and C reciprocate; for A C can be demonstrated by the middle,[2] B; again,[3] A B (the major) through the conclusion, and through the proposition B C, (the minor) being converted; likewise[4] also B C the minor through the conclusion, and the proposition A B converted. We must however demonstrate the proposition C B,* and B A,† for we use these alone undemonstrated, if then B is taken as present with every C,‡ and C with every A, there will be a syllogism of B in respect to A.§ Again, if C is assumed present with every A, and A with every B,‖ it is necessary that C should be present with every B, in both[5] syllogisms indeed, the proposition C A is taken undemonstrated, for the others were demonstrated. Wherefore if we should show this, they will all have been shown by each other. If then C is assumed present with every B,¶ and B with every A, both propositions are taken demonstrated, and C is necessarily present with A, hence it is clear that in convertible propositions alone, demonstrations may be formed in a circle, and through each other, but in others as we have said before,[6] it occurs also in these[7] that

* The minor of of the 2nd syllogism.

† The major of the 6th syllogism.

‡ The 5th syllogism, B C A.

§ i. e. that B is with A.

‖ The 3rd syllogism, C A B.

¶ The 4th syllogism, C B A.

[1] Premises in the first syllogism.

[2] The first syllogism of a circle, A B C.

[3] The second syllogism, A C B.

[4] The sixth syllogism, B A C.

[5] i. e. in the fifth and third.

[6] One proposition is not demonstrated in a circle.

[7] i. e. in the 3rd, 4th, and 5th, in which the converse propositions are proved. It must be remembered that a circle consists of six syllogisms, the others flowing from the first: of these, the 2nd proves the major, and the 6th the minor of the first, but both assume the conclusion of the first, to which the 2nd adds the converse minor, and the 6th the converse major of the first: hence the 2nd and 6th prove directly the propositions of the first, but assume two converse propositions, which have also to be proved to make the circle complete. This is done by the third

we use the same thing demonstrated for the purpose of a demonstration. For C is demonstrated of B,* and B of A,† assuming C to be predicated of A,‡ but C is demonstrated of A § by these propositions,‖ so that we use the conclusion [1] for demonstration.

* The major of 4th.
† The minor of 4th.
‡ The major of 3rd.
§ In the 4th.
‖ C B and B A.

3. Case of negatives.

In negative syllogisms a demonstration through each other is produced thus: let B be with every C, but A present with no B, the conclusion that A is with no C. If then it is again necessary to conclude that A is with no B, which we took before, A will be with no C, but C with every B, for thus the proposition becomes converted. But if it is necessary to conclude that B is with C, the proposition A B must no longer be similarly converted, for it is the same proposition,¶ that B is with no A, and that A is with no B, but we must assume that B is present with every one of which A is present with none. Let A be present with no C, which was the conclusion, but let B [2] be assumed present with every of which A is present with none, therefore B must necessarily be present with every C, so that each of the assertions which are three becomes a conclusion, and this is to demonstrate in a circle, namely, assuming the conclusion and one premise converse to infer the other.[3] Now in particular syllogisms we cannot demonstrate universal proposition through others, but we can the particular, and that we cannot demonstrate universal is evident, for the universal is shown by universals, but the conclusion is not universal, and we must demonstrate from the conclusion, and from the other proposition. Besides, there is no syllogism produced at all when the proposition is converted, since both premises become particular.

¶ Æquipollent.

4. In particulars the major is not demonstrated, but the minor is.

1.

and fifth syllogisms, the major of the 3rd and the minor of the 5th being identical, as well as the latter being the converse conclusion of the first, proved by the 4th. Thus a circle may be divided into two parts, of which the conclusion of the 1st, 2nd, and 6th are direct, but those of the 3rd, 4th, and 5th are converse.

[1] Of the 4th, i. e. in order to prove the propositions of the same fourth.

[2] Omitted by Taylor. [3] Vide Whately and Hill.

Ex. 1. Every B is A
Some C is B
∴ Some C is A.

But we can demonstrate a particular proposition, for let A be demonstrated of a certain C through B, if then B is taken as present with every A, and the conclusion remains, B will be present with a certain C, for the first figure is produced, and A will be the middle.* Nevertheless if the syllogism is negative, we cannot demonstrate the universal proposition for the reason adduced before, but a particular one cannot be demonstrated, if A B is similarly converted as in universals, but we may show it by assumption,[1] as that A is not present with something, but that B is, since otherwise there is no syllogism from the particular proposition being negative.

2.

* Example (1.)

CHAP. VI.—*Of the same in the second Figure.*

1. In universals of the second figure an affirmative proposition is not demonstrated.

IN the second figure we cannot prove the affirmative in this mode, but we may the negative; the affirmative therefore is not demonstrated, because there are not both propositions affirmative, for the conclusion is negative, but the affirmative is demonstrated from propositions both affirmative, the negative however is thus demonstrated. Let A be with every B, but with no C, the conclusion B is with no C, if then B is assumed present with every A, it is necessary that A should be present with no C, for there is the second figure, the middle is B. But if A B be taken negative, and the other proposition affirmative, there will be the first figure, for C is present with every A, but B with no C, wherefore neither is B present with any A, nor A with B, through the conclusion then and one proposition a syllogism is not produced, but when another proposition is assumed there will be a syllogism. But if the syllogism is not universal, the universal proposition[2] is not demonstrated for the reason we have given before,[3] but the particular[4] is demonstrated

2. But the negative is.

3. In particulars the particular proposition alone is

[1] That is, hypothetically. As regards the concluding sentence of this chapter, I have followed Bekker, Buhle, and Taylor, in preference to Waitz and Averrois, since though I favour the grammatical construction of the two latter, the sense of the context is against them. [2] The major.

[3] Because the conclusion being assumed, and the minor of Festino or Baroko, both propositions are particular, hence there is no conclusion.

[4] The minor.

when the universal is affirmative. For let A be with every B, but not with every C, the conclusion that B is not with a certain C, if then B is assumed present with every A, but not with every C, A will not be with a certain C, the middle is B. But if the universal is negative, the proposition A C will not be demonstrated, A B being converted, for it will happen either that both[1] or that one[2] proposition will be negative, so that there will not be a syllogism. Still in the same manner there will be a demonstration, as in the case of universals, if A is assumed present with a certain one, with which B is not present.

demonstrated when the universal is affirmative.

2.

CHAP. VII.—*Of the same in the third Figure.*

IN the third figure, when both propositions are assumed universal, we cannot demonstrate reciprocally, for the universal is shown through universals, but the conclusion in this figure is always particular, so that it is clear that in short we cannot demonstrate an universal proposition by this figure. Still if one be universal and the other particular, there will be at one time and not at another (a reciprocal demonstration); when then both propositions are taken affirmative, and the universal belongs to the less extreme, there will be, but when to the other,[3] there will not be. For let A be with every C, but B with a certain (C), the conclusion A B, if then C is assumed present with every A, C has been shown to be with a certain B, but B has not been shown to be with a certain C. But it is necessary if C is with a certain B, that B should be with a certain C, but it is not the same thing, for *this* to be with that, and *that* with *this*, but it must be assumed that if *this* is present with a certain *that*, *that* also is with a certain *this*, and from this assumption there is no longer a syllogism from the conclusion and the other proposition. If

1. In this figure, when both propositions are universal there is no demonstration in a circle.

2. There will be demonstration where the minor is universal and the major particular.

1.

[1] If the conclusion is assumed and the major premise.

[2] If a negative conclusion is assumed, with a minor affirmative.

[3] When the major is universal and the minor particular there will not be a true circle, because from the conclusion and the major premise the minor is not proved.

2. however B is with every C, but A with a certain C, it will be possible to demonstrate A C, when C is assumed present with every B, but A with a certain (B). For if C is with every B, but A with a certain B, A must necessarily be with a certain C, the middle is B. And when one is affirmative, but the other negative, and the affirmative universal, the[1] other will be demonstrated; for let B be with every C, but A not be with a certain (C), the conclusion is, that A is not with a certain B. If then C be assumed besides present with every B, A must necessarily not be with a certain C, the middle is B. But when the negative is universal, the other is not demonstrated, unless as in former cases, if it should be assumed that the other is present with some individual, of what this is present with none, as if A is with no C, but B with a certain C, the conclusion is, that A is not with a certain B. If then C should be assumed present with some individual of that with every one of which A is not present, it is necessary that C should be with a certain B. We cannot however in any other way, converting the universal proposition, demonstrate the other, for there will by no means be a syllogism.[2]

3. When the affirmative is universal there is demonstration of the particular negative.

4. Not when the negative is universal (exception).

5. Recapitulation of the preceding chapters.

It appears then, that in the first figure there is a reciprocal demonstration effected through the third and through the first figure, for when the conclusion is affirmative, it is through the first, but when it is negative through the last,[3] for it is assumed that with what this* is present with none, the other† is present with every individual. In the middle figure however, the syllogism being uni-

* The predicate.

† The subject.

[1] The particular negative.

[2] Thus in Ferison, the minor, being I, cannot be demonstrated in a circle, the conclusion and major being negative, except by converting both these into affirmative. In the cases of the particular modes of the third figure, where there is an universal minor, i. e. Disamis and Bokardo, there may be a perfectly circular demonstration, but not in those which have the major universal, as Datisi and Ferison.

[3] Aristotle does not mean the third figure of categoricals, because in the syllogisms mentioned by him, there are a negative minor and an universal conclusion, contrary to the rules of the third figure. He intends therefore an hypothetical syllogism, wherein there are two predicates and one subject, as in the third figure.

versal, (the demonstration) is through it and through the first figure,[1] and when it is particular, both through it and through the last.[2] In the third all are through it, but it is also clear that in the third and in the middle the syllogisms, which are not produced through them, either are not according to a circular demonstration, or are imperfect.

Chap. VIII.—*Of Conversion of Syllogisms in the first Figure.*

1. Definition of conversion of syllogism (ἀντιστρέφειν).

Conversion is by transposition of the conclusion to produce a syllogism, either that the major is not with the middle, or this (the middle) is not with the last (the minor term).[3] For it is necessary when the conclusion is converted, and one proposition remains, that the other should be subverted, for if this (proposition) will be, the conclusion will also be.[4]

2. Difference whether this is done contradictorily or contrarily. The distinction between these shown.

But there is a difference whether we convert the conclusion contradictorily or contrarily, for there is not the same syllogism, whichever way the conclusion is converted, and this will appear from what follows. But I mean to be opposed (contradictorily) between, to every individual and not to every individual, and to a certain one and not to a certain one, and contrarily being present with every and being present with none, and with a certain one, not with a certain one.[5] 1. For let A be demonstrated of C, through the middle B; if then A is assumed present with no C, but with every B, B will be with no C, and if A is with no C, but B with every C, A will not be with every B, and not altogether with none, for the universal was not concluded through the last figure. In a word, we cannot subvert universally the major

[1] For the major of Cesare is proved in Celarent.

[2] For the minor of Ferison is proved hypothetically. See above.

[3] The minor term is here called τὸ τελευταῖον, lower down in this chapter it is called τὸ ἔσχατον. By transposition of the conclusion, is intended the change of it into its contradictory or contrary, when a proposition is enunciated, to which the other proposition is added, and thus a new syllogism in subverting the former is produced. Vide Whately and Hill's Logic.

[4] This has been shown above, that we cannot infer falsity from true premises; if then we admit the conclusion to be false, and take its opposite, one proposition must be false.

[5] i. e. these are *sub*-contraries.

premise by conversion, for it is always subverted through the third figure, but we must assume both propositions to the minor term, likewise also if the syllogism is negative. For let A be shown through B to be present with no C, wherefore if A is assumed present with every C,[1] but with no B, B will be with no C, and if A and B are with every C, A will be with a certain B, but it was present with none.[2]

2. If however the conclusion is converted contradictorily, the (other) syllogisms also will be contradictory,[3] and not universal, for one premise is particular, so that the conclusion will be particular. For let the syllogism be affirmative, and be thus converted, hence if A is not with every C, but with every B, B will not be with every C, and if A is not with every C, but B with every C, A will not be with every B. Likewise, if the syllogism be negative,* for if A is with a certain C,[4] but with no B, B will not be with a certain C, and not simply † with no C, and if A is with a certain C,[5] and B with every C, as was assumed at first,[6] A will be with a certain B.

* i. e. Celarent.

† Universally.

3. In particulars, of the first figure when the conclusion is converted contradictorily both propositions are subverted, if contrarily, neither.

In particular syllogisms, when the conclusion is converted contradictorily, both propositions are subverted, but when contrarily, neither of them; for it no longer happens, as with universals, that through failure of the conclusion[7] by conversion, a subversion is produced, since neither can we subvert it[8] at all. For let A be demonstrated of a certain C,‡ if therefore A is assumed present with no C,[9] but B with a certain C, A will not be with a certain B,[10] and if A

‡ Darii.

[1] i. e. by converse of the conclusion and assumption of the minor.

[2] By hypothesis in the major premise of Celarent.

[3] In their opposition, for they will prove a particular conclusion contradicting the previously assumed universal proposition.

[4] The subversion of the minor in Ferison.

[5] The subversion of the major in Disamis.

[6] In the minor proposition of Celarent.

[7] ἐλλείποντος τοῦ συμπεράσματος, deficiente conclusione. Buhle. This expression signifies the change from an universal to a particular in the conclusion, because in the latter case it comprehends fewer things.

[8] Because there is no syllogism from particular premises.

[9] The subversion of the minor in Camestres—while the major of the first syllogism is retained.

[10] The contradictory of the major will be concluded.

is with no C, but with every B, B will be with no C,[1] so that both propositions are subverted. If however the conclusion be converted contrarily, neither (is subverted), for if A is not with a certain C, but with every B, B will not be with a certain C, but the original proposition is not yet subverted,* for it may be present with a certain one, and not present with a certain one. Of the universal proposition A B there is not any syllogism at all,[2] for if A is not with a certain C, but is with a certain B, neither premise is universal. So also if the syllogism be negative, for if A should be assumed present with every C, both are subverted, but if with a certain C, neither; the demonstration however is the same.

2.

* Viz. the minor premise of Darii.

CHAP. IX.—*Of Conversion of Syllogisms in the second Figure.*

1. In universals we cannot infer the contrary to the major premise, but we may the contradictory—the minor dependent upon the assumption of the conclusion.

IN the second figure we cannot subvert the major premise contrarily, whichever way the conversion is made, since the conclusion will always be in the third figure, but there was not in this figure an universal syllogism. The other proposition indeed we shall subvert similarly to the conversion, I mean by similarly, if the conversion is made contrarily (we shall subvert it contrarily), but if contradictorily by contradiction. For let A[3] be with every B and with no C, the conclusion B C, if then B is assumed[4] present with every C, and the proposition A B remains, A will be with every C, for there is the first figure. If however B is[5] with every C, but A with no C, A is not with every B, the last figure. If then B C (the conclusion) be converted contradictorily, A B may be demonstrated similarly,[6] and A C contradictorily. For if B is with a certain C,[7] but A with no C, A will not be present with a certain B; again, if B[8] is with a certain C, but A

2.

[1] That is, by assuming a contradictory conclusion of the first syllogism, and retaining the major premise of the same, a conclusion will be drawn, contradictory of the minor.

[2] In which the major premise of Darii is subverted.

[3] This is in Camestres. [4] Barbara subverting the minor of Camestres.

[5] Felapton subverting the major of Camestres.

[6] i. e. subverted by a contrary.

[7] Darii subverting the minor. [8] Ferison subverting the major.

with every B, A is with a certain C, so that there is a syllogism produced contradictorily.[1] In like manner it can be shown, if the premises are vice versâ,[2] but if the syllogism is particular, the conclusion being converted contrarily, neither premise is subverted, as neither was it in the first figure, (if however the conclusion is) contradictorily (converted), both (are subverted). For let A be assumed present with no B, but with a (certain) C,[3] the conclusion B C; if then B is assumed present with a certain C, and A B remains, the conclusion will be that A is not present with a certain C, but the original would not be subverted, for it may and may not be present with a certain individual. Again, if B is with a certain C, and A with a certain C, there will not be a syllogism, for neither of the assumed premises is universal, wherefore A B is not subverted. If however the conversion is made contradictorily, both are subverted, since if B is with every C, but A with no B, A is with no C, it was however present with a certain (C).[3] Again, if B is with every C, but A with a certain C, A will be with a certain B, and there is the same demonstration, if the universal proposition be affirmative.

3.

2. In particulars, if the contrary of the conclusion is assumed, neither proposition is subverted; if the contradictory, both are.

CHAP. X.—*Of the same in the third Figure.*

IN the third figure, when the conclusion is converted contrarily, neither premise is subverted, according to any of the syllogisms, but when contradictorily, both are in all the modes. For let A be shown to be with a certain B, and let C be taken as the middle, and the premises be universal: if then A is assumed not present with a certain B, but B with every C, there is no syllogism of A and C,[4] nor if A is not present with a certain B, but with every C, will there be a syllogism of B and C.[5] There will also be a similar demonstration, if the premises

1. In this figure, if the contrary to the conclusion is assumed, neither premise is subverted, but if the contradictory, both.

1. Universals.

[1] Because Darii proves a contradictory conclusion to the minor, and Ferison a contradictory conclusion to the major—of the same Camestres.

[2] That is, if the major is negative, but the minor affirmative, hence a syllogism produced in Cesare.

[3] A was assumed present with a certain C, in the minor of Festino.

[4] Because the major is particular. [5] Because the major is particular.

are not universal, for either both must be particular by conversion, or the universal be joined to the minor, but thus there was not a syllogism neither in the first nor in the middle figure. If however they are converted contradictorily, both propositions are subverted; for if A is with no B, but B with every C, A will be with no C; again, if A is with no B, but with every C, B will be with no C. In like manner if one proposition is not universal; since if A is with no B, but B with a certain C, A will not be with a certain C, but if A is with no B, but with every C, B will be present with no C. So also if the syllogism be negative, for let A be shown not present with a certain B, and let the affirmative proposition be B C, but the negative A C, for thus there was a syllogism; when then the proposition is taken contrary to the conclusion, there will not be a syllogism. For if A were with a certain B, but B with every C, there was not a syllogism of A and C,*[1] nor if A were with a certain B, but with no C was there a syllogism of B and C,† so that the propositions are not subverted. When however the contradictory (of the conclusion is assumed) they are subverted. For if A is with every B, and B with C, A will be with every C, but it was with none.[2] Again if A ‡ is with every B, but with no C, B will be with no C, but it was with every C.[3] There is a similar demonstration also, if the propositions are not universal,§ for A C ‖ becomes universal negative, but the other,¶ particular affirmative. If then A is with every B, but B with a certain C, A happens to a certain C, but it was with none;[4] again, if A is with every B, but with no C,* B is with no C, but if A is with a certain B, and B with a certain C, there is no syllogism,[5] nor if A is with a certain B, but with no C, (will there thus be a syllogism):[6] Hence in that way,† but not in this,‡ the propositions are subverted.

2.

3.

* Vide ch. iv. b. i. Anal. Pr.

† Vide ch. v. b. i. Anal. Pr.

4.

‡ Camestres.

2. Particulars the same.

§ Ferison.

‖ The major prop.

¶ The minor pr

* Camestres.

† The contradictory.

‡ The contrary.

1 Because the major is particular.
2 So assumed in the major proposition of Felapton.
3 In the minor of Felapton.
4 In the major of Ferison.
5 Because of part. premises.
6 Because of the part. major.

3. Recapitulation.

From what has been said then it seems clear how, when the conclusion is converted, a syllogism arises in each figure, both when contrarily and when contradictorily to the proposition, and that in the first figure syllogisms are produced through the middle and the last, and the minor premise is always subverted through the middle (figure), but the major by the last (figure): in the second figure, however, through the first and the last, and the minor premise (is) always (subverted) through the first figure, but the major through the last: but in the third (figure) through the first and through the middle, and the major premise is always (subverted) through the first, but the minor premise through the middle (figure). What therefore conversion is, and how it is effected in each figure, also what syllogism is produced, has been shown.

CHAP. XI.—*Of Deduction to the Impossible in the first Figure.*

1. How syllogism διὰ τοῦ ἀδυνατοῦ is shown, and its distinction from conversion (ἀντιστροφή).

A SYLLOGISM through the impossible is shown, when the contradiction of the conclusion is laid down, and another proposition is assumed, and it is produced in all the figures, for it is like conversion except that it differs insomuch as that it is converted indeed, when a syllogism has been made, and both propositions have been assumed, but it is deduced to the impossible, when the opposite is not previously acknowledged but is manifestly true. Now the terms subsist similarly[1] in both, the assumption also of both is the same, as for instance, if A is present with every B, but the middle is C, if A is supposed present with every or with no B, but with every C, which was true, it is necessary that C should be with no or not with every B. But this is impossible, so that the supposition is false, wherefore the opposite[2] is true. It is a similar case with other figures, for whatever are capable of conversion, are also capable of the syllogism per impossibile.

2. The universal affirm. in the first figure not demonstra-

All other problems then are demonstrated through the impossible in all the figures, but the universal affirmative is demonstrated in the mid-

[1] That is to say, both in the converse syllogism and in that per impossibile.

[2] The contradictory.

dle, and in the third, but is not in the first. For let A be supposed not present with every B, or present with no B, and let the other proposition be assumed from either part, whether C is present with every A, or B with every D, for thus there will be the first figure. If then A is supposed not present with every B, there is no syllogism,[1] from whichever part the proposition is assumed, but if (it is supposed that A is present with) no (B), when the proposition B D is assumed, there will indeed be a syllogism of the false, but the thing proposed is not demonstrated. For if A is with no B, but B with every D, A will be with no D, but let this be impossible, therefore it is false that A is with no B. If however it is false that it is present with no B, it does not follow that it is true that it is present with every B. But if C A is assumed, there is no syllogism,[2] neither when A is supposed not present with every B, so that it is manifest that the being present with every, is not demonstrated in the first figure per impossibile. But to be present with a certain one, and with none, and not with every is demonstrated, for let A be supposed present with no B, but let B be assumed to be present with every or with a certain C, therefore is it necessary that A should be with no or not with every C, but this is impossible, for let this be true and manifest, that A is with every C, so that if this is false, it is necessary that A should be with a certain B. But if one proposition should be assumed to A,[3] there will not be a syllogism,[4] neither when the contrary to the conclusion is supposed as not to be with a certain one, wherefore it appears that the contradictory must be supposed. Again, let A be supposed present with a certain B, and C assumed present with every A, then it is necessary that C should be with a certain B, but let this be impossible, hence the hypothesis is false, and if this be the case, that A is present with no B is true.

ble per impossibile.

3. But the par. affir. and univ. nega. may be demonstrated, when the contradictory of the conclusion is assumed.

[1] Because of a particular nega. prem. being inadmissible in the first fig.

[2] Because from the hypothesis being negative it cannot be the minor in the first fig.

[3] So that it becomes the major.

[4] Because the negative hypothesis becomes the minor prem. contrary to the rule.

In like manner, if C A is assumed negative; if however the proposition be assumed to B, there will not be a syllogism, but if the contrary be supposed, there will be a syllogism, and the impossibile (demonstration), but what was proposed will not be proved. For let A be supposed present with every B, and let C be assumed present with every A, then it is necessary that C should be with every B, but this is impossible, so that it is false that A is with every B, but it is not yet necessary that if it is not present with every, it is present with no B. The same will happen also if the other proposition[1] is assumed to B, for there will be a syllogism, and the impossible (will be proved), but the hypothesis is not subverted, so that the contradictory must be supposed. In order however to prove that A is not present with every B, it must be supposed present with every B, for if A is present with every B, and C with every A, C will be with every B, so that if this impossible, the hypothesis is false. In the same manner, if the other proposition is assumed to B,[2] also if C A is negative in the same way, for thus there is a syllogism, but if the negative be applied to B, there is no demonstration. If however it should be supposed not present with every, but with some one, there is no demonstration that it is not present with every, but that it is present with none, for if A is with a certain B, but C with every A, C will be with a certain B, if then this is impossible it is false that A is present with a certain B, so that it is true that it is present with none. This however being demonstrated, what is true is subverted besides, for A was present with a certain B, and with a certain one was not present. Moreover, the impossibile does not result from the hypothesis, for it would be false, since we cannot conclude the false from the true, but now it is true, for A is with a certain B, so that it must not be supposed present with a certain, but with every B. The like also will occur, if we should show that A is not present with a certain B, since if it is the same thing not to be with a certain individual, and to be not with every, there is the same demonstration of both.

4. Also the par. neg. is demonstrated, but if the sub-contrary to the conclusion is assumed, what was proposed is subverted.

[1] A proposition evidently true.
[2] If the true proposition becomes the minor.

5. Summary and reason of the above assumption.

It appears then, that not the contrary, but the contradictory must be supposed in all syllogisms,[1] for thus there will be a necessary (consequence), and a probable axiom,[2] for if of every thing affirmation or negation (is true), when it is shown that negation is not, affirmation must necessarily be true. Again, except it is admitted that affirmation is true, it is fitting to admit negation; but it is in neither way fitting to admit the contrary, for neither, if the being present with no one is false, is the being present with every one necessarily true, nor is it probable that if the one is false the other is true.

It is palpable, therefore, that in the first figure, all other problems are demonstrated through the impossible; but that the universal affirmative is not demonstrated.

CHAP. XII.—*Of the same in the second Figure.*

1. In the second figure A is proved per absurdum, if the contradictory is assumed, not if the contrary.

IN the middle, however, and last figure, this[3] also is demonstrated. For let A be supposed not present with every B, but let A be supposed present with every C, therefore if it is not present with every B, but is with every C, C is not with every B, but this is impossible, for let it be manifest that C is with every B, wherefore what was supposed is false, and the being present with every individual is true. If however the contrary be supposed, there will be a syllogism, and the impossible, yet the proposition is not demonstrated. For if A is present with no B, but with every C, C will be with no B, but this is impossible, hence that A 1.

[1] Leading to the impossible. Taylor gives rise to much confusion, by using the word opposite as antithetical to contrary, instead of the word contradictory.

[2] ἀξίωμα ἔνδοξον—dignitas probabilis, Averr.—axioma rationi consentaneum, Buhle; the latter notes, that Aristotle refers to the principle, that of two contradictories, one is true and the other false, from which it follows that when the contradictory of the first conclusion is proved false, the original conclusion itself is proved true. As to the words themselves, it may be sufficient to remark, that ἀξιώματα are the original premises, from which demonstration proceeds, and are a branch of the κοιναί 'Αρχαί; and that taken purely, per se, Aristotle regards τὰ ἐνδόξα as among the elements of syllogism, some of which are necessary. See also Waitz, vol. i. p. 505.

[3] An universal affirmative.

is with no B is false. Still it does not follow, that if this is false, the being present with every B is true, but when A is

2. with a certain B, let A be supposed present with no B, but with every C, therefore it is necessary that C should be with no B, so that if this is impossible A must necessarily be present with a certain B. Still if it* is supposed not present with a certain one,† there will be the same[1] as in the first figure. Again, let A be supposed present with a certain B, but let it be with no C, it is necessary then that C should not be with a certain B, but it was with every, so that the supposition is false, A then will be with no B.

* A.

† B.

3. When however A is not with every B, let it be supposed present with every B, but with no C, therefore it is necessary that C should be with no B, and this is impossible, wherefore it is true that A is not with every B. Evidently then all syllogisms are produced through the middle figure.[2]

CHAP. XIII.—*Of the same in the third Figure.*

1. In this figure both affirmatives and negatives are demonstrable per absurdum.

THROUGH the last figure also, (it will be concluded) in a similar way. For let A be supposed not present with a certain B, but C present with every B, A then is not with a certain C, and if this is impossible, it is false that A is not with a certain B, wherefore that it is present with every B is true. If, again, it should be supposed present with none, there will be a syllogism, and the impossible, but the proposition is not proved, for if the contrary is supposed there will be the same[3] as in the former (syllogisms). But in order to conclude that it is present with a certain one, this hypothesis must be assumed, for if A is with no B, but C with a certain B, A will not be with every C, if then this is false, it is true that A is with a certain B. But when A is with no B, let it be supposed present with a certain one, and let C be assumed present with every B, wherefore it is necessary that A should be with a certain C, but it was with no C, so that it is false that A is with a certain B. If however A is supposed

[1] The proposition will not be so much confirmed as subverted, for if O is false, A is true, and vice versâ. [2] By a deduction to an absurdity.
[3] A will not be demonstrated universal, but particular.

present with every B, the proposition is not demonstrated,[1] but in order to its not being present with every, this hypothesis must be taken.[2] For if A is with every B, and C with a certain B, A is with a certain C, but this was not so, hence it is false that it is with every one, and if thus, it is true that it is not with every B, and if it is supposed present with a certain B, there will be the same things as in the syllogisms above mentioned.

2. Recapitulation.

It appears then that in all syllogisms through the impossible the contradictory must be supposed, and it is apparent that in the middle figure the affirmative is in a certain way[3] demonstrated, and the universal in the last figure.

Chap. XIV.—*Of the difference between the Ostensive, and the Deduction to the Impossible.*[4]

1. Difference between direct demonstration and that per impossibile.

A demonstration to the impossible differs from an ostensive, in that it admits what it wishes to subvert, leading to an acknowledged falsehood, but the ostensive commences from confessed theses. Both therefore assume two allowed propositions, but the one[5] assumes those from which the syllogism is formed, and the other[6] one of these, and the contradictory of the conclusion. In the one case* also the conclusion need not be known, nor previously assumed that it is, or that it is not, but in the other it is necessary[7] (previously to assume) that it is not; it is of no consequence however whether the conclusion is affirmative or

* The ostensive.

[1] Because if A is with every B is false, that A is with no B is not immediately true, but only the particular negative is true.

[2] A, i. e. the hypothesis of being universally present.

[3] By a deduction to an absurdity.

[4] Compare Prior Anal. i. 23; Hessey's Logical Tables, No. 4; Whately's Treatise on Rhetoric, part i. c. 3; Rhetoric, xi. 22. It is clear from the remark in the text, that the demonstration per impossibile is one kind of the hypothetical syllogism, the object of which is to prove the truth of a problem, by inferring a falsity from its contradiction being assumed. (Vide An. i. 23, and 29; also Waitz, vol. i. p. 430.) The reader will find the question fully discussed in note G, Appendix to Mitchell's Logic.

[5] The ostensive.

[6] The per impossibile.

[7] i. e. we must assume the contradictory of the conclusion, to be proved.

negative, but it will happen the same about both.[1] Now whatever is concluded ostensively can also be proved per impossibile, and what is concluded per impossibile may be shown ostensively through the same terms, but not in the same figures.

2. What is demonstrated per absurdum in the first figure, is proved in the second, ostensively, if the problem be negative, and in the third figure if it be affirmative.

For when the syllogism[2] is in the first figure,[3] the truth will be in the middle, or in the last, the negative indeed in the middle, but the affirmative in the last. When however the syllogism is in the middle figure,[4] the truth will be in the first in all the problems, but when the syllogism is in the last, the truth will be in the first and in the middle, affirmatives in the first, but negatives in the middle. For let it be demonstrated through the first figure* that A is present with no, or not with every B, the hypothesis then was that A is with a certain B, but C was assumed present with every A, but with no B, for thus there was a syllogism, and also the impossible. But this is the middle figure, if C is with every A, but with no B, and it is evident from these that A is with no B. Likewise if it has been demonstrated to be not with every,† for the hypothesis is that it is with every, but C was assumed present with every A, but not with every B. Also in a similar manner if C A were assumed negative, for thus also there is the middle figure.‡ Again, let A be shown present with a certain B,§ the hypothesis then is, that it is present with none, but B was assumed to be with every C, and A to be with every or with a certain C, for thus (the conclusion) will be impossible, but this is the last figure, if A and B‖ are with every C. From these then it appears that A must necessarily be with a certain B, and similarly if B or A is assumed present with a certain C.

1. * Darii.

2. † Barbara.

3. ‡ Cesare or Festino.

4. § In Celarent.

5. ‖ Darapti.

Again, let it be shown in the middle figure¶ that A is with every B, then the hypothesis was that A is not with every B, but A was assumed present with

6. ¶ Baroko.

[1] The conclusion is called negative when it is false, whether it affirms or denies, hence if it affirm a falsity, it is said "not to be," and when it denies a truth, it is equally said "not to be." Waitz omits "not" in the same figures; I read with Bekker, Buhle, and Taylor.

[2] Per impossibile. [3] The thing proposed will be proved.—Taylor.

[4] Sometimes also in the 3rd, in fact what Arist. here states are the principal modes of demonstration, and are not to be too generally assumed.

every C, and C with every B, for thus there will be the impossible. And this is the first figure,* if A is 7. * Barbara.
with every C, and C with every B. Likewise if
it is demonstrated to be present with a certain one,† 8. † Camestres.
for the hypothesis was that A was with no B, but A was assumed present with every C, and C with a certain B, but if
the syllogism ‡ should be negative,[1] the hypothesis 9. ‡ Festino, inferring the impossible.
was that A is with a certain B, for A was assumed
to be with no C, and C with every B, so that
there is the first figure. Also if in like manner the syllogism § is not universal, but A is demonstrated not
to be with a certain B,‖ for the hypothesis was § per impossibile.
that A is with every B, but A was assumed present 10. ‖ in Cesare.
with no C, and C with a certain B, for thus there ¶ Ferio.
is the first figure.¶

Again, in the third figure,* let A be shown to 11. * Bokardo.
be with every B, therefore the hypothesis was
that A is not with every B, but C has been assumed to be with every B, and A with every C, for thus there will be the
impossible, but this is the first figure.† Likewise † Barbara.
also, if the demonstration is in a certain thing,[2]‡ ‡ In Ferison.
for the hypothesis would be that A is with no B,
but C has been assumed present with a certain B, and A with
every C, but if the syllogism is negative,§ the hypothesis § Disamis.
pothesis is that A is with a certain B, but C has
been assumed present with no A, but with every B, and this is the middle figure. In like manner also,[3] if the demonstration is not‖ universal, since the hypothesis will
be that A is with every B, and C has been as- ‖ In Datisi.
sumed present with no A, but with a certain B, ¶ Festino.
and this is the middle figure.¶

It is evident then that we may demonstrate 3. What is demonstrable per absurdum is so also ostensive-
each of the problems through the same terms, both
ostensively[4] and through the impossible, and in

[1] If it should prove a conclusion in E, which contradicts the minor of Festino.

[2] This will prove a conclusion in I.

[3] If the syllogism per impossibile in Datisi should prove O.

[4] Buhle, Bekker, and Taylor insert "and through the impossible," which Waitz omits. It may be remarked, that though in some cases the demonstration per impossibile is advantageous, yet that it is more open to fallacy, especially to that of "a non-causa pro causa," a deception

ly, and vice versâ.

like manner it will be possible when the syllogisms are ostensive, to deduce to the impossible in the assumed terms when the proposition is taken contradictory to the conclusion. For the same syllogisms arise as those through conversion, so that we have forthwith figures through which each (problem) will be (concluded). It is clear then that every problem is demonstrated by both modes, (viz.) by the impossible and ostensively, and we cannot possibly separate the one from the other.

Chap. XV.—*Of the Method of concluding from Opposites in the several Figures.*

1. Of the various figures from which a syllogism is deducible from opposite propositions, the latter (κατα τὴν λεξιν) of four kinds, (cf. Herm. 7,) but κατὰ τὴν ἀληθειαν, of three.

In what figure then we may, and in what we may not, syllogize from opposite propositions[1] will be manifest thus, and I say that opposite propositions are according to diction four, as for instance (to be present) with every (is opposed) to (to be present) with none; and (to be present) with every to (to be present) not with every; and (to be present) with a certain one to (to be present with) no one; and (to be present with) a certain one to (to be present) not with a certain one; in truth however they are three, for (to be present) with a certain one

which is very frequent in dialectical disputation when the opponent is asked to grant certain premises. Vide the 17th ch. of this book, also Rhet. ii. 24.

[1] ἀντικειμέναι πρότασεις, is an expression sometimes limited to contradictories, the κατὰ τὴν λέξιν, opposition is properly subcontrary: that of subalterns is not recognised by Aristotle (ὑπάλληλοι); the laws of this last are first given by Apuleius de Dogmate Plat. lib. iii. anonymously; also by Marcian Capella. Vide Whately's and Hill's Logic. Taylor, from his extreme fondness for the expression "opposites," certainly does not "what is dark in this, illumine, nor what is low, raise and support."

Ex. 1. Every science is excellent
No science is excellent
∴ No science is science.

Ex. 2. Every science is excellent
No medicine (a certain science) is excellent
∴ No medicine (a certain science) is science.

Ex. 3. No science is opinion
All medicine (a certain science) is opinion
∴ No medicine (a certain science) is science.

is opposed to (being present) not with a certain one according to expression only. But of these I call such contraries as are universal, viz. the being present with every, and (the being present) with none, as for instance, that every science is excellent to no science is excellent, but I call the others contradictories.

2. No conclusion from opposites of either kind in the first figure.

In the first figure then there is no syllogism from contradictory propositions, neither affirmative nor negative; not affirmative, because it is necessary that both propositions should be affirmative, but affirmation and negation are contradictories: nor negative, because contradictories affirm and deny the same thing of the same,* but the middle in the first figure is not predicated of both (extremes), but one thing is denied of it, and it is predicated of another; these propositions however are not contradictory.

* Vide Aldrich's Logic, ch. ii. sect. 4. Soph. Elench. v. 5.

3. But from both in the second.

But in the middle figure it is possible to produce a syllogism both from contradictories and from contraries, for let A be good, but science B and C; if then any one assumed that every science is excellent, and also that no science is, A will be with every B, and with no C, so that B will be with no C, no science therefore † is science. It will be the same also, if, having assumed that every science is excellent, it should be assumed that medicine is not excellent, for A is with every B, but with no C, so that a certain science will not be science.‡ Likewise if A is with every C, but with no B, and B is science, C medicine, A opinion, for assuming that no science is opinion, a person would have assumed a certain science to be opinion.§ This[1] however differs from the former[2] in the conversion of the terms, for before the affirmative was joined to B,[3] but now it is to C.‖ Also in a similar manner, if one premise is not universal, for it is always the middle which is predicated negatively of the one and affirmatively of the other. Hence it happens that contradictories are

† Example (1.)

‡ Example (2.)

§ Example (3.)

‖ The minor.

[1] Cesare. [2] Camestres.
[3] That is, in Camestres the major of course was affirmative, the minor negative.

concluded, yet not always, nor entirely, but when those which are under the middle* so subsist as either to be the same, or as a whole to a part:[1] otherwise it is impossible, for the propositions will by no means be either contrary or contradictory.

* i. e. the extremes, being subject to the middle in 2nd figure.

4. In the third no affirmative is deduced.

In the third figure there will never be an affirmative syllogism from opposite propositions, for the reason alleged in the first figure; but there will be a negative, both when the terms are and are not universal. For let science be B and C, and medicine A, if then a person assumes that all medicine is science, and that no medicine is science, he would assume B present with every A, and C with no A, so that a certain science will not be science.† Likewise, if the proposition A B is not taken as universal, for if a certain medicine is science, and again no medicine is science, it results that a certain science is not science.‡ But the propositions are contrary, the terms being universally taken,[2] if however one of them is particular,[3] they are contradictory.

† Example (4.)

‡ Example (5.)

We must however understand that it is possible thus to assume opposites as we have said, that every science is good, and again, that no science is good, or that a certain science is not good, which does not usually lie concealed. It is also possible to conclude either (of the opposites), through other interrogations, or as we have observed in the Topics,§ to assume it. Since however the oppositions of affirmations are three, it results that we may take opposites in six ways, either with every and with none, or with every and not with every individual, or with a certain and with no one; and to convert

§ Top. book viii. ch. 1.

5. Opposition six-fold.

[1] As genus to species—thus science is related to medicine.

Ex. 4. No medicine is science
All medicine is science
.·. A certain science is not science.

A B
Ex. 5. A certain medicine is not science.
A C
All medicine is science
C B
.·. A certain science is not science.

[2] In Felapton. [3] In Bokardo.

this in the terms, thus A (may be) with every B but with no C, or with every C and with no B, or with the whole of the one, but not with the whole of the other; and again, we may convert this as to the terms. It will be the same also in the third figure, so that it is clear in how many ways and in what figures it is possible for a syllogism to arise through opposite propositions.

But it is also manifest that we may infer a true conclusion from false premises, as we have observed* before, but from opposites we cannot, for a syllogism always arises contrary to the fact, as if a thing is good, (the conclusion will be,) that it is not good, or if it is an animal, that it is not an animal, because the syllogism is from contradiction, and the subject terms are either the same, or the one is a whole,† but the other a part.‡ It appears also evident, that in paralogisms[1] there is nothing to prevent a contradiction of the hypothesis arising, as if a thing is an odd number, that it is not odd, for from opposite propositions there was a contrary syllogism; if then one assumes such, there will be a contradiction of the hypothesis. We must understand, however, that we cannot so conclude contraries from one syllogism, as that the conclusion may be that what is not good is good, or any thing of this kind, unless such a proposition is immediately assumed,[2] as that every animal is white and not white, and that man is an animal.[3] But we must either presume contradiction,[4] as that all science is opinion,[5] and is not opinion, and afterwards assume that medicine is a science indeed, but is no opinion, just as Elenchi[6] are produced, or (conclude) from two syllo-

* Vide this book, chapters 2, 3, and 4.

6. No true conclusion deducible from such propositions.

† Genus.

‡ Species.

7. From contradictories a contradiction to the assumption is inferred.

8. To infer contradiction in the conclusion, we must have contradiction in the premises. (Vide Whately, b. ii. c. 2 and 3.)

[1] All reasoning from opposites is faulty, because one proposition is necessarily false.

[2] A proposition opposed.

[3] The minor; the conclusion will be, man is white and not white.

[4] That is, at first suppose an axiom contradictory of subsequent conclusion, e. g. all science is opinion.

[5] This clause is omitted by Waitz, it is the conclusion contradicting the hypothesis.

[6] In the 20th chapter of this book, an Elenchus is defined to be a syllogism of contradiction, or (b. i. c. 1, Soph. Elen.) "a syllogism with con-

gisms.[1] Wherefore, that the things assumed should really be contrary, is impossible in any other way than this, as was before observed.

* De impotentiis syllogisticis. (Averrois.)

CHAP. XVI.—*Of the "Petitio Principii," or Begging the Question.*[2] *

1. What the "petitio principii" is—τὸ ἐν ἀρχῇ αἰτεισθαι.

To beg and assume the original (question) consists, (to take the genus of it,) in not demonstrating the proposition, and this happens in many ways, whether a person does not conclude at all, or whether he does so through things more unknown, or equally unknown, or whether (he concludes) what is prior through what is posterior; for demonstration is from things more creditable and prior.† Now of these there is no begging the question from the beginning, but since some things are naturally adapted to be known through themselves, and some through other things, (for principles[3] are known through themselves, but what are under principles‡ through other things,) when a person endeavours to demonstrate by itself what cannot be known by itself, then he begs the original question. It is possible however to do this so as immediately to take the thing proposed for granted, and it is

† Vide Post. An. b. i. ch. 2, 10, 32.

‡ Conclusions.

2. How this fallacy is effected. See Hill's Logic, p. 331, et seq. Rhet. ii. 24.

tradiction of the conclusion," "proprie syllogismus est adversarium redarguens, confirmando scil. quod illius sententiæ contradicat." Aldrich. It is well observed by Dr. Hessey, that the ἐλεγκτικὸν ἐνθύμημα of the Rhetoric seems to include the two processes, ἡ εἰς τὸ ἀδυν. ἀπαγωγή and συλλογις. διὰ τοῦ ἀδυν., An. Pr. i. 38, and to correspond to the εἰς τὸ ἀδυν. ἂγουσα ἀποδείξις, An. Post. i. 26. Vide Hessey's Tables, 4, Rhet. ii. 22, and ii. 24.

[1] Proving affirmation in one, and negation in the other.

[2] This takes place when one of the premises (whether true or false) is either plainly equivalent to the conclusion, or depends on that for its own reception. The most plausible form of this fallacy is arguing in a *circle*, (vide supra,) and the *greater* the circle, the harder to detect. Whately, b. iii. sect. 4. Aristotle enumerates five kinds of it, these however do not concur with those given by Aldrich in his Fallaciæ extra dictionem. As to the identity of the syllogism with a petitio principii, see Mansel's Logic, Appendix, note D. Conf. Top. 8; also Pacius upon this chap.

[3] These precede all demonstration: for their relative position refer to note p. 81; also Meta. v. 1, x. 7, vi. 4, and Sir W. Hamilton Reid's Works, p. 16.

also possible, that passing to other things which are naturally adapted to be demonstrated by that (which was to be investigated), to demonstrate by these the original proposition; as if a person should demonstrate A through B, and B through C, while C was naturally adapted to be proved through A, for it happens that those who thus syllogize, prove A by itself. This they do,[1] who fancy that they describe parallel lines, for they deceive themselves by assuming such things as they cannot demonstrate unless they are parallel. Hence it occurs to those who thus syllogize to say that each thing is, if it is, and thus every thing will be known through itself, which is impossible.

2. Example given of mathematicians.

If then a man, when it is not proved that A is with C, and likewise with B, begs that A may be admitted present with B, it is not yet evident whether he begs the original proposition, but that he does not prove it is clear, for what is similarly doubtful is not the principle of demonstration. If however B so subsists in reference to C as to be the same,[2] or that they are evidently convertible, or that one is present with the other,[3] then he begs the original question. For that A is with B, may be shown through them, if they are converted, but now[4] this prevents[5] it, yet not the mode; if however it should do this,* it would produce what has been mentioned before,† and a conversion would be made through three terms.[6] In like manner if any one should take B to be present with C, whilst it is equally doubtful if he assumes A also (present with C), he

3.

4.

* i. e. convert the minor, and prove A of B through C.

5. † Beg the question.

[1] Those beg the question who endeavour to show that certain lines are parallel because they never meet, for they ought to prove that equi-distant lines do not meet; so that it is tantamount merely to saying that lines are equi-distant because they are equi-distant, and they prove the same thing by the same, and beg the question.

[2] The same in reality, as a vestment and a garment. Taylor.

[3] B predicated of C, as genus of species.

[4] i. e. when this is done, viz. B predicated thus of C.

[5] That is, B being of wider extension than A, prevents the demonstrating A of B through C, though the syllogistic mode does not prevent conversion taking place, but rather favours it, since it is Barbara, wherein alone a perfect circle is produced by this kind of conversion.

[6] Not always really three, but sometimes one term is assumed for two, and therefore in one respect there are three terms.

does not yet beg the question, but he does not prove it. If however A and B should be the same, or should be converted, or A should follow B, he begs the question from the beginning for the same reason, for what the petitio principii can effect we have shown before, viz. to demonstrate a thing by itself which is not of itself manifest.

3. This fallacy may occur in both the 2nd and 3rd figures, but in the case of an affirmative syllogism by the 3rd and first.

If then the petitio principii is to prove by itself what is not of itself manifest, this is not to prove, since both what is demonstrated and that by which the person demonstrates are alike dubious, either [1] because the same things are assumed present with the same thing, or the same thing with the same things;[2] in the middle figure, and also in the third, the original question may be the objects of petition, but in the affirmative syllogism, in the third and first figure.[3] Negatively when the same things are absent from the same, and both propositions are not alike,[4] (there is the same result also in the middle figure,) because of the non-conversion of the terms in negative syllogisms.[5] A petitio principii however occurs in demonstrations, as to things which thus exist in truth, but in dialectics as to those (which so subsist) according to opinion.

[1] i. e. when A and B are the same, thus A is said to be with C in the conclusion, but B with C in the minor, and in Barbara.

[2] i. e. when B and C are the same with which in Barbara A is present, the latter being predicated of B in the major, and of C in the conclusion.

[3] Because there is no affirmative syllogism in the 2nd figure.

[4] A petitio principii can only occur in an affirmative proposition.

[5] i. e. the terms of a negative proposition, being different in signification, cannot be converted, which would be necessary if a petitio principii could occur in an affirmative proposition. For whenever this fallacy occurs in the other proposition, the subject and attribute should be identical, or nearly so. After all, it must be remembered that the Pet. Prin. is a material, and non-logical, not a formal fallacy.

CHAP. XVII.—*A Consideration of the Syllogism, in which it is argued, that the false does not happen—"an account of this,"* παρὰ τοῦτο συμβαίνειν, τὸ ψεῦδος.[1]

1. This happens in a deduction to the impossible, which is contradicted not in ostensive demonstration.

THAT the false does not happen on account of this (which we are accustomed to say frequently in discussion) occurs first in syllogisms leading to the impossible, when a person contradicts that which was demonstrated by a deduction to the impossible. For neither will he who does not contradict assert that it is not (false) on this account, but that something false was laid down before;[2] nor in the ostensive (proof), since he does not lay down a contradiction. Moreover when any thing is ostensively subverted through A B C,* we cannot say that a syllogism is produced not on account of what is laid down, for we then say *that* is not produced on account *of this*, when *this* being subverted, the syllogism is nevertheless completed, which is not the case in ostensive syllogisms, since the thesis being subverted the syllogism which belongs to it will no longer subsist. It is evident then that in syllogisms leading to the impossible, the assertion, "not on account of this," is made, and when the original hypothesis so subsists in reference to the impossible as that both when it is, and when it is not, the impossible will nevertheless occur.

* i. e. ostensively through those terms.

2. The perfect example of this is when the prop. of which the syllo. consists do not concur.

Hence the clearest mode of the false not subsisting on account of the hypothesis, is when the syllogism leading to the impossible[3] does not conjoin with the hypothesis by its media, as we have observed in the † Topics. For this is to assume as a cause, what is not a cause, as if any one wishing to show that the diameter of a square is incom-

† Sop. Elen. ch. v.

[1] "Non penes hoc." Averr.—"non per hoc." Waitz. Confer. Sop. Elen. v. 11, 29, 1; Rhet. ii. 24; Whately, iii. 3 and 4; Hill's ed. Aldrich, p. 336.

[2] Viz. of the propositions anterior to the conclusion. He also who uses an ostensive proof, of course does not adduce a proposition contradictory of what he wishes to prove.

[3] Taylor translates this passage somewhat differently, but I prefer the rendering of Buhle. Aristotle joins the Sop. Elen. with the Topics, because the former contain sophistical, as the other dialectic, places.—Note Julius Pacius.

mensurate with its side should endeavour to prove the argument of Zeno,* that motion has no existence, and to this should deduce the impossible, for the false is by no means whatever connected with what was stated from the first.[1] There is however another mode, if the impossible should be connected with the hypothesis, yet it does not happen on account of that, for this may occur, whether we assume the connexion up or down, as if A is placed present with B, B with C, and C with D, but this should be false, that B is with D. For if A being subverted B is nevertheless with C, and C with D, there will not be the false from the primary hypothesis. Or again, if a person should take the connexion upward, as if A should be with B, E with A, and F with E, but it should be false that F is with A, for thus there will be no less the impossible, when the primary hypothesis is subverted. It is necessary however to unite the impossible with the terms (assumed) from the beginning, for thus it will be on account of the hypothesis ;† as to a person taking the connexion downward, (it ought to be connected) with the affirmative term ; for if it is impossible that A should be with D, when A is removed there will no longer be the false. But (the connexion being assumed) in an upward direction, (it should be joined) with the subject, for if F cannot be with B, when B is subverted, there will no longer be the impossible, the same also occurs when the syllogisms are negative.

* Sop. Elen. x. 2, 33, 4.

3. Another mode.

2.

4. Necessity of connecting the impossible with the terms assumed from the first.

† i. e. the impossible will be deduced.

It appears then that if the impossible is not connected with the original terms, the false does not happen on account of the thesis, or is it that neither thus will the false occur always on account of the hypothesis? For if A is placed present not with B but with K, and K with C, and this with D, thus also the impossible remains ; and in like manner when we take the terms in an upward direction, so that since the impossible happens whether this is or this is not, it will not be on account

[1] That the diameter of a square is not commensurable with its side. Upon the argument called Achilles, which Zeno used to support the leading tenet of Parmenides, viz. the unity of all things ; a sophism which after all turns upon the falsity of the major premise. See Plato, Parm. 128, Cousin, Nouv. Frag., and Mansel, p. 125. Ar. Phys. lib. vi.

of the position.* Or if this is not, the false nevertheless arises; it must not be so assumed, as if the impossible will happen from something else being laid down, but when this being subverted, the same impossible is concluded through the remaining propositions, since perhaps there is no absurdity in inferring the false through several hypotheses, as that parallel lines meet,[1] both whether the internal angle is greater than the external, or whether a triangle has more than two right angles.

* i. e. the hypothesis.

5. This not to be employed as if a deduction to the impossible arises from other terms.

CHAP. XVIII.—*Of false Reasoning.*

FALSE reasoning arises from what is primarily false. For every syllogism consists of two or more propositions, if then it consists of two, it is necessary that one or both of these should be false, for there would not be a false syllogism from true propositions.† But if of more than two, as if C (is proved) through A B, and these through D E F G, some one of the above[2] is false, and on this account the reasoning also, since A and B are concluded through them. Hence through some one of them the conclusion and the false occur.[3]

1. False conclusion arises from error in the primary propositions.

† Vide this book, chap. 2—4.

CHAP. XIX.—*Of the Prevention of a Catasyllogism.*[4]

To prevent a syllogistical conclusion being adduced against us, we must observe narrowly when (our opponent) questions the argument[5] without conclusions, lest the same thing should be twice granted in the propositions, since we know that

1. Rule to prevent the advancement of a catasyllogism is to watch against the same term

[1] This is a false conclusion from two false hypotheses; the one, that when a line falls on two parallel lines the internal angle is greater than the external angle; the other is, if a triangle has three angles greater than two right angles.

[2] i. e. D E F G.

[3] i. e. the false conclusion C. Vide Aldrich and Huyshe for the rules of syllogism.

[4] καρασυλλογίζεσθαι vox dialectica, disputationum et interrogationum laqueis aliquem irretire. Waitz.

[5] i. e. the propositional matter.

being twice admitted in the prop.

a syllogism is not produced without a middle, but the middle is that of which we have frequently spoken. But in what manner it is necessary to observe the middle in regard to each conclusion, is clear from our knowing what kind of thing is proved in each figure, and this will not escape us in consequence of knowing how we sustain the argument.[1]

2. Necessity and method of masking our design in argument—two ways of effecting this.

Still it is requisite, when we argue, that we should endeavour to conceal that which we direct the respondent to guard against,[2] and this will be done, first, if the conclusions are not pre-syllogized, but are unknown when necessary propositions are assumed, and again, if a person does not question those things which are proximate, but such as are especially immediate,* for instance, let it be requisite to conclude A of F, and let the media be B C D E; therefore we must question whether A is with B, and again, not whether B is with C, but whether D is with E, and afterwards whether B is with C, and so of the rest. If also the syllogism arises through one middle, we must begin with the middle, for thus especially we may deceive the respondent.

* Vide Mansel's Logic.

CHAP. XX.—*Of the Elenchus.*[3]

1. The elenchus (redargutio) is a syllo-

SINCE however we have when, and from what manner of terminal subsistence syllogism is produced, it

[1] We shall know the principal conclusion, as being the subject matter of our dispute.

[2] i. e. if we wish to infer an indefinite conclusion, we should secretly endeavour that our opponent may grant us two propositions, in which the middle is latent; if however we wish to infer a definite conclusion, we must assume propositions containing the middle from which the conclusion is inferred mediately and remotely. Taylor, from whom the above note is chiefly taken, appears to have fallen into the same error as Buhle, Boeth, and some of the older interpreters, by reading *μέσα* instead of *ἄμεσα*, which I have followed from Waitz and Averrois, and which the former evidently proves to be the right reading. Vide Waitz, tom. i. p. 521; Aver. vol. i. p. 159; Top. 8. *Immediate* inference is that with which opposition and conversion are connected; *mediate* pertains to induction and syllogism.

[3] An *ἐπιχείρημα* admits of a species of this, which is called *ἀπόρημα* The original meaning of *ἔλεγχος* is, as Dr. Hessey observes, (Table 4,) the refutation of an *actual* adversary's position, and so indirectly a con-

is also clear when there will and will not be an Elenchus. For all things being granted, or the answers being arranged alternately, for instance, the one being negative and the other affirmative, an elenchus may be produced, since there was a syllogism when the terms were as well in this as in that way, so that if what is laid down should be contrary to the conclusion, it is necessary that an elenchus should be produced, for an elenchus is a syllogism of contradiction. If however nothing is granted, it is impossible that there should be an elenchus, for there was not a syllogism when all the terms are negative, so that there will neither be an elenchus, for if there is an elenchus, it is necessary there should be a syllogism, but if there is a syllogism, it is not necessary there should be an elenchus. Likewise, if nothing should be universally laid down in the answer,* for the determination of the elenchus and of the syllogism will be the same.[1]

gism of contradiction, to produce which there must be a syllogism—though the latter may subsist without the former. (Conf. Sop. Elen. 6.)

* i. e. if the respondent should not concede any universal proposition.

Chap. XXI.—*Of Deception, as to Supposition—κατὰ τὴν ὑπόληψιν.*[2]

Conf. Meta. lib. vi. and iii., and de Animâ, iii. 3, 7.

Sometimes it happens, that as we are deceived in the position of the terms,† so also deception arises as to opinion, for example, if the same thing happens to be present with many things primary,[3] and a person should be ignorant of one, and think that it is present with nothing, but should know the other. For let A be present with B and with C, per se, (that is, essentially,) and let these, in like manner, be with every D; if then somebody thinks that A is with every B, and this with every D, but A with no C, and this with every D; he will have knowledge‡ and ignorance § of the same thing,|| as to the same.¶

1. This kind of deception twofold.

† Vide ch. 33, Pri. An. i.

1.

‡ Through B.
§ C.
|| D.
¶ A.

firmation of our own; but, practically, the process of meeting a real or supposed opponent, is the same. Vide Rhet. ii. 22 and 24.

[1] The reader will profitably read upon this chapter, Hill's notice and examples of the Elenchus, given at p. 322 of his Logic.

[2] See Hill and Whately on Fallacies.

[3] So Waitz; Buhle, and Taylor read πρώτως; the latter adds, i. e. "without a medium," a meaning which is evidently concurred in by Waitz.

2. Again, if one should be deceived about those things which are from the same class,[1] * as if A is with B, but this with C, and C with D, and should apprehend A to be with every B, and again with no C, he will at the same time both know and not apprehend its presence. Will he then admit nothing else from these things, than that he does not form an opinion on what he knows?[2] for in some way, he knows that A is with C through B, just as the particular is known in the † universal, so that what he somehow knows, he admits he does not conceive at all, which is impossible. In what, however, we mentioned before,‡ if the middle is not of the same class, it is impossible to conceive both propositions, according to each of the media,[3] as if A were with every B,§ but with no C,‖ and both these with every D.¶ For it happens that the major proposition assumes a contrary, either simply or partially,[4] for if with every thing with which B is present a person thinks A is present, but knows that B is with D, he also will know that A is with D. Hence, if, again, he thinks that A is with nothing with which C is, he will not think that A is with any thing with which B is, but that he who thinks that it is with every thing with which B is, should again think that it is not with something with which B is, is either simply or partially contrary. Thus however it is impossible to think, still nothing prevents (our assuming) one proposition according to each (middle),[5] * or both according to one, as that A is with every B, and B with D, and again, A with no C. For a deception of this kind resembles that by which we are deceived about particulars, as if A is with every B, but B with every C, A will be with every C.[6] If then a man knows that A is

* ἐκ τῆς αὐτῆς συστοιχίας.

† C being a part of B.

‡ i. e. in the first deception.

2. Case of the middles in Barbara and Celarent, not being subaltern.

§ The major of Barbara.

‖ Major of Celarent.

¶ The minor of both.

* i. e. B and C.

[1] Taylor says, "co-ordinatum;" Waitz, "ex eadem serie." It is clear, that subalterns are intended.

[2] For in the major of Celarent, he assumes no C is A, whereas he knows, as will be shown, that C is A.

[3] That is, he cannot, at one and the same time, assume both the prop. of Barbara, and both of Celarent.

[4] i. e. by reason of D, the subject of both B and C.

[5] i. e. one prop. for B, the other for C, as every B is A, no C is A, the minors not being added.

[6] Vide Post An. i. 1; Eth. Nicom. b. vi. c. 3.

with every thing with which B is, he knows also that it is with C; still nothing prevents his being ignorant of the existence of C, as if A were two right angles, B a triangle, and C a perceptible triangle.* For a man may think that C does not exist, knowing that every triangle has two (equal to) right angles, hence he will know and be ignorant of the same thing at once; for to know that every triangle has angles equal to two right, is not a simple thing,† but in one respect arises from possessing universal science, in another, particular science. Thus therefore he knows by universal science, that C has angles equal to two right angles, but by particular science he does not know it, so that he will not hold contraries. In like manner is the reasoning in the Meno,‡ that discipline is reminiscence, for it never happens that we have a pre-existent knowledge of particulars, but together with induction,§ receive the science of particulars as it were by recognition; since some things we immediately know, as (that there are angles) equal to two right angles, if we know that (what we see) is a triangle, and in like manner as to other things.

* Example (1.)

3. Distinction between universal and particular knowledge.

† i. e. it is "anceps ambiguum." Waitz.

‡ Meno, (Plat.) p. 81. Ritter, vol. ii. p. 293.

§ Cf. Eth. vi. 4.

By universal knowledge then we observe particulars,[1] but we do not know them by an (innate)

4. Our observation of parti-

Ex. 1. Every triangle (B) has angles equal to two right angles (A) (known)

This (C) is a triangle (B) (unknown)

∴ This (C) has angles equal to two right angles (A) {known by universal / unknown by particular} knowledge. Vide Post. An. i. 4. 253. 255

[1] It would weary the reader, and far exceed the limits to which, necessarily, we confine our remarks, to enter fully into the analysis of the distinction here drawn. In the Post An. i. 6, the subject is again entered upon, but for all necessary understanding of the matter, the reader is referred to Sanderson upon Certainty, book iii., and to Mansel's notes upon Syllogism quoad Materiam, artic. Opinio, p. 97, et seq. Although we have translated ὑπόληψις, supposition, yet as it approaches nearest to our idea of logical *judgment*, (see Trendelenburg de Animâ, p. 469,) the latter term shows at once, not only the nature, but frequently the causes, of error, (An. Post. i. 6, 8,) which may be individual, that is, connected with the person's own constitution of mind or circumstances, and, both as to universals and particulars, partake much of the character of

culars, derived from our knowledge of universals, a peculiarity noticed. (Met. book vi. 9.) Locke's Ess. vi. 4, v. 5, and vi. 2.

peculiar knowledge, hence we may be deceived about them, yet not after a contrary manner, but while possessing the universal, yet are deceived in the particular. It is the same also as to what we have spoken of, for the deception about the middle is not contrary to science about syllogism, nor the opinion as to each of the middles. Still nothing prevents one who knows that A is with the whole of B, and this again with C, thinking that A is not with C, as he who knows that every mule is barren, and that this (animal) is a mule, may think that this is pregnant; for he does not know that A is with C from not at the same time surveying each. Hence it is evident that if he knows one (of the propositions), but is ignorant of the other, he will be deceived as to how the universal subsists with reference to the particular sciences. For we know nothing of those things which fall under the senses as existent apart from sense,[1] not even if we happen to have perceived it before, unless in so far as we possess universal and peculiar knowledge, and not in that we energize. For to know is predicated triply, either as to the universal or to the peculiar (knowledge), or as to energizing, so that to be deceived is likewise in as many ways. Nothing therefore prevents a man both knowing and being deceived about the same thing, but not in a contrary manner,* and this happens also to him, who

5. A deception from knowing one prop. and being ignorant of the other.

6. Scientific knowledge is predicated triply.

* i. e. so as not to hold a self-either. What however Aristotle here means is, that scientific knowledge, or that of particulars, is said of truths deduced from higher truths; hence to each of these there is a foundation, in universal knowledge (νοεῖν), viz. we originally begin our speculation upon them, ἐξ ἀληθῶν καὶ πρώτων, or intuitively perceived truths, though these generals will not of themselves suffice to prevent error in particulars, seeing that to each of the last its own peculiar study and examination is appropriately necessary. This is fully borne out by the relative meanings of ἐπιστήμη and νοῦς. The word "innate" we have inserted from Buhle; by a contrary manner is not only meant, as Taylor says, "not in a manner contrary to science," but without holding a contradictory opinion, we may know the general, yet mistake the particular truth. (Cf. Hill's note on Objective and Subjective Certainty. Leibnitz de Stylo Nizolii. Sir W. Hamilton Reid's Works, p. 671.)

[1] Vide de Animâ, lib. ii. 5 and 6.—αἴσθησις is perception by the senses, as νοῦς is the intellectual element. Vide Eth. vi. 1 and 12; in the latter, αἰσθ. is reckoned intuition.

knows each proposition, yet has not considered before;[1] for thinking that a mule is pregnant, he has not knowledge in energy,* nor again, on account of opinion,[2] has he deception, contrary to knowledge, since deception, contrary to universal (knowledge), is[3] syllogism.

contradictory opinion.

* κατὰ τὸ ἐνεργεῖν. "Scientiam actu." Buhle. (Vide Met. 8.)

Notwithstanding, whoever thinks that the very being of good is the very being of evil, will apprehend that there is the same essence of good and of evil; for let the essence of good be A, and the essence of evil B; and again, let the essence of good be C. Since then he thinks that B and C are the same, he will also think that C is B; and again, in a similar manner, that B is A, wherefore that C is A.† For just as if it were true that of what C is predicated B is, and of what B is, A is; it was also true that A is predicated of C; so too in the case of the verb "to opine." In like manner, as regards the verb "to be," for C and B being the same, and again, B and A, C also is the same as A. Likewise, as regards to opine, is then this necessary,[4] if any one should grant the first? but perhaps that is false,[5] that any one should think that the essence of good is the essence of evil, unless accidentally,[6] for we may opine this in many ways, but we must consider it better.[7]

7. From a deception of this kind, a person may imagine that a thing concurs with its contrary.

† Example (2.)

[1] i. e. he has not considered both propositions together.

[2] i. e. because he thinks the mule parturient.

[3] i. e. as Taylor says, it is a deceptive syllogism, which proves no mule barren, because the universals are contrary. The opinion proposed is however particular, because it thinks this particular mule barren.

Ex. 2. He thinks the essence of evil (B) is the essence of good (A)
He thinks the essence of good (C) is the essence of evil (B)
∴ He thinks the essence of good (C) is the essence of good (A).

[4] That one who conjointly considers both propositions should hold contrary opinions, if a person should state the essence of good and of evil to be identical.

[5] Vide the opinion of Heraclitus, upon the nature of contraries; also Met. books ix. and xiii.

[6] That is, what is essentially good, for instance, to return a person's property, may be in a certain case bad, as to give a sword to a madman.

[7] In the Ethics and Metaphysics.

CHAP. XXII.—*On the Conversion of the Extremes in the first Figure.*

1. If the terms connected by a certain middle are converted, the middle must be converted with both.

* The major.

† The minor.

WHEN the extremes are converted, the middle must necessarily be converted with both. For if A is present with C through B, if it is converted, and C is with whatever A is, B also is converted with A,* and with whatever A is present, B also is through the middle C, and C is converted with B † through the middle A. The same will occur with negatives, as if B is with C,[1] but A is not with B,[2] neither will A be with C, if then B is converted with A, C also will be converted with A. For let B not be with A,[3] neither then will C be[4] with A, since B was with every C, and if C is converted with B, (the latter) is also converted
2. with A; for of whatever B is predicated, C also is, and if C is converted with A, B also is converted with A, for with whatever B is present, C also is,[5] but C is not present with what[6] A is. This also alone begins from the conclusion, (but the others not similarly,) as in the case of an affirmative syllogism. Again, if A and B are converted, and C and D likewise; but A or C must necessarily be present with every individual; B and D also will so subsist, as that one of them will be present with every individual. For since B is present with whatever A is, and D with whatever C is, but A or C with every individual, and not both at the same time, it is evident that B or D is with every individual, and not both of them at the same time; for two syllogisms are conjoined.‡ Again, if A or B is with every individual and C or D, but they are not
2. present at the same time, if A and C are converted B also and D are converted, since if B is not present with a certain thing with which D is, it is evident that A is present

3. The mode of converting a negative syllogism, begins from the conclusion, as in Barbara.

‡ Omitted by Waitz.

[1] The minor of Celarent. [2] The major of Celarent.

[3] The minor of Camestres. [4] The conclusion of Camestres.

[5] i. e. every B is C, this is the major of Camestres, inferred from the conversion of the minor of Celarent.

[6] i. e. no A is C, the minor of Camestres, taken from the conversion of the conclusion of Celarent.

with it. But if A is, C also will be, for they are converted, so that C and D will be present at the same time, but this is impossible;[1] as if what is unbegotten is incorruptible, and what is incorruptible unbegotten, it is necessary that what is begotten should be corruptible, and the corruptible begotten. But when A is present with the whole of B and C, and is predicated of nothing else, and B also is with every C, it is necessary that A and B should be converted, as since A is predicated of B C alone, but B itself is predicated both of itself and of C, it is evident that of those things of which A is predicated, of all these B will also be predicated, except of A itself. Again, when A and B are with the whole of C, and C is converted with B, it is necessary that A should be with every B, for since A is with every C, but C with B in consequence of reciprocity, A will also be with every B. But when of two opposites A is preferable to B, and D to C likewise, if A C are more eligible than B D, A is preferable to D, in like manner A should be followed and B avoided, since they are opposites, and C (is to be similarly avoided) and D (to be pursued), for these are opposed. If then A is similarly eligible with D, B also is similarly to be avoided with C, each (opposite) to each, in like manner, what is to be avoided to what is to be pursued. Hence both (are similar) A C with B D, but because (the one are) more (eligible than the other they) cannot be similarly (eligible), for (else) B D would be similarly (eligible) (with A C). If however D is preferable to A, B also is less to be avoided than C, for the less is opposed to the less, and the greater good and the less evil are preferable to the less good and the greater evil, wherefore the whole B D is preferable to A C. Now however this is not the case, hence A is preferable to D, consequently C is less to be avoided than B. If then every lover according to love chooses A, that is to be in such a condition as to be gratified, and C not to be gratified, rather than be gratified, which is D, and yet not be in a condition to be gratified, which is B, it is evident that A, i. e. to be in a condition to be gratified,

4. Case of election of opposites.

5. The greater good and less evil preferable to the less good and greater evil.

[1] He had before shown B to be predicated of D universally, though it does not hence follow that they are convertible unless D is shown to be predicated of B universally; this is omitted for brevity, as the proof is the same as the other.

is preferable to being gratified.[1] To be loved then is preferable according to love to intercourse, wherefore love is rather the cause of affection than of intercourse, but if it is especially (the cause) of this, this also is the end. Wherefore intercourse either, in short, is not or is for the sake of affection, since the other desires and arts are thus produced.* How therefore terms subsist as to conversion, also in their being more eligible or more to be avoided, has been shown.

6. The desire of the end, the incentive to the pursuit. (Eth. b. i. c. 7.)

* Waitz concludes the chapter here.

Chap. XXIII.—*Of Induction.*[2]

1. Not only dialectic and apodeictic syllogisms, but also rhetorical, and every species of demonstration, are through the above-named figures.

We must now show that not only dialectic and demonstrative syllogisms are produced through the above-named figures, but that rhetorical are also, and in short, every kind of demonstration and by every method. For we believe all things either through syllogism or from induction.

Induction, then, and the inductive syllogism is to prove one extreme in the middle through the other,[3] as if B is the middle of A C, and we show through C that A is with B, for

[1] This confirms the opinion of Plato in the Symposium. The demonstration is thus; if of four terms the first is preferable to the 2nd, and the 4th to the third, but the 1st and 3rd together preferable to the 2nd and 4th together, then the 1st is preferable to the 4th, hence to be in a condition adapted to be gratified is preferable to being gratified.

[2] Aristotle attributes the discovery of induction and also of definition to Socrates, but the induction of the latter (who exhibited both dialectically) comes closer to the "example" of Aristotle. Vide Gorgias 460, also Metaph. xii. 4, 5.

[3] i. e. to prove the major term of the middle by the minor. The expression ἐξ ἐπαγωγῆς συλλ.—used here, does not (as Mansel justly remarks) denote the syllogism proper, or reasoning from a whole to its parts, but comprehends formal reasoning generally, as in Rhet. ii. 25, Enthymem is spoken of as including example. For induction properly is an inverted syllogism, which argues from the individuals collected to the universal or whole class they constitute, whereas syllogism does just the reverse. Upon the various kinds of induction see Hill's Logic, 229, where some examples are given; also Mansel's Logic, Appendix note F. Inasmuch as we seldom can enumerate all the individuals of a class, we rarely meet with a specimen of perfect induction, but we agree with Whately in believing, that the cause of the opposition of induction to syllogism, arises entirely from the inaccuracy in the use of the word. Vide Whately, Log. b. iv. c. i. 1. Even however the distinction between perfect and imperfect induction is extra-

thus we make inductions. Thus let A be long-lived, B void of bile, C every thing long-lived, as man, horse, mule; A then* is present with the whole of C, for every thing void of bile is long-lived, but B† also, or that which is void of bile, is present with every C, if then C is converted with B,‡ and does not exceed the middle, it is necessary that A should be with B. For it has been before shown,[1] that when any two things are present with the same thing, and the extreme is convertible with one of them, that the other predicate will also be present with that which is converted. We must however consider C as composed of all singulars, for induction is produced through § all. A syllogism of this kind however is of the first, and immediate proposition; for of those which have a middle, the syllogism is through the middle, but of those where there is not (a middle) it is by induction.[2] In some way also induction is opposed to syllogism, for the latter demonstrates the extreme ‖ of the third through the middle, but the former the extreme of the middle through the third.¶ To nature therefore the syllogism produced through the middle is prior or more known, but to us that by induction is more evident.[3]

2. Induction is proving the major term of the middle by the minor.

* The major of the induction in the 3rd figure.

† The minor of the induction.

‡ A reduction to the 1st figure.

§ Example (1.)

3. Induction is occurrent in those demonstrations, which are proved without a middle.

‖ i. e. the major.

¶ The minor.

logical. The reader may profitably consult on this subject the Edinburgh Review, No. 115, p. 229; Bacon, Nov. Orga. lib. 2, Aph. x.; Sir W. Hamilton Reid's Works, p. 712. The word ἐπαγωγη, or induction, is clearly taken from the Socratic accumulation of instances, serving as antecedents to establish the requisite conclusion. Confer. Cicero de Inventione i. 32.

[1] In the preceding ch.

```
                C                       A
Ex. 1. Every man, horse, mule, is long-lived
                              B              C
         Whatever is void of bile is man, horse, mule
                           B                  A
    ∴ Whatever is void of bile is long-lived.
```

[2] Vide Aldrich's Logic upon the second species of demonstration, v. 5, 1; also remarks made before upon the use of the terms mediate and immediate.

[3] Some things are more known to nature, but others more known to us. Vide Post. An. i. 1, 2; Pliny, b. i. c. 1; Metaph. b. ii. c. 1. Com-

CHAP. XXIV.—*Of Example.*[1]

1. παράδειγμα, or example, is proving the major of the middle by a term resembling the minor.

EXAMPLE is when the extreme is shown[2] to be present with the middle through something similar to the third,[3] but it is necessary to know that the middle is with the third, and the first with what is similar.[4] For example, let A be bad, B to (make war) upon neighbours, C the Athenians against the Thebans, D the Thebans against the Phocians. If then we wish to show that it is bad to war against the Thebans, we must assume that it is bad to war against neighbours, but the demonstration of this is from similars, as that (the war) by the Thebans against the Phocians (was bad). Since then war against neighbours is bad, but that against the Thebans is against neighbours, it is evidently bad to war against the Thebans, so that it is evident that B is with C, and with D, (since both are to war against neighbours,) and that A is with D, (for the war against the Phocians was not advantageous to the Thebans,) but that A is with B will be

2. * Example.

pare also the whole chapter with Rhet. b. i. c. 2, b. ii. c. 23; and Ethics, Nic. b. vi. c. 3.

[1] Compare Rhet. b. ii. c. 20, 24, and b. iii. c. 17. Example differs from induction, 1st, in that the latter proves the universal from a complete enumeration of individuals, whilst example selects single cases; 2nd, Induction stops at the universal, whilst example infers syllogistically a conclusion regarding another individual: in fact, example includes an imperfect (therefore illogical) induction and a syllogism. Sometimes it is called loosely reasoning from analogy, but as logic recognises only formal consequence, neither analogy nor example have any logical force. (Vide Mill's Logic, b. iii. ch. 20; also Mansel, p. 82.) The distinction is however better drawn by Hill, p. 243, comprehending, 1st, the antecedent, which in induction consists of several singular cases, but in example frequently of only one. 2nd, the conclusion, being universal in induction, but singular in example: he adds as usual various examples. See also Whately, b. iv. ch. 1 and 2. As to the place which παράδειγμα occupies with regard to the relation of the subject matter of a premise to the subject matter of the conclusion, in the consideration of Enthymem, the excellent Tables of Dr. Hessey, 2, Div. 1, and Table 5, give a complete scheme of their position, also the statement of the argument given in the text. It is evident, as Aristotle shows, that example consists of two elements, a quasi inductive syllogism apparently in Fig. 3, and a deductive syllogism in Fig. 1, so it is assailable in each of these.

[2] i. e. the major. [3] The minor.

[4] i. e. with what is similar to the minor.

shown through D. In the same manner also if the demonstration of the middle as to the extreme should be through many similars, wherefore it is evident that example is neither as part to a whole, nor as whole to a part, but as part to part,[1] when both are under the same thing,[2] but one is known. It (example) also differs from induction, because the latter shows from all individuals that the extreme[3] is present with the middle, and does not join the syllogism to the extreme, but the former,[4] both joins it, and does not demonstrate from all (individuals).

3. Example subsists as part to part, (ὡς μέρος προς μέρος,) wherein it differs from induction. (Vide note above.)

CHAP. XXV.—*Of Abduction.*[5]

1. Ἀπαγωγὴ a syllogism with a major prem. certain, and the minor more credible than the conclusion.

ABDUCTION is when it is evident the first is present with the middle,[6] but it is not evident that the middle is with the last, though it is similarly credible, or more so, than the conclusion; moreover if the media of the last and of the middle be few, for it by all means happens that we shall be nearer to knowledge. For instance, let A be what may be taught, B science, C justice; that science then may be taught is clear, but not whether justice is science. If

2. Moreover when the minor is proved by the interposition

[1] "Exemplo utemur ut singula demonstremus per singula."—Waitz. A is a whole, B part of A, C D parts of B, when therefore example proceeds from D to C, it proceeds from part to part.

[2] As C and D under the same A, but D more than C is known to be under A.

[3] i. e. the major A with the middle B, and does not join the syllogism with the minor, in other words, it does not prove A of C.

[4] Example proves A of C, and does not demonstrate from all individuals, but only from some of them, under B.

[5] This term (ἀπαγ.) must not be confounded when it occurs alone, with the meaning it bears, in reference to the impossible, for when it is by itself, as here, it signifies a syllogism with a major premise certain, and a minor more probable, or demonstrable, than the conclusion. Aldrich is so far right in using the word "oblique," as applied to it, (though utterly wrong in limiting its sense only to the "ducens ad impossibile,") in that the word means "a turning off," from the immediate point to be proved, to something else on which it may depend, this is the foundation of the meaning it bears here, and the more general acceptation of it as a deduction per impossibile. Syllogistically it holds a place between the demonstration and the dialectic syllogism. Confer. Mansel and Hill's Logic. [6] i. e. when the major is known.

of few middle terms.

* Example (1.)

therefore B C is equally or more credible than A C,[1] it is abduction, for we are nearer knowledge because of our assuming A C, not possessing science before.* Or again, if the media of B C should be few, for thus we are nearer knowledge, as [2]if D should be to be squared, E a rectilinear figure, and F a circle, then if, of E F there is only one middle, for a circle to become equal to a rectilinear figure, through lunulæ, will be a thing near to knowledge.† But when neither B C is more credible than A C, nor the media fewer, I do not call this abduction, nor when B C is immediate, for such a thing is knowledge.

Vide Waitz in An. Pr. c. 24.

† Example (2.)

CHAP. XXVI.—*Of Objection.*[3]

1. Ἐνστασις (Instantia,) a proposition contrary to a proposition, it

OBJECTION is a proposition contrary to a proposition, it differs however from a proposition be-

[1] The minor than the conclusion.

B A
Ex. 1. Every science may be taught.—Known.
C B
All justice is science. { Equally or more credible than the conclusion.
C A
∴ All justice may be taught.—Unknown.

[2] As Taylor remarks, Arist. here refers to the quadrature of the circle by Hippocrates of Chius.

E D
Ex. 2. Every rectilinear figure may be squared.—Known.
F E
Every circle may become a rectilinear figure. { proved through one middle, i. e. per lunulas.
F D
Every circle may be squared. { This is proved through many media.

[3] We assail an adversary either by bringing an ἔνστασις to show his conclusion is *not proved*, or by *disproving* his conclusion, by an ἀντισυλλογισμος, (objection to consequent,) i. e. by proving its contradictory by means of a new middle term. Now Ἔνστασις may either be material, or objection to antecedent, or formal objection to consequent. If material, it may be either ἐκ ταὐτοῦ, ἐκ τοῦ ἐναντίου, ἐκ τοῦ ὁμοιου ἐκ κρισεως, or ἐκ τοῦ κατα δοξὰν: (see by this ch.) the relative position of which the reader will find admirably laid down in Dr. Hessey's Schema Rhetorica, wherefrom this note is chiefly taken. The present ch. causes us chiefly to notice the Ἔνστασις ἐκ ταυτου, and this may be either καθολου, or κατὰ μέρος. In proving the first we assume as a new middle, a term

cause objection may be partial, but proposition cannot be so at all, or not in universal syllogisms. Objection indeed is advanced in two ways, differs from a proposition in that it may be

more extensive, and καθόλου, as compared with the subject of the original προτασις; in proving the ἐνστ. κατα μέρος, we assume as a new middle, a term less extensive than the subject of the original πρότασις. Now A may be assailed by proving its contrary, or contradictory, in Fig. 1, or its contradictory in Fig. 3. E may be assailed by proving its contrary (or contradictory) in Fig. 1, or its contradictory in Fig. 3. Lastly, an affirmative proposition (but not a negative) may be assailed by an Enstatic Enthymem, in Fig. 2, but Arist. objects to do so. Conf. upon this ch., Julius Pacius; Whately on the Nature and Fallacy of Objections; Anal. Post. i. 12; Rhet. ii. 26; Waitz, p. 535, in loc. Hermogenes, in his treatise upon Invention, does not consider objection in the same respect as Arist. The apparent discrepancy between this chap. and the account of objection in the Rhetoric is noticed by Dr. Hessey, Table 5.

Ex. 1. Proposition.

A B
There is one science of contraries.

Objection.

A C
There is not one science of opposites
B C
Contraries are opposites
A B
∴ There is not one science of contraries.

Ex. 2. Proposition.

A B
There is one science of contraries.

Objection.

A C
There is not one science of the known, and of the unknown
C B
The known and the unknown are contraries
A B
There is not one science of contraries.

Ex. 3. Proposition.

A B
∴ There is not one science of contraries.

Objection.

A C
There is one science of opposites
B C
Contraries are opposites
A B
∴ There is one science of contraries.

either καθόλου or ἐπὶ μέρος.

and by two figures; in two ways, because every objection is either universal or particular, and by two figures, because they are used opposite to the proposition, and opposites* are concluded in the first and third figure alone. When then a person requires it to be admitted that any thing is present with every individual, we object either that it is with none, or that it is not with a certain one, and of these, the being present with none, (is shown) by the first figure,† but that it is not with a certain one by the last.‡ For instance, let A be "there is one science, and B contraries;" when therefore a person advances that there is one science of contraries, it is objected either that there is not the same science of opposites, altogether, but contraries are opposites, so that there is the first figure;§ or that there is not one science of the known and of the unknown, and this is the third figure,‖ for of C, that is, of the known, and of the unknown, it is true that they are contraries, but that there is one science of them is false.¶ Again, in like manner in a negative proposition, for if any one asserts that there is not one science of contraries, we say either that there is the same science of all opposites, or that there is of certain contraries, as of the salubrious, and of the noxious; that there is therefore (one science) of all things is by the first figure,* but that there is of certain by the third.† In short, in all (disputations) it is necessary that he who universally objects should apply a contradiction of the propositions to the universal,‡ as if some one should assert that there is not the same science of all contraries, (the objector) should say, that there is one of opposites. For thus it is necessary that there should be the first figure, since the middle becomes an universal to that

* i. e. affirmatives and negatives.

2. Method of alleging the ἔνστασις.

† Celarent.

‡ Felapton.

§ Example (1.)

‖ Felapton.

¶ Example (2.)

* Barbara.

† Darapti.

‡ Example (3.)

3. Rule for the καθόλου ἔνστασις.

4. And for that

Proposition the same.

Objection.

A C
There is one science of the salubrious and noxious
C B
The salubrious and noxious are contraries
A B
∴ There is one science of certain contraries.

(which was proposed) at first, but he who objects in part (must contradict) that which is universal,§ of which the proposition is stated, as that there is not the same science of the known, and the unknown, for the contraries are universal with reference, to these.* The third figure is also produced, for what is particularly assumed is the middle, for instance, the known and the unknown; as from what we may infer a contrary syllogistically, from the same we endeavour to urge objections. Wherefore we adduce then (objections) from these figures only,† for in these alone opposite syllogisms are constructed, since we cannot conclude affirmatively through the middle figure.[1] Moreover, even if[2] it were (possible), yet the (objection), in the middle figure would require more (extensive discussion), as if any one should not admit A to be present with B, because C is not consequent to it, (B). For this is manifest through other propositions, the objection however must not be diverted to other things, but should forthwith have the other proposition apparent,[3] wherefore also from this figure alone there is not a sign.[4]

ἐν μερει. Vide note.

§ Subject.

* Contraries attributed to the known and unknown, as universal to particular.

5. Objection adduced in the first and third figures alone.

† Hence if the prop. is negative, an objection to it cannot be proper in the 2nd figure since the objection ought to affirm.

We must consider also other objections, as those adduced from the contrary, from the similar, and from what is according to opinion,[5] also whether it is possible to assume a particular objection from the first, or a negative from the middle figure.

6. Objections of other kinds to be noticed, vide not. 1, supra; Rhet. ii. 25.

[1] In self-defence upon this "vexed place," I am obliged to quote the note of Julius Pacius as corroborative of the sense I have given in the text; Waitz however in most obscure phraseology comes, as Dr. Hessey remarks, to the same point. The following is from Pacius: "Aristoteles loquens de universali objectione inquit hoc *simpliciter;* id est, generaliter in omnibus disputationibus obtinere, ut necesse sit, eum qui universaliter objicit, id est, affert objectionem universalem dirigat contradictionem propositorum, id est, suam objectionem, quæ opponitur propositioni adversarii; dirigat (inquam) ad universale, id est in eâ objectione sumat terminum universalem, qui attribuatur, subjecto propositionis, ut in exemplo antea dato, sumebamus hunc terminum, *ἀντικείμενα* qui est universalis, et attribuitur subjecto propositionis, id est *ἐναντΐοις*." (Vide Julius Pacius in h. l.; also Waitz, p. 536, An. Pr.)

[2] i. e. when the prop. is affirmative. [3] i. e. the prop. understood.

[4] See the following ch.

[5] Examples of all these are given in Table v., Hessey's Schema Rhet.

CHAP. XXVII.—*Of Likelihood, Sign, and Enthymeme.*[1]

1. Εἰκὸς—consentaneum ar- LIKELIHOOD and sign, however, are not the same, but the likely is a probable proposition for

[1] For writers upon the subjects of this chapter we may refer to the commentary of Julius Pacius, (Excerpta,) and Crakanthorpii Logica, lib. v., both annexed to the Schema Rhetorica of Dr. Hessey; No. 115, in the Edinburgh Review, attributed to Sir W. Hamilton; Mansel's Logic, Appendix, note E.; Whately's Rhetoric and Buckley's note, Bohn's edition of the Rhetoric, book i. chap. 2. The older writers upon it are Rodolphus Agricola, 1485, Phrissemius, 1523, J. Pacius, Scaynus, 1599, and Majoragius, (1572). We now proceed to the words themselves.

The term Εἰκὸς, we prefer, with Sir W. Hamilton, to interpret "likelihood" to the other senses given by commentators we have named in the margin, since the former approaches nearer to its Aristotelian definition as a proposition stating a general probability. This indeed is a proposition nearly, though not quite, universal, and when employed in an Enthymeme, will form the major premise of a syllogism such as the following:

Most men who envy, hate.
This man envies:
Therefore this man (probably) hates.

Aristotle limits it to contingent matter, and its relation to the conclusion is that of an universal to a particular.

Σημεῖον, on the other hand, in a propositional sense, is a *fact* which is known to be an indication, more or less certain, of the truth of some further statement, whether of a single fact or of a general belief. We say in a propositional sense, for sometimes Εἰκός, σημεῖον, and τεκμηρίον, are used for the Enthymemes drawn from each; it is, in fact, a singular proposition employed relatively to some other proposition which may be inferred from it, and will form one premise of a syllogism, which may be in either of these figures which Aristotle discusses, having respect in this division to the extent of the so-called middle term, as compared with the other two terms. In the first and second figures it is the minor premise, in the third it seems more naturally to belong to the major. Whately considers the εἴκος (or διοτι) of Aristotle to be an a priori argument, which may be employed to account for the fact, whereas the σημεῖον (or ὃτι) could not be so employed; he has however glanced at this point but generally. Aristotle tells us that we may either class τεκμήριον, as he does in the Rhet. c. 2, as a species of σημεῖον, or contradistinguish two σημεῖα—in necessary matter as in the relation of a particular to an universal, or of an universal to a particular, and class the τεκμήριον as a species under a genus. By a reference to Dr. Hessey's Tables the exact position of each in the enthymematic system may be clearly perceived: we may merely add that, as propositions, it is no where stated that εικος and Σημεῖον may not be combined in the same syllogism, and that much of apparent contradiction between the places in the Analytics and Rheto-

what men know to have generally happened or not, or to be or not to be; this is a likelihood, for instance, that the envious hate, or that lovers love: but a sign seems to be a demonstrative proposition, necessary or probable, for that which when it exists a thing is, or which when it has happened, before or after, a thing has happened, this is a sign of a thing happening or being. Now an Enthymeme is a syllogism from likelihoods or signs, but a sign is assumed triply in as many ways as the middle in the figures, for it is either as in the first, or as in the middle, or as in the third, as to show that a woman is pregnant because she has milk is from the first figure, for the

gumentum, Buhle and Taylor; "verisimile" and "verisimilitudo," Averrois, Waitz; "probabile," Cicero; "likelihood," Sir W. Hamilton;—is a probable proposition. Σημεῖον is a demonstrative proposition, either necessary or probable. Enthymeme is a syllogism drawn from either of

ric may be solved by a careful study of the tabular view given by the Doctor, of the consideration of these elements of Enthymeme, first as propositions, next as terms.

In regard to Enthymeme, it is no wonder that difficulties should not vanish, when even the abandonment of the word ἀτελής, ejected as a gloss by Pacius, and discountenanced by the best MSS. of the old Latin version, is still clung to by some authors. Enthymeme is composed of εἰκότα, or σημεῖα, and without circumscribing our notion of it within the limits absurdly laid down of its etymology by Aldrich, we may conceive it in a general sense as comprehending πίστεις of every kind; and at other times limited to a special kind of syllogism designated rhetorical. Various senses have been attributed to it by Cicero, Quintilian, and others, but Aristotle in general describes it as one sort of argument on moral matters distinguished carefully as to its principle from example, a collateral sort of argument. In the words of Sir W. Hamilton, "Enthymeme is distinguished from pure syllogism as a reasoning of peculiar matter from signs and likelihoods;" whether therefore a premise of it be suppressed or not, an argument agreeing with this description is an Enthymeme. The words ἀποδεικτικὴ ἀναγκαια ἢ ἔνδοξος, applied to σημεῖον as a προτασις, do not relate to the modal character of the proposition in itself, but to its logical validity when the other premise is added, without which addition expressed or understood, there is no Enthymeme at all. Lastly, Σημεῖον is called a demonstrative proposition, because it professes to enunciate what is absolutely true, i. e. what Aristotle calls *necessary*, (Rhet. i. c. 2,) the latter word being used in two senses, 1st, of a premise which states a fact, 2nd, of a consequence which is logically unassailable.

B A
Ex. 1. Whatever woman has milk is pregnant
C B
This woman has milk
C A
∴ This woman is pregnant.

these. Cf. Rhet. b. i. c. 2. Soph. Œd. Col. 292 and 1199.

2. A sign assumed triply, according to the number of figures.

* Example (1.)

† Example (2.) (a paralogism.)

middle is to have milk. Let A, be to be pregnant, B to have milk, C a woman.* But that wise men are worthy, for Pittacus is a worthy man, is through the last figure, let A be worthy, B wise men, C Pittacus. It is true then A and B are predicated of C, except that they do not assert the one[1] because they know it, but the other they assume.† But that a woman is pregnant because she is pale, would be through the middle figure, for since paleness is a consequence of pregnancy, and also attends this woman, they fancy it proved that she is pregnant. Let A be paleness, to be pregnant B, a woman C.‡ If then one proposition should be enunciated, there is only a sign, but if the other also be assumed, there is a syllogism, as for instance that Pittacus is liberal, for the ambitious are liberal, and Pittacus is ambitious, or again, that the wise are good, for Pittacus is good and also wise. Thus therefore syllogisms are produced, except indeed that the one in the first figure is incontrovertible if it be true, (for it is universal,) but that through the last is controvertible though the conclusion should be true, because the syllogism is not universal nor to the purpose, for if Pittacus is worthy, it is not necessary that on this account other wise men also should be worthy. But that which is by the middle figure is always and altogether controvertible, for there is never a syllogism, when the terms thus subsist,§ for it is not necessary, if

‡ Example (3.)

3. If one prop. be enunciated, there is only a sign.

4. Syllogism, if it be true, is incontrovertible in the 1st fig., but not so in the last or 2nd fig.

§ i. e. when both premises affirm.

[1] Viz. "That Pittacus is a wise man," but they assume the other, viz. "That Pittacus is a worthy man."

C A
Ex. 2. Pittacus is a worthy man
C B
Pittacus is a wise man
B A
∴ Wise are worthy men.

B A
Ex. 3. Whatever woman is pregnant is pale
C A
This woman is pale
C B
∴ This woman is pregnant.

she who is pregnant be pale, and this woman be pale, that this woman should be pregnant; what is true therefore will be in all the figures,* but they have the above-named differences.

* Bekker and Waitz σημείοις. Taylor, Buhle, and Averrois, σχημασιν.

5. τεκμηριον, (indicium,) a syllogism in the first figure. (Cf. Quintilian, lib. v. c. 9, sec. 8.)

Either therefore the sign must be thus divided, but of these the middle must be assumed as the[1] proof positive, (for the proof positive they say is that which produces knowledge, but the middle is especially a thing of this[2] kind,) or we must call those from the[3] extremes, signs, but what is from the middle a proof positive, for that is most probable, and for the most part true, which is through the first figure. We may however form a judgment of the disposition by the body, if a person grants that whatever passions are natural, change at once the body and the soul,[4] since perhaps one who has learned music has changed his soul in some respect, but this passion is not of those which are natural to us, but such as angers and desires, which belong to natural emotions. If therefore this should be granted, and one thing should be a sign of one (passion), and we are able to lay hold of the peculiar passion and sign of each genus, we shall be able

6. By the example of physiognomy Aristotle shows that signs especially probable belong to the 1st figure.

[1] The τεκμηριον is a σημεῖον in fig. 1, necessarily conclusive, (vide Rhet. i. c. 2,) derived by Arist. from τέκμαρ, a boundary. The argument διὰ τεκμηρίου is logical, but rarely occurs, since its advancement settles the question. He speaks of "the middle," &c., as referring to the first figure, in which the middle term obtains the middle place. Τεκμηρια can only be refuted by assailing the premises.

[2] Cf. Waitz, Tom. i. p. 538. Biese, i. 227, also ch. 14, book i. Anal. Post.

[3] Which are referred to the second or third figure; "quæ extrema sunt (ut utrobique subjecti aut utrobique predicati locum habeant,") ea signa dicenda sunt; quod autem e medio (sumtum est) ut partim subjecti, partim prædicati vicem gerat indicium dicendum est. Buhle.

[4] Cf. Arist. Physio. Eth. ii. c. 1, and 5. Buhle, Anal. i. ch. v. Dan. iii. 19. Gen. xxxi. 2.

"——My grief lies all within;
And those external manners of laments
Are merely shadows to the unseen grief
That swells with silence in my tortured soul.
There lies the substance."— Shaks. Richd. II.

The same sentiment is met with in our dramatists passim. The acquisition of *knowledge* of course changes the soul; since, to take a high view, it is the first *human* element of all religion.

7. The first physiognomic hypothesis is that natural passion changes at one time the body and soul. The 2nd, that there is one sign of one passion. The 3rd, that the proper passion of each species of animal may be known.

to conjecture from nature. For if a peculiar passion is inherent in a certain individual genus, as fortitude in lions, it is necessary also that there should be a certain sign, for it is supposed that they (the body and soul) sympathize with each other, and let this be the having great extremities, which also is contingent to other, not whole, genera.[1] For the sign is thus peculiar, because the passion is a peculiarity of the whole genus, and is not the peculiarity of it alone,[2] as we are accustomed to say. The same (sign) then will also be inherent in another genus, and man will be brave, and some other animal, it will then possess that sign,[3] for there was one (sign) of one (passion). If then these things are so, and we can collect such signs in those animals, which have one peculiar passion alone, but each (passion) has its (own) sign, since it is necessary that it should have one, we may be able to conjecture the nature from the bodily frame. But if the whole genus have two peculiarities, as a lion has fortitude and liberality, how shall we know which of those signs that are peculiarly consequent is the sign, if either (passion)? Shall we say that we may know this, if both are inherent in something else, but not wholly,[4] and in what each is not inherent

[1] Other species, he means, also have this sign, but it is not possessed by every individual in the species.

[2] That is, though it may even happen to every individual, it does not happen to that genus *alone*. This mere sketch presents the outlines, in comparative anatomy, of the strongest evidence upon which modern phrenologists can rest their claim to credence; it must be remembered however that the whole case falls, if the identification of the peculiar mark with the passion is not *fully proved*. His further question, of how we are to apportion each passion to its own mark, when many are present in one genus, seems unanswerable:—yet we have presumed even to measure the prominence which marks each passion, (if it does mark it,) and to set one over against the other, e. g. benevolence against destructiveness, almost to a hair's breadth!

[3] Viz. great extremities.

[4] i. e. If both passions and both signs are inherent in another genus of animals, yet so as not both to be inherent in all the individuals of that genus; for instance, both courage and liberality, and their signs, are in horses as well as in lions, but not in all horses, for some are brave and not liberal, others liberal and not brave.

Ex. 4. Whatever has great extremities is brave
Every lion has great extremities
∴ Every lion is brave.

geometry, & algebra, were text books for 100 years, was on
among the earliest adherents of Copernicus System.
Chambers

wholly, when they have the one, they have not the other; for if a (lion) is brave, but not generous, but has this* from two signs, it is evident that in a lion also this is the sign of fortitude. But to form a judgment of the natural disposition by the bodily frame, is, for this reason, in the first figure, because the middle reciprocates with the major term, but exceeds the third, and does not reciprocate with it; as for instance, let fortitude be A, great extremities B, and C a lion. Wherefore B is present with every individual with which C is, but with others* also, and A is with every individual of that with which B is present, and with no more, but is converted, for if it were not, there would not be one sign of one (passion).†

* i. e. great extremities.

8. Whatever is inferred in this respect is collected in the 1st figure.

* As with D, or some "man."

† Example (4.)

Whatever has great extremities is brave
Some man has great extremities
∴ Some man is brave.

rus Ramus, or Pierre de la Ramee 1515–1572. French
manist. Born village of Cuth, Picardy (Somme)
mber of noble but impoverished family. His father
charcoal burner. Admitted to College of Navarre, in
menial capacity. When had to do battle with Schola-
ic Aristotelianism, outdid his predecessors in the
volt. Took degree 1536. Said "everything Aristotle
ught is false". Accused of undermining foundati-
s of philosophy & religion, brought before par-
ment of Paris & Francis I, found guilty of acting ras-
y. Lectures interdicted 1544. Sentence cancelled
Cardinal Lorraine. — Appointed professor of Philo-
phy & eloquence 1551 by Henry II. at College de France. — Publis-
d 50 works in his life-time, & 9 appeared after. — In 1561
dopted Protestantism, had to leave Paris, murdered
Bartholomew massacre. — Emendations of syllogi-
no his work. Ramus set the modern fashion of deducing
figures from the positions of the middle term in the premises, instead of basing them, as Aristotle does, upon the
fferent relation of the middle to the so-called major
minor. — Had little ground to claim superiority to
istotle." Encyc. Brit.: "Ramus born at Cuth in Verman-
is. Got situation as servant to rich scholar at College
Navarre. — Placed higher value on reason than author-
. Undertook to reform logic. Assailed by Sorbonne, Ca-
dinals Bourbon & Lorraine. 1545 appointed principal
College de Presles. Wrote treatises on arithmetic

theory of the Syllogism) & being demonstrative reason
Encyclop. Brit: 492
n P.80

THE POSTERIOR ANALYTICS.

BOOK I.

CHAP. I.—*Upon the Nature of Demonstration.*

1. All dianœtic discipline is produced from previous knowledge, possessed in a two-fold respect. (Cf. Mag.Moral.lib. i. 18, and Eth. Eude. lib. v. c. 1, 2, 3.)

ALL doctrine, and all intellectual discipline,[1] arise from pre-existent knowledge. Now this is evident, if we survey them all, for both mathematical sciences are obtained in this manner, and also each of the other arts. It is the same also with arguments, as well those which result through syllogisms, as those which are formed through induction, for both teach through things previously known, the one assuming as if from those who understood them,[2] the other* demonstrating the universal by that which is evident as to the singular. Likewise also do rhetoricians persuade, for they do so either through examples, which is induction, or through enthymems, which is syllogism.†[3] It is necessary however to possess previous knowledge in a twofold respect; for with some things we must pre-suppose that they are, but with others we must understand what that is which is spoken of; and with others both must be

* Induction.

† Vide Prior Anal. b. ii. c. 27.

[1] Doctrine and discipline are the same in reality, but differ in relation, being called "doctrine" when applied to teaching, and "discipline" as pertaining to learning. Taylor defines Διανοία, that power of the soul which reasons scientifically, deriving the principles of its reasoning from intellect: and these principles are axioms and definitions. Comp. Poetic. ch. 6, where the word is applied to a certain part of tragedy. Ethics, b. vi. c. 2. Waitz notices the similarity between the commencement of this ch. and the opening ch. of the Ethics. For the principle stated, consult Hill's Logic, p. 137, and for the word, see Biese, i. p. 89.

[2] That is, syllogisms contain propositions, assumed to be known either by demonstration or per se.

[3] Vid. Rhet. b. i. ch. 2. It was shown (b. ii. ch. 24, Anal. Pri.) that example is reduced to a syllogism in the 1st figure, the major prop. of which is proved by an imperfect deduction; wherefore as the whole force of the example consists in that induction, it is not undeservedly said to be a certain induction. Taylor.

known, as for instance, (we must pre-assume,) that of every thing it is true to affirm or deny that it is, but of a triangle, that it signifies so and so, and of the monad (we must know) both, viz. what it signifies and that it is, for each of these is not manifest to us in a similar manner.[1] It is possible however to know from knowing some things previously,[2] and receiving the knowledge of others at the same time, as of things which are contained under universals, and of which a man possesses knowledge.[3] For he knew before that every triangle has angles equal to two right angles, but that this which is in a semi-circle is a triangle, he knew by induction at the same time. For of some things knowledge is acquired after this manner, nor is the extreme known through the middle, as such things as are singulars, and are not predicated of any subject. Perhaps however we must confess that we possess knowledge after a certain manner before induction or the assumption of a syllogism, but in another manner not.[4] For what a man is ignorant about its existence at all, how could he know at all that it has two right angles? But it is evident that he thus knows because he knows the universal, but singly he does not know it. Still if this be not admitted, the doubt which is mentioned in the Meno* will occur, either he will learn nothing, or those things which he knows,[5]

2. What we know universally and generally we may not know singly, although not in the same manner.

* Meno, Plato.

[1] Quæ antequam disciplina ipsa quæcunque nobis tradatur, cognoscere debemus ὅτι ἔστιν, axiomata sunt, quæ vero cognoscere debemus τί τὸ λεγόμενόν ἐστι, definitiones sunt: unde fit ut disciplinam ipsam quamcunque, præcede redebeant, axiomata et definitiones.—Nam etsi definitio rei naturam non patefaciat, tamen quam vim habeat nomen quo res significetur exponit, ut etiam definitio nominalis, quæ dicitur utilitatem quandam habeat. Waitz. See also Meditationes de cognitione Veritatis et Ideis: Leibnitz Opera, p. 80, ed. Erdmann.

[2] i. e. to prove the principal conclusion, from certain propositions being proved, pro-syllogistically.

[3] Learning them not from antecedent knowledge nor pro-syllogistically, but immediately, just as sensibles are known by the senses. Taylor. Compare also Ethics, b. vi. ch. 3, and Whately's Logic.

[4] i. e. the conclusion may be known by universal, yet it cannot be by proper or peculiar knowledge; for instance, in the case below he knows that this triangle has angles equal to two right, because he knows this to be the case universally of a triangle, but he does not know it singly, absolutely, and perfectly by proper knowledge.

[5] The passage in the Meno of Plato is that commencing καὶ τίνα τρόπον

nis Opera, Bekker's ed. tom. iv. p. 32.

for he must not say, as some endeavour to solve the doubt, "Do you know that every duad is an even number or not?" for since if some one says that he does, they would bring forward a certain duad which he did not think existed, as therefore not even; and they solve the ambiguity, not by saying that he knew every duad to be even, but that he was ignorant as to what they know is a duad. Nevertheless they know that of which they possess and have received the demonstration, but they have received it not of every thing which they know to be a triangle or a number, but of every number and triangle singly, for no proposition is assumed of such a kind as the number which you know, or the rectilinear figure which you know, but universally. Still there is nothing (I think) to prevent a man who learns, in a certain respect knowing and in a certain respect being ignorant,[1] for it is absurd, not that he should in some way know what he learns, but that he should thus know it, as he does when he learns it, and in the same manner.

Chap. II.—*Of Knowledge, and Demonstration, and its Elements.*

* Soph. Elenc. xi. 1. Metap. lib. v.

1. Scientific knowledge is possessed, when we know the necessary connexion between a thing and its cause. Definition of Demonstration. (Vide Ethics, vi. 3, 4.)

We think that we know each thing singly, (and not in a sophistical manner,* according to accident,) when we think that we know the cause on account of which a thing is, that it is the cause of that thing, and that the latter cannot subsist otherwise; wherefore it is evident that knowledge is a thing of this kind, for both those who do not, and those who *do* know, fancy, the former, that they in this manner possess knowledge, but those who know, possess it in reality, so that it is impossible that a thing of which there is know-

ζητήσεις. The doubt (ἀπόρημα) is, that if we can learn nothing, therefore that nothing is to be investigated, since what we know we need not investigate, and it is vain to search after what we know not, since not knowing the object of our search, we shall be ignorant of it, even when found. Socrates solves this (λύει) by declaring that to discover and to learn, are nothing else than to remember, because the soul, being immortal, formerly knew every thing, of which knowledge, becoming oblivious by being merged in the body, she endeavours to recall knowledge to memory by investigation.

[1] Knowing by universal, being ignorant by proper knowledge.

ledge simply should subsist in any other way.[1] Whether therefore there is any other mode of knowing we shall tell hereafter, but we say also that we obtain knowledge through demonstration, but I call demonstration a scientific* syllogism, and I mean by scientific that according to which, from our possessing it, we know. If then to know is what we have laid down, it is necessary that demonstrative science should be from things true, first, immediate, more known than, prior to, and the causes of the conclusion, for thus there will be the appropriate first principles of whatever is demonstrated.[2] Now syllogism will subsist even without these, but demonstration will not, since it will not produce knowledge. It is necessary then that they should be true, since we cannot know that which does not subsist, for instance, that the diameter of a square is commensurate with its side. But it must be from things first and indemonstrable, or otherwise a man will not know them, because he does not possess the demonstration of them,[3] for to know those things of which there is demonstration not accidentally is to possess demonstration. But they must be causes, and more known, and prior; causes indeed, because we then know scientifically when we know the cause; and prior, since they are causes; previously known also, not only according

* Syllog. qui scire facit. Buhle.

2. Specified elements of true demonstrative science.

1. True.

2. First and indemonstrable.

3. Causes of the conclusion.

[1] True science requires, 1st, that the cause of a thing be known, i. e. that the middle term be the cause of the conclusion; 2nd, that the cause be compared with the effect, so that we know it to be the cause of the conclusion; 3rd, that we know the conclusion to subsist thus necessarily, and that it cannot subsist otherwise. Taylor. Comp. Rhet. i. c. 7. Magna Moralia, i. c. 34. Metap. i. 1, and 10, 3, and 7. Cause and ἀρχη must not be confounded, since the cause precedes the ἀρχὴ; vide Buckley's note in Bohn's edition of the Rhetoric quoted above.

[2] Vide Hill's Logic, page 289, also Mansel, p. 104, et seq.; in the appendix note H. of the latter's work, the reader will find the statement of the nature of demonstrative syllogism fully set forth. The words first and immediate, signify that they are not demonstrable by a middle term from any higher truth. The demonstration, "propter quid sit per causam non primam," would only form a subordinate portion of a complex demonstration. Vide Wall's Log. lib. iii. cap. 22. As post demonstrations depend upon those prior, therefore all are said to be from things first.

[3] Either they would be unknown or not be principles, because they might be demonstrated by other things prior to them, ad infinitum. Vide Whately's Logic, book iv.

4. Prior and more known, in a two-fold respect.

to the other mode by understanding (what they signify), but by knowing that they are.[1] Moreover they are prior and more known in two ways, for what is prior in nature, is not the same as that which is prior in regard to us, nor what is more known (simply) the same as what is more known to us. Now I call things prior and more known to us, those which are nearer to sense, and things prior and more known simply, those which are more remote from sense; and those things are most remote * which are especially universal,[2] and those nearest which are singular, and these are mutually opposed. That again is from things first, which is from peculiar principles,[3] and I mean by first, the same thing as the principle, but the principle of demonstration is an immediate proposition, and that is immediate to which there is no other prior. Now a proposition is one part of enunciation, one of one,[4] dialectic indeed, which similarly assumes either (part of contradiction), but demonstrative which definitely (assumes) that one (part) is true. Enunciation is either part of contradiction, and contradiction is an opposition † which has no medium in respect to itself. But that part of contradiction (which declares)

* i. e. from sense.

5. Immediate.

3. Distinction of proposition.

† Vide ch. 10. Categories.

[1] Principles are prior in a two-fold respect, they cause a thing to be, and also cause the same to be known. Taylor. Comp. Anal. Post. i. 24. The inquiry into the definition of a thing is identical with that of its cause, with the difference that the cause of attributes is to be sought in their subject, but in the case of substances per se the cause must be sought in themselves only. Cf. Metap. v. 1, 2; x. 7, 2.

[2] Aristotle here intimates his concurrence with the Platonic theory, that the soul contains in itself essentially the "universal," or true principle of demonstration; vide the Commentary of Proclus on the Parmenides of Plato, in which he exhibits the priority of universals to singulars, and the method of their reception by the dianœtic faculty. Cf. also Ritter and Cousin upon the Old Academy. Arist. Ethics, b. vi. c. 11, and Metap. books i. iv. vi. and xii. (Leip. ed.) If demonstration be from universals prior by nature, it follows, according to Aristotle, that it is alone from forms essentially inherent in the soul, since abstract forms are not *naturally* prior, because they are universals of a *posterior* origin.

[3] That principles ought to be peculiar to the science, and to what is to be demonstrated, he shows, ch. vii. and ix.

[4] One enunciation signifies one thing of one. Vide ch. 8, on Interpretation.

something, of somewhat, is affirmation, and that (which signifies) something from somewhat is negation.* Of an immediate syllogistic principle, I call that the thesis, which it is not possible to demonstrate, nor is it necessary that he should possess it, who intends to learn any thing; but what he who intends to learn any thing must necessarily possess, that I call an axiom,[1] for there are certain things of this kind, and in denominating these, we are accustomed generally to use this name. But of thesis, that which receives either part of contradiction, as for instance, I mean that a certain thing is, or that it is not, is hypothesis, but that which is without this, is definition. For definition is a thesis, since the arithmetician lays down unity to be that which is indivisible, according to quantity, yet it is not hypothesis, since *what* unity is, and *that* unity is, are not the same thing.

* Ch. 6, on Interpretation.

4. Definition of thesis, considered by Pacius and Waits as synonymous with πτῶσις.

5. Of axiom.

6. Of hypothesis.

Notwithstanding, since we must believe in and know a thing from possessing such a syllogism as we call demonstration, and this is, because these are so, of which syllogism consists—it is necessary not only to have a previous knowledge of the first, or all, or some things, but that they should be more known, for that on account of which any thing exists, always exists itself in a greater degree; for example, that on account of which we love is itself more beloved. Hence if we know and believe on account of things first, we also know and believe those first things in a greater degree, because through them (we know and believe) things posterior. A man however cannot believe more than what he knows, those things which he does not know, nor with respect to which he is better disposed

[1] Axioms are common, according to Aristotle, to several classes, but in the case of a single science need only be assumed to an extent commensurate with the object-matter of that science. As Mansel well observes, the places in which the axioms are mentioned in connexion with demonstration, have never been satisfactorily explained on the usual scholastic interpretation. I entirely agree with him, that the supposition that axioms are *virtually*, but not *actually*, employed in demonstration, and the distinction drawn between immediate propositions and axioms, are equally unfounded; in fact, it subverts Aristotle's own expression. Vide Mansel's Logic, App. 66. Compare also Zabarella in I. An. Post. Cont. 57, 58. Crakanthorpe, Logic, lib. iv. c. 1. Aquinas Opusc. 48, de Syllo. Dem. cap. 6.

than if he knew.[1] This however will happen, unless some one should previously know of those who give credence through demonstration, since it is more necessary to believe either in all or in certain first principles, than in the conclusion. It is not only however requisite that he who is to possess knowledge through demonstration, should know in a greater degree first principles, and believe rather in them than in the thing demonstrated, but also that nothing else should be more credible or more known to him than the opposites of the principles, from which a syllogism of contra-deception may consist, since it behoves him who possesses knowledge singly to be unchangeable.[2]

7. The necessity of knowing principles and their opposites, in order to possess science by demonstration.

CHAP. III.—*Refutation of certain opinions as to Science and Demonstration.*

1. Refutation of those who deny the existence of science.

To some, because it is necessary that first things should be known, science does not appear to exist, but to others to exist indeed, yet (they think) there are demonstrations of all things, neither of which opinions is true or necessary.[3] For those who suppose

[1] By being better disposed, Aristotle, who is here speaking of demonstrative knowledge, means the intuitive apprehension of intellect. Cf. Waitz and Biese in loc.

[2] That is, free from lapsing into error, which he would fall into by not knowing opposites, since he might believe that the opposites to true principles are true. For the better elucidation of the above chapter, the following table of the principles of science is given:

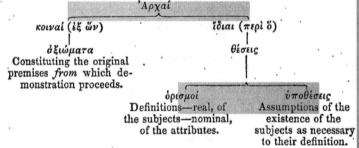

Ἀρχαί

- *κοιναί* (ἐξ ὧν)
  - *ἀξιώματα*
    Constituting the original premises *from* which demonstration proceeds.
- *ἴδιαι* (περὶ ὅ)
  - *θέσεις*
    - *ὁρισμοί*
      Definitions—real, of the subjects—nominal, of the attributes.
    - *ὑποθέσεις*
      Assumptions of the existence of the subjects as necessary to their definition.

[3] The argument is as follows: there are, or are not, certain *πρῶτα*; if there are not, but we admit a process ad infinitum, there is no science, since the latter ultimately depends on certain *πρῶτα*: if there are

that knowledge does not subsist at all, these think that we are to proceed to infinity as if we may not know things subsequent by things prior, of which there are no first, reasoning rightly, since it is impossible to penetrate infinites.[1] And if (they say) we are to stop, and there are principles, these are unknown, since there is no demonstration of them, which alone they say is to know scientifically; but if it is not possible to know first things, neither can we know either simply or properly things which result from these, but by hypothesis, if these exist. Others however assent with respect to knowledge, for (they assert) that it is only through demonstration, but that nothing prevents there being a demonstration of all things, for demonstration may be effected in a circle, and (things be proved) from each other. We on the contrary assert, that neither is all science demonstrative, but that the science of things immediate is indemonstrable. And this is evidently necessary, for if it is requisite to know things prior, and from which demonstration subsists, but some time or other there is a stand made at things immediate, these must of necessity be indemonstrable. This therefore we thus assert, and we say that there is not only science,* but also a certain principle of science, by which we know terms.[2] But that it is impossible to demonstrate in a circle simply is evident, since demon-

2. Also of those who declare all things capable of demonstration.

* That is, demonstrative science.

3. We cannot demonstrate in a circle things

"firsts" on the other hand, still there is no science, for the latter being from things prior, there can be nothing prior to "firsts."

[1] They are right in saying we cannot know things posterior through the prior, unless the progress of investigation stop at certain "firsts;" they are wrong in asserting that these firsts cannot be known. Cf. Physics, lib. i. and iii.

[2] A certain knowledge antecedent to demonstrative science. The word ὅροι, here, Pacius mistakes for "simple terms;" it signifies rather, as St. Hilaire observes, "les propositions immediates," i. e. axioms. The following is the interpretation by Ammonius of this place. The principle of science is intellect, not our intellect, but that which is divine and above us; but terms are intelligible and divine forms, which are called terms in consequence of being the boundaries of all things. For as multitude originates from the monad, and is dissolved into the monad, and tens are the boundaries of hundreds, and hundreds of thousands, but the monad is the common boundary of all numbers; thus also with respect to things, we may say that the boundaries of sensibles are the celestial bodies, of the celestial bodies intelligible essences, and of all things in common the first cause. And this may be said in answer to those who

which do not reciprocate.

stration must consist of things prior and more known, as it is impossible that the same should be prior and posterior to the same, unless in a different way, as for instance, some things with reference to us, but others simply in the manner in which induction makes known.* If however this be so, to know simply will not be well defined, but it is two-fold,[1] or the other demonstration is not simply so which is produced from things more known to us.† Still there happens to those who assert there is demonstration in a circle, not only what has now been declared, but that they say nothing else than this is if it is, and in this manner we may easily demonstrate all things. Nevertheless it is evident that this occurs, when three terms are laid down, for to assert that demonstration recurs through many or through few terms, or whether through few or through two, makes no difference. For when A existing, B necessarily is, and from this last C, if A exists C will exist, if then, when A is, it is necessary that B should be, but this existing, A exists, (for this were to demonstrate in a circle,) let A be laid down in the place of C. To say therefore that because B is A is, is equivalent to saying that C is, and this is to say that A existing C is, but C is the same as A, so that it happens that they who assert there is demonstration in a circle, say nothing else than that A is because A is, and thus we may easily demonstrate all things. Neither however is this possible, except in those things which follow each other as properties: from one thing however being laid down, it has been proved‡ that there will never necessarily result something else, (I mean by one thing, neither one term, nor one thesis being laid down,) but from two first and least theses, it is possible (to infer necessarily something else), since we may syllogize. If then A is consequent to B and to C, and these to each

* Vide Whately, b. iv. ch. 1, also Metap. lib. ii.

† i. e. of the ὅτι, see ch. 13.

4. Example.

‡ Anal. Prior, book i. ch. 24.

subvert demonstration by a procession to infinity, that we not only say there is demonstration, but that things do not proceed to infinity, because there is a certain principle of demonstration by which we know the terms or boundaries of things, when we obtain illumination from thence. Perhaps, however, by a "certain principle of science," Aristotle means our intellect, and by terms, axioms. Cf. Metap. lib. ii. and x.

[1] The one from things more known and prior, according to nature; the other from those more known and prior, according to us.

other, and to A, thus indeed it is possible to demonstrate all those things which are required from each other in the first figure, as we have shown in the books on Syllogism.* It has also been shown † that in the other figures there is either not a syllogism,‡ or not one concerning the subjects assumed ;[1] but it is by no means possible to demonstrate in a circle those which do not reciprocate. Hence, since there are but few such in demonstrations, it is evidently vain and impossible to say, that there is demonstration of things from each other, and that on this account universal demonstration is possible.

* Anal. Prior, book ii. ch. 5.
† Ibid. ch. 5, et seq.
‡ (circulo.) Buhle.

CHAP. IV.—*Upon the terms "every," "per se," and "universal."* 225

1. Definition of demonstration.

SINCE it is impossible that a thing, of which there is simply science, should have a various subsistence, it will be also necessary that what we know should pertain to demonstrative science, and demonstrative science is that which we possess from possessing demonstration, hence a syllogism is a demonstration from necessary (propositions). We must comprehend then of what, and what kind (of propositions), demonstrations consist; but first let us define what we mean by "of every," and "per se," and "universal."

2. Of predication "de omni." τὸ κατὰ παντός.

I call that "of every," which is not in a certain thing, and in another certain thing is not, nor which is at one time, and not at another; as if animal is predicated of every man, if it is truly said that this is a man, it is true also that he is an animal, and if now the one is true, so also is the other; and in like manner, if a point is in every line. Here is a proof, for when we are questioned as it were of every, we thus object, either if a thing is not present with a certain individual, or if it is not sometimes. But I call those "per se" which are inherent in (the definition of) what a thing

3. Of "τὸ καθ' αὑτό," "per se."

[1] Both assumed prop. are not proved, because in the 2nd fig. the conclusion is negative, wherefore we cannot prove an affirmative prop. in a circle; and in the 3rd fig. the conclusion is particular, wherefore an universal cannot be demonstrated in a circle.

is,[1] as line is in triangle, and point in line, (for the essence of them is from these,* and they are in the definition explaining what it is:)[2] also those things which are inherent in their attributes in the definition declaring what a thing is,[3] as the straight and the curved are inherent in a line, and the odd and even in number, and the primary† and composite,‡ the equilateral § and the oblong:[4] and they are inherent in all these, in the definition declaring what a thing is, there indeed line, but here number. In a similar manner, in other things, I say that such are per se inherent in each, but what are in neither way inherent (I call) accidents, as the being musical, or white in an animal. Moreover, that which is not predicated of any other subject, as that which walks being something else, is that which walks, and is white, but essence and whatever things signify this particular thing, not being any thing else, are that which they are. Now those which are not predicated of a subject, I call "per se," but those which are so predicated, I call accidents. Again, after another manner, that which on account of itself is present with each thing is "per se," but that which is not on account of itself is an accident;[5] thus it is an accident if while any body was walking it should lighten, for it did not lighten on account of his walking, but we say that it accidentally happened. If, however, a thing is present on account of itself, it is per se, as if any one having his throat

* i. e. from line and point.

† As 3, 5, 7, &c.

‡ As 9, i. e. 3, 3, 3, &c.

§ i. e. a square number. Taylor.

4. Of accidents. συμβεβηκότα. (Cf. Phys. lib. ii., et Metap. lib. v.)

[1] Four senses are given of this expression, τὸ καθ' αὑτό: 1. When the predicate is part of the definition of the subject. 2. When the subject is part of the definition of the predicate. 3. When existence is predicated of a substance. 4. When the subject is the external efficient cause of the predicate. In proper demonstration, propositions must be "per se" either in the first or second meaning. Cf. Mansel's Logic, note H. on the Demonstrative Syllogism.

[2] Thus a triangle is defined to be a figure contained by three straight lines.

[3] As, to use Aristotle's graphic illustration, in the definition of nose, flatness of nose is not employed, but flatness of nose is defined to be a curvature of nose.

[4] An oblong number is that which a number produces, not multiplied by itself, but by another number, as six is from twice three. Taylor.

[5] This relates to the efficient cause.

cut should die, and through the wound, because he will die in consequence of his throat being cut, but it did not accidentally happen that he whose throat was cut died. Those therefore which are predicated in things which are simply objects of science per se, so as to be inherent in the things predicated,* or which are themselves inherent in subjects,† are on account of themselves, and from necessity, for it does not happen that they are not inherent either simply or as opposites, as the straight and the curved in a line, and the even or odd in number. For a contrary is either privation or contradiction in the same genus, as that is even which is not odd in numbers, so far as it follows:[1] hence if it is requisite to affirm or deny, it is also necessary that those which are per se should be inherent.

5. "Per se," recapitulation.

* 1st mode.

† 2nd mode.

6. What is a contrary.

Let then the expressions "of every" and "per se" be thus defined: I call that universal, however, which is both predicated "of every" and "per se," and so far as the thing is.[2] Now it is evident that whatever are universal are inherent in things necessarily, but the expressions "per se," "and so far as it is," are the same; as a point and straightness are per se present in a line, for they are in it, in as far as it is a line, and two right angles in a triangle, so far as it is a triangle, for a triangle is per se equal to two right angles. But universal is then present, when it is demonstrated of any casual and primary thing, as to possess two right angles is not universally inherent in figure, yet it is possible to demonstrate of a figure that it has two right angles, but not of any casual figure, nor does a demonstrator use any casual figure, for a square is indeed a figure, yet it has not angles equal to two right. But

7. τὸ ᾗ αὐτό, "quatenus ipsum," and το καθόλου, explained.

[1] Contraries may, however, be both absent from a subject, as a body may be neither white nor black; but the even and odd are opposed as contradictories, so that one of them must be present in a subject. Vide Categ. ch. 10. The even is compared to the not odd, because it is necessarily consequent to it.

[2] As man is risible, because every man is, both "per se" and "quatenus ipsum;" upon the apparent inconsistency of Aristotle in the use of the word καθολου, see Waitz, 1. Ana. Post. p. 315. The reader will find some valuable remarks upon the demonstratio potissima, especially in reference to this place, in Mansel's Logic, Appendix, note H., where the example is regularly stated.

any isosceles has angles equal to two right, yet not primarily, for triangle is prior. Whatever therefore is casually first demonstrated to possess two right angles, or any thing else, in this first is the universal inherent, and the demonstration per se of this is universal, but of other things after a certain manner not per se, neither is it universally present in an isosceles, but extends farther.

CHAP. V.—*Of Errors about the primary Universal.*[1]

WE ought not to be ignorant that frequently error arises, and that what is demonstrated is not primarily universal, in so far as the primarily universal appears to be demonstrated.

1. Sources of error in effecting universal demonstration. Example.

Now we are deceived by this mistake, when either nothing higher can be assumed, except the singular or singulars, or when something else can be assumed, but it wants a name in things differing in species, or when it happens to be as a whole in a part, of which the demonstration is made, for demonstration will happen to particulars, and will be of every individual, yet nevertheless it will not be the demonstration of this first universal. Still I say the demonstration of this first, so far as it is this, when it is of the first universal. If then any one should show that right lines do not meet, it may appear to be (a proper) demonstration of this, because it is in all right lines, yet this is not so, since this does not arise from the lines being thus equal, but so far as they are in some way or other equal. Also if a triangle should be no other than isosceles, so far as isosceles it may appear to be inherent:

[1] All universals are gained by abstraction, i. e. by separating the phenomena in which a certain number of individuals resemble each other, from those in which they differ; Locke calls all universals, abstract ideas. Upon generalization as distinguished from abstraction, vide Stewart, Phil. of the Human Mind; Whately's Logic, Outline of Laws of Thought, p. 44. The causes of the error which a person commits who demonstrates of the inferior as of species, what he ought to demonstrate of the superior as of genus, are four. 1st, When one particular being under universal, we demonstrate the former instead of the latter: 2nd, when we demonstrate of all contained under a proper subject when we seem to do so of the proper subject itself: 3rd, when the particular is demonstrated because the universal has no name: 4th, when we conclude that an universal demonstration of a thing has been given because the demonstration is of every individual. Cf. Waitz, p. 387, et seq.

alternate proportion also, so far as regards numbers and lines and solids and times (as was once shown separately) it is possible at least to be demonstrated of all by one demonstration, but inasmuch as all these, numbers, length, time, are not one denominated thing, and differ from each other in species, they were assumed separately. But now the demonstration is universal, for it is not in so far as they are lines or numbers, that it is inherent, but in so far as this thing which they suppose to be universally inherent. For this reason neither if one should demonstrate each several triangle by one or another demonstration, that each has two right angles, equilateral, the scalene, and the isosceles separately, would he yet know that the triangle (itself) has angles equal to two right, except in a sophistical manner,* nor triangle universally, though there should be no other triangle besides these. For he does not know it so far as it is triangle, nor does he know every triangle, except according to number, but not every, according to species, even if there be no one that he does not know.[1] When then does he not know universally, and when knows he simply? It is clear that if there is the same essence of a triangle, and of an equilateral either of each or of all, he knows,†[2] but if there is not the same, but different, and it is inherent so far as it is triangle, he does not know.[3] Whether however is it inherent, so far as it is triangle, or so far as it is isosceles? And when, according to this, is it primary? And of what is the demonstration universally? It is evident that it then is, when, other things being taken away, it is inherent in the primary, thus two right angles will be inherent in a brazen isosceles triangle, when the being brazen and the being isosceles are taken away, but not if the figure or boundary is taken away, nor if the primary are. But what pri-

* Vide supra.

† i. e. universally.

[1] That is, in number. Triangles are here said to be as many in number as in species.

[2] Universally and simply mean nearly the same thing, because when a man knows not sophistically, i. e. simply, he knows universally, hence Taylor and Buhle insert, the one "universally," the latter "simpliciter," as equivalent in this place.

[3] That is, by demonstration of a species of triangle, he does not know the universal property as demonstrated of triangle, viz. the possession of three angles equal to two right.

mary? if indeed triangle (is taken away); according to this it is inherent in others, and of this universally is the demonstration.

25

CHAP. VI.—*Demonstration consists of Principles per se; and of a necessary Medium.*[1]

1. Recapitulation; true demonstration only from necessary propositions.

IF then demonstrative science is from necessary principles, (for what is scientifically known cannot subsist otherwise,) and those which are per se inherent are necessarily so in things, (for some are inherent in the definition of what a thing is, but others are they in the very nature of which the subjects are inherent, of which they are so predicated, that one of opposites is necessarily present,) it is evident that the demonstrative syllogism will consist of certain things of this kind,* for every thing is either thus inherent, or according to accident, but accidents are not necessary.

* i. e. of propositions per se.

Either therefore we must say this, or that demonstration is a necessary thing, if we lay down this principle, and that if demonstration is given that a thing cannot subsist otherwise, wherefore the† syllogism must be from necessary (matter). For it is possible without demonstration to syllogize from what are true, but we cannot do so from things necessary, except by demonstration, for this is now (the essence) of demonstration. An indication also that demonstration is from things necessary is, that we thus object to those who think they demonstrate that (the conclusion) is not necessary, whether we think that the matter may altogether be otherwise possible, or on account of the argument. Hence too the folly of those appears, who think they assume principles rightly, if the proposition be probable and true, as the Sophists (assume) that to know is to possess knowledge.[2] For it is not the probable or improbable, which

† i. e. the demonstrative.

2. Proof of this.

1. Reply to objection.

[1] If things per se or essential are necessary, and the principles of demonstration are necessary; therefore the principles of demonstration are per se. As Taylor observes, by conversion of the major, Aristotle's argument here may become a syllogism in Barbara.

[2] It was thus argued by Protagoras: Whoever knows any thing, pos-

is the principle, but that which is primary of the genus about which the demonstration is made, nor is every thing true appropriate. But that it is necessary that the syllogism should consist of necessary things appears also from these; for if he who cannot assign a reason why a thing is,* when there is a demonstration, does not possess knowledge,† let A‡ be necessarily predicated of C, but B the medium through which it is demonstrated not of necessity, (in this case) he does not know the cause. For this is not on account of the medium, for the latter may not exist, yet the conclusion is necessary. Besides, if some one does not know, though he now possesses a reason, and is safe, the thing also being preserved, he not having forgotten it, neither did he before know it. But the medium may perish if it is not necessary, so that he, being safe, will have a reason,§ the thing being preserved, and yet not know it, wherefore neither did he know it before.[1] But if the medium is not destroyed, yet may possibly perish, that which happens will be possible and contingent, it is impossible however that one so circumstanced should know.[2]

2nd proof.

* The major.
† Vide 2nd ch.
‡ The minor.

3.

§ Conclusionem. Buhle.

When therefore the conclusion is from necessity, there is nothing to prevent the medium through which the demonstration was made from being not necessary, since it is possible to syllogize the necessary even from things not necessary, just as we may the true from things not true. Still when the medium is from necessity the conclusion is also from necessity, as the true (results) from the true always: for let A be of necessity predicated of B, and this of C, then it is

3. If the conclusion be necessary, the premises need not be so, but when the latter are so the conclusion must be necessary.

sesses science: he who possesses science knows what science is: therefore, he who knows any thing knows what science is.

[1] Scientia quam quis habet, non perditur, nisi aut ipse perit aut obliviscitur aut res quam scivit, interit. Waitz. For a general analysis of the argument, see Waitz, page 320, in locum.

[2] Vide Prior Anal. book ii. chap. 2—4. The argument that the medium, the source of science as containing the cause, does not perish, though it may do so, and therefore by its remaining that science may be possessed, Aristotle shows to be ineffectual, since they who advance it are compelled to confess that to be possible, viz. that the medium may perish, which is impossible, and hence that we may be ignorant of what we know. By being "so circumstanced," is meant "to be ignorant without forgetfulness." Cf. Whately's Logic, b. iv. c. ii. sec. 2.

necessary that A should be with C. But when the conclusion is not necessary, neither possibly can the medium be necessary: for let A be present with C, not of necessity, but let it be with B, and this with C of necessity; A then will also be of necessity present with C, yet it was not supposed so.[1] Since therefore what one knows demonstratively must be inherent of necessity, we must evidently obtain the demonstration through a necessary medium also, for otherwise, he will neither know why a thing exists, nor that it is necessary for it to exist, but he will either imagine not knowing, if he assumes what is not necessary as if it were necessary,[2] or in like manner he will not imagine if he knows *that* it is through media, and *why* it is through the immediate.*[3]

* Cf. ch. 2.

Of accidents however which are not per se after the manner in which things per se have been defined, there is no de-

[1] The necessary relations between premises and conclusion may be considered as four:

1. If the conclusion is necessary, the propositions may be non-necessary.
2. If the conclusion is non-necessary, the prop. are non-necessary.
3. If the prop. are necessary, the conclusion is always necessary.
4. If the prop. are non-necessary, the conclusion may be necessary.

Granting that the last (number 4.) may be true, yet Aristotle denies that in such a case the person who thus infers demonstrates, because demonstration produces true science, but such a man is ignorant that the conclusion is necessary. Vide also Hill's Logic, p. 285, et seq.

[2] Sanderson defines thus: Error est habitus quo mens inclinatur ad assentiendum sine formidine falsitati. Opinio est habitus quo mens inclinatur ad assentiendum cum formidine alicui propositioni propter probabilitatem quam videtur habere. Error, therefore, as Mansel observes, implies certainty of the subject, but not of the object; whilst opinion cannot consist with certainty of the subject, nor yet, strictly, with that of the object. It is of course clear, that what one may scientifically know, another may only think, but to constitute real science two things are necessary: 1. A correct ascertainment of the data from which we are to reason: 2. Correctness in deduction of conclusions from them. Cf. Whately, b. iv. c. 2, sect. 3. Error, as defined above, comes under the state of mind described in the text by Aristotle.

[3] Cf. Aquinas, Op. 48, cap. 1; Occam, Log. p. 3, c. 2. If the premise is not the first cause, though it contains the cause of the conclusion, the syllogism is not δι' ἀμέσων, and there is no demonstration: neither if the premise be an effect and not a cause of the conclusion, nor if the premise, though immediate, be a remote cause of it, since in all these cases we know the fact only, but not the cause. Cf. Mansel and Wall's Log. lib. iii. cap. 22.

monstrative science, since it is not possible to demonstrate the conclusion of necessity, because accident may possibly not be present, for I speak of accident of this kind.[1] Still some one may perhaps doubt why we must make such investigations about these things, if it is not necessary that the conclusion should be, for it makes no difference if any one interrogating casual things*[2] should afterwards give the conclusion: nevertheless we must interrogate not as if (the conclusion) were necessary on account of things interrogated, but because it is necessary for him who asserts these should assert this, and that he should speak truly if the things are truly inherent.

4. The non-necessary, not to be neglected in disputation.

* τὰ τυχόντα. (Cf. Rhetoric, b. i. c. 5, and 10; Phy. lib. ii.)

Since, however, whatever are inherent per se are necessarily inherent in every genus, and so far as each is, it is clear that scientific demonstrations are of things "per se" inherent, and consist of such as these. For accidents are not necessary:† wherefore it is not necessary to know the conclusion why it is, nor if it always is, but not "per se,"[3] as, for instance, syllogisms formed from signs.‡ For what is "per se" will not be known "per se," nor why it is, and to know why a thing is, is to know through cause, wherefore the middle must "per se" be inherent in the third, and the first in the middle.

5. Necessity of the minor and major propositions being "per se."

† An. Post. ii. 8.

‡ Vide Rhet. b. ii. c. 24.

CHAP. VII.—*That we may not demonstrate by passing from one Genus to another.*[4]

It is not therefore possible to demonstrate passing from one genus to another, as, for instance,

1. Three things in demonstration, viz. a de-

[1] i. e. about common accident—for proper accident is predicated in the second mode per se of a subject. Taylor.

[2] Ad veram demonstrationem nihil attinet si quis sumat quæ in casu posita, et mutationi obnoxia sint et quæ inde consequantur, declaret. Waitz. The casual, here alluded to, are propositions not belonging to the conclusion.

[3] If it always is inherent, i. e. if the propositions be always true.

[4] Cf. Anal. Post. i. 10. Eth. i. 2. Keckermann Syst. Log. iii. Tract. 2. cap. 1. Zabarella de Meth. lib. ii. cap. 7. Genus here signifies the object or materia circa quam, often, but improperly, called the subject; the species are the subdivisions of the general subject. In the

monstrated conclusion, axioms, and the subject genus.

* The attribute concluded of the subject.

† Cf. Aquinas Opusc. 48, c. 11.

‡ Vide ch. 11.

§ Vide ch. 9.

(to demonstrate) a geometrical (problem) by arithmetic, for there are three things in demonstrations, one the demonstrated conclusion, and this is that which is per se inherent in a certain genus.* Another are axioms, but axioms are they from which (demonstration is made), the third is the subject genus, whose properties and essential accidents demonstration makes manifest.† Now it is possible that the things from which demonstration consists may be the same,‡ but with those whose genus is different, as arithmetic and geometry, we cannot adapt an arithmetical demonstration to the accidents of magnitudes, except magnitudes are numbers, and how this is possible to some shall be told hereafter.§ But arithmetical demonstration always has the genus about which the demonstration (is conversant), and others in like manner, so that it is either simply necessary that there should be the same genus, or in a certain respect,[1] if demonstration is about to be transferred; but that it is otherwise impossible is evident, for the extremes and the middles must necessarily be of the same genus, since if they are not per se, they will be accidents. On this account we cannot by geometry demonstrate that there is one science of contraries, nor that two cubes make one cube,[2] neither can any science (demonstrate) what belongs to any science, but such as are so related to each other as to be the one under the other, for instance, optics to geometry, and harmonics to arithmetic. Nor if any thing is inherent in lines not so far as they are lines, nor as they are from proper principles, as if a straight line is the most beautiful of lines, or if it is contrary to circumference, for these things are inherent not by reason of their proper genus, but in so far as they have something common.

2. That the extremes and media must be of the same genus.

demonstrative syllogism, the minor term is the subject; the major, the attribute; the middle, the cause.

[1] Of subaltern sciences, the subject is not *entirely* the same, as the subject of geometry is a line, but of optics an optical line. Taylor. Vide also Trendelenburg, p. 118.

[2] That is, geometry cannot teach a method of doubling the cube. Vide Reimer de Duplicatione Cubi. Omnis demonstratio genus suum, non excedere sed in eo consistere debet. Waitz.

CHAP. VIII.—*Things which are subject to Change are incapable of Demonstration per se.*

1. That there is no demonstration nor definition "per se" of mutable natures, because of the universal being non-existent.

IT is also evident that if the propositions of which a syllogism consists are universal, the conclusion of such a demonstration, and in short of the demonstration of itself, must necessarily be perpetual. There is not then either demonstration, nor in short science of corruptible natures, but so as by accident, because there is not universal belonging to it, but sometimes, and after a certain manner. But when there is such, it is necessary that one proposition should not be universal, and that it should be corruptible, corruptible indeed, because the conclusion will be so if the proposition is so, and not universal, because one of those things of which it is predicated will be, and another will not be,[1] hence it is not possible to conclude universally, but that it is now. It is the same in the case of definitions, since definition is either the principle of demonstration, or demonstration, differing in the position (of the terms), or a certain conclusion of demonstration. The demonstrations and sciences however of things frequently occurrent, as of the eclipse of the moon, evidently always exist, so far as they are such, but so far as they are not always, they are particular,[2] and as in an eclipse, so also is it in other things.

CHAP. IX.—*That the Demonstration of a thing ought to proceed from its own appropriate Principles: these last indemonstrable.*

1. That true demonstration

SINCE however it is evident that we cannot demonstrate each thing except from its own prin-

[1] Hoc quidem (tempore) erit quod asseritur, hoc vero (tempore) non erit. Buhle. I prefer Buhle's translation for its clearness, but have followed Taylor's on account of its exactness. The science of things subject to change is not simply science, but with the addition of κατὰ συμβεβηκός. Upon the relation of science to its subject-matter, see Rhet. book i. ch. 7. Cf. also Rhet. ii. ch. 24. Anal. Prior, i. ch. 13. The subject of science, he expressly says in the Ethics, (b. vi. ch. 4,) has a necessary existence, therefore it is eternal and indestructible.

[2] Particular cases, (of eclipses, for instance,) as they are not always the same, do not fall under demonstration.

Ab Boll 11.563
Syllogism leading to the impossible P. 219

only results from principles appropriate to the subject of demonstration: the terms must either be homogeneous, or from two genera, of which one is contained in the other.

ciples, if what is to be demonstrated is inherent in a subject so far as the subject is that (which it is), to have a scientific knowledge of that thing is not this, if it should be demonstrated from true, indemonstrable, and immediate (propositions).[1] For we may so demonstrate possibly, as Bryso did, the quadrature of the circle, since such reasonings prove through something common, that which is inherent in another thing, hence these arguments are adapted to other things not of the same genus.[2] Wherefore that thing would not be scientifically known, as far as it is such, but from accident, for otherwise the demonstration would not be adapted also to another genus.

* Cf. Eth. b. vi. ch. 3.

† The possession of three angles equal to two right.

‡ Of triangle.

§ πάθος, or property, like ἴδιον here.

|| i. e. with the extremes, subject, and property.

We know however each thing not accidentally when we know it according to that, after which it is inherent from principles which are those of that thing, so far as it is that thing;[3]* as that a thing has angles equal to two right angles, in which the thing spoken of† is essentially inherent from the principles of this thing.‡ Hence if that§ is essentially inherent in what it is inherent, it is necessary that the middle should be in the same affinity,|| but if not, yet it will be as harmonics are proved through an arithmetical principle.[4] Such things however are demonstrated after a similar manner,

[1] That is, the propositions must also be appropriate to the subject of demonstration.

[2] According to Alexander Aphrodisiensis—Bryso endeavoured to demonstrate the quadrature of the circle thus: Where the greater and less are found, there also is the equal found, but a square greater and less than a circle is found, therefore a square equal to the circle may also be found. The minor is proved, because a square *in*scribed in a circle is less, and *circum*scribed about a circle is greater than the circle, but the demonstration is founded on a common principle, because the greater, the less, and the equal are found not only in a square and circle, but also in other things. Neither is the major universally true, because a rectilinear angle may be given greater or less than the angle in a semicircle, but one equal to it cannot be given. Vide Euclid Elem. Prop. xvi. b. 3.

[3] The examples of Aristotle are principally taken from the Mathematics, and the tests of καθ' αὑτό and ᾗ αὐτό are expressly applied to a geometrical theorem. Mansel. Vide the 4th chap. of this book.

[4] That is, by the application of the principle of a superior science, to a problem belonging to a subaltern science, as music is subaltern to arithmetic.

yet they differ,[1] for *that* they are, is part of another science,* (for the subject genus is another,†) but *why* they are, is a province of a superior science, of which they are the essential qualities. Hence from these things also it is apparent that we cannot demonstrate each thing simply, but from its proper principles, and the principles of these‡ have something common.

* Inferior science.

† i. e. differs from the subject of superior science.

‡ Of subaltern sciences.

2. That the appropriate principles of each thing are themselves incapable of demonstration. What is the especial science.

If then this is evident, it is also clear that it is impossible to demonstrate the proper principles of each thing, for they will be the principles of all things, and the science of them the mistress of all (sciences):[2] for the man has more scientific knowledge who knows from superior causes, since he knows from prior things when he knows not from effects, but from causes. So that if he knows more, he knows also most, and if that be science, it is also more, and most of all such. Demonstration however is not suitable to another genus, except as we have said, geometrical to mechanical or optical, and arithmetical to harmonical demonstrations.

3. Difficulty of deciding whether a thing is really known.

Nevertheless it is difficult to know whether a man possesses knowledge or not, since it is hard to ascertain if we know from the principles of each thing or not, which indeed constitutes knowledge. We think however that we know, if we have got a syllogism from certain primary truths, but it is not so, since it is necessary that they§ should be of a kindred nature with the primary.

§ i. e. the conclusions with principles.

[1] Where the principle is assumed from the same science, or from a superior one, the difference is, that, in the former case, the ὅτι and διότι are known; but in the latter, the διότι is known in the superior, the ὅτι in the inferior science.

[2] Metaphysics. See the third book of Aristotle's treatise on that subject; also Magna Moralia, lib. i.; De Animâ, books i. ii. iii.

* Cf. Metaph. books v. vi. x.

CHAP. X.—*Of the Definition and Division of Principles.**

1. Definition of principles, (ἀρχαί,) their existence to be assumed. Example.

† Vide ch. 2.

I CALL those principles in each genus, the existence of which it is impossible to demonstrate. What then first things,† and such as result from these signify, is assumed, but as to principles, we must *assume* that they are, but *demonstrate* the rest, as what unity is, or what the straight and a triangle are; it is necessary however to assume that unity and magnitude exist, but to demonstrate the other things.[1]

2. What are peculiar to each science, and what common.

Of those which are employed in demonstrative sciences, some are peculiar to each science, but others are common, and common according to analogy, since each is useful, so far as it is in the genus under science. The peculiar indeed are such as, that a line is a thing of this kind, and that the straight is, but the common are, as that if equals be taken from equals the remainders are equal. Now each of these is sufficient, so far as it is in the genus, for (a geometrician) will effect the same, though he should not assume of all, but in magnitudes alone, and the arithmetician in respect of numbers[2] (alone).

2. ἴδια.

Proper principles, again, are those which are assumed to be, and about which science considers whatever are inherent per se, as arithmetic assumes unities, and geometry points and lines, for they assume that these are, and that they are this particular thing.‡ But the essential properties of these, what each signifies, they assume, as arithmetic, what the odd is, or the even, or a square, or a cube; and geometry,

‡ They assume *that* they are, and *what* they are.

[1] The above clears Aristotle from the charge unjustly brought against him by Mill, since the former states here the necessity of *assuming* the existence of the subject, as clearly as the latter asserts it. (Vide Mill's Logic, vol. i.) The principles (ἐξ ὧν) from which Aristotle demonstrates are axioms of which he gives a specimen below: "If equals, &c." Vide the table of the principles of science, given before. Cf. also Euclid, b. vi. Prop. 11.

[2] The geometrician and arithmetician each assume the principle, only so far as it is analogous to his subject science; thus the former does not assume every whole to be greater than its part, but that every *magnitude* is so, and the latter that every whole *number* is greater than its part. Cf. Waitz in loc.

what is not proportionate, or what is to be broken, or to incline; but *that* they are, they demonstrate through things common,* and from those which have been demonstrated.† So also astronomy, for all demonstrative science is conversant with three things, those which are laid down as existing, and these are the genus,‡ (the essential properties of which the science considers,) and common things called axioms, from which as primaries they demonstrate; and thirdly, the affections,§ the signification of each of which the demonstrator assumes.[1] There is nothing however to prevent certain sciences overlooking some of these, as if the genus is not supposed to be, if it be manifest[2] that it exists, (for it is not similarly manifest that number is, as that the cold and hot are,) and if (the science) does not assume what the affections signify, if they are evident, as neither does it assume what things common signify, (as what it is) to take away equals from equals, because it is known; nevertheless these things are naturally three, viz. that about which demonstration is employed, the things demonstrated, and the principles from which they are.

* i. e. principles.

† i. e. conclusions.

3. All demonstration conversant with three things, of which we sometimes may neglect two.

‡ i. e. the subject.

§ Properties. Taylor.—Affectiones. Buhle.—Passiones. Averrois.

Neither however hypothesis nor postulate is that which it is necessary should exist per se, and be necessarily seen,‖ for demonstration does not belong to external speech, but to what is in the soul,[3] since neither does syllogism. For it is always possible to object to external discourse,

4. Of the difference between ἀξίωμα, ὑπόθεσις, and αἴτημα.

‖ Vide Mansel, p. 38, App. Waitz in loc.

[1] Vide Trendelenburg Erlaüteringen, p. 118. For a full enunciation of the statement made here by Aristotle, the reader is referred to Mansel's Logic, p. 109, and Appendices.

[2] It is not made the subject of hypothesis, if it is manifest; in other words, it is tacitly assumed.

[3] The two kinds of speech were, 1st, λόγος ὁ ἔξω, καὶ προφορικὸς, καὶ κατὰ τὴν φωνὴν, i. e. the external, and (2nd) the internal, ὁ ἔσω, καὶ ἐνδιάθετος, καὶ κατὰ τὴν ψυχὴν. Plut. in Philo. et Damascen. Both Whately and Aldrich regard language as the principal object of logic; the former declares that "if any process of reasoning can take place in the mind without any employment of language, orally or mentally, such a process does not come within the province of the science here treated of." Mansel, on the contrary, considers "the laws of such process, equally with any other, matters of logical investigation." The reader may pro-

but not always to internal. Whatever things then, being demonstrable, a man assumes without demonstration, these, if he assumes what appear probable to the learner, he supposes, and this is not an hypothesis simply, but with reference to the learner alone; but if, there being no inherent opinion, or when a contrary is inherent, the demonstrator assumes, he requires the same thing to be granted to him. And in this hypothesis and postulate differ, for postulate is any thing sub-contrary to the opinion of the learner, which though demonstrable a man assumes, and uses without demonstration.

5. That definition is not hypothesis. Definitions then are not hypotheses, (for they are not asserted to be or not to be,) but hypotheses are in propositions. Now it is only necessary that definitions should be understood, but this is not hypothesis, except some one should say that the verb to hear is hypothesis. But they are hypotheses, from the existence of which, in that they are, the conclusion is produced. Neither does the geometrician suppose falsities, as some say, who assert, that it is not right to use a false (principle), but that the geometrician does so, when he calls a line a foot long when it is not so, or the line which he describes a straight line when it is not straight. The geometrician indeed concludes nothing from the lines being so and so, as he has said, but concludes those, which are manifested through these (symbols). Moreover postulate and every hypothesis are either as a whole or as in a part, but definitions are neither of these.[1]

fitably compare Locke's Essay, b. iv. 5, 5, and 6, 2; also Sanderson. The former's distinction between mental and verbal propositions is well known. The words in the text are only enunciative of oral as contrasted with mental reasoning, but are not decisive against Whately's opinion. Vide De Animâ, b. i. and iii.; Eth. b. i. c. 13. Dr. Hessey speaks sensibly enough of the "absurdity of maintaining that logic regards the accident of the external language, and not the necessity of the internal thought" (p. 4, Intro. Schem. Rhet.). It appears to be, after all, "splitting a straw;" for such an opinion is not only "absurd," but self-destructive, we never *do*, because we never *can*, practically adopt it.

[1] Definitio ab hypothesi eo differt quod nihil edicit de existentia rei quæ definitur: nam si quis contendat definitionem, licet non ponat aliquid esse vel non esse, sed intelligi tantum velit id quod dicat, tamen esse hypothesin, quodcunque auribus percipimus, si quod dictum est intelleximus, hypothesis dicenda erit. Verum ὑποθέσεις dicuntur quibus positis (ὅσων ὄντων) et ex quibus aliud quid colligitur. Alia causa cur

Faith as an intellectual act & its reconciliation with the Aristotelian origin of ideas. Idea of Plato's "bed" not practical. see Republic

CHAP. XI.—*Of certain Common Principles of all Sciences.*

THAT there should then be forms,* or one certain thing besides the many, is not necessary, to the existence of demonstration,[1] but it is necessary truly to predicate one thing of the many, for there will not be the universal unless this be so, and if there be not an universal, there will not be a medium, so that neither will there be a demonstration. It is essential then that there should be one and the same thing, which is not equivocal in respect of many: no demonstration however assumes that it is impossible to affirm and deny the same thing at one and the same time, unless it is requisite also thus to demonstrate the conclusion. It is demonstrated however by assuming the first † to be true of the middle, and that it is not true to deny it, but it makes no difference

* Εἴδη—species. Buhle.

1. Demonstration may exist without εἰδη, but not without an universal conception.

† i. e. the major prop.

definitio non appellari possit hypothesis in eo est, quod hæc aut universalis est aut particularis, in illa, vero quod subjectum est æquale esse debet ei quod prædicatur. Waitz. Vide also scheme of principles of science. Cf. Locke's Essay, b. iii. 4, 7. Occam's Logic, part i.

[1] The Platonic theory of Idea, to which Aristotle here refers, so highly commended by St. Augustine, is not free from much error, arising from Plato's opinion that the ideas in man's soul are inherently good. The remark which Aristotle makes in this place, seems chiefly, as Taylor thinks, to prevent the misconception of Plato's theory, by those who imagined his ideas to be corporeally separate from matter, and not incorporeal forms residing in a divine intellect; but the real case is, that Aristotle elsewhere impugns the doctrine of the idea as not practical. Vide Ethics, lib. i. c. 6, Browne's note, Bohn's edition; also Metaphysics, lib. xii. De Animâ; Brewer's Ethics; Ritter, vol. ii. The province of the Platonic dialectic was to investigate the true nature of that connexion, which existed between each thing and the archetypal form or idea which made it what it was, and to awaken the soul to a full remembrance of what she had known prior to her being imprisoned in the body. Hence, dialectic, with Plato, is the science of the immutable, and takes cognizance of the universal principle; in fact, is an object identical with the Metaphysics of Aristotle, whereas the dialectic of the latter partook of the essentially practical nature of his mind, and is merely "the art of disputing by question and answer." Cf. Gorgias, Theætetus, Meno, and the Commentaries of Syrianus, and upon the doctrine of universals, see Locke's Essay, b. iv.; Stewart, Phil. of Human Mind; Whately's and Mansel's Logics.

Ethics I. 6

271

Callias is a Man

whether we assume the middle to be or not to be, and in a similar manner also in respect of the third.[1] For if that be granted* in respect of which it is true to predicate man, even if (some one should think that man is) not man, (the conclusion) will be true, if only it is said that man is an animal, and not that he is not an animal, for it will be true to say that Callias, even if he be not Callias,† yet is still an animal,‡ but not that which is not an animal. The cause however is, that the first is not only predicated of the middle, but also of something else, in consequence of its being common to many, so that neither if the middle be that thing itself, or not that thing, does it make any difference in respect to the conclusion. But the demonstration which leads to the impossible, assumes that of every thing affirmation or negation is true,§ and these‖ it does not always (assume) universally, but so far as is sufficient, and it is sufficient (which is assumed) in respect of the genus. I mean by the genus, as the genus about which a person introduces demonstrations, as I have observed before.¶

* The major.

† Supply the minor—Callias is a man.

‡ The conclusion.

2. Of the use of what is called the principle of contradiction in demonstration.

§ Vide An. Prior, book ii.

‖ (Axioms.) Taylor.

¶ Vide ch. 10.

3. Of the common principles of the several sciences.

All sciences communicate with each other according to common (principles), and I mean by common those which men use as demonstrating from these, but not those about which they demonstrate, nor that which they demonstrate, and dialectic is (common) to all (sciences). If also any one* endeavours to demonstrate universally common (principles), as that of every thing it is true to affirm or deny, or that equals remain from equals, or others of this kind. Dialectic however does not belong to certain things thus definite, nor to one particular genus;† for it would not interrogate, since it is impossible for the demonstrator to interrogate, because the same thing is not proved from opposites:[2] this however has been shown in the treatment of syllogism.‡

* (Science.) Taylor. i. e. metaphysics. Vide Metap. b. iii.

† i. e. it is conversant with all subjects.

‡ Pr. An. b. ii. ch. 15.

[1] Though the minor should not be assumed both to be and not to be that which it is, nevertheless the conclusion will be right.

[2] Here is a proof of the difference between the dialectic of Plato and

CHAP. XII.—*Of Syllogistic Interrogation.*

1. Method of deciding what proposition belongs to each science.

IF syllogistic interrogation is the same as a proposition of contradiction,[1] but there are propositions in each science, from which the syllogism which belongs to each consists, there will be a certain scientific interrogation, from which the syllogism,* which is appropriate to each science, is drawn. It is clear, then, that not every interrogation would be geometrical, or medical, and so of the rest, but from what any thing is demonstrated about which geometry is conversant, or which are demonstrated from the same principles as geometry, as optics, and in like manner with other sciences. These† also must be discussed from geometrical principles and conclusions,‡ but the discussion of principles is not to be carried on by the geometrician so far as he is such; likewise with other sciences. Neither is every one who possesses science to be interrogated with every question, nor is every question about each to be answered, but those which are defined about the science. It is evident then that he does well, who disputes with a geometrician thus, so far as he is such, if he demonstrate any thing from these principles, but if not, he will not do well. Again, it is clear that neither does he confute the geometrician except by accident, so that there cannot be a discussion of geometry by those who are ignorant of geometry, since the bad reasoner will escape detection, and it is the same with other sciences.

* i. e. the demonstrative syllogism.

† What are proved in geometry, &c.

‡ i. e. the conclusions from the former become principles to the subsequent demonstrations.

2. Of discovering the science to which each

Since there are geometrical interrogations, are there also those which are ungeometrical? and

that of Aristotle, pointed out above. Moreover the dialectician interrogates so that his opponent may either affirm or deny, but the demonstrator proves or interrogates in order to make the thing evident from principles better known to his hearer; again, the dialectician may employ affirmation or negation, but the demonstrator has to prove a certain conclusion.

[1] Interrogation and proposition are the same in reality, but differ in definition. A proposition is such as, "Every man is an animal;" an interrogation is such as, "Is not every man an animal?" Taylor.

false syllogism appertains.

in each science are those ignorant questions which are of a certain quality[1] geometrical? whether also is a syllogism, from ignorance, a syllogism composed from opposites or a paralogism,[2] but according to geometry, or from another art, as a musical interrogation is ungeometrical, about geometry, but to imagine that parallel lines meet is in a certain respect geometrical,* and after another manner ungeometrical?† For this‡ is two-fold, in the same way as what is without rhythm; and the one is ungeometrical because it possesses not (what is geometrical), as what is without rhythm; but the other because it possesses it wrongly—and this ignorance which is from such principles,§ is contrary.‖ In mathematics however there is not in like manner a paralogism, because the middle is always two-fold,[3] for (one thing) is predicated of every individual of this, and this again of another every, but the predicate is not called universal;[4] those, nevertheless, it is possible, we may see by common perception,¶ but in argument they escape us. Is then every circle a figure? If any one should delineate it, it is clear. But what, are verses a circle? They are evidently not so.[5]

* Because the subject terms are so.
† Because it is false.
‡ i. e. the ungeometrical.
§ From false prop. with geometrical terms.
‖ To science.
¶ Mente.

[1] Ignorance is two-fold; 1st, From pure negation; 2nd, From a depraved disposition. Vide chapters 16, 17, and 18; also Eth. b. iii. ch. 1. Cf. Metap. lib. iii.

[2] Utrum syllogismus ἀγεωμέτρητος dicendus est is, qui fiat ex propositionibus veritati repugnantibus, sive etiam qui ex propositionibus veris non recte colligat (ὁ παραλογισμός) dummodo propositiones ex quibus fiat geometriæ sint propriæ an syll. qui ex aliâ doctrinâ desumtus ad geometriam omnino non pertineat? Waitz. Aristotle says (afterwards) that certain interrogations, entirely geometrical, are assumed from another art or science, and correspond to the ignorance which is said to be of pure negation, as "Is number even or odd?" but that there are others which are in a certain respect geometrical, and in a certain respect not, and which are falsely conceived of geometrical points, as "Will not parallel lines meet?" Cf. Philop. fol. 34.

[3] That is, the middle term is twice assumed, viz. in the major and in the minor prop.

[4] The majus extremum is universally attributed to the middle term in the major prop. in the first figure, (to which Aristotle refers,) and the middle term is universally attributed to the minor extreme in the minor proposition; but the expression of universality is not added to the predicate, but to the subject only.

[5] I read the concluding paragraph according to Waitz's stopping. Aris-

Still it is improper to object to it, if it be an inductive proposition;* for as neither is that a proposition which is not in respect of many things, (since it will not be in all, but syllogism is from universals,) neither, it appears clear, is that an objection, for propositions and objections are the same, as the objection which one adduces, may become either a demonstrative or a dialectic proposition.[1] †

* πρότασις ἐπακτική.

3. When an objection is not to be made.

† Cf. ch. 4.

It occurs that some argue contrary to syllogism, from assuming the consequences of both (extremes), as Cæneus does,[2] that fire is in a multiple proportion, because, as he says, both fire and this proportion are rapidly generated. But thus there is no syllogism,[3] though there will be, if

4. Instance of a syllogistic argument, by employing a syllogism with both prop. affirm. in the 2nd figure.

totle says, they may be seen by common perception, (τῇ νοήσει,) the verb νοεῖν being said of self-evident truths, because mathematicians represent these things by diagrams, and therefore if a circle was similarly described, it would be manifest; κύκλος however signifies both a mathematical figure and a kind of period or verse. Vide Hermo. et Demet.

[1] The following is the note of Julius Pacius on Anal. Prior, c. 28, (Pacian Division,) as to the apparently conflicting statement made by Aristotle here. "Discrimen ponit Aristoteles (lib. ii. Prior, cap. 28) inter objectionem et propositionem, id est propositionem illam cui objicitur: alioquin etiam ipsa objectio est propositio, ut dictum fuit in definitione. Discrimen est, quod objectio est universalis, vel particularis: propositio verò, si sit pars syllogismi universalis, necessario est universalis. Sensus est propositiones constituentes syllogismum esse universales: everti autem vel per objectiones universales, ut contrarias; vel per particulares ut contradicentes. Huic sententiæ opponitur quod ait Aristoteles, lib. i. Post. cap. 12, par. 11, omnem instantiam esse universalem. Existimo hæc loca per distinctionem esse concilianda. Aristoteles in Prior. considerat instantiam sive objectionem quatenus evertit propositionem contrariam; hæc objectio potest esse tam universalis quam particularis. In Poster. autem considerat objectionem quatenus per eam, non solum evertitur propositio adversarii, sed etiam demonstratio erigitur. Quoniam igitur demonstratio constat ex propositionibus universalibus, etiam hæc objectio necessario est universalis." On the consideration of the enstatic enthymeme, and of the passages relative to the Ἔνστασις, vide Dr. Hessey's Schem. Rhet. Supple. Table 5. Cf. also Waitz in loc.

[2] Cæneus argued: "That which is increased by multiple proportion is rapidly increased
Fire is rapidly increased
∴ Fire is increased by multiple proportion."
The last expression means that by every addition it becomes double or triple, etc.

[3] Because both prop. affirm. in the 2nd fig.

the multiple is consequent to the most rapid proportion, and the most rapid proportion to fire in motion. Sometimes it does not happen that a conclusion is made from the assumptions, and sometimes it happens, but is not perceived: if however it were impossible to demonstrate the true from the false, it would be easy to resolve,* for (the terms) would be necessarily converted.[1] Thus let A† exist, and this existing, these things also exist‡ the existence of which I know, as B, from these then § I will demonstrate that that‖ exists. What pertain however to mathematics, are rather converted, because they take nothing accidental, (and in this they differ from dialectical subjects,) but definitions.

* ἀναλύειν. Cf. Prior An. b. ii. ch. 2—4.
† Propositions.
‡ This conclusion which I know is true.
§ The conclusion: B.
‖ The propositions: A.

5. Mathematical demonstrations rarely prove the same, by many media.

Yet they are increased, not through media, but through additional assumption, as A of B, this of C, this again of D, and so on to infinity. Also transversely, as A both of C and of E, as there is a number so great or even infinite, which is A, an odd number so great B, and an odd number C. A then is (true) of C, and the even is a number so great D, the even number is E, wherefore A is (true) of E.¶

¶ Example (1).

Chap. XIII.—*The difference between Science, "that" a thing is, and "why" it is.*

1. A two-fold difference if the syllogism be

Now there is a difference between knowing that a thing is, and why it is, first in the same

[1] Difficilius est ad dijudicandum ex quibus propositionibus coactum sit, quod syllogismus confecit (τὸ ἀναλύειν). Waitz. Aristotle means that the truth of the prop. might easily be collected from the truth of the conclusion, for they might be converted.

Ex. 1. Every odd number (B) is finite or infinite (A)
Every ternary (C) is an odd number (B)
∴ Every ternary (C) is finite or infinite (A).
Every even number (D) is finite or infinite (A)
Every binary (E) is an even number (D)
∴ Every binary (E) is finite or infinite (A).

science, and in this in two ways, the one, if the syllogism is not formed through things immediate, (since the primary cause is not assumed, but the science of the why has respect to the first cause,) but the other if it is through things immediate indeed, yet not through the cause, but through that which is more known of the things, which reciprocate.[1] Now nothing prevents that which is not a cause being sometimes more known amongst things which are mutually predicated, so that demonstration shall accrue through this, as that the planets are near, because they do not twinkle. Let C be the planets, B not to twinkle, A to be near, B therefore is truly predicated of C, since the planets do not twinkle, A also of B, for what does not twinkle is near, but this* may be assumed by induction or by sense.[2] It is neces-

not through things immediate: next, if it be, but not through cause, in the same science.

* i. e. the two propositions.

[1] When the effect immediately follows the cause, the two are said to reciprocate, because one being admitted, the other is necessarily so, though sometimes the effect is more known than the cause, as he says below. For the two senses of the word ἄμεσος, cf. Anal. Post. i. 2, and ii. 19; here it signifies a premise immediate, as regards its conclusion, i. e. not requiring the insertion of *lower* middle terms, to connect its terms with those of the conclusion. On the particular meaning of the word "cause," and in fact in relation to the whole chapter, see Hill's Logic, under "Demonstrationis species," pp. 287, et seq., and Mansel's Logic, 106, Appendix, pp. 63, et seq.

[2] The major by induction, because a lamp, gold, etc., when they are near, do not twinkle; the minor by sense, because we see the planets do not twinkle. Taylor.

Ex. 1. Whatever does not twinkle (B) is near (A)
The planets (C) do not twinkle (B)
∴ The planets (C) are near (A).

Ex. 2. Whatever is near (B) does not twinkle (A)
The planets (C) are near (B)
∴ The planets (C) do not twinkle (A).

Ex. 3. What is spherical (B) is thus increased (A)
The moon (C) is spherical (B)
∴ The moon (C) is thus increased (A).

sary then that A should be present with C, so that it is demonstrated that the planets are near.* This syllogism then is not of the "why," but of the "that" (a thing is), for the planets are not near because they do not twinkle, but they do not twinkle because they are near. It happens indeed that the one may be proved through the other, and the demonstration will be of the "why," as let C be the planets, B to be near, A not to twinkle, B then is present with C, so that A "not to twinkle" will be with C.† It is also a syllogism of the "why," for the first cause was assumed. Again, as they show the moon to be spherical through increments (of light), for if what is thus increased be spherical, and the moon is increased, it is evident that the moon is spherical, thus then a syllogism of the "that" is produced, but if the middle is placed contrarily,‡ there is a syllogism of the "why," for it is not spherical on account of the increments, but from being spherical she receives such increments: let the moon be C, spherical B, increase A.§ Where again the media do not reciprocate,[1] and what is not the cause is more known, the "that" is indeed demonstrated, but not the "why;" further, where the middle is placed externally,[2] for in these the demonstration is of the "that," and not of the "why," as the cause is not assigned. For example, why does not a wall breathe? because it is not an animal, for if this was the cause of its not breathing, it would be necessary that animal should be the cause of its breathing, since if negation is the cause of a thing not being, affirmation is the cause of its being, thus if the disproportion of hot and cold is the cause of not being well, the proportion of these is the cause of being well. Likewise if affirmation is the cause of being, negation is the cause of not being, but in things which have been thus explained, what has been stated does not occur, for not

* Example (1.) of the ὅτι.

† Example (2.) of the διότι.

‡ i. e. the former middle becomes the major, and the former major becomes the middle.

§ Example (3.)

2. Where the media do not reciprocate the ὅτι is demonstrated, also where the middle is externally placed.

[1] The cause is the middle, in the demonstration of the "*why*," and the effect is the middle, in the demonstration of the "*that*." By media not reciprocating, is meant when we reason affirmatively, from the effect to the remote cause; as, man is risible, therefore he is animal: here we miss the proximate cause, "is rational."

[2] i. e. before both extremes, in the 2nd figure, in which demonstration through a remote cause (as he will show) occurs.

every animal respires.[1] A syllogism of such a cause is nevertheless produced in the middle figure, for example, let A be animal, B to respire, C a wall, A then is present with every B, (for whatever respires is animal,) but with no C, so that neither is B present with any C, wherefore a wall does not respire.* Such causes however resemble things spoken hyperbolically,[2] and this is, when we turn aside to speak of the middle, which is more widely extended, as for instance, that saying of Anacharsis, that amongst the Scythians there are no pipers, since neither are there any vines.[3]

* Example (4.)

3. Another difference between a syllogism of the ὅτι and the διότι, in respect of each belonging to a different science.

As to the same science then, and the position of the media, these are the differences between a syllogism of, that a thing is, and of why it is, but in another respect the why differs from the that, because each is beheld in a different science. Now such are those things which so subsist with reference to each other, as that the one is under the other, such as optics with reference to geometry, mechanics to the measurement of solids, harmonics to arithmetic, and celestial phenomena to astronomy. Some of these sciences are almost synonymous, as astronomy is both the mathematical and the nautical; and harmony is both mathematical and

[1] But only those which have lungs, hence the proximate cause of respiration is not animal, but the possession of lungs, which cause however is not assigned.

B A
Ex. 4. Whatever respires is an animal
C A
No wall is an animal
C B
∴ No wall respires.

[2] Remote causes being adduced resemble hyperboles, in that more is said than is requisite, for a remote is of wider extension than a proximate cause.

[3] When we leave (the proximate cause) to speak of that middle which is more widely extended than (cause). Taylor. The demonstration of Anacharsis is thus framed in the 2nd figure. There are no pipers where there are no vines, but there are no vines among the Scythians, ∴ among the Scythians there are no pipers. Now the successive causes to the first or major premise are, there are no vines because there are no grapes; no grapes is the cause of no wine; no wine is the cause of no intoxication; no intoxication cause of no pipers; but these intermediate causes are omitted, and the effect is at once connected with the remote cause.

4. The knowledge of the ὅτι belongs to the perceptive, of the διότι to the mathematical, arguer.

that which belongs to the ear. For here to know *that* a thing is, is the province of those who exercise the sense, but to know *why* it is, belongs to mathematicians, since these possess the demonstrations of causes, and often are ignorant of the *that*, as they who contemplating universals, frequently are ignorant of singulars from want of observation. But these* are such as being essentially something else† use forms, for mathematics are conversant with forms, since they do not regard one certain subject, for though the geometrical are of a certain subject, yet not so far as they are geometrical are they in a subject.‡ As optics also to geometry, so is some other science related to optics, as for example, the science about the rainbow, for to know that it is, appertains to the natural philosopher, but why it is, to the optician either simply or mathematically. Many sciences also which are not arranged under each other subsist thus,§ for example, medicine with regard to geometry, for to know *that* circular wounds heal more slowly is the province of the physician, but *why* (they do so) of the geometrician.[1]

* i. e. the superior sciences.
† Essentially different from their subject sciences.
‡ Cf. Procli. Con. in Euclid. Elem.
§ i. e. the ὅτι is known in one science, but the διότι in another.

CHAP. XIV.—*The first Figure most suitable to Science.*

1. Mathematical demonstra-

OF the figures, the first is especially adapted to science, for both the mathematical sciences carry

[1] Viz. because he knows that the capacity of the circle is the largest of all figures, having equal perimeters, hence the parts of a circular wound coalesce more slowly. For the development of the chapter, the following scheme of demonstration is introduced:

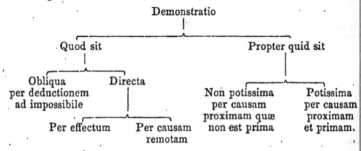

Demonstratio
- Quod sit
  - Obliqua per deductionem ad impossibile
  - Directa
    - Per effectum
    - Per causam remotam
- Propter quid sit
  - Non potissima per causam proximam quæ non est prima
  - Potissima per causam proximam et primam.

out their demonstrations by this, as arithmetic, geometry, optics, and nearly, so to speak, whatsoever sciences investigate the "why," since either entirely or for the most part, and in most sciences, the syllogism of the why is through this figure. Wherefore also, on this account, it will be specially adapted to science, for it is the highest property of knowledge to contemplate the "why;" in the next place, it is possible through this figure alone to investigate the science of what a thing is; for in the middle figure, there is no affirmative syllogism, but the science of what a thing is belongs to affirmation,* and in the last figure, there is an affirmative, but not an universal; but the what a thing is belongs to universals, for man is not a biped animal *in a certain respect.* Moreover this has no need of those, but they are condensed† and enlarged‡ through this, till we arrive at things immediate:§ it is evident, then, that the first figure is in the highest degree adapted to scientific knowledge.

tions effected through this figure.

2. Also the syllogism of the διότι. Cf. book 2nd.

3. Also the science of τοῦ τί ἐστιν.

* i. e. the definition affirms.

4. The other figures condensed by this one.

† i. e. they are reduced to the first figure.

‡ By prosyllogisms.

§ i. e. indemonstrable.

CHAP. XV.—*Of immediate negative Propositions.*

As it happened that A was present with B individually, so also it may happen not to be present, and I mean by being present with, or not, individually, that there is no medium between them, for thus the being present with or not, will not be according to something else. When then either A or B is in a certain whole,‖ or when both are, it is impossible that A should not be primarily present with B. For let A be in the whole of C, if then B is not in the whole of C, (for it is possible that A may be in a certain whole, but that B may not be in this,) there will be a syllogism¶ that A is not present with B, for if C is present with every A, but with no B A will be present with no B. In like manner also, if B is in a certain whole, as for instance, in D, for D is with every B, but A with no D, so that A will be present with no B by a syllogism.* In the same way† it can be

1. That one thing may possibly not be individually present with another. Examples.

‖ Vide Anal. Prior i. ch. 1.

¶ In Camestres.

* In Cesare.

† In either Ce-

sare or Camestres. * That A is not with B. † συστοιχίαι. ‡ Example (1.)

shown* if both also are in a certain whole, but that it is possible that B may not be in the whole in which A is, or again A in which B is, is evident from those co-ordinations† which do not interchange.[1] For if none of those, which are in the class A C D, is predicated of any of those in B E F, but A is in the whole of H, which is co-arranged with it, it is evident that B will not be in H, for otherwise the co-ordinates would intermingle.‡

§ This prop., B is not A, is indemonstrable. || i. e. A or B. ¶ Both prop. negative in 2nd figure. * In 2nd figure.

2. Likewise also if B is in a certain whole, but if neither is in any whole, and A is not present with B, it is necessary that it should not be present individually,§ for if there shall be a certain middle, one of them must necessarily be in a certain whole, for there will be a syllogism either in the first, or in the middle figure. If then it is in the first, B will be in a certain whole, (for it is necessary that the proposition in regard to this should be affirmative,) but if in the middle figure either of them|| may be (in the whole), for the negative being joined to both,¶ there is a syllogism,* but there will not be when both the propositions are negative.

It is manifestly possible then, that one thing may not be individually present with another, also when, and how this may happen, we have shown.

CHAP. XVI.—*Of Ignorance,[2] according to corrupt position of the Terms, where there are no Media.*

† Cf. ch. 12; also Eth. b. iii. ch. 1.

THE ignorance† which is denominated not according to negation, but according to disposition,

[1] By co-ordinations, he means the series deduced from each of the ten categories, as substances, body, etc. Now what belongs to one class cannot be arranged in another; thus body, which is in the category of substance, cannot be in the category of quality.

Ex. 1.	Substance. H.	B. Quality.
	Body. A.	E. *Colour.*
	Animated. C.	F. *Whiteness.*
	Rational. } D. *Animal.* }	

[2] Vide Whately, b. iii. sec. 15—19.

1. Definition of ἄγνοια ἡ κατὰ διάθεσιν, and its kinds.

is a deception produced through syllogism, and this happens in two ways, in those things which are primarily present, or not present; for it happens either when one simply apprehends the being present, or not being present, or when he obtains this opinion through syllogism: of simple opinion, then, the deception is simple, but of that which is through syllogism, it is manifold. For let A not be present with any B individually, if then A is concluded to be present with B, assuming C as the middle, a person will be deceived through syllogism. Hence it is possible that both propositions may be false, but it is also possible that only one may be so, for if neither A is present with any C, nor C with any B, but each proposition is taken contrary, both will be false. But it may be that C so subsists with reference to A and B, as neither to be under A nor universally (present) with B, for it is impossible that B should be in a certain whole, since it was said that A is not primarily present with it; but A need not be universally present with all beings, so that both propositions are false. Nevertheless, we may assume one proposition as true, not either of them casually, but the proposition A C, for the proposition C B will be always false, because B is in none; but A C may be (true), for instance, if A is present individually, both with C and B, for when the same thing is primarily predicated of many things, neither will be predicated of neither; it makes no difference however if it (A) be not individually present with it (C).

2. Examples of affirmative deception.

3. Negative deception instanced in the first and middle figures.

The deception then of being present, is by these and in this way only, (for there was not a syllogism of being present in another figure,*) but the deception of not being present with, is in the first and middle figure.† Let us first then declare in how many ways it occurs in the first, and under what propositional circumstances. It may then happen when both propositions are false, e. g. if A is present individually with C and B, for if A should be assumed present with no C, but C with every B, the propositions will be false. But (deception) is possible, when one proposition is false, and either of them casually; for it is possible that A C may be true, but C B false; A C true, because A is not present with all beings, but C B false,

* Vide Anal. Prior, b. i.

† 3rd figure omitted because no universal conclusion proved in it.

because it is impossible that C should be with B, with nothing of which A is present; for otherwise the proposition A C will be no longer true,* at the same time, if both are true, the conclusion also will be true.† But it is also possible that C B may be true, when the other proposition is false, as if B is in C and in A, for one‡ must necessarily be under the other,§ so that if A should be assumed present with no C, the proposition will be false.‖ It is clear then, that when one proposition is false, and also when both are, the syllogism will be false.¶

* Because A is with some C, viz. with B contained under C.
† Vide An. Prior i. ch. 2—4.
‡ A.
§ C.
‖ i. e. partially.
¶ i. e. the conclusion will be false.

2. Middle fig.

In the middle figure, however, it is not possible that both propositions should be wholly false, for when A is present with every B, it will be impossible to assume any thing,* which is present with every individual of the one, but with no individual of the other;† but we must so assume the propositions that the (middle) may be present with one (extreme), and not be present with the other, if indeed there is to be a syllogism.‡ If then, when they are thus assumed, they are false, it is clear that, when taken contrarily, they will subsist vice versâ, but this is impossible.[1] Still there is nothing to prevent each being partly false, as if C is with A, and with a certain B; for if it should be assumed present with every A, but with no B, both propositions indeed would be false, yet not wholly, but partially. The same will occur when the negative is placed vice versâ.§ But it is possible that one proposition, and either of them, may be false, for what is present with every A, will be also with B,‖ if then C is assumed present with the whole of A, but not present with the whole of B, C A will be true, but the proposition C B false. Again, what is present with no B, will not be present with every A; for if with A, it would also be with B, but it was not present; if then C should be assumed present with the whole of A, but with no B, the proposition C

* Any term.
† With every A and no B in Camestres, or with no A and every B in Cesare.
‡ In 2nd figure.
§ So that the neg. prop. is major.
‖ Because B is species of A.

[1] They will be true when the arrangement is such that negation results from affirmation, and affirmation from negation; but this will be impossible, because when the conclusion is false, the prop. cannot be true.

B will be true, but the other false.* The same will happen if the negative is transposed,† for what is in no A, will neither be in any B; if then C is assumed not present with the whole of A, but present with the whole of B, the proposition A C will be true, but the other false.‡ Again, also, it is false to assume that what is present with every B, is with no A; for it is necessary, if it is with every B, that it should be also with a certain A; if then C is assumed present with every B, but with no A, the proposition C B will be indeed true, but C A false.§ Hence, it is evident that when both propositions are false, and when one only is so, there will be a syllogism deceptive in individuals.[1]

* Either wholly or partially.
† If the negative becomes the major.
‡ Wholly false.
§ Either wholly or partially.

CHAP. XVII.—*Continuation of the same with Media.*

IN those which are not individually present,‖ or which are not present, when a syllogism of the false is produced through an appropriate medium, both propositions cannot be false, but only the major. But I mean by an appropriate medium, that through which there is a syllogism of contradiction.¶ For let A be with B through the medium of C, since then we must take C B as affirmative, if there is to be a syllogism, it is clear that this will be always true, for it is not converted.* A C, on the other hand, will be false, for when this is converted, a contrary syllogism arises.[2] So also if the middle is assumed from another affinity, as for instance, if D is in the whole of A, and is predicated of every B, for the proposition D B must necessarily remain,[3] but the other proposition must be converted,[4] so that the one (the minor) will be always true, but the other (the major) always false. Deception also of this kind is almost the same

1. Syllogism of the false produced in mediates, when the major is false.
‖ But by a medium.
¶ i. e. a conclusion contradictory of the original false conclusion.
* It is not changed into a negative.

[1] In those cases which have no medium.
[2] A syllogism with a conclusion opposite to the true conclusion, and which produces deception opposed to true science.
[3] Because the minor in the 1st fig. must continue affirm.
[4] i. e. the major must be changed into a negative.

2. Case of both propositions being false.

as that which is through an appropriate medium, but if the syllogism should not be through an appropriate medium,[1] when indeed the middle is under A, but is present with no B, it is necessary that both propositions should be false. For the propositions must be assumed contrary to the way in which they subsist, if a syllogism is to be formed,[2] for when they are thus assumed both are false, as if A is with the whole of D, but D present with no B, for when these are converted, there will be a syllogism, and both propositions will be false. When however the medium is not under A, for instance, D, A D will be true, but D B false, for A D is true, because D was not in A, but D B false, because if it were true the conclusion also would be true,* but it was false.

* Vide An. Prior, b. i. ch. 2—4.

3. Both prop. cannot be wholly false in the middle figure, when deception is produced.

Through the middle figure however, when deception is produced, it is impossible that both propositions should be wholly false, (for when B is under A, it is possible for nothing to be present with the whole of the one, but with nothing of the other, as has been observed before,†) but one proposition may be false whichever may happen. For if C is with A and with B, if it be assumed present with A, but not present with B, the proposition A C will be true, but the other false; again, if C be assumed present with B, but with no A, the proposition C B will be true, but the other false.

† Vide preceding chapter.

4. Affirmative deception.

If then the syllogism of deception be negative, it has been shown when and through what the deception will occur, but if it be affirmative,‡ when it is through an appropriate medium, it is impossible that both should be false, for C B must necessarily remain,§ if there is to be a syllogism,‖ as was also observed before. Wherefore C A will be always false, for it is this which is converted.¶ Likewise

‡ In Barbara.
§ Affirmative.
‖ In the 1st figure.
¶ From being true is made false.

[1] When it is through a medium by which a true conclusion cannot be proved: thus, through "brute," it can never be proved that "man is a living being." Taylor.

[2] i. e. to form a negative in the 1st figure, (Celarent,) it is necessary in the major prop. that the first be denied of the middle, and in the minor that the middle should be affirmed of the last.

also, if the middle be taken from another class, as was observed in negative deception, for the proposition D B must of necessity remain, but A D be converted, and the deception is the same as the former. But when it is not through an appropriate medium, if D be under A, this* indeed will be true, but the other† false, for A may possibly be present with many things which are not under each other.[1] If however D is not under A, this‡ will evidently be always false, (for it is assumed affirmative,) for D B may be as well true as false, since nothing prevents A being present with no D, but D with every B, as animal with (no) science, but science with (all) music. Again, (nothing prevents) A from being present with no D, and D with no B: it is clear then that when the medium is not under A, both propositions, and either of them, as it may happen, may be false.

* The major.

† The minor.

‡ The major.

In how many ways then, and through what, syllogistic deceptions are possible, both in things immediate, and in those which are demonstrated, has been shown.

CHAP. XVIII.—*Of the Dependence of Universals upon Induction, and of the latter upon Sense.*

1. Universals from which demonstration proceeds, depend upon induction, the latter upon sense. (Cf. Eth. b. vi. ch. 3; Rhet. b. i. ch. 2, and b. ii. ch. 23.

IT is clear, also, that if any sense be deficient, a certain science must be also deficient, which we cannot possess, since we learn either by induction or by demonstration. Now demonstration is from universals, but induction from particulars, it is impossible however to investigate universals, except through induction, since things which are said to be from abstraction, will be known through induction;[2] if any one desires to make it ap-

[1] The expression, present with, must be taken generally, for the being attributed, whether affirmatively or negatively, to many things not under each other; thus "brute" is affirmatively attributed to "quadruped," but negatively to "man;" but "man" is not subjected to "brute." Taylor.

[2] Vide Hill's Logic, and Aldrich de Prædicab. form.; Whately's Logic, book ii. ch. 5, and book iv. ch. 1. Universals are gained by abstraction, because we separate the points of concord, concomitant with a certain number of individuals, from those points in which they differ, hence Locke calls all universals abstract terms. Properly speaking, abstraction

parent that some things are present with each genus, although they are not separable, so far as each is such a thing. Nevertheless, it is impossible for those who have not sense to make an induction, for sense is conversant with singulars, as the science of them cannot be received, since neither (can it be obtained) from universals without induction, nor through induction without sense.

CHAP. XIX.—*Of the Principles of Demonstration, whether they are Finite or Infinite.*

EVERY syllogism consists of three terms, and one indeed is able to demonstrate that A is with C from its being present with B, and this last with C, but the other is negative, having one proposition (to the effect) that one certain thing is in another, but the other proposition (to the effect) that it is not with it. Now it is clear, that the same are principles, and what are called hypotheses, since it is necessary to demonstrate by thus assuming these,[1] e. g. that A is present with C through B, and again, that A is with B through another medium, and that B is with C in like manner. By those then who syllogize according to opinion only, and dialectically, this alone it is clear must be

1. By those who syllogize κατὰ δόξαν it is to be consider-

is the separation of one portion of the attributes co-existing in any object from the rest; hence, in this sense, Aristotle applies the expression here, τὰ ἐξ ἀφαιρέσεως, to geometrical magnitudes, because the geometer considers only the properties of the figure, separating them from those of the material in which it is found. (Cf. An. Post. i. ch. 5.) "Induction," says Taylor, "is so far subservient to the acquisitions of science, as it evocates into energy in the soul, those universals from which demonstration consists. For the universal, which is the proper object of science, is not derived from particulars, since these are infinite, and every induction of them must be limited to a finite number. Hence the perception of *the all* and *the every* is only *excited*, and not *produced*, by induction." Cf. Trendelen. de An. p. 478. Biese 1. Sententia nostri loci hæc est. Universales propositiones omnes inductione comparantur, quum etiam in iis quæ a sensibus maxime aliena videntur et quæ ut mathematica (τὰ ἐξ ἀφαιρέσεως) cogitatione separantur a materiâ quâcum conjuncta sunt, inductione probentur ea quæ de genere, ad quod demonstratio pertineat prædicentur καθ' αὑτά et cum ejus naturâ conjuncta sint. Inductio autem iis nititur quæ sensibus percipiuntur; nam res singulares sentiuntur, scientia vero rerum singularium, non datur sine inductione, non datur inductio, sine sensu. Waitz. Cf. Metap. b. ii. and vi.; De Animâ, b. iii. iv.

[1] So that both prop. affirm, or one affirms and the other denies.

considered, viz. whether the syllogism is produced from propositions as probable as possible, so that if there is in reality a medium between A and B, but it does not appear, he who syllogizes through this, will have syllogized dialectically. But as to truth, it behoves us to make our observations from things inherent:[1] it happens thus. Since there is that, which is itself predicated of something else, not according to accident,* but I mean by according to accident, as we say sometimes, that that white thing is a man, not similarly saying, that a man is a white thing, for man not being any thing else is white, but it is a white thing, because it happens to a man to be white:[2] there are then some such things as are predicated per se. Let C be a thing of this kind which is not itself present with any thing else, but let B be primarily† present with this, without any thing else between. Again, also let E be present in like manner with F, and this with B, is it then necessary that this should stop, or is it possible to proceed to infinity?[3] Once more, if nothing is predicated of A per se, but A is primarily present with H, nothing prior intervening, and H with G, and this with B, is it necessary also that this should stop, or can this likewise go on to infinity?[4] Now this so much differs from the former, that the one is, whether it is possible by beginning from a thing of that kind,‡ which is present with nothing else, but something else present with it, to proceed upward to infinity; but the other is, beginning from that which is itself predicated of another, but nothing predicated of it,§ whether it is possible to proceed to infinity downward. Besides, when the extremes are finite, is it possible that the media may be infinite? I mean, for instance, if A is present with C, but the medium of them is B, and of B and A there are other media, and of these again others, whether it is possible or impossible for these also to proceed to infinity? To consider this however

ed whether the syllogisms arise from propositions especially probable.

* Cf. ch. 6.

† Immediately.

2. An inquiry whether a stated series of terms proceeds to infinity.

‡ i. e. from a last subject.

§ A supreme attribute.

[1] Whether the propositions are really immediate.

[2] I read this sentence with Buhle, Bekker, and Waitz.

[3] So that a first predicate may not be found.

[4] So that a last subject may not be found.

* Cf. ch. 3.
† If so, there are no first principles, for these are indemonstrable. Cf. Metap. lib. i. and ii.

is the same as to consider whether demonstrations proceed to infinity,* and whether there is demonstration of every thing,† or whether there is a termination (of the extremes) relatively to each other.[1]

3. The same as to negatives.

I say also the same in respect of negative syllogisms and propositions, for instance, whether A is primarily present with no B, or there will be a certain medium with which it was not before present, as if G (is a medium), which is present with every B; and again, with something else prior to this, as whether (the medium is) H, which is present with every G; for in these also, either those are infinite with which first they are‡ present, or the progression stops.

‡ So Waitz and Bekker; but Taylor and Buhle read "*not* present."

4. The doubt does not exist in the case of reciprocals.

The same thing however does not occur in things which are convertible, since in those which are mutually predicated of each other, there is nothing of which first or last a thing is predicated;[2] for in this respect all things subsist similarly with respect to all, whether those are infinite, which are predicated of the same, or whether both§ subjects of doubt are infinite, except that the conversion cannot be similarly made; but the one is as accident, but the other as predication.[3]

§ The predicates and subjects.

[1] i. e. whether there may be found a last subject, which is the boundary of the progression downward from the first attribute; and also whether there may be found a first attribute, by which the progression from the last subject upward will be terminated. Πρὸς ἄλληλα περαίνεσθαι, dicuntur quorum termini medii non infiniti sunt, ut sive uno sive pluribus terminis mediis interjectis major cum minore continuâ ratiocinatione connectatur in conclusione. Waitz.

[2] In circular proofs, as in the circle itself, there is not a first nor last.

[3] Whether the attributes are infinite, in terms convertible, they may become subjects, or whether both attributes and subjects are infinite, the effect is the same, and Aristotle shows that these investigations may be adapted to reciprocals, when one is per se predicated of the other, and the other from accident. Excluding the last, the inquiry is whether the subjects and predicates which are so per se, are finite or infinite. A thing is attributed from accident, as man to a white thing; but per se as risibility to a man. Predication therefore is now assumed for attribute per se, as will be shown in chap. 22.

CHAP. XX.—*Of Finite Media.*

THAT media cannot be infinite, if the predications, both downward and upward, stop, is evident: I call indeed the predication upward, which tends to the more universal, but the downward that which proceeds to the particular. For if when A is predicated of F, the media are infinite, that is B,* it evidently may be possible that from A in a descending series, one thing may be predicated of another to infinity, (for before we arrive at F, there are infinite media,) and from F in an ascending series, there are infinite (attributes) before we arrive at A. Hence, if these things are impossible,† it is also impossible that there should be infinite media between A and F; for it does not signify if a man should say that some things of A B F‡ so mutually adhere, as that there is nothing intermediate, but that others cannot be assumed.§ For whatever I may assume of B,[1] the media with reference to A or to F,|| will either be infinite or not, and it is of no consequence from what the infinites first begin,[2] whether directly or not directly, for those which are posterior to them are infinite.

1. Media not infinite where the predications stop—Explanation and example.

* A is the highest predicate, F the last subject, B the media.

† That there should be infinite subjects to A, and infinite attributes to F.

‡ So Waitz; Taylor and Bekker, A B; Buhle, A B C.

§ Because they are infinite.

|| The media between B and F, or between B and A.

CHAP. XXI.—*It is shown that there are no Infinite Media in Negative Demonstration.*

IT is apparent also, that in negative demonstration the progression will stop, if indeed in affirmative it is stopped in both (series),¶ for let it be impossible to proceed to infinity upward from the last,[3] (I call the last that which is itself not present with any thing else, but something else with it, for instance, F,) or from the first* to the

1. That there is not an infinity of media in negative demonstration, proved in the several figures.

¶ i. e. both ascending and descending.

* Predicate.

[1] i. e. whatever medium is assumed between A and F; for the infinite media between A and F are signified by the letter B.

[2] Whether from either (A or F) of the extremes, or from some medium. Infinites are *di*rectly or *im*mediately placed from A or from F, but not *di*rectly when they are from some medium.

[3] That is, in affirmative syllogisms, upward from the last subject.

last, (I call the first that which is indeed itself predicated of something else, but nothing else of it). If then these things are so, the progression must stop in negation, for the not being present is demonstrated triply,* since either B is present with every individual with which C is, but A is present with none with which B is. In B C therefore, and always in the other proposition,† it is necessary to proceed to immediates, for this proposition is affirmative.[1] With regard to the other‡ however it is clear, that if it is not present with something else prior, for instance, with D, it will be requisite that this (D) should be present with every B.§ Also if again it‖ is not present with something else prior to D,¶ it will require that* to be present with every D, so that since the upward progression stops, the downward progression will also stop, and there will be something first with which it is not present.† Moreover if B is with every A, but with no C, A will be with no C; again, if it is required to show this,‡ it is evident, that it may be demonstrated either through the superior mode,§ or through this, or through the third, now the first has been spoken of, but the second shall be shown. Thus indeed it may demonstrate it,[2] as, for instance, that D is present with every B, but with no C, if it is necessary that any thing‖ should be with B,[3] and, again, if this¶ is not present with C,* something else† is present with D, which is not present with C, wherefore since the perpetually being present with something superior stops, the not being present will also stop. But the third mode was if A indeed is present with every B, but C is not present, C will not be present with every A;[4] again,

* In the three figures.

† In the proof of the minor. Taylor.

‡ A; the predicate of the major.

§ Because in 1st figure the middle is predicate of the minor.

‖ i. e. A.

¶ As with E.

* E.

† Of which A is immediately denied.

‡ Viz. prop. B C.

§ i. e. figure.

2.

‖ As D.

¶ i. e. D.

* Which will be shown.

† As E.

[1] It is assumed that there is no infinite progression in affirmative prop., because this will be proved in the following chapter.

[2] The syllogism in the 2nd fig. will prove B to be predicated of no C.

[3] In order that a syllogism may be formed in Camestres; if, on the other hand, D is predicated of every C, and of no B, it would be in Cesare.

[4] This is a particular prop., in order to effect a syllogism in Bokardo, as Aristotle will shortly prove it in the third figure; if it were universal in Felapton, it could not be proved in this figure.

this will be demonstrated either through the above-mentioned modes,* or in a similar manner,† in those modes the progression stops,‡ but if thus, it will again be assumed that B is present with E, with every individual of which C is not present. This § again, also, will be similarly demonstrated,|| but since it is supposed that the downward progression stops, C also, which is not present with,¶ will evidently stop.

* The 1st or 2nd figure.
† Through the 3rd.
3.
‡ Vide above.
§ That C is not with every E.
|| In the 3rd figure.
¶ That is, a negative prop.

Nevertheless, it appears plain, that if it should not be demonstrated in one way, but in all, at one time from the first figure, at another from the second or the third, that thus also the progression will stop, for the ways are finite,* but it is necessary that finite things being finitely assumed should be all of them finite.

* Viz. three.

That in negation then the progression stops, if it does so in affirmation, is clear,† but that it must stop in them ‡ is thus manifest to those who consider logically.[1]

† Taylor and Buhle end here.
‡ In affirmations.

CHAP. XXII.—*That there are no Infinite Media in Affirmative Demonstration.*

1. Of predications, as to what a thing is, there cannot be infinity—a difference of predication pointed out.

IN things predicated therefore as to what a thing is, this is clear, for if it is possible to define, or if the very nature of a thing may be known, but infinites cannot be passed through, it is necessary that those things should be finite which are predicated with respect to what a thing is. We must however speak universally thus: a white thing we may truly say walks, also that that great thing is wood; moreover, that the wood is great, and that the man walks, yet there is a difference between speaking in this way and in

[1] Aristotle calls those arguments logical which are not derived from the nature of a thing, but analytical are opposed to them, because they resolve things into their principles; the one method is, as Waitz says, an accurate demonstration, which depends upon the true principles of the thing itself; the other, that which is satisfied with a certain probable ratiocination. Cf. Philop.; also Biese i. p. 261; Waitz in loc. Cicero (de Finib. i. 7) calls the "logical" that part of philosophy, "quæ sit quærendi ac disserendi."

that. For when I say that that white thing is wood, then I say that what happens to be white is wood, but what is white is not, as it were, a subject to wood, since neither being white, nor what is a certain white thing, became wood, so that it is not (wood) except from accident. But when I say that the wood is white, I do not say that something else is white, but it happens to that* to be wood, (as when I say that a musician is white, for then I mean that the man is white, to whom it happens to be a musician,) but wood is the subject which became (white), not being any thing else than what is wood, or a certain piece of wood. If indeed it is necessary to assign names, let speaking in this way † be to predicate, but in that way ‡ be either by no means to predicate, or to predicate indeed, not simply, but according to accident. That which is predicated is as white, but that of which it is predicated as wood; now let it be supposed that the predicate is always spoken of what it is predicated of simply, and not according to accident, for thus demonstrations demonstrate. Therefore when one thing is predicated of one, it will be predicated either in respect of what a thing is, or that it is a quality, or a quantity, or a relative, or an agent, or a patient, or that it is some where, or at some time.

* To that something else.

† As the wood is white.

‡ As that which is white is wood. Cf. Met. lib. v. Phy. lib. ii.

2. True predications either define what the subject is, or are accidents.

Moreover, those which signify substance, signify that the thing of which they are predicated, is that which it is, or something belonging to it, but whatever do not signify substance, but are predicated of another subject, which is neither the thing itself, nor something belonging to it, are accidents, as white is predicated of man, since man is neither white, nor any thing which belongs to white, but is perhaps animal, for man is that which is a certain animal. Such as do not signify substance it is necessary should be predicated of a certain subject, and not be something white, which is white, not being any thing else. For, farewell to ideas, for they are mere prattlings,§ and if they exist, are nothing to the subject, since demonstrations are not about such things.[1]

§ Cf. ch. 11.

[1] Taylor tells us quaintly, "that Aristotle is not serious in the ob-

Again, if this is not a quality of this, and that of this, neither a quality of a quality, it is impossible that they should be thus mutually predicated of each other, still they may possibly be truly said, but cannot truly be mutually predicated. For will they be predicated as substance, as being either the genus or the difference of what is predicated? It has been shown that these will not be infinite, neither in a descending nor in an ascending progression, as for instance, man is a biped, this an animal, this something else; neither can animal be predicated of man, this of Callias, this of something else,* in respect to what a thing is. For we may define the whole of this to be substance, but we cannot penetrate infinites by perception,† wherefore neither are there infinites upwards or downwards, for we cannot define that of which infinites are predicated. They will not indeed be mutually predicated of each other as genera, for genus would be a part itself, neither will quality nor any of the other categories be (mutually) predicated, except by accident, for all these are accidents, and are predicated of substances. But neither will there be infinites in ascending series,‡ for of each thing, that is predicated, which signifies either a certain quality, or a certain quantity, or something of this kind, or those which are in the substance, but these are finite, and the genera of the categories are finite, since (a category) is either quality, or quantity, or relation, or action, or passion, or where, or when. One thing is however supposed to be predicated of one,§ but those not to be mutually predicated which do not signify what a thing is, since all these are accidents, but some are per se, others after a different manner, and we say all these are predicated of a certain subject,

2.

* i. e. in an infinite series. Cf. Phys. lib. iii.

† Hence they are incapable of definition.

3. In either case there cannot be an infinite series shown from the nature of category.

‡ There will not be infinite accidents.

§ i. e. propositions are not multiplied by the conjunction of attributes.

jections which he urges against Plato's theory of ideas; for that demonstration cannot exist (from the testimony of Aristotle himself) unless the existence of ideas be admitted conformably to the doctrine of Plato," in total opposition to what is stated in the 11th chap. What Aristotle means is, that ideas, even if they exist, are of little use to effect demonstration, because the latter cannot subsist unless there be ἓν κατὰ πολλῶν; but since ideas subsist per se, (χωριστά ἐστιν,) they cannot be predicated of others. Vide also Metap. lib. ix. (x.) and lib. xii. (xiii.) ed. Leipsic.

but that accident is not a certain subject, for we do not assume any thing of this kind to be, which not being any thing else, is said to be what it is said to be, but we say that it is predicated of something else, and certain other things of another thing.[1] Neither then can one thing be predicated of one (infinitely) upwards, nor downwards, for those of which accidents are predicated, are such as are contained in the substance of each thing, but these are not infinite. Both these indeed and accidents are ascending, and both are not infinite, wherefore it is necessary that there should be something* of which primarily † something ‡ is predicated, and something else § of this, also that this should stop, and that there should be something ‖ which is neither predicated of another prior thing,¶ nor another prior thing of it.*

* A last subject, e. g. D.
† i. e. immediately.
‡ As C.
§ As B.
‖ A first predicate, as A.
¶ Prior to B.
* So that there is nothing prior to A.

4. Hypothesis that a mediate proposition may be proved.

This then is said to be one mode of demonstration, but there is another besides, if there is a demonstration of those of which certain things are previously predicated, but of what there is demonstration, it is not possible to be better affected towards them than to know them, nor can we know without demonstration.[2] Still if this † becomes known through these,‡ but these we do not know, nor are better affected towards them than if we knew them, neither shall we obtain scientific knowledge of that which becomes known through these. If then it is possible to know any thing simply through demonstration, and not from certain things, nor from hypothesis,§ it is necessary that the intermediate predications should stop; for if they do not stop, but there is always something above what is assumed, there will be a demonstration of all things, so that if we cannot pass through infinites, we shall not know by demonstration those things of which there is demonstration. If then we are not better affected towards them than if we knew them, it will be impossible to know

† The conclusion.
‡ The premises.
§ Cf. Prior An. ii. ch. 18.

5. If there is an infinity of predication, demonstration cannot exist.

[1] As whiteness of a swan, blackness of a crow.

[2] To first principles (indemonstrable) we are better affected than if we knew them through demonstration, as was shown in ch. 2.

any thing by demonstration simply, but by hypothesis.*[1]

* If the propositions are true.

Logically then from these things a person may believe about what has been said, but analytically[2] it is more concisely manifest thus, that there cannot be infinite predicates in demonstrative sciences, the subject of the present treatise, either in an ascending or descending series. For demonstration is of such things as are essentially present with things, essentially in two ways, both such as are in them in respect of what a thing is, and those in which the things themselves are inherent in respect of what a thing is, thus the odd in number which indeed is inherent in number, but number itself is inherent in the definition of it,† again also, multitude or the divisible is inherent in the definition of number. Still neither of these can be infinites, nor as the odd is predicated of number, for again there will be something else in the odd,‡ in which § being inherent,‖ (the odd) would be inherent, and if this be so, number will be first inherent in those things which are inherent in it. If then such infinites cannot be inherent in the one,¶ neither will there be infinites in ascending series. Still it is necessary that all should be inherent in the first,* for example, in number, and number in them,† so that they will reciprocate, but not be more widely extensive. Neither are those infinite which are inherent in the definition of a thing,‡ for if they were, we could not define, so that if all predicates are predicated per se, and these are not infinite, things in an upward progression will stop, wherefore also those which descend.

5. The same proved analytically from the nature of those things which are predicated καθ' αὑτά.

† i. e. of the odd.

‡ e. g. inequality.

§ In the definition of which.

‖ i. e. in the odd.

¶ Cf. Met. As the finite cannot contain infinity.

* Thus the third is in the second, and the second in the first.

† In their definition.

‡ Cf. Metap. lib. ix. (x.).

[1] Jam si vera scientia demonstratione comparari potest, quæ necessario vera sit, ut non pendeat ex aliis conditionibus quibuscunque, quæ et esse possint, et non esse, terminorum mediorum, quibus demonstratio utitur, numerus non erit infinitus: nam si esset, et omnia demonstrari possent, et, quia infinitam demonstrationem perficere non liceret, quædam demonstrari non possent, ut demonstratio non efficeret veram scientiam, sed hypotheticam, h. e. non cogeretur quod demonstratur ex propositionibus certis, sed ex propositionibus quæ, quamquam ipsæ demonstrari deberent, tamen pro certis sumtæ essent. Waitz. By hypothesis, he alludes to what is not self-evidently certain, but is assumed to be so.

[2] From the principles and essence of demonstration. Vide supra.

6. That there is not infinity of media.

If then this be so, those also which are between the two terms will be always finite, but if this be the case, it is clear now that there must necessarily be principles of demonstrations, and that there is not demonstration of all things, as we observed in the beginning,* certain persons assert. For if there be principles, neither are all things demonstrable, nor can we progress to infinity, since that either of these should be, is nothing else than that there is no proposition immediate and indivisible, but that all things are divisible, since what is demonstrated is demonstrated from the term† being inwardly introduced, and not from its being (outwardly) assumed.‡[1] Wherefore if this § may possibly proceed to infinity, the media between two terms‖ might also possibly be infinite, but this is impossible, if predications upwards and downwards stop, and that they do stop, has been logically shown before, and analytically now.

* Vide ch. 3.
† The middle.
‡ Extrinsecus definitio. Buhle.
§ The demonstration of propositions.
‖ i. e. between the subject and attribute of the first prop.

CHAP. XXIII.—*Certain Corollaries.*

1. Case where no common ground of inherency subsists.

FROM what has been shown it appears plain that if one and the same thing is inherent in two, for instance, A in C and in D, when one is not predicated of the other,¶ either not at all or not universally, then it is not always inherent according to something common.* Thus to the isosceles and to the scalene triangle, the possession of angles equal to two right, is inherent according to something common,† for it is inherent so far as each is a certain figure,‡ and not so far as it is something else.§ This however is not always the case, for let B be that according to which A is

¶ As C of D.
* Some term in common predicated of C and D.
† Viz. triangle.
‡ i. e. triangle.
§ Viz. scalene, isosceles, etc.

[1] Being assumed between the subject and attribute of the prop. to be proved. Thus the middle term is assumed in the first figure, in which it is subjected to the attribute, i. e. to the greater extreme, and is attributed to the subject, i. e. to the less extreme. Taylor. By the middle being inwardly introduced, he means that in order to demonstrate A B, A must be predicated of C, and C of B, but A of B, and B of C. Upon the above chap., compare Metap. lib. iii. iv. vi. ix. xiii.; Eth. book i. ch. 6; De Anim. b. iii. Vide also Hill's Logic, de Definitione, and Whately's Logic, b. ii. ch. 5, and b. iii. sec. 10.

inherent in C D, then it is evident[1] that B is also inherent in C, and in D, according to something else common,* and that also † according to something else,‡ so that between two terms,§ infinite terms may be inserted, but this is impossible.‖ It is not then necessary that the same thing should always be inherent in many, according to something common, since indeed there will be immediate propositions; it is moreover requisite that the terms should be in the same genus, and from the same individuals, since that which is common will be of those which are essentially inherent, for it is impossible to transfer things which are demonstrated from one genus to another.¶

* As E.
† E is in C and D.
‡ As F.
§ Viz. between B and C, or B and D.
‖ Vide ch. 22.
¶ Vide ch. 6.

2. Cases of propositional demonstration, when a certain medium is granted.

But it is also manifest that when A is with B, if there is a certain middle, we may show that B is with A, and the elements of this* are these and whatever are media, for immediate propositions, either all of them, or those which are universal, are elements.[2] Yet if there is not (a medium) there is no longer demonstration, but this is the way to principles.† In like manner, if A is not with B, if there is either a middle, or something prior to which it‡ is not present,§ there is a demonstration,[3] but if not, there is no demonstration, but a principle, and there are as many elements as terms,‖ for the propositions of these are the principles of demonstration. As also there are certain indemonstrable principles, that this is that, and that this is present with that, so there are also that this is not that, and that this is not

* Of the conclusion B is A.
† To first principles.
‡ So Waitz and Bekker.
§ A.
‖ With B.

[1] Because if a thing is inherent in two things, it is inherent mediately. Taylor.

[2] Immediate particular propositions are not the principles of demonstrations, but of inductions. Upon the use of the word στοιχεῖα, by Aristotle, cf. Ammonius upon Catego. ch. 12; also Biese i. p. 381, note 5, Trendelenburg Platonis de Ideis. In the Topics, as Waitz observes, he uses στοιχεῖα as synonymous with τόποι, for certain universal arguments, from which, with some appearance of truth, a thing may be either proved or refuted. Top. lib. iv. ch. 1, etc. The sense here, of elements, seems most suggestive of their meaning, viz. that of certain principles of disputation, which when provided, enable us rightly to conduct an argument.

[3] If there is a certain middle (C) through which A is proved not present with B, A will first be denied of C in the major premise, and afterwards of B in the conclusion; thus a syllogism will result in Celarent: No C is A, every B is C; therefore no B is A.

present with that, so that there will be some principles that a thing is, but others that it is not. Still when it is required to demonstrate,* that which is first predicated of B must be assumed; let this be C, and let A, in like manner, (be predicated) of this;† by always proceeding thus,[1] there is never a proposition externally, nor is that‡ which is present with A assumed in the demonstration, but the middle is always condensed till they become indivisible and one.[2] They are one indeed when the immediate is produced, and one proposition simply, an immediate one, and as in other things the principle is simple, but this is not the same every where, but in weight it is a minor, in melody a demi-semi-quaver,[3] and something else in another thing, thus in syllogism, "the one" is an immediate proposition, but in demonstration and science it is intuition.§[4] In syllogisms then, which demonstrate the being inherent, nothing falls beyond (the middle), but in negatives here,‖ nothing falls external of that which ought to be inherent,[5]¶ as if A is not present with B through C. For if C is present with every B,* but A with no C,† and if, again, it should be requisite to show that A is with no C,‡ we must assume the medium of A and C, and thus we must always proceed.[6] If

* As that A is with B.

† A syllogism in Barbara.

‡ The middle D.

3. What position the connecting term should occupy in an affirmative and negative proposition.

§ Cf. An. Post. ii. ch. 19, and Eth. b. vi. ch. 1, 2, and 5.

‖ In 1st figure.

¶ Seu medium non sumitur externum. Buhle.

* The minor prem.

† The major.

‡ The conclu-

[1] By assuming a new term, as predicate of the minor, and subject of the major.

[2] Until we arrive at an indemonstrable and immediate proposition.

[3] *Δίεσις*. The least perceptible sound we have therefore expressed it; by its closest representative in music.

[4] For we know principles by "*νοῦς*." Cf. de Anim. iii. ch. 4—6, ubi cf. Trende., Biese, and Rassow. I have translated the word "intuition," agreeing as I do with Professor Browne, (vide Ethics, b. vi. ch. 6, Bohn's edition,) that no other word conveys with the same exactitude Aristotle's own definition of it in the Magnâ Moralia (i. 35), Ὁ *νοῦς ἐστι περὶ τὰς ἀρχας τῶν νοητῶν καὶ τῶν ὄντων, ἡ μὲν γὰρ ἐπιστήμη τῶν μετ' ἀποδεῖξεως ὄντων ἐστὶν, ἄρα δ' ἀρχαὶ ἀναπόδεικτοι.*

[5] Thus Waitz, Buhle, and Bekker. Taylor evidently reads, ὃ, *δει, μὴ ὑπάρχειν*, an amendment which Waitz approves in his note, and so do I, for the conclusion of the syllogism is of course negative; the meaning is, that a middle term is never assumed, which is predicated of the major extreme, since the major is that in which the conclusion is negatively predicated of the minor.

[6] Assume a middle term which does not fall externally to the major extreme, in order to demonstrate the negative proposition.

however it should be required to show * that D is not with E, because C is with every D,† but with no, or not with every E,‡ the medium will never fall external to E, and this § is with what it need not be present.[1] As to the third mode,‖ it will never proceed external to that from which, nor which it is necessary to deny.[2]

sion of the pro-syllogism.
* In Camestres.
† The major.
‡ The minor.
§ E.
‖ The 3rd figure.

CHAP. XXIV.—*The superiority of Universal to Particular Demonstration proved.*

1. The question stated.

As one demonstration is universal, but another particular, one also affirmative, but the other negative, it is questioned which is preferable, likewise also about what is called direct demonstration, and that which leads to the impossible. Let us first then consider the universal and the particular, and having explained this, speak of what is called direct demonstration, and that to the impossible.

2. Reasons why particular demonstration may appear eligible.

Perhaps then to some considering the matter in this way, the particular may appear the better, for if that demonstration is preferable, by which we obtain better knowledge, for this is the excellence of demonstration, but we know each thing better when we know it per se, than when through something else, (as we know Coriscus is a musician, when we know that Coriscus is a musician rather than when we know that a man is a musician, and likewise in other things,) but the universal demonstrates because a thing is something else, not because it is that which it is, as that an isosceles triangle (has two right angles), not because it is isosceles, but because it is a triangle,) but the particular demonstrates because a thing is what it is, if then the demonstration per se is preferable, and the particular is such rather than the universal, particular demonstration would be the better. Besides, if the universal is nothing else than

[1] It is the subject of the negative conclusion, of which D is denied.

[2] A middle will never be assumed above the greater or less extreme, nor be predicated of either, because in the 3rd figure the middle term is always the subject of both premises. As Taylor remarks, in the whole of this chapter, the middle is said to fall external to the extreme, when it changes its situation; so that if it was before the subject of the major extreme, afterwards in the pro-syllogism, it becomes the predicate of the major.

2\. particulars, but demonstration produces opinion that this thing is something according to which it demonstrates, and that a certain nature of this kind is in things which subsist, (as of triangle besides particular (triangles), and of figure besides particular (figures), and of number besides particular (numbers), but the demonstration about being is better than that about non-being, and that through which there is no deception than that through which there is, but universal demonstration is of this sort, (since men proceeding demonstrate as about the analogous,[1] as that a thing which is of such a kind as to be neither line nor number, nor solid nor superficies, but something besides these, is analogous,) if then this is more universal, but is less conversant with being than particular, and produces false opinion, universal will be inferior to particular demonstration.

* i. e. the first.

3\. Reply to the above.

First then may we not remark that one of these arguments* does not apply more to universal than to particular demonstration? For if the possession of angles equal to two right angles is inherent, not in respect of isosceles, but of triangle, whoever knows that it is isosceles knows less essentially[2] than he who knows that it is triangle. In short, if not so far as it is triangle, he then shows it, there will not be demonstration, but if it is,† whoever knows a thing so far as it is what it is, knows that thing more.[3] If then triangle is of wider extension (than isosceles), and there is the same definition,‡ and triangle is not equivocal, and the possession of two angles equal to two right angles is inherent in every triangle, triangle will have such angles, not so far as it is isosceles, but the isosceles will have them, so far as it is triangle. Hence he who knows the uni-

† Supply—inherent, or is demonstrated so far as it is triangle.

‡ So that all species of it are synonymously called triangle.

[1] They who employ universal demonstration do not keep within the exact limits of demonstration, but appear to go beyond them in the same way as those who reason ἐκ του ἀνὰ λόγον, for if they have demonstrated any thing of lines, body, etc., they apply the proof as equally conclusive to every thing similar, and thus extend the demonstration unfairly.

[2] Minus scit quatenus ipsum (tale est ut habere duos rectos angulos illi insit). Buhle.

[3] As Mansel observes, (Appendix, note B,) the office of logic is to contribute to the distinctness of a conception, by an analysis and separate exposition of the different parts contained within it. The mind, like the sky, has its nebulæ, which the telescope of logic may resolve into their component stars.

versal, knows more in regard to the being inherent than he who knows particularly, hence too the universal is better than the particular demonstration. Moreover if there is one certain definition, and no equivocation, the universal will not subsist less, but rather more than certain particulars, inasmuch as in the former there are things incorruptible, but particulars are more corruptible.[1] Besides, there is no necessity that we should apprehend this (universal) to be something besides these (particulars), because it shows one thing, no more than in others which do not signify substance, but quality, or relation, or action, but if a person thinks thus, it is the hearer, and not demonstration, which is to blame.[2]

2.

3. Universal alone is cognizant of cause. * Therefore more causal. Cf. An. Post. ii. 5; Eth. vi. 3. † The first subject in which a property is per se inherent.

Again, if demonstration is a syllogism, showing the cause and the why, the universal indeed is rather causal, for that with which any thing is essentially present, is itself a cause to itself,* but the universal is the first,† therefore the universal is cause. Wherefore the (universal) demonstration is better, since it rather partakes of the cause and the why, besides up to this we investigate the why, and we think that then we know it, when this is becoming, or is, not because something else (is), for thus there is the end and the last boundary. For example, on what account did he come? that he might receive money, but this that he might pay his debts, this that he might not act unjustly, and thus proceeding, when it is no longer on account of something else, nor for the sake of another thing, then we say that he came, and that it is, and that it becomes on account of this as the end, and that then we especially know why he came. If then the same occurs, as to all causes and inquiries into the why, but as to things which are so causes as that for the sake

[1] So Waitz, who has this note, "Notiones universales, si unitatem quandam exprimunt et si alius earum est usus quam ut orationem ambiguam faciant, quum singula quæ illis subjecta sint pereant, illæ vero non corrumpantur, etiam rectius ipsæ existere dicentur quam τὰ ἄτομα." Cf. Metap. lib. ii. (iii.), v. (vi.), vi. (vii.), ix. (x.), and xi. (xii.), Leipsic; Phys. lib. iii. and viii.; also Crakanthorpe's Logic, lib. ii., and upon this chapter generally, Aquinas in Periherm. sect. i.

[2] That is, if a man thinks that universal is something besides particulars. By universal here, he means, that which is "co-ordinated" with the many, and which when abstracted out of the many by the mind, produces the universal, which is of posterior origin. Taylor.

* (Aliquid sit aut fiat.) Buhle.

of which,* we thus especially know, in other things also we then chiefly know, when this no longer subsists because another thing does.[1] When therefore we know that the external angles are equal to four right angles, because it is isosceles, the inquiry yet remains, why because isosceles, because it is a triangle, and this because it is a rectilinear figure. But if it is this no longer on account of something else, then we pre-eminently know, then also universally, wherefore the universal is better.

4. It is true "non per aliud," but "per se."

Again, by how much more things are according to the particular, do they fall into infinites, but the universal tends to the simple and the finite, so far indeed as they are infinite, they are not subjects of science, but so far as they are finite they may be known, wherefore so far as they are universal, are they more objects of scientific knowledge, than so far as they are particular.

5. Universals tend to the simple and finite, hence are more scientific.

Universals however are more demonstrable, and of things more demonstrable is there pre-eminent demonstration, for relatives are at one and the same time more,† whence the universal is better, since it is demonstration pre-eminently. Besides, that demonstration is preferable, according to which this and something else are known, to that, by which this alone is known, now he who has the universal knows also the particular, but the latter does not know the universal, wherefore even thus the universal will be more eligible.

† i. e. if one is more, the other is more.

6. They come closer in demonstration to the principle.

Again, as follows: it is possible rather to demonstrate the universal, because a person demonstrates through a medium which is nearer to the principle, but what is immediate is the nearest and this is the principle; if then that demonstration which is from the principle is more accurate than that which is not from the principle, the demonstration which is in a greater degree from the principle, is more accurate than that which is from it in a less degree. Now the more universal is of this kind, wherefore the universal will be the better, as if it were required to demonstrate A of D, and the media should be B C, but B the higher, wherefore the demonstration through this is more universal.

[1] A verbose exemplification of the terse truism of Swift, that "we unravel sciences, as we do old stockings, *by beginning at the foot.*"

Some of the above arguments are logical, it is chiefly clear however that the universal is more excellent, because when of two propositions we have that which is the prior,* we also in a certain degree know and possess in capacity that which is posterior; thus if a man knows that every triangle has angles equal to two right, he also in a certain respect knows in capacity that an isosceles triangle has angles equal to two right, even if he does not know that the isosceles is a triangle,† but he who has this proposition by no means knows the universal, neither in capacity nor in energy. The universal proposition also is intuitively intelligible, but the particular ends in sense.[1] ‡

7. The universal is above all superior, in that it comprehends the particular, and is more intellectual.

* The universal proposition.

† The particular proposition.

‡ An. Post. ii. ch. 19.

CHAP. XXV.—*The Superiority of Affirmative to Negative Demonstration proved.*

THAT universal is better than particular demonstration, let so much be alleged, but that the affirmative is preferable to the negative, will be evident from this. Let that demonstration be better, cæteris paribus,§ which consists of fewer postulates, or hypotheses, or propositions. For if they[2] are similarly known, quicker knowledge will be obtained through these, which is more eligible. The reason however of this proposition, that that which consists of fewer is better, universally is this; for if the media are similarly known, but things prior are more known, let the demonstration be through the media of B C D, that A is present with E, but through F G, that A is present with E.[3] That A is present with D, and that A is present with E subsists similarly,‖ but that A is with D, is prior and more known than that A is with E, for that¶ is demonstrated

1. That the demonstration which is through fewer postulates, etc., is, "cæteris paribus," the better—proved by example, and applied to affirmatives.

§ As it may be from unknown principles.

‖ Each is the conclusion.

¶ Viz. A E.

[1] Cf. de An. iii. 6; Metaph. ix. 1; and upon the conception of universal notions, Reid's Works, Hamilton's ed.; Mill's Logic; Whately's Rhet.; Trende. Biese i. p. 327, note 4; Rassow, p. 72.

[2] Viz. the propositions of both demonstrations.

[3] B C and F G are the same, but they are called B C, so far as they form parts of the syllogism concluding A E; and they are called F G, so far as they belong to the syllogism A D.

through this,* and that is more credible through which (a thing is demonstrated). Also the demonstration which is through fewer things is therefore better cæteris paribus; both † then are demonstrated through three terms, and two propositions, but the one assumes that something is,‡ and the other that something is and is not,[1] hence through a greater number of things (the demonstration is made) so that it is the worse.

* i. e. A D.

† i. e. both affirmatives and negatives.

‡ Affirmative.

Moreover since it has been shown impossible for a syllogism to be produced with both propositions negative,§ but that one must of necessity be such (negative), and the other that a thing is present with, (that is affirmative,) we must in addition to this assume this,‖ for it is necessary that affirmative (propositions) when the demonstration is increased,¶ should become more, but it is impossible that the negatives should be more than one in every syllogism. For let A be present with nothing of those with which B is, but B be present with every C, if indeed, again, it should be necessary to increase both propositions,* a middle must be introduced.[2] Of A B then let the middle be D, but of B C let the middle be E, E then is evidently affirmative,† but D is affirmative indeed of B, yet is placed negatively as regards A, since it is necessary that D should be present with every B, but A with no D; there is then one negative proposition, viz. A D.‡ The same mode also subsists in other syllogisms, for the middle of affirmative terms is always affirmative in respect of both (extremes),§ but in the case of a negative (syllogism), the middle must be necessarily negative in respect to one of the two,‖ so there is one proposition of this kind,¶ but the others are affirmative. If then that is more known and credible through which a thing is demonstrated, but the negative is shown through the

2. The negative requires the affirmative, but the latter does not need the former.

§ Vide Pr. An. i. ch. 7 and 24.

‖ That negation is proved by affirmation.

¶ By pro-syllogisms.

* To prove them by pro-syllogisms.

† B may be affirmed of E, and E of C.

‡ The major.

§ Subject of the major, and predicate of the minor—both affirmatively.

‖ Of the major extreme to which it is subject in the major prem.

¶ The major is negative.

[1] Because of negative demonstration, one premise affirms, but the other denies.

[2] This is done when a pro-syllogism is constructed in the 1st figure because here alone the middle term occupies the middle place.

affirmative, and the latter not through the former, this, since it is prior, more known, and more credible, will be better. Again, since the principle of syllogism is an universal immediate proposition, but the universal proposition in an ostensive (demonstration) is affirmative, but in a negative is negative, and since the affirmative is prior to, and more known than, the negative, for negation is known through affirmation, and affirmation is prior, just as being is prior to not being, therefore the principle of affirmative is better than that of negative demonstration, but that which uses better principles is better. Moreover it partakes more of the nature of principle,* since without affirmative there is no negative demonstration.[1]

3. Affirmative comes nearer than negative to the nature of a principle.

* ἀρχοειδεσ-τέρα.

CHAP. XXVI.—*The Superiority of the same to Demonstration ad impossibile proved.*[2]

SINCE affirmative is better than negative demonstration, it is evidently also better than that which leads to the impossible,† it is necessary however to know what the difference between them is. Let A then be present with no B, but let B be with every C, wherefore it is necessary that A should be with no C, (the terms) then being thus assumed, the negative proposition proving that A is not present with C will be ostensive. The demonstration however to the impossible is as follows: if it is required to show that A is not present with B it must be assumed present,‡ also that B is with C so that it will happen that A is with C. Let this however be known and acknowledged impossible, then it is impossible that A should be with B; if then B is acknowledged present with C, it is im-

1. The difference proved by example, between direct demonstration and that which leads "ad absurdum."

† Vide infra.

‡ In order to a right syllogism in 1st figure.

[1] An affirmative partakes more of the nature of principle than a negative demonstration, because the minor prem. of a negat. is proved through an affirmative.

[2] Vide Hill's and Mansel's Logic, article Demonstration; also Whately, App. I. xi., upon "Impossibility," and Rhetoric, part i. ch. 3, sec. 7. The *εἰς τὸ ἀδύνατον ἄγουσα ἀπόδειξις* here, seems to correspond with the *ἐλεγτικὸν ἐνθύμημα* of the Rhetoric, upon which see Dr. Hessey's Schem. Rhet. Table 4. Cf. also Anal. Pr. i. 22 and 38; Rhet. ii. 22—24 and 30; iii. 17, 13.

possible that A should be with B. The terms then indeed are similarly arranged,* but it makes a difference which negative proposition is more known, viz. whether that A is not present with B, or that A is not present with C. When then the conclusion is more known that it is not, there is a demonstration to the impossible produced, but when that which† is in the syllogism (is more known) the demonstration is ostensive. Naturally, however, that A is not present with B is prior to A is not present with C, for those things are prior to the conclusion, from which the conclusion (is collected), and that A is not with C is the conclusion, but that A is not with B is that from which the conclusion is derived. For neither if a certain thing happens to be subverted, is this the conclusion, but those (the premises) from which (the conclusion is derived). That indeed from which (it is inferred) is a syllogism, which may so subsist as either‡ a whole to a part, or as a part to a whole,§ but the propositions A C and A B do not thus subsist with regard to each other. If then that demonstration which is from things more known and prior be superior, but both are credible from something not existing, yet the one from the prior, the other from what is posterior, negative demonstration will in short be better, than that to the impossible, so that as affirmative demonstration is better than this,‖ it is also evidently better than that leading to the impossible.

* In the ostensive as in the ad impossibile.

† The negation that A is not in C.

‡ One proposition is to the other as a whole to a part, i. e. the major as to the minor.

§ As the major in Disamis.

2. Scale of demonstrative superiority. 1st, Affirmative. 2nd, Negative. 3rd, Ad absurdum.

‖ Than negative.

CHAP. XXVII.—*Upon the Nature of more Accurate Science.*[1]

1. That one science is more subtle and accurate than another.

ONE science is more accurate than, and prior to, another, both the science that a thing is, and the same why it is, but not separately that it is, than the science of why it is, also that which is not of a subject[2] than that which is of a subject, for instance, arith-

[1] Cf. ch. 13; Plato, Phileb.; Rhet. b. i. ch. 7. In the last place, he says that the precedence of one science over another is dependent upon the higher elevation of its subject matter. Met. lib. i. and x.

[2] Not conversant with a *material* subject, as arithmetic, which is conversant with number. Taylor.

metic then harmonic science, and that which consists of fewer things than that which is from addition, as arithmetic than geometry. I mean by "from addition," as unity is a substance without position, but a point is substance with position,[1] this is from addition.

Chap. XXVIII.—*What constitutes one, and what different Sciences.*

1. Whatever things are demonstrated from principles of a common genus, these constitute one science. Nature of diverse sciences.

One science is that which is of one genus of those things which are composed of first (principles), and are the parts or affections of these per se;[2] but a science is different from another, whose principles are neither from the same things, nor one from the other.[3] A token of this is when any one arrives at things indemonstrable, for it is necessary* that they should be in the same genus with those that are demonstrated; it is also a sign of this when things demonstrated through them are in the same genus and are cognate.

* If it is one science.

Chap. XXIX.—*That there may be several Demonstrations of the same thing.*

1. The same thing demonstrable in many

There may possibly be many demonstrations of the same thing, not only when one assumes an

[1] A point was defined by the Pythagoreans, unity with position: cf. Categ. ch. 6; Procl. in Euc. Elem. lib. ii. Θέσιν ἔχειν dicuntur ea quorum partes simul intuemur ac si oculis subjectæ essent; quæ dum fluunt, manent et quorum quasi imagines ita animo representantur, ut quæ præterierint mente repeti possint simul cum iis, quæ præsto sint. Waitz, in Cat. cap. 6.

[2] Thus natural productions, though they possess their own proper principles, are ultimately composed of the first and common principles, matter and form: these last constitute the parts of body, but body and soul the parts of animal. Also in the sciences we must consider the subjects of them, their parts, and their proper affections.

[3] That is, their principles neither issue from a common source, nor are so intermingled that the one may be derived from the other: thus physics and arithmetic are different sciences, but the science of motion and of the heavens are not entirely different. Vide Physics.

modes, both when the middles are taken from the same, or from a different genus.

* When one is subaltern to the other.

† The conclusion.

un-continued medium from the same class,* as if C D and F (were assumed) of A B,† but also from another (series).[1] Thus, let A be to be changed, D to be moved, B to be delighted, and again G to be tranquillized. It is true then to predicate D of B and A of D, for whoever is delighted is moved, and what is moved is changed: again, it is true to predicate A of G, and G of B, for every one who is delighted is tranquillized, and he who is tranquillized is changed. Wherefore there is a syllogism through different media,[2] and not from the same class, yet not so that neither is predicated of neither medium, since it is necessary that both‡ should be present with something§ which is the same. We must also consider in how many ways|| there may be a syllogism of the same thing through the other figures.

‡ D and G.

§ B.

|| Through how many media.

Chap. XXX.—*That there is no Science of the Fortuitous.*[3]

1. This class does not come under the proper subjects of demonstration.

There is no science through demonstration of that which is fortuitous, since the fortuitous is neither as necessary nor as for the most part, but that which is produced besides these, and demonstration is of one of these. For every syllogism is through premises, either necessary, or through those which are for the most part (true), and if indeed the propositions are necessary, the conclusion also is necessary; but if for the most part (true), the conclusion also is of the same character. Hence if the fortuitous is neither as for the most part nor necessary, there cannot be demonstration of it.

¶ Vide Ethics, b. vi. ch. 2 and 3.

Chap. XXXI.—*That we do not possess Scientific Knowledge through Sensation.*¶

1. The perception of the

Neither is it possible to have scientific knowledge through sensation, for although there is

[1] That is, it is possible to effect this when the one is not subaltern to the other, as it may be shown that man is an essence if we take biped as a medium, or walking, or disputing, for these are not from the same class as the former.

[2] That is, D and G, media, the same conclusion A B is proved.

[3] Cf. Metap. lib. v. (vi.).

sensible perception of such a thing as this, and not of this particular thing,* yet it is necessary to have a sensible perception of this particular thing, and some where and now.[1] But it is impossible sensibly to perceive the universal and in all things, for it is not this particular thing, nor now, otherwise it would not be universal, since we call the universal that which is always and every where. Since then demonstrations are universal, but these cannot be perceived by sense, it is plain that neither can scientific be possessed through sense. In fact, it is clear, that even if we could perceive by sense that a triangle has angles equal to two right, we should require demonstration, and not, as some say, know this scientifically, for it is necessary sensibly to perceive the singular, but science is from the knowledge of the universal.† Wherefore also if we were above the moon, and saw the earth opposite, we should not know the cause of an eclipse (of the moon). For we should perceive that it is eclipsed, but in short should not perceive *why*, since there would not be a sensible perception of the universal. Nevertheless, from observing this frequently to happen, by investigation of the universal, we should obtain demonstration, for the universal is manifest from many singulars, but is valuable, because it discloses the cause, wherefore the universal (knowledge) about such things, of which there is another cause, is more honourable than the senses and apprehension: about first principles however there is another reason.‡[2]

senses is not science.

* Nec certæ hujus rei. Buhle.

† Cf. Meta. lib. i. ch. 1.

‡ Cf. An. Post. ii. ch. 9.

[1] Aristotle intends to show that sense is not science; otherwise since sense apprehends qualities, as sounds, etc., it may seem that sense and science are the same; but the fact is, that though they are employed about the same things, yet they are not so after the same manner, for sense apprehends particularly, but science universally. Moreover the perception of the senses is limited by time and place, but science, or universal knowledge, is not so restricted, so that the ascertainment of the universal is beyond the scope of sensuous perception. Cf. Physics; De Animâ, lib. ii. and iii.; Metap. lib. i. ch. 1; Magna Moral. lib. i. 34, and Moral. Eud. lib. v. c. 3.

[2] The nearest approach to simple apprehension is ἡ τῶν ἀδιαιρέτων νόησις, but νόησις is variously used, and in its widest sense will embrace all the logical operations. Mansel. See also Reid's Works, pp. 242, 692. Waitz observes upon the passage, "Quare in iis quorum causa aliunde suspensa est, cognitio quam maxime universalis potior est omni alia, quæ vel ex sensuum affectione gignatur vel ex cognitione solâ originem habeat: eorum vero quæ non aliunde probantur, quippe quibus nitatur

2. Though there are certain things unknown, from the deficiency of sensible perception.

It is clearly then impossible to possess scientific knowledge of any thing demonstrable by sensible perception, unless some one should affirm that sensible perception is this, to possess science through demonstration. There are indeed certain problems which are referred to the deficiency of our sensible perception,[1] for some if we should see them we should not investigate, not as knowing from seeing, but as possessing the universal from seeing. For instance, if we saw glass perforated, and the light passed through it, it would be also manifest why it illuminates in consequence of our seeing separately in each,* and at the same time perceiving that it is thus with all.†

* piece of glass.
† pieces.

(Cf. An. Post. i. 1, 10.)

CHAP. XXXII.—*On the Difference of Principles according to the Diversity of Syllogisms.*

1. The impossibility of principles of all syllogisms being identical, proved.

THAT there should be the same principles of all syllogisms is impossible, first (this will be seen) by those who consider logically. For some syllogisms are true, others false, since it is possible to conclude the true from the false, yet this but rarely happens, for instance, if A is truly predicated of C, but the middle B is false, for neither is A present with B nor B with C.‡ If however the media of these propositions are assumed, they will be false,[2] because every false conclusion is from false principles, but the true from true principles, and the false and the true are different. Next, neither are the false (deduced) from the same (principles) with themselves, for they are false and contrary to each

‡ Example (1.)

omnis ratiocinatio, alia ratio est: hæc enim mente ipsâ intuemur et quasi amplectimur.

[1] Philoponus observes that Aristotle added this observation lest any discrepancy should appear to exist between what he has stated here and at chapter 18. Philop. Schol.

B A
Ex. 1. Every stone is an animal
C B
Every man is a stone
C A
∴ Every man is an animal.

[2] i. e. the propositions of the prosyllogisms, if the former are to be proved by the latter.

other, and cannot be simultaneous, for instance, it is impossible that justice should be injustice or timidity, that man should be a horse or an ox, or that the equal should be greater or less. From these positions indeed (we may prove it) thus,* since neither are there the same principles of all the true (conclusions), for the principles of many are different in genus, and are not suitable, as units do not suit points, for the former have not position, but the latter have it. At least it is necessary to adapt (either) to media or from above or below, or to have some terms within but others without.[1]† Nor can there possibly be certain common principles from which all things may be demonstrated: I mean by common as to affirm or to deny every thing, for the genera of beings are different, and some are present with quantities, but others with qualities alone, with which there is demonstration through the common. Again, principles are not much fewer than conclusions, for the propositions are principles, but the propositions subsist when a term is either assumed or introduced. Moreover, conclusions are infinite, but terms finite; besides, some principles are from necessity, but others contingent.

* i. e. that there are not the same principles of all things.

† The extremes. (Syllogismum,) Buhle.

2.

2. Reply to objection founded upon mistaken identity.

To those therefore who thus consider, it will be impossible that there should be the same finite principles when the conclusions are infinite, but if any one should reason in some other way, for instance, that these are the principles of geometry, but these of reckoning,‡ and these of medicine, what is this statement other than that there are principles of the sciences?§ but to say that there are the same principles because they are the same with themselves is ridiculous,‖ for thus all things become the same. Still neither is to demonstrate any thing from all things to investigate whether there are the same principles of all, since this would be

‡ λογισμῶν, Waitz. ἀριθμῶν, Taylor and Buhle.

§ i. e. peculiar principles of the several sciences.

‖ Because nothing differs from itself.

[1] That is, if principles are to be accommodated to another science, we must so arrange the terms as that the demonstrations may be formed either in the 1st figure, wherein the middle term holds the middle place; or in the 2nd figure, where it occupies the first place, and is *above* both the extremes; or in the 3rd figure, where it holds the last place *under* each extreme. Moreover, some must be formed in the first, but others in the second or third figure.

* i. e. Mathematics.

very silly. For neither does this happen in evident disciplines,* nor is it possible in analysis,[1] since immediate propositions are principles, and another conclusion arises, when an immediate proposition is assumed.† If however any one should say that the first immediate propositions are the same principles, there is one in each genus, but if it is neither possible that any thing can be demonstrated as it ought to be from all (principles), nor that they should be so different, as that there should be different ones of each science, it remains that the principles of all are the same in genus,‡ but that from different principles different sciences (are demonstrated). Now this is evidently impossible, for it has been shown § that the principles are different in genus of those things which are generically different, for principles are two-fold, viz. *from which* and *about which*, those indeed *from which* are common,[2] but those *about which* are peculiar, for instance, number and magnitude.

† So that he assumes the principles of many conclusions.

‡ but differ in species.

§ Ch. 7.

3. Principles (ἀρχαὶ) two-fold, ἐξ ὧν and περὶ ὅ.

|| Vid. Ethics, b. vi. ch. 3, and b. iii. ch. 2.

CHAP. XXXIII.—*Upon the Difference between Science and Opinion.*||

1. Science is universal, and subsists through things necessary: intellect the principle of science.

THE object of scientific knowledge and science (itself) differs from the object of opinion, and from opinion, because science is universal, and subsists through things necessary, and what is necessary cannot subsist otherwise than it does: some things however are true, and subsist, yet may possibly subsist otherwise. It is evident then that science is not conversant with these, (for else things which are capable of subsisting otherwise, could not possibly subsist otherwise). Yet neither is intellect¶ conversant with such, (for I call intellect the principle of science,[3]) nor indemonstrable science, and this is the notion * of an imme-

¶ See Ethics, b. vi. ch. 2 and 3, Brown's Notes, Bohn's edit.

* ὑπόληψις.

[1] If any one were to analyze the different sciences into their principles, he would not be able to analyze them into the same, but into different principles.

[2] As axioms, see ch. 10; also table of the principles of science. Cf. Sanderson's Logic, b. iii. ch. 11; Mill's Logic, vol. i. p. 197; Metap. v. and vi.

[3] Because of our cognizance of axioms by it

diate proposition. But intellect, science, and opinion, and what is asserted through these, are true, wherefore it remains that opinion is conversant with the true or false, which yet may have a various subsistence, but this is the notion of an immediate and not necessary proposition. This also agrees with what appears, for both opinion is unstable, and its nature is of this kind,[1] besides, no one thinks that he opines, but that he knows, when he thinks it impossible for a thing to subsist otherwise than it does, but when he thinks that it is indeed thus, yet that nothing hinders* it being otherwise, then he thinks that he opines; opinion as it were being conversant with a thing of this kind, but science with what is necessary.

See Mansel's Logic, p. 5, note.

2. Opinion conversant with the non-necessary.

* So Waitz, κωλυεῖν. Taylor and Buhle, κωλυεῖ.

How then is it possible† to opine and know the same thing, and why will opinion not be science, if a person admits that every thing which he knows he may opine? for both he who knows and he who opines will follow through media till they come to things immediate, so that if the former knows, he also who opines knows. For as it is possible to opine *that* a thing is, so likewise *why* it is, and this is the medium. Or ‡ if he so conceives things which cannot subsist otherwise, as if he had the definitions through which the demonstrations are framed, he will not opine, but know; but if that they are true, yet that these are not present with them essentially, and according to form, he will opine and not know truly both the *that* and the *why*, if indeed he should opine through things immediate; but if not

† Taylor and Buhle insert οὐκ—"non licet," "it is not possible." Waitz and Bekker omit it.

3. Solution of an inquiry why in certain cases opinion may not be science.

‡ Supply, "shall we say." Taylor. Waitz omits, but Bekker retains the question.

[1] In fact, as Aldrich observes, "ei (opinioni) nulla competit certitudo sed in ipsa sui ratione includit formidinem oppositi: sunt opinioni tamen gradus quidam ad certitudinem." For the most admirable example of all the vacillation of opinion from surmise to certainty, and of the desire for that full knowledge and assurance which after all will crush the heart, "the doom it dreads, yet dwells upon," see Shakspeare's Othello, passim, but especially act iii. scene 3:

"OTH. By the world,
I think my wife be honest; and think she is not;
I think that thou art just; and think thou art not;
I'll have some proof."

See also Butler's Analogy, Introduction on Probable Evidence. Cf. Top. i. 1; Aldrich, Whately, Sanderson's and Hill's Logic, in verb.

through the immediate, he will only opine *that* they are. Still opinion and science are not altogether conversant with the same thing, but as both the true and the false opinion are in a manner about the same thing, thus also science and opinion are conversant with the same.[1] For as some say that true and false opinion are of the same; absurd consequences follow both in other respects, and also that he who opines falsely does not opine.[2] * Now since the same thing is stated in several ways, in one way there may be, and in another there cannot be (a true and false opinion of the same). For to opine truly that the diameter of a square is commensurate with its side, is absurd, but because the diameter about which there are (contrary) opinions is the same thing, thus also they are of the same thing, but the essence of each according to the definition is not the same.[3] In like manner also knowledge and opinion are conversant with the same thing, for the former is so conversant with animal as that it is impossible animal should not exist, but the latter so as that it may possibly not exist, as if the one should be conversant with that which is man essentially, but the other with man indeed, yet not with what is man essentially; † for it is the same thing, that is, man, but not the same as to the manner.

* Cf. Met. b. iii. ch. 5.

† But accidentally.

4. We cannot, at one and the same time, know, and opine.

From these then it is clearly impossible to opine and know the same thing at the same time, for otherwise at one and the same time a man might have a notion that the same thing could and could not subsist otherwise, which is impossible. In different (men) indeed each (of these) may be possible about the same thing,

[1] Science is however distinguished from opinion, by the certainty of its subject: error also consists with certainty of the subject, but opinion cannot consist with it. Vide Mansel's note, p. 102; Sanderson's definitions. Cf. also Anal. Post. i. 6. The whole subject is well discussed by Hill (Logic, p. 275, et seq.), and upon the distinction of the dialectic and demonstrative syllogism, as enunciative of opinion and science, the reader will find some valuable remarks in Mansel, and Crakanthorpe's Logic. Cf. Top. i. 1.

[2] He here glances at the opinion entertained by Protagoras and the sophists, who asserted that truth and falsehood were only in opinion, and that if every opinion is true, false opinion is not opinion.

[3] From the thing being considered in two ways, there are two essences of the thing, and the diameter is assumed in true opinion in one way, and in false opinion in another. Taylor.

as we have said,* but in the same (man) it is impossible even thus, since he would have a notion at the same time, for instance, that man is essentially animal, (for this it is to be impossible not to be an animal,) and is not essentially an animal, for this it is to be possible not to be an animal.

* Vide Aldrich in verb. "opinio." Top. i. 1.

For the rest, how it is necessary to distinguish between discourse and intellect, and science and art, and prudence and wisdom, belongs rather partly to the physical, and partly to the ethical theory.[1]

CHAP. XXXIV.—*Of Sagacity.*†

† Cf. Ethics, b. vi. ch. 9

1. Definition of sagacity. ἐυστοχία τις ἐν ἀσκεπτῷ χρόνῳ τοῦ μέσου: instances.

SAGACITY is a certain happy extempore conjecture of the middle term, as if a man perceiving that the moon always has that part lustrous which is towards the sun, should straightway understand why this occurs, viz. because it is illuminated by the sun, or seeing a man talking to a rich person, should know that it is in order to borrow money of him, or that persons are friends, because they are enemies of the same man; for he who perceives the extremes‡ knows all the middle causes. Let to be lustrous in the part toward the sun be A, to be illuminated by the sun B, the moon C. Wherefore B to be illuminated by the sun is present with the moon C, but A to be lustrous in the part turned towards that by which it is illuminated is present with B, hence also A is present with C through B.§

‡ i. e. conclusions.

§ Example (1.)

[1] Cf. Biese, vol. i. p. 89, 327; Hamilton's Reid, p. 768. Διάνοια is the progress of the intuitive intellect (νοῦς) in investigating truth, and is perhaps best rendered here "discourse," though the latter applies both to it and to λογισμος. Upon these terms, cf. Mansel's note, pp. 4—6, and upon the powers or energies themselves, see Ethics, b. vi., Bohn's edition, and De Animâ.

Ex. 1. Whatever is illuminated (B) by the sun shines in the part towards the sun (A)
The moon (C) is illuminated by the sun (B)
∴ The moon (C) shines in the part towards the sun (A).

BOOK II.

CHAP. I.—*That the subjects of Scientific Investigation are four.*

1. Subjects of investigation: the that; the why; the if; and the what. A thing is τὸ ὅτι τὸ, διότι, εἰ ἔστιν, τί ἐστιν. Instances.

THE subjects of investigation are equal in number to the things which we scientifically know; but we investigate four things; *that* a thing is, *why* it is, *if* it is, *what* it is. For when we inquire whether it is this, or that, having reference to a number (as whether the sun is eclipsed or not) we investigate the *that*, and a sign of this is that when we have found that it is eclipsed we desist from our inquiries, and if we knew from the first that it is eclipsed, we do not inquire whether it is so. But when we know the *that*, we investigate the *why*, for instance, when we know that there is an eclipse, and there is an earthquake, we inquire why there is an eclipse, and an earthquake. These things indeed we investigate thus,* but some after another manner,† for instance, if there is, or is not, a centaur or a God. I say if there is or is not, simply,[1] and not if it is white or not. When however we know *that* a thing is, we inquire what it is, for instance, what God, or what man is.‡

* i. e directing our attention to many things.
† Simply considering one thing.
‡ Bekker and Waitz end here: Taylor and Buhle add the opening sentence of the next chapter.

CHAP. II.—*That all Investigation has reference to the Discovery of the Middle Term.*

1. The former four investigations may be reduced to two,

THE things then which we investigate, and which having discovered we know, are such and so many, but when we inquire the *that* or if a thing

[1] Vide Trendelen. Elem. Log. p. 74. By simply, he means an investigation into the mere existence of the thing, but when an inquiry as to the τὸ ὅτι is made, then it becomes a question of the quality. Upon the argument of this whole book, see Kuhn's work, Hal. 1844; we may remark that the question or τὸ ζητούμενον here, has a more extensive application than what Aldrich assigns to it, since two of the questiones scibiles, "an sit," and "quid scit," cannot in all cases be determined syllogistically. Cf. ch. 3, of this book. See also Mansel's Appendix, note B.

is simply, then we inquire whether there is a medium of it or not, but when knowing, either *that* it is, or *if* it is, either in part or simply,[1] we again investigate *why* it is, or *what* it is, then we inquire what the middle is. But I mean by the *that* if it is in a part and simply, in a part indeed (as) is the moon eclipsed or increased? for in such things we inquire if a thing is or is not; but simply (as) if there is a moon or not, or if night is or not.* In all these inquiries it occurs that we investigate either if there is a middle or what the middle is, for the cause is the middle, and this is investigated in all things. Is there then an eclipse? is there a certain cause or not? after this, when we know that there is, we inquire what this is. For the cause of a thing not being this or that, but simply substance, or not simply, but something of those which subsist per se, or accidentally, is the middle. I mean by what is simply (substance) the subject, as the moon, or the earth, or the sun, or a triangle, but by a certain thing, (as) an eclipse, equality, inequality † if it is in the middle or not.‡ For in all these it is evident that *what* a thing is and *why* it is are the same; *what* is an eclipse? a privation of light from the moon through the interposition of the earth. *Why* is there an eclipse, or *why* is the moon eclipsed? because its light fails through the interposition of the earth.[2] *What* is symphony? a ratio of numbers in sharp and flat. *Why* does the sharp accord with the flat? because the sharp and flat have the ratio of numbers. Do then the sharp and flat accord? is there then a ratio of them in numbers? assuming that there is, what then is the ratio?

concerning the middle term, if there be one, and what it is.

* A question of the whole, not of an accident.

2. The middle is that which expresses the cause why the major is predicated of the minor.

† Referring to the angles of a triangle.

‡ Referring to the earth, as in the centre of the spheres.

That the inquiry is of the middle those things prove whose middle falls within the cognizance of the senses, since we inquire when we have not a sensible perception, as of an eclipse, whether it is or not. But if we were above the moon we should not inquire neither if, nor why, but it would be immediately evident, as from sensible perception we should also obtain knowledge of the universal;

3. We do not investigate the middle, if the thing itself, and its cause, fall within the cognizance of our senses. (Vide Waitz, note, p. 381.)

[1] In part *that* it is, or simply *if* it is.

[2] Upon the reduction of this demonstration to syllogistic form, see Aquinas Opusc. 38, and Crakanthorpe Log. lib. iv. cap. 4.

for sense (would show us) that the earth is now opposed, for it would be evident that there is now an eclipse, and from this there would arise the universal.[1] *

* Cf. Metap. lib. i.

As therefore we say, the knowledge of the *what* is the same as the knowledge of the *why*, and this is either simply, and not somewhat of things inherent, for it is of things inherent, as that there are two right angles or that it is greater or less.

CHAP. III.—*Upon the Difference between Demonstration and Definition.*

THAT all investigations then are an inquiry of the middle is evident, but let us show how *what* a thing is, is demonstrated, and what is the method of training up a thing to its principles,[2] † also what a definition is, and of what subjects doubting first about these. But let the commencement of the future (doubts) be that which is most appropriate to the following discussion, since perhaps a man might doubt whether it is possible to know the same thing, and according to the same by definition and demonstration, or whether it is impossible? For definition seems to be of *what* a thing is, but every thing (which signifies) what a thing is, is universal and affirmative, but some syllogisms are negative, others not universal; for instance, all those in the second figure are negative, but those in the third not universal. Next, neither is there definition of all affirmatives in the first figure, as that every triangle has angles equal to two right angles; the reason of this is, because to know

† ἀναγωγῆς, h. e. ἀναλύσεως. Waitz.

1. We cannot know by definition every subject capable of demonstration.

[1] By sensible perception that of the universal is produced.

[2] That is, how definition is reduced to demonstration, for every definition is either the principle or the conclusion of demonstration, or it alone differs from demonstration in the position of terms, as was shown in ch. 8, of the preceding book. Taylor. Upon the subject of this chapter, and the subsequent ones, the reader is referred to the truly valuable remarks in Mansel's Appendix, note B., which want of room prevents my fully quoting, and justice to the excellent treatment the author has shown of his subject, forbids me to abridge. In many cases I have been compelled to give only references, where otherwise I would have entered into greater detail. The student will do well also to consult Rassow, Aristot. de notionis def. doctr., and Crakanthorpe's Logic. Cf. also Top. i. 5 and 6, 4 and 14; Metap. vi. 11; De Animâ, i. 1.

scientifically that which is demonstrable, is to possess demonstration, so that if there is demonstration in regard to things of this kind, there can evidently not be also definition of them, for a person might know by definition without demonstration, since nothing prevents the possession of it at one and the same time. A sufficient evidence of this is also derived from induction, for we have never known by definition, any of those which are inherent per se nor which are accidents; besides, if definition be a certain indication of substance, it is evident that such things are not substances.

2. Nor by demonstration all those which are capable of definition.

Clearly then, there is not definition of every thing of which there is also demonstration, but what, is there then demonstration of every thing of which there is definition or not? there is one reason and the same also of this.* For of one thing, so far as it is one, there is one science, so that if to know that which is demonstrable be to possess demonstration, an impossibility would happen, for he who possesses definition would know scientifically without demonstration. Besides, the principles of demonstration are definitions, of which it has been shown before, there will not be demonstrations,† since either principles will be demonstrable, and principles of principles, and this would proceed to infinity, or the first (principles) will be indemonstrable definitions.

* Proposed above.

† See Part i. ch. 3 and 22.

3. In fact, nothing capable of definition admits demonstration.

Yet if there are not of every thing and the same, may there not be definition and demonstration of a certain thing and the same? or is it impossible? since there is not demonstration of what there is definition. For definition is of what a thing is, and of substance, but all demonstrations appear to suppose and assume what a thing is, as mathematics, what is unity and what an odd number, and the rest in like manner. Moreover every demonstration shows something of somewhat, as that it is, or that it is not, but in definition one thing is not predicated of another, as neither animal of biped, nor this of animal, nor figure of superficies, for superficies is not figure, nor figure superficies. Again, it is one thing to show *what* a thing is, but another to show *that* it is, definition then shows what a thing is, but demonstration that this thing, either

4. One part of a definition is not predicated of another. Vide Hill's Logic, and Whately on "Definition."

is or is not of this. Of a different thing indeed there is a different demonstration, unless it should be as a certain part of the whole. I say this because the isosceles has been shown (to have angles equal) to two right, if every triangle has been shown (to have them), for that is a part, but this a whole:* these however, that a thing is, and *what* it is, do not thus subsist in reference to each other, since the one is not a part of the other.

* The isosceles being a species of triangle, is to it as a part to a whole.

5. Recapitulation.

Evidently then there is neither entirely demonstration of what there is definition, nor entirely definition of what there is demonstration; hence in short it is impossible to have both † of the same thing, so that it is also evident that definition and demonstration will neither be the same, nor the one contained in the other, otherwise their subjects[1] would subsist similarly.‡

† Definition and demonstration.

‡ The things defined and demonstrated.

CHAP. IV.—*That the Definition of a thing cannot be demonstrated.*

1. In order to collect by a syllogism what a thing is, the middle term ought to express the definition.

LET then so far these things be matters of doubt, but as to *what* a thing is whether is there, or is there not, a syllogism and a demonstration of it, as the present discussion supposed? for a syllogism shows something in respect of somewhat through a medium, but the (definition) what a thing is, is both peculiar and is predicated in respect of what it is. Now it is necessary that these should reciprocate: ‖ for if A is the property of C, it is evidently also that of B, and that of C, so that all § reciprocate with each other. Nevertheless, if A is present with every B in respect of what it is, and universally B is predicated of every C in respect of what it is, it is also necessary that A should be predicated of C in the question what it is. Still if some one should assume without this reduplication,[2] it will not be necessary that A should be predicated of C in the question what a thing is, though A should be predicated of B ¶ in the same question, but not of those of which B is predicated in this question.* Now both these † will signify what a thing (C) is,

‖ The nature of the thing and that of which it is the nature.
§ A B C.

¶ In the major.
* In the minor.
† A and B.

[1] τὰ ὑπο κείμενα, h. e. finis ad quem tendit utraque vel id quod utraque conficere vult. Waitz.

[2] That is, simply saying that A is attributed to B, and B to C.

wherefore B will also be the definition of C, hence if both signify what a thing is, and what the very nature of it is, there will be the very nature of a thing prior in the middle term. Universally also, if it is possible to show what man is, let C be man, but A what he is, whether biped animal, or any thing else; in order then that a conclusion should be drawn, A must necessarily be predicated of every B, and of this there will be another middle definition, so that this also will be a definition of a man, wherefore a person assumes what he ought to show, for B also is the definition of a man.

2. A twofold consideration.

We must however consider it in two propositions, and in first and immediate (principles), for what is stated becomes thus especially evident: they therefore who show what the soul is, or what man or any thing else is, by conversion, beg the question,[1] as if a man should assume the soul to be that which is the cause to itself of life,* and that this is number moving itself,† he must necessarily so assume as a postulate that the soul is number moving itself, as that it is the same thing. For it does not follow if A is consequent to B, and this to C, that A will therefore be the definition of the essence of C, but it will be only possible to say that this is true, nor if A is that which is predicated essentially of every B. For the very nature of animal is predicated of the very nature of man, since it is true that whatever exists as man, exists as animal, (just as every man is animal,) yet not so, as for both to be one thing.‡ If then a person does not assume this, he will not

* The minor.
† The major.
Cf. de Anim. b. i. ch. 4, 16.

‡ Because one is genus, the

[1] In the minor in fact the terms so reciprocate as to become identical, and the very nature of a thing, and that of which it is the very nature, are the same. The whole argument goes to show that no definition, as such, can be proved, but the endeavour necessarily results in a petitio principii, and the reason is simply because a definition can be predicated essentially (ἐν τῷ τί ἐστι) of nothing but that, of which it is the definition; and since to prove a conclusion concerning the essence, the premises must be of the same character, the assumed middle must be identical with the minor, and the major premise with the conclusion. The argument is used against Xenocrates. Cf. Scholia, p. 242, b. 35. Trendelenburg, de An. p. 273. Kuhn, de Notionis Definitione, p. 11. Mansel's Logic, Appendix B. In some passages (Metap. vi. 5, 5; vi. 4, 12) Aristotle declares substances alone capable of definition, but in a wider sense, as used throughout the Post. Anal., the remark is applicable both to substances and attributes.

other species. 3. He who proves the definition by a syllogism begs the question.

conclude that A is the very nature and substance of C, but if he thus assume it, he will assume prior to the conclusion that B is the definition of the essence of C. Therefore there has been no demonstration, for he has made a "petitio principii."

CHAP. V.—*That there is no Conclusion by Divisions proved.*

1. That the method by division is inconclusive. * An. Prior, i. 31. † The members of division. ‡ The definition to be proved. § The admitted premises.

NEVERTHELESS, neither does the method through divisions infer a conclusion, as we observed in the analysis about figures,* since it is never necessary that when these things exist,† that‡ should exist, as neither does he demonstrate who forms an induction. For the conclusion ought not to inquire nor to exist from being granted, but it necessarily is, when they§ exist, although the respondent does not acknowledge it. Is man (for instance) animal or inanimate,[1] if he has assumed him to be an animal, it has not been syllogistically concluded. Again, every animal is either pedestrian or aquatic, he assumes it pedestrian, and that man is that whole animal pedestrian, is not necessary from what is said, but he assumes also this. It signifies nothing however, whether he does this in respect of many things or few, since it is the same thing; to those therefore who thus proceed, and in what is capable of syllogistic conclusion, this use is unsyllogistic. For what prevents the whole of this‖ being true of man, yet without enunciating what a thing is, or the very nature of it? Again, what prevents something being added to, or taken away from, or exceeding the essence?[2]

2. The same reasoning good in long or short definition. ‖ Pedestrian.

3. A rule applied for divisional definition.

Negligence then happens about these things, but we may avoid it by assuming all things (as granted) in respect of what a thing is, and the first being made a postulate by arranging the order

[1] This is an interrogation of one, investigating a definition by division.

[2] That is, that something may be superfluous or defective in the definition. Cf. rules for definition in the common Logics; also Passow, Arist de Notionis Defin. Doct., Crakanthorpe, and Sanderson, and especially Boethius de Divisione.

in division, omitting nothing. This however is requisite, for it is necessary that there should be an individual, yet nevertheless there is not a syllogism, but if so it indicates after another manner. And this is not at all absurd, since neither perhaps does he who makes an induction demonstrate, though at the same time he renders something manifest, but he who selects definition from division does not state a syllogism.[1] For as in conclusions without media, if a man state that from such things being granted, this particular thing necessarily exists, it is possible to inquire why, thus also is it in definitions by division. What is man? A mortal animal, pedestrian, biped, without wings. Why? according to each addition,[2] for he will state and show by division as he thinks that every one is either mortal or immortal. The whole however of such a sentence is not definition,* wherefore though it should be demonstrated by division, yet the definition does not become a syllogism.[3]

4. By constant division, when a perfect definition is arrived at, we are said to arrive at the individual.

* For the definition has to be selected from it, i. e. a mortal animal.

CHAP. VI.—*Case of one Proposition defining the Definition itself.*

Is it however possible to demonstrate what a thing is according to substance, but from hypothesis assuming that the very nature of a thing in the question what it is, is something of its

1. It is proved that there is no demonstration of the definition, neither if one proposition

[1] Οὐ λέγει ὁ ἐκλέγων. A paronomasia; a definition is said to be selected from division, because not all the members of the division are assumed in the definition, but always from two opposite members, the one is assumed and the other relinquished. Taylor.

[2] That is, we may question each part of the definition, which is added successively, e. g. why is man animal? why mortal? etc. παρ' ἑκάστην πρόσθεσιν.

[3] Syllogism here, as in other places continually, means the conclusion, and, as Waitz remarks, Aristotle would more accurately have written ἀλλ' ὁ συλλογισμὸς οὐχ ὁρισμὸς γίνεται. Division was a favourite method with Plato, for the demonstration of definitions, but Aristotle considers it only a weak kind of syllogism; in fact, that its chief use is to test definitions when obtained. Andronicus Rhodius wrote a separate treatise on division, and amongst the later Peripatetics, the system was apparently held in higher estimation. Cf. Cic. Top. ch. 6; Quintil. v. 10; vii. 1; Hamilton's Reid; Trendelen. Elem. and Abelard Dialectica, ed. Cousin.

defines the definition itself. peculiar principles, and that these alone[1] indicate its substance, and that the whole[2] is its peculiarity? for this is its essence. Or again, has a person assumed the very nature of a thing in this also? for we must necessarily demonstrate through a middle term.[3] Moreover, as in a syllogism, we do not assume what is to have been syllogistically concluded, (for the proposition is either a whole or a part, from which the syllogism consists,) thus neither ought the very nature of a thing to be in a syllogism, but this should be separate from the things which are laid down, and in reply to him who questions whether this has been syllogistically concluded or not, we must answer that it is, for this was the syllogism.[4] And to him who asserts that the very nature of the thing was not concluded, we must reply that it was, for the very nature of the thing was laid down by us, so that it is necessary that without the definition of syllogism, or of the definition itself, something should be syllogistically inferred.

2. Nor by any other hypothetical syllogism. Also, if a person should demonstrate from hypothesis, for instance, if to be divisible is the essence of evil; but of a contrary, the essence is contrary of as many things as possess a contrary; but good is contrary to evil, and the indivisible to the divisible, then the essence of good is to be indivisible. For here he proves assuming the very nature of a thing, and he assumes it in order to demonstrate what is its very nature:* let however something be different, since in de-

* Therefore "begs the question." Cf.

[1] The things assumed as constituting the definition.

[2] The composite from many attributes. It may be observed that there are two ways of investigating definition; one by division, and the other by induction; the first took a wide genus, including the object to be defined, and contracted it by the addition of successive differentiæ, until we obtain a complex notion, co-extensive with that of which the definition is sought; this was Plato's favourite method, though rejected by Speusippus. Vide Scholia, p. 179, b. xi. The other method was by induction, which consisted in examining the several individuals of which the term to be defined is predicable, and observing what they have in common; the definition sought, being the one common notion which is thus obtained. Vide Mansel's Logic, Appendix B.; Locke's Essay, book ii. ch. 23.

[3] The medium being the essence, the latter is thus assumed to demonstrate itself.

[4] i. e. from the definition of syllogism, it must be shown that the syllogism was rightly constructed, and the conclusion properly inferred.

monstrations it is assumed that this is predicated of that, yet not that very thing, nor that of which there is the same definition,* and which reciprocates.† To both however there is the same doubt against him who demonstrates by division, and against the syllogism thus formed, why man will be an animal biped pedestrian,[1] but not an animal and pedestrian,‡ for from the things assumed, there is no necessity that there should be one predicate, but just as the same man may be both a musician and a grammarian.§

Prior. An. b. ii. ch. 16.

* Equally unknown as the conclusion.

† When the proposition can be equally proved by, as prove the conclusion.

‡ So that one thing is not proved from these.

§ Cf. Interpretation, ch. 11.

CHAP. VII.—*That what a thing is can neither be known by Demonstration nor by Definition.*

How then will he who defines show the essence of a thing, or what it is? for neither as demonstrating from things‖ which are granted will he render it evident that when they exist, it is necessary that something else¶ should be, for demonstration is this, nor as forming an induction by singulars which are manifest, that every thing thus subsists, from nothing * subsisting otherwise; since he does not show what a thing is, but that it is, or is not. What remaining method is there? for he will not indicate by sense nor by the finger.

1. An inquiry into the method of concluding definition. Objections.

‖ Propositions.

¶ The conclusion.

* No individual.

Moreover how will he show what it † is? for it is necessary that he also who knows *what* man is, or any thing else, should also know *that* he is,[2] ‡ for no one knows with respect to non-being that it is, but what the definition or the name signifies, as when I say "tragelaphos," it is impossible to

2\.

† So Waitz and Bekker. Buhle and Taylor read what "man" is.

‡ Cf. next chapter.

[1] So that one thing is produced from these, according to the nature of definition. Cf. on Interpretation, ch. 5.

[2] Before we can determine the real definition of any object (τι ἐστι) we must of necessity ascertain that it exists (ὅτι ἔστι). (Vide next chapter.) Now the existence of attributes and that of substances being determined in two different ways, there is a corresponding variety in the form of definition, the former being defined by the same cause which served as a middle term to prove their existence, a mode of definition described as συλλογισμὸς τοῦ τί ἐστι, πτώσει διαφέρων τῆς ἀποδείξεως—four causes being recognised by Aristotle (cf. An. Post. b. ii. ch. 11): but

know what tragelaphos is. Moreover, if he should show what a thing is, and that it is, how will he show this in the same sentence? for both definition and also demonstration manifest one certain thing, but what man is is one thing, and the essence of man is another.

3. "Esse" is not the substance to any thing.

We next say that it is necessary to show by demonstration every thing, that it is, except it be substance, but to be, is not substance to any thing, for being is not the genus. There will then be demonstration that it is,* and this the sciences now effect. For *what* a triangle means, the geometrician assumes, but *that* it is, he demonstrates. What then will he who defines what it is, prove? that it is a triangle? he then who knows what it is by definition, will not know if it is,† but this is impossible.

* Not a definition of "what" it is.

† Pecause it is not yet chosen to be a triangle.

4. Error of present modes.

Evidently then those who define according to the present methods of definition, do not demonstrate *that* a thing is, for although those lines be equal which are drawn from the middle, yet why is it the thing defined?‡ and why is this a circle?§ for we might say that there is the same definition of brass.‖ For neither do definitions demonstrate that it is possible for that to be which is asserted, nor that that thing is, of which they say there are definitions,[1] but it is always possible to say why.¶

‡ i. e. a circle.

§ Why is the circle a figure having equal lines from the centre to the circumference.

‖ ὀρειχάλχου.

¶ i. e. to interrogate, why is this a circle.

5.

If then he who defines shows either what a thing is or what the name signifies, except there is, by no means (an explanation) of what a thing is, definition will be a sentence signifying the same thing as a name, but this is absurd.[2] For in the first place

the definition of substances is determined by the formal cause, in reference to the essential constituents of the general notion, the possession of which entitles the individual to be reckoned under it. Aristotle makes summa genera, and individuals alone indefinite. Locke avers that simple ideas only cannot be defined. Cf. Metap. books vi. and x.; Locke's Essay, b. iii. 4, 7; Descarte's Princip. i. 10; Occam's Logic, Part I.

[1] Definition does not teach that the proposed thing, the essence of which is investigated, exists in the nature of things, nor does it teach that the thing is that, the essence of which the definition unfolds. Taylor.

[2] Cf. Top. vi. 4 and 6, 14; Metap. vi. 11; Albert de Præd. Tract. i.; Occam, Part I. ch. 26; Whately's Logic, and Aldrich upon nominal and

there would be a definition of non-essences and of non-entities, since it is possible even for non-entities to have a signification. Again, all sentences will be definitions, for we might give a name to any sentence, so that we might all discuss in definitions, and the Iliad would be a definition. Besides, no science would demonstrate that this name signifies this thing, neither therefore do definitions manifest this.

6. Recapitulation. It is proved that we can know "quid res sit" neither by definition nor by demonstration.

From these things therefore it appears that neither definition nor syllogism are the same thing, nor are syllogism and definition of the same thing, moreover that definition neither demonstrates nor shows any thing, and that we can know what a thing is neither by definition nor by demonstration.

CHAP. VIII.—*Of the logical Syllogism of what a thing is.*

1. Questions propounded for consideration.

MOREOVER we must consider which of these things is well, and which is not well asserted, also what definition is, and whether there is in a certain way or by no means a demonstration and definition of what a thing is. Now since it is the same thing as we have said to know what a thing is, and to know the cause wherefore* it is, and the reason of this is, that there is a certain cause,† and this is either the same or another,‡ and if it is another, it is either demonstrable or indemonstrable; if then it is another, and is capable of demonstration,[1] it is necessary that the cause should be a medium, and should be demonstrated in the first figure, for that which is demonstrated is both universal and affirmative.§ Now one method will be that which has been now investigated, viz. to demonstrate what a thing is through something else, for of those things which

* αἴτιον τοῦ τί ἐστιν. Cf. ch. 2.

† Essentiæ rei.

‡ Different from the essence of which it is the cause.

§ i. e. the nature of a thing is universally affirmed of that of which it is the nature.

real definition. It will be found from various places cited, that physical definition was rejected by Aristotle, and that nominal definition is one in which the existence of the objects to which the definition is applicable is not proved; in fact, it is questionable whether the name "nominal definition" is sanctioned by Aristotle (Cf. Trendelen. Elem. 55, upon ch. 10 of this book, and Mansel, Appendix B.

[1] If being different from the "what" a thing is, it can be demonstrated "what" it is.

* e. g. an eclipse.
† e. g. defect of light.
‡ e. g. the opposition of the earth.

are predicated in respect of what a thing is, it is necessary that the medium should be what it is, and a property in respect of properties, wherefore of two essential natures of the same thing,* it will demonstrate the one,† but not the other.‡

2. The logical syllogism "de eo, quid sit." The "why" and the "that" sometimes simultaneously known. The "if" sometimes known. κατὰ συμβεβηκός. How "what a thing is" is assumed and known.

§ Vide last chapter: otherwise the definition will be only nominal.

That this method then is not demonstration, has been shown before, but it is a logical syllogism of what a thing is, still let us show in what method this is possible, discussing it again from the beginning. For as we investigate *why* a thing is, when we know *that* it is, but sometimes those become evident at the same time, but it is not possible to know why it is, prior to knowing that it is, it is clear that in like manner the very nature of a thing, or *what* it is, cannot be known, without knowing that it is, since it is impossible to know what a thing is, when ignorant if it is.§ We sometimes indeed know if it is, accidentally, knowing sometimes something belonging to the thing,[1] as thunder we know, because it is a certain sound of the clouds, and an eclipse, because it is a cer-

[1] This passage is doubtful: it has nevertheless been used for the decision of the question as to whether the class of definitions described as τῆς τοῦ τί ἐστιν ἀποδείξεως συμπέρασμα, is to be regarded as nominal, or as imperfect real definition; the question is of less importance as Aristotle elsewhere condemns their use (De Animâ ii. 2, 2). The instances he gives here may refer either to the one or the other description. The authorities who hold the first view of the subject are Averroes, Zabarella, and St. Hilaire; those who hold up their pens "on the contrary," are the Greek commentators, Pacius, Rassow, and Kuhn.

Ex. 1. That to which the earth is opposed (B) is eclipsed (A).
The earth is opposed (B) to the moon (C).
∴ The moon (C) is eclipsed (A).

Ex. 2. What does not produce a shadow when nothing intervenes (B) is eclipsed (A).
The moon (C) does not produce a shadow, &c. (B)
∴ The moon (C) is eclipsed (A).

tain privation of light, and a man, because it is a certain animal, and soul, because it moves itself. As regards then whatever we know accidentally *that* they are, it is by no means necessary that we should possess any thing by which to know what they are, for neither do we (really) know that they are, and to inquire what a thing is, when we do not know that it is, is to inquire about nothing. In those things however of which we know something, it is easy (to inquire) what they are; hence as we know that a thing is, so also are we disposed to know *what* it is, now of those things, of whose essential nature we know something, let this be first an example, an eclipse A, the moon C, the opposition of the earth B.* To inquire then whether there is an eclipse or not, is to inquire whether B is or not, but this does not at all differ from the inquiry if there is a reason of it, and if *this* is, we say that *that* also is. Or we (inquire) of which contradiction there is a reason, whether of possessing, or of not possessing, two right angles, but when we have discovered, we know at the same time, *that* it is, and *why* it is, if it is inferred through media;† but if it is not so inferred, we know the *that*, but not the *why*. Let C be the moon, A an eclipse, not to be able to produce a shadow when the moon is full and nothing is seen interposed between us, B, if then B, that is, not to be able to produce a shadow when there is nothing between us, be present with C, and A, to be eclipsed, present with this, *that* there is an eclipse, is indeed evident, but *why* is not yet so, and *that* there is an eclipse, we indeed know, but *what* it is we do not know.‡ Yet as it is clear that A is with C, (to inquire) why it is, is to investigate what B is, whether it is the opposition (of the earth), or the turn of the moon, or the extinction of light, but this is the definition of the other extreme, as in those (examples) of A, since an eclipse is the interposition of the earth. What is thunder? the extinction of fire in a cloud: why does it thunder? because fire is extinguished in a

* Example (1.)

† So Bekker, Buhle, and Taylor; but Waitz, δι' ἀμέσων.

‡ Example (2.)

B A
Ex. 3. Where there is an extinction of fire there is thunder.
C B
In a cloud there is extinction of fire.
C A
∴ In a cloud there is thunder.

cloud. Let C be a cloud, A thunder, B the extinction of fire, hence B is present with C, that is, with the cloud, for fire is extinguished in it, but A, sound, is present with this, and B is the definition of A, the first extreme;* if there be again another medium of this † it will be from the remaining definitions.[1]

* Example (3.)
† i. e. another prior cause of the opposition of the earth.

3. Of what a thing is, there is neither a syllogism nor demonstration, but it is manifested by both. Cf. ch. 3.

We have shown therefore thus, how what a thing is, is assumed, and becomes known, wherefore there is neither syllogism nor demonstration of what a thing is, still it will become evident through syllogism, and through demonstration; and hence without demonstration it is neither possible to know what a thing is, of which there is another cause, nor is there demonstration of it, as we have already observed in the doubts.

CHAP. IX.—*Of certain Natures or Principles incapable of Demonstration.*

1. A two-fold division of things—the method used in each.

OF some things indeed there is a certain other cause, but of others there is not, so that it is plain that some of them are immediate, and principles, whose existence and what they are, we must suppose, or make manifest after another manner,[2] which indeed the arithmetician does, for he both supposes *what* unity is, and *that* it is. Of those however which have a medium,[3] and of whose essence there is another cause, it is possible, as we have said, to produce a manifestation through demonstration, yet not by demonstrating *what* they are.

[1] Sin autem etiam alius terminus medius inveniri potest per quem cogatur propositio A B, is quoque una ex reliquis definitionibus notionis A non esse non poterit. Waitz. If *what a thing* is, may be proved by another *what*, this last may also be proved by another, so that there will be three causes of an eclipse, of which the 1st proves the 2nd, and the 2nd the 3rd, and if all are joined there will be a perfect definition. Cf. ch. 10.

[2] As by induction, or a demonstration of the "*that*." He shows here that definitions are assumed prior to all demonstration, and are real, inasmuch as the existence of the objects is assumed with them. The ground of the assumption will vary according to the nature of the object to be defined. Cf. Metap. x. 7.

[3] A cause different from themselves.

CHAP. X.—*Upon Definition and its kinds.*

1. Definition either explains the name of a thing;

SINCE definition is said to be a sentence (explanatory) of what a thing is, it is evident that one definition will be of what a name signifies, or another nominal sentence, as what a thing signifies, which is so far as it is a triangle, which when we know *that* it is, we inquire why it is.[1] Still it is difficult thus to assume things, the existence of which we do not know, and the cause of this difficulty has been explained before, because neither do we know whether it is or is not, except accidentally. One sentence is indeed in two ways, the one by conjunction, as the Iliad, but the other from signifying one thing of one, not accidentally.

2. Or shows its cause. A distinction drawn.

The above-named then is one definition of a definition, but the other definition is a sentence showing why a thing is, so that the former signifies, but does not demonstrate, but the latter will evidently be, as it were, a demonstration of what a thing is, differing from demonstration in the position (of the terms). For there is a difference between saying, why does it thunder? and what is thunder? for thus a person will answer, because fire is extinguished in the clouds; but what is thunder? the sound of fire extinguished in the clouds; hence there is the same sentence spoken in another manner, and in the one way there is a continued demonstration, but in the other there is a de-

[1] Vide Aldrich, Hill's and Whately's Logics upon nominal and real definition. With regard to the expression λόγος ἕτερος ὀνοματώδης, (oratio diversa nominalis, Buhle,) Trendelenburg's, (Elementa, 55,) the literal rendering, gives the idea that nominal as well as real definitions must be *sentences*, but Mansel thinks the context seems rather to mean "a definition of the signification of a name, or of another sentence having the force of a name;" yet on the other hand fairly allows that in this way the word ἕτερος "is superfluous," and the example given "unintelligible." There is no doubt therefore that by λόγος ὀνοματώδης is meant a sentence whose signification, like that of a single noun, is *one;* a description which includes all real definitions, of which the example is a specimen. We subjoin the places he refers to: Int. v. 2; Metap. vi. 4, and 12, and vii. 6; Alex. Scholia, p. 743, a. 31. In the Greek commentators λόγος ὀνομ. is clearly used for nominal definitions: see Philop. Schol. p. 244, b. 31, also Mansel, Appendix B. p. 19. For the different uses of the word λόγος by Aristotle, as enunciative of definition, cf. Waitz upon this chapter.

finition. Moreover the definition of thunder is, a sound in the clouds, but this is the conclusion of the demonstration of what it is; now the definition of things immediate is, the indemonstrable thesis of essence.* [1]

* Cf. ch. 8. (Vide also Mansel's Logic, page 16, App. note.)

3. Brief summary—three forms of definition.

One definition then is, an indemonstrable sentence (significative) of essence, but another is a syllogism of essence, differing from demonstration in case,† and a third is the conclusion of the demonstration of what a thing is. Wherefore, from what we have said, it is evident how there is, and how there is not, a demonstration of what a thing is, also of what things there is, and of what there is not; moreover in how many ways definition is enunciated, and how it demonstrates the essence of a thing, and how it does not; also of what things there is, and of what there is not, definition; yet more, how it subsists with respect to demonstration, and how it may, and how it may not be, of the same thing.

† i. e. in grammatical form, or in the position of the terms.

CHAP. XI.—*Of Causes and their Demonstration.*

1. Causes of things are four, which are all expressed by

SINCE we think that we scientifically know, when we are cognizant of the cause, but causes are four,[2] one indeed as to the essence of a

[1] "Of things immediate," such as the definition of a subject. Waitz and Pacius consider πτῶσις and θέσις synonymous. Upon the kinds of definition referred to here, the reader will find ample information in Mansel's Appendix B., where they are ably and fully discussed.

[2] Upon the four causes of things, see Forchhammer Verhandlungen der sechsten, Versammlung deutscher Philoll. und Schulmm. Cassel, 1844, p. 84—89. Although Aristotle allows any of the four to be used as a middle term, yet it by no means follows that each may be a definition of the major, for while he has not decidedly expressed his opinion, it is probable that he regarded the *formal* cause only, as available for definition. For not only has a material cause no place in attributes, but in physical substances (Metap. vii. 4); in this chapter he gives a material cause, instanced as a middle term, as in fact identical with the formal. The efficient and final causes seem, as Mansel says, to be excluded, as not being contemporaneous with their effects, so that from the existence of the one we cannot certainly infer that of the other. Vide Waitz, vol. ii. p. 411; Trendelenburg, de Anim. p. 355; Mansel, App. B. 17. Cf. also next chapter; Metap. books vi., xi., xii., xiii.; De Anim. i.; Physic. lib. i. and ii.

thing,* another that which from certain things existing, this necessarily exists,† a third that which first moves something,‡ and a fourth on account of which a thing (exists); § all these are demonstrated through a medium.‖ For the one that this existing it is necessary that that should be, is not from one proposition being assumed, but from two at the least, but this is, when they have one medium; this one therefore being assumed,¶ there is necessarily a conclusion, which is evidently thus: Why is the angle a right one in a semicircle, or from the existence of what, is it right?* Let then A be a right angle, B the half of two right angles, and the angle in the semicircle C. Hence B is the cause why A the right angle is inherent in C, i. e. in the angle of a semicircle; for this angle is equal to A, but C is equal to B, for it is the half of two right angles; B then being the half of two right angles, A is inherent in C, and this was for the angle in a semicircle to be a right angle.† This‡ however is the same as the explanation of the essence of a thing,§ because definition signifies this, but the cause of the essence of a thing has been shown to be the middle.‖ Why was there a Median war with the Athenians? What was the cause of waging war with the Athenians? Because the latter with the Eretrians attacked Sardis; this was the first cause of the movement. Let war then be A, first made the attack B, the Athenians C, B then is present with C, i. e. to have first made the attack is present with the Athenians, but A is also with B, for they make war with the aggressors, A then is present with B, i. e. to wage war is present with the aggressors, but this, B, is present with the Athenians, for they were the aggressors. Wherefore the middle is the cause here, and that which first moves; but of those things, whose cause is for the sake of something, as, why does he walk? that he may be well: why is a

the middle term.
* το τί ἦν εἶναι —the formal cause.
† The material cause.
‡ The efficient cause.
§ The final.
‖ When one of these is assumed for a middle. (Vide note.)
¶ The middle.

* Vide Euclid, b. iii. prop. 31.

† Example (1.)
‡ The conclusion.
§ Because a thing is the same as its nature.
‖ Ch. 8, and 10.

Ex. 1. Every angle which is the half of two right angles (B) is a right angle (A)
Every angle described in a semicircle (C) is the half of two right angles (B)
∴ Every angle described in a semicircle (C) is a right angle (A).

house built? that furniture may be preserved; the one is for the sake of health, but the other for the sake of preservation. Still there is no difference between why is it necessary to walk after supper, and for the sake of what is it necessary? but let walking after supper be C, the food not to rise B, to be well A. Let then walking after supper be the cause why the food does not rise to the mouth of the stomach, and let this be healthy; for B, that is, for the food not to rise, appears to be present with walking, C, and with this A, salubrious. What then is the cause that A, which is that for the sake of which (the final cause), is present with C? B (is the cause), that is, the food not rising, this* however is as it were, the definition of it,† for A will be thus explained.[1]‡ Why is B present with C? because to be thus affected is to be well: we must nevertheless change the sentences,§ and thus the several points will be more clear.‖ The generations here¶ indeed, and in causes respecting motion,* subsist vice versâ, for there† it is necessary that the middle‡ should be first generated, but here§ C, which is the last,‖ and that for the sake of which is generated the last.¶

* B.
† A.
‡ Example (2.)
§ The premises and conclusion.
‖ Example (3.)
¶ In final causes.
* Efficient causes.
† In the latter.
‡ The cause.
§ Final cause.
‖ The effect.
¶ The last in *time*, not in *nature*.

2. The same thing may sometimes possess two causes.

Possibly indeed the same thing may be for the sake of something, and from necessity; for instance, why does light pass through a lantern? for necessarily that which consists of smaller particles passes through larger pores, if light is produced by transit, also (it does so) on account of something, that we may not fall. If then it possibly may be, is it also possible to be generated?

[1] That is, the healthy will be explained to be that which does not suffer the food to rise.

Ex. 2. For the food (B) not to rise in the stomach is healthy (A)
Walking after supper (C) does not suffer the food to rise (B), etc.
∴ Walking after supper (C) is healthy (A).

Ex. 3. That which is healthy (A) causes the food not to rise (B)
Walking after supper (C) is healthy (A)
∴ Walking after supper (C) causes the food not to rise (B).

as if it thunders, fire being extinguished, it is necessary that it should crash and rumble, and, as the Pythagoreans say, for the sake of threatening, that those in Tartarus may be terrified. Now there are many things of this kind, especially in those which are constituted and consist from nature, for nature produces one thing for the sake of something,* and another from necessity;† but necessity is two-fold, one according to nature and impulse,‡ another with violence, contrary to impulse; thus a stone is borne from necessity both upward and downward, yet not from the same necessity.§ In things however which are from reason,|| some never subsist from chance, as a house, or a statue, nor from necessity,[1] but for the sake of something, whilst others are also from fortune, as health and safety.[2]¶ Especially in those which are capable of a various subsistence, as when the generation of them is not from fortune, so that there is a good end, on account of which it takes place, and either by nature or by art: from fortune however nothing is produced for the sake of something.

3. Necessity is two-fold; instances. Cf. Rhet. i. 11.

* For the sake of the end or form.

† The necessity of matter.

‡ ὁρμή, i. e. natural impulse.

§ Because it descends naturally, but rises by force.

|| Artificial things.

¶ Cf. Poetics, ch. 9.

CHAP. XII.—*Upon the causes of the Present, Past, and Future.*

(Cf. Phys. lib. iv.)

THE cause of things which are, is the same also as that of things which are generated, which have been generated, and which will be, for the middle is the cause, except that being is the cause to be, what is generated, to those which are generated, what has been, to those which

1. Identity of cause.

[1] Not from the necessity of matter; because though there are wood, stones, and cement, yet there is no necessity on that account that there should be a house.

[2] "As health," which is either from the medicinal art, or from chance, e. g. when Pheræus Jason was healed by a dart thrown by an enemy, as Cicero relates in book iii., de Naturâ Deorum; "and safety," which so happens to a ship when it is preserved, either on account of the art and skill of the pilot, or fortuitously. Taylor. Upon necessity, chance, and the principles generally alluded to at the close of this chapter, cf. Physics, book ii.; Metaph. books iv. v; Rhet. i. 6 (Bohn's ed., where see note); also i. 10, and Ethics i. 9. See also Montaigne's Essays, pp. 50 and 105, Hazlitt's ed.

have been, and what will be to those that will be. Thus why *was* there an eclipse? because the earth *was* interposed, but an eclipse *is generated*, because an interposition of the earth *is generated*, but there *will be*, because the earth *will be*, and there *is*, because it *is* interposed. What is ice? Let it be assumed to be congealed water; let water be C, congealed A, the middle cause B, a perfect defect of heat; B then is present with C, but with this A, viz. to be congealed,* but ice *is* generated, when B *is* generated, it was so, when the latter was so, and it *will* be, when the latter *will* be.

* Example (1.)

2. Causes and effects properly simultaneous—an inquiry into causes of things not simultaneous.

Hence that which is thus a cause, and that of which it is the cause, are generated at one and the same time, when they are generated; are simultaneously when they are; and in like manner, in respect to the having been, and the will be, generated. In the case of things which are not simultaneous, are there in a continued time, as it seems to us, different causes of different things? for instance, is another thing having been generated the cause of this thing having been generated, and another thing which will be, the cause that this will be, and of this being, something which was generated before? the syllogism however is from what was afterwards generated.† And the principle of these are those things which have been generated, wherefore the case is the same as to things which are generated. From the prior indeed there is no (syllogism), as that this thing was afterwards generated, because that thing was generated,‡ it is the same also in regard to the future. For whether the time be indefinite or definite,§ it will not result that because that thing was truly said to have been generated, this which is posterior is truly said to have been generated,

† It is concluded the foundation was laid from the house being built.

3. The posterior not collected from the prior.

‡ That because the foundation was laid the house was built.

§ That is, the interval between the

Ex. 1. That, the heat of which fails, is congealed (B … A)
The heat fails of water (B … C)
∴ Water is congealed. (C … A)

since in the interval it will be false to say this,[1] when already another thing* has been produced. The same reasoning also happens to what will be, nor because that† was produced, will this‡ be, as the middle must be generated at the same time;[2] of things that have been that which has been, of the future the future, of what are produced that which is produced, of things which are that which is, but of what was generated, and of that which will be, the middle cannot possibly be produced at one and the same time. Moreover neither can the interval§ be indefinite, nor definite,[3] since it will be false to assert it in the interval;[4] but we must consider what is connected with it, so that after the having been generated, to be generated may exist in things.[5] Or is it evident that what is generated is not connected with what was generated? for the past does not cohere with what was generated, since they are terms and individuals. As then neither points are mutually connected, those things which have been produced are not so, for both are indivisible; nor for the same reason does that which is, cohere with that which has been generated, for that which is generated is divisible, but that which has been is indivisible. As a line then is to a point, so is that which is to that which was generated, for infinite things which have been, are inherent in that which is;‖ we must however enunciate these matters more clearly in the universal discussions about motion.¶

former and the latter generation.

* The foundation.

† The foundation.

‡ The house.

4. Medium must be simultaneous with those of which it is the medium.

§ Between the past and future.

‖ As infinite points in a line.

¶ Vide Physics, b. vi.

Concerning then the manner in which, when there is a successive generation, the middle cause subsists, let so much be assumed, for in these also it is necessary that the middle and the first should be immediate, thus A was generated because C was so, but C was after, A before. The principle indeed is

5. In the cases of past and futures, some principle or first must be taken.

[1] As that the house was produced.

[2] Supply—with that of which it is the medium. Vide Waitz on this chap., vol. ii. p. 411; and Cf. An. Prior ii. 5.

[3] Supply—in which we may justly infer, that one will be, because another is.

[4] Since the future does not exist in that time.

[5] So that there may be a continual successive production.

C, because it is nearer to the now, which is the principle of time, but C was generated if D was, hence from D having been, it is necessary that A should have been. The cause however is C, for from D having been, it is necessary that C should have been generated, but C having been, A must of necessity have been produced before. When however we thus assume the middle, will (the process) at any time stop at the immediate, or on account of the infinity will a medium always intervene? for, as we have stated, what has been generated is not connected with what has been; nevertheless we must commence at least from the immediate* and from the first *now*.[1] Likewise with regard to the "will be," for if it is true to say that D will be, it is necessary that, prior to this, it should be true to say that A will be, the cause however of this is C, for if D will be, prior to it C will be, but if C will be, prior to it A will be. Likewise also in these the division is infinite, for things which will be, are not mutually coherent, but an immediate principle must also be assumed in these. It is thus in the case of works, if a house has been built, stones must necessarily have been cut, and formed; and why this? because the foundation must of necessity have been laid, if the house was built, but if the foundation was laid, stones must necessarily have been prepared before. Again, if there shall be a house, in like manner there will be stones prior to this, still the demonstration is in like manner through a medium, for the foundation will have a prior subsistence.

* So Waitz. Mediate, Taylor, Buhle, and Bekker.

6. Things generated in a circle must have a similar demonstration.

Notwithstanding, since we see in things which are, that there is a certain generation in a circle,† this happens when the middle and the extremes follow each other, for in these there is a reciprocation; this however was shown in the first treatise,‡ viz. that the conclusions are converted;§ but the case of being in a circle is thus. In works it appears after this manner, when the earth has been moistened, vapour is necessarily produced, from the production of this, there is a cloud, from this last, water, and from the presence of this, the earth is necessarily moistened, this however was the (cause) at first, so that it has come round

† i. e. mutually.

‡ Pr. An. b. ii. ch. 5—7; also Post. An. b. i. ch. 3.

§ Changed into prem.

[1] Compare Waitz upon this place.

in a circle, for any one of these existing, another is, and if that is, another, and from this, the first.

7. Of things which are not universally, but usually, the principles should be non-necessary, but for the most part true. Cf. Wallis, iii. 23.

There are some things which are generated universally, (for always, and in every thing, they either thus subsist, or are generated,) but others not always, but for the most part; thus not every vigorous man has a beard, but this is generally the case, now of such things it is necessary that the medium also should be for the most part; for if A is universally predicated of B, and this of C universally, it is necessary that A also should be predicated always, and of every C, (for the universal is that which is present with every individual and always,) but it was supposed to be for the most part, wherefore it is necessary that the medium also, B, should be for the most part: hence of those which are for the most part, the principles are immediate, as many as thus subsist for the most part, or are generated.

CHAP. XIII.—*Upon the Method of investigating Definition.*

WE have before shown how *what a thing is*, is attributed to definitions, and in what way there is or is not a demonstration or definition of it, how therefore it is necessary to investigate[1] things which are predicated in respect to what a thing is, let us now discuss.

1. Division of things quoad extension.

Of those then, which are always present with each individual, some have a wider extension, yet are not beyond the genus.* I mean those have a wider extension, as many as are present with each individual universally, yet also with another thing, thus there is something which is present with every triad, and also with that which is not a triad, as being is present with a triad, but also to that which is not number. Nevertheless the odd is present with every triad, and is of wider extension, for it is with five, but it is not beyond the genus,† for the five is number, and nothing out of number is odd. Now such things we must take so far

* Of the subject.

† i. e. number.

2. For the attainment of de-

[1] He uses the term θηρεύειν: see also Mansel's note (Appendix B.) in reference to the expressions κατασκευάζειν and ζητεῖν as applied separately to the two methods of "hunting for" and "testing" the definition, viz. Division and Induction.

finition those to be taken, each of which is of wider extension than, but all together equal to, the thing to be defined.
* Taken separately.
† Than the thing to be defined.

until so many are first assumed, each of which* is of wider extension,† but all of them together are not of greater extent, for it is necessary that this should be the substance of a thing.[1] For example, number, the odd is present with every triad, the first in both ways, both as not being measured by number and as not being composed of numbers.[2] Now therefore the triad is this, viz. the first odd number, and the first in this way, for each of these is present, the one with all odd numbers, but the last also with the dual, yet all of them (together) with none (but the triad). Since however we have shown above,‡ that those things which are predicated in respect of what a thing is are necessary, but universals are necessary, but what are thus assumed of a triangle, or any other thing, are assumed in respect to what a thing is, thus from necessity the triad will be these things. That this however is its essence appears from this, since it is necessary, unless the very nature of a triad were not this, that this should be a certain genus, either denominated or anonymous. It will be therefore of wider extension than to be with a triad alone, for let the genus be supposed of that kind as to be more widely extended according to power, if then it is present with nothing else than individual triads, this will be the essence of the triad. Let this also be supposed, that an ultimate predication like this of individuals is the essence of each thing, wherefore in like manner, when any thing is thus demonstrated, it will be the essence of that thing.

‡ Last book, ch. 4.

3. Method of dividing the genus.
§ Which can-

Nevertheless it is right when any one is conversant with a certain whole,[3] to divide the genus into the individuals which are first in species,§

[1] As some discrepancy has been supposed to exist between this passage and Metap. vi. 12, it may be well to observe that, although in the latter passage he seems to maintain that the last differentia must be co-extensive with the subject, he is there apparently speaking not of the specific difference *per se*, but of the difference regarded as dividing the genus: this is in fact equivalent to saying, that the whole must be co-extensive, which no one would think of denying. Vide Mansel's Appendix, note B.; Boethius, Hill, and Whately upon logical definition and decision; also Waitz's remarks.

[2] Because the triad is the first number, the monad being the principle of number, and the dual, a medium between 1 and 3.

[3] In investigating the definition of a subaltern species.

for instance, number into triad and dual, then to endeavour thus to assume the definitions of these, as of a straight line, of a circle,[1] and of a right angle; afterwards assuming what the genus is,[2] for instance, whether it is quantity or quality, he should investigate the peculiar passions* through common first (principles.)[3] For those which happen to the composites from individuals will be evident from the definitions,† because definition and that which is simple[4] are the principles of all things, and accidents are essentially present with simple things alone, but with others according to them. The divisions indeed by differences[5] are useful for our progression in this way, but how indeed they demonstrate we have shown before,‡ but they would thus be useful only for syllogizing what a thing is, and indeed they may appear to do nothing, but to assume every thing immediately,§ just as if any one assumed from the beginning without division. It makes some difference, however, whether what is predicated be so, prior or posterior,[6] as for instance, whether we call animal, mild biped, or biped, animal mild, for if every thing consists of two,‖ and one certain thing is animal mild, and again from this, and the difference, man or any thing else which is one, consists, we must necessarily make a postulate by division. Besides, thus only is it possible to leave out nothing in the definition, since when the first genus is assumed, if a person takes a certain inferior division,[7] every thing will not fall into this; for instance, not every animal has entire or divided wings, but every animal which is winged, for this is the difference of it,¶ but the first difference of animal is that into which every

not be divided into species.

* Of the first species.

† Of the first species.

4. Differential division useful in the investigation of definition.

‡ An. Prior i. ch. 31, and this book, ch. 5.

§ i. e. without proof.

‖ Genus and difference.

¶ i. e. the division of it. Taylor.

[1] A circle is first amongst figures, because it is circumscribed by one line, other figures by many lines.
[2] In what category the thing defined is contained.
[3] Principles common to the first and remaining lowest species, for the principles of the subaltern are those of the infinia species.
[4] The defin. of the first simple species. [5] Specific differences.
[6] Therefore division is useful for the arrangement of things properly in regard to priority, etc. Cf. Waitz.
[7] In which there is not the peculiarity of genus, but of some lower species.

animal falls. Likewise in regard to each of the rest, both of those genera* which are external to animal, and of those which are contained under it, as of bird,† is that into which every bird falls, and of fish that into which every fish falls. Thus proceeding we may know that nothing is omitted,‡ but otherwise we must omit something, and not know it.

* The first division is to be assumed.

† The first division of bird.

‡ In the definition.

5. It is not requisite that he who defines should know all other subjects from which he distinguishes the thing defined.

It is not at all necessary that he who defines and divides, should know all things that subsist,[1] though some say it is impossible to know the differences of each thing without knowing each; but it is impossible to know each thing without differences, for that from which this does not differ, is the same with this, but that from which it differs is something else than this. In the first place then this is false, for it is not something else according to every difference, since there are many differences in things which are the same in species, yet not according to substance, nor per se. Next, when any one assumes opposites, and difference, and that every thing falls into this or that, and assumes also that the question is in one part of the two, and knows this, it is of no consequence whether he knows or does not those other things of which the differences§ are predicated. For it is evident that thus proceeding,‖ if he should arrive at those of which there is no longer a difference, he will obtain the definition of the substance; but that every thing will fall into division, if there should be opposites of which there is no medium, is not a postulate,¶ since every thing must necessarily be in one of them, if indeed it will be the difference of it.

6. A division into opposite members, as of animal into rational and irrational.

§ Rational, etc.

‖ From genus to species by differences.

¶ Not a petitio principii.

7. Three things to be attended to, in divisional definition—how to effect these. Vide Whately, Hill, and Aldrich.

In order to frame definition by divisions, we must attend to three things, viz. to assume the things predicated in respect of what a thing is; to arrange these, which shall be first or second; and that these are all. Now the first of

[1] We find from the scholia that Aristotle here glances at Speusippus: he proceeds to show that it does not signify to the proper knowledge of the thing defined, whether a person knows, or does not know, other things included in either species; since if he carries on division he will arrive at those which have no difference, and will then have attained the desired definition.

these arises from our being able as syllogistically to collect accident, that it is inherent,* so to construct through genus.† There will however be a proper arrangement if what is first be assumed, and this will be if that be taken which is consequent to all, but all not consequent to it; for there must be something of this kind. This then being taken, there must now be the same method in the things inferior, since the second will be that which is first of the rest, and the third that which is first of the following, for what is superior being taken away, whatever succeeds will be the first of the others; there is also similar reasoning in the other cases. Still that all these should be, is clear from assuming what is first in the division, that every animal is either this or that,‡ but this is inherent; § and again the difference of this whole[1] but that of the last[2] there is no longer any difference, or immediately with the last difference[3] this‖ does not differ in species from the whole:[4] for it is clear that neither more (than is necessary) is added, for every thing has been assumed in reference to what a thing is, nor is any thing deficient, for it would be either genus or difference. Both the first then is genus, and this assumed together with differences, but all the differences are contained, for there is no longer any posterior difference.¶ Otherwise the last* would differ in species, this however has been shown not to differ.†

* Vide Topics, book ii.

† Topics, book iv.

‡ e. g. rational or irrational.

§ e. g. rational.

‖ Being assumed.

8. The summum genus assumed in the definition.

¶ Essential.

* Animal, rational, mortal, black.

† Essentially from the whole animal, rational, mortal.

Still we must investigate, looking to those which are similar and do not differ, first (considering) what that is which is the same in all these, then again in other things which are in the same genus with them, and which are among themselves the same in species, but different from those. Yet when in these that is

9. Method to be applied in the case of several species with something common.

[1] Subdivision of rational animal into mortal, immortal, etc.

[2] As of mortal rational animal.

[3] This may be some accidental difference, e. g. "black," united to the last, as animal rational mortal *black*.

[4] That is, from animal rational mortal, but as it does not differ from it essentially, the last accidental difference (black) ought not to be admitted. He uses the term τὸ σύνολον, when the definition is composed of the genus and its differences. Cf. Waitz, Boethius, and Keckermann's Lyst. Log. Min. lib. i. cap. 17. Wallis, Log.

assumed which all have the same, and in others similarly, we must consider in the things assumed whether it is the same, until we arrive at one reason, for this will be the definition of the thing. Yet if we do not arrive at one, but at two or more, it is evident that the question will not be one, but many, for instance, I mean if we should inquire what magnanimity * is, we must consider in the cases of certain magnanimous persons, whom we know what one thing they all possess, so far as they are such. Thus if Alcibiades is magnanimous, or Achilles, or Ajax, what one thing have they all? intolerance of insult, for one of them fought,[1] † another sulked,[2] another slew himself.‡ Again, in other instances, as in that of Lysander or Socrates. If then (it is common to these) to behave in the same manner, in prosperity and adversity, taking these two, I consider what indifference with regard to fortune, and what impatience under insult possess in common; if they have nothing there will be two species of magnanimity.

* μεγαλοψυχία. Cf. Eth. Nic. iv. 3 and 4, and Shaks. Coriolanus, passim.

† Alcibiades.

‡ Ajax.

10. The especially universal most difficult to be defined.

Every definition is nevertheless universal, for the physician does not prescribe what is wholesome for a certain eye, but defines what is fit for every eye, or for the species. The singular however is easier to define than the universal, wherefore we must pass from singulars to universals, for equivocations lie more concealed in universals, than in things without a difference. But as in demonstrations the power of syllogizing must necessarily be inherent, so also perspicuity must be in definitions,§ and there will be this, if through things which are singularly enunciated, what is in each genus be separately defined; as with the similar, not every similar, but that which is in colours and in figures, and the

§ Vide logical rules for definition in Aldrich.

[1] Alcibiades, to revenge the preference given by his countrymen to Lysias, revolted to Lacedæmon, and brought war on his country.

[2] Achilles, for Briseis. The reader may smile at the graphic term used here for εμήνισεν, as descriptive of the "angry boy" in the Iliad, but will confess that its use is warranted, both verbally, by Johnson, and circumstantially, by Shakspeare (Troilus and Cressida). Upon the freaks and follies of Ajax, see the speech of Thersites in the same play, act iii. scene 3, and Sophocles (Ajax) passim. Zell observes that magnanimity was a conspicuous element in Aristotle's own character: upon Christian magnanimity, see St. Paul's Epistles.

sharp that which is in voice, and so to proceed to what is common, taking care that equivocation does not occur. But if it is not right to use metaphors in disputation, we must clearly not define by metaphors,* nor by those things which are spoken by metaphor, otherwise it will be necessary to use metaphors in disputation.†

* Because of ambiguity.

† Because definition is sometimes employed in discussion. (Cf. Waitz, vol. ii. p. 420.)

CHAP. XIV.—*Rules for Problems.*‡

‡ Cf. An. Prior i. 4, and i. 26; also Topics i. 4, and i. 11.

1. Need of division for rightly appropriating problems to each science.

Now that we may have problems, we must select sections and divisions, and thus select, the common genus of all being supposed, as for example, if animals were the subjects of consideration, (we must first consider,) what kind of things are present with every animal.[1] When these have been taken, we must again see what kind of things are consequent to every first individual of the rest,[2] thus if this is a bird, what things follow every bird, and so always that which is nearest,[3] for we shall evidently now be able to say why things are present, which are consequent to those under what is common, as why they are present with man or horse.[4] Let then animal be A, B things consequent to every animal, C D E certain animals, why then B is present with D is evident, for it is present through A: in a similar manner with the rest, and in others there is always the same reasoning.§

§ Example (1.)

[1] For the word problem and its uses, see Alexander Scholia, p. 150, b. 40. What he means here, is that we ascertain the questions or problems to be discussed in every system, by the use of proper divisions and sections, (which Aristotle assumes for the same thing,) and by proceeding from universals to singulars. Vide Biese i. p. 314.

[2] Of the first species.

[3] To the first species, which is next to the proposed genus. Taylor.

[4] i. e. the properties of animal.

A B
Ex. 1. Every animal is sentient
D A
Every horse is an animal
D B
∴ Every horse is sentient.

The proof may be applied in the same manner to every species of animal.

* Synonyms. 2. Also of investigating that which is inherent in the singulars as something common.

Now then we speak according to presented common names,[1] * but we must not only consider in these, but also assume if any thing else should be seen to be common, afterwards consider to what things this is consequent, and the quality of the things consequent to this,[2] as those consequent to having horns are the possession of a rough muscular lining to the stomach, and the not having teeth in both jaws. Moreover to what things the possession of horns is consequent, for it will be evident why what has been mentioned† is present with them,‡ for it will be so in consequence of their possessing horns.

† Viz. to have teeth in one jaw only, etc.
‡ With the species of horned animals.

3. Selection κατὰ τὸ ἀνάλογον.
§ i. e. to assume a common analogous thing.

There is yet another mode of selection by analogy,§ since it is impossible to assume one and the same thing, which it is necessary to call sepium, spine, and bone, there are also things consequent to these, as if there were one certain nature of this kind.[3]

Chap. XV.—*Of Identical Problems.*

1. Problems are identical which have either the same middle

Some problems are the same from having the same medium, for instance, because all things are an antiperistasis,[4] but of these some are the same in

[1] Cf. Top. i. 5; Categ. ch. 1. Synonyms are not allowed to be real definitions, in the proper sense, by Aristotle, though admitted to be ὁρικα; as nominal definitions, they are recognised by Alexander on Metaph. vi. 4, p. 442, Bonitz ed., but the genuineness of this portion of the commentary has been questioned. Vide Mansel's Logic on Definition.

[2] We must not only use this method in things synonymous, and investigate the common generic properties, and afterwards the specific peculiarities, but if there be any thing common without a name, yet we must assume it, in order to investigate its properties, and afterwards to consider to what species it is attributed, and the quality of the things which are consequent to the anonymous genus.

[3] The instances given are analogous, because there is the same relation of the sepium in a particular kind of fish; of the spine in fish generally, and of bone in quadrupeds. He means that from a certain analogy, which is expressive of some common nature in things, we may ascertain what is common to various individuals. Cf. Scholia, p. 42, a. 37, 47.

[4] Quod omnia fiant quia contraria qualitas cerminus instat. Buhle. Compressio undique circumfusa. Scap. Theoph. de Caus. pl. 1, 2. The

genus, which have differences from belonging to other things, or from subsisting differently, e. g. why is there an echo, or why is there a reflection, and why a rainbow? for all these are the same problem in genus, (for all are reflection,) but they differ in species.[1] Other problems differ from the medium being contained under another medium, as why does the Nile have a greater flow during the fall of the month?[2] because the fall of the month is more winterly: but why is the fall more winterly? because the moon fails, for thus do these subsist towards each other.

term, or of which the one is subjected to the other.

Chap. XVI.—*Of Causes and Effects.*

1. Solution of a difficulty—the middle term should always express the cause of the inference. (Cf. Aldrich's Log., p. 104, Mansel's ed. and Wallis's Log.)

Some one may perhaps doubt concerning cause and that of which it is the cause, whether when the effect is inherent, the cause also is inherent, as if the leaves fall from a tree, or there is an eclipse, will there also be the cause of the eclipse, or of the fall of the leaves? As if the cause of this, is the having broad leaves, but of an eclipse the interposition of the earth, for if this be not so, something else will be the cause of these, and if the cause is present, at the same time the effect will be, thus if the earth be interposed, there is an eclipse, or if a tree have broad leaves, it sheds them. But if this be so, they would be simultaneous, and demonstrated through each other, for let the leaves to fall be A, the having broad leaves B, and a vine C, if then A is present with B, (for whatever has broad leaves sheds them,) but B is present with C, for every vine has broad leaves, A is present with C, and every vine sheds its leaves, but the cause is B;

word signifies the effect produced from a thing being surrounded by its contrary. Thus why is hail produced? Because the cold is contracted by the surrounding heat. Why are subterranean places cold in summer and hot in winter? Because in winter the heat is contracted on account of the surrounding cold, and in summer the cold, on account of the surrounding heat. Taylor. Cf. Physic, b. iv. v. vi.; also Lucretius.

[1] Reflection of the air produces the echo; of the figure in the mirror produces the image; of the sun's rays produces the rainbow.

[2] During the fall of the month there is more rain; hence the Nile rises, and there is more rain during the decrease of the moon, because when her light fails, she more powerfully excites humid bodies. Taylor. Cf. also Herod. lib. ii. c. 19—25.

* Example (1.)

the middle.* We may also show that the vine has broad leaves, from its shedding them, for if D be what has broad leaves, E to shed the leaf, F a vine, E then is present with F, (for every vine sheds its leaf,) but D with E, (for every thing which sheds its leaf, has broad leaves,) every vine then has broad leaves, the cause is, its shedding them.† Nevertheless if they cannot be the cause of each other, (since cause is prior to that of which it is the cause,) the cause of an eclipse indeed is the interposition of the earth, but an eclipse is not the cause of the earth interposing. If then the demonstration by cause (shows) *why* a thing is, but that which is not through cause, *that* it is, one knows[1] indeed that the earth is interposed, but why it is, he does not know.[2] Yet that an eclipse is not the cause of the interposition, but this of an eclipse, is plain, since in the definition of an eclipse, the interposition of the earth is inherent, so that evidently that is known through this,[3] but not this through that.[4]

† Example (2.)

2. There is only one cause of one and the same thing, from which it is inferred.

Or may there be many causes of one thing? for if the same thing may be predicated of many primary, let A be present with B a first, and with C another first, and these with D E, A then will be present with D E, but the cause why it is with D will be B, and C the cause why it is with E, hence from the existence of the cause there is necessarily the ex-

* Ex. 1. Whatever consists of broad leaves (B) sheds its leaves (A)
Every vine (C) consists of broad leaves (B)
∴ Every vine (C) sheds its leaves (A).

† Ex. 2. Whatever sheds its leaves (E) has broad leaves (D)
Every vine (F) sheds its leaves (E)
∴ Every vine (F) has broad leaves (D).

[1] i. e. he who through an eclipse proves the interposition of the earth.

[2] That is, one kind of knowledge (that of the ὅτι) is empirical, but the other (that of the διότι) is scientific. Cf. Ethic. Nic. b. i. c. 5.

[3] The eclipse is proved through the interposition of the earth.

[4] Cause is not truly proved through effect, because the true demonstration is of the "*why*," but demonstration from effect is of the "*that*."

istence of the thing, but when the thing exists, it is not necessary that every cause should exist, still some cause indeed, yet not every cause. Or if the problem is always universal, is the cause also a certain whole, and that of which it is the cause universal?[1] as to shed the leaf is present definitely with a certain whole,* though there should be species of it,[2] and with these universally, i. e. either with plants or with such plants.† Hence in these, the medium and that of which it is the cause must be equal, and reciprocate,[3] for instance, why do the trees shed their leaves? if indeed through the concretion of moisture, whether the tree casts its leaf, there must of necessity be concretion, or whether there is concretion not in any thing indiscriminately, but in a tree, the latter must necessarily shed its leaf.

* Or genus.

† e. g. plants with broad leaves.

CHAP. XVII.—*Extension of the same subject.*

1. If the same thing is predicated of many, except there is an accidental demonstration, it must be shown from the same cause. If the conclusion is equivocal, the middle

WHETHER however may there not be possibly the same cause of the same thing[4] in all things,[5] but a different one, or is this impossible? or shall we say it cannot happen, if it is demonstrated per se and not by a sign or accident?[6] for the middle is the definition of the extreme,[7] but if it is not thus, (shall we say that) it is possible?[8] We may however consider that of which[9] and to which[10]

[1] "Universal" is here used in the same sense as in ch. iv. of the preceding book, when a property is predicated of every subject and primarily, so as to reciprocate with it. Cf. Waitz, vol. ii. 424.

[2] The property may be in the several species as in the genus, but its presence in the latter does not prevent its predication of the former.

[3] Reciprocals are called equals because they are identical in quantity.

[4] Property—which in the demonstration is the major extreme.

[5] In subjects which are the minor extremes—by cause understand, the middle term.

[6] Cf. Anal. Pr. ch. xxvii. and Waitz, p. 425, vol. ii.

[7] Of the major, see below.

[8] That if it is not demonstrated per se, but from accident, there may be many causes.

[9] The property.

[10] The subject, it is possible to consider these from accident, just as if a grammarian was proved visible, because man is visible. Taylor.

termi will be so. Cf. An. Post. i. 13.

it is the cause by accident, still they do not appear to be problems,[1] but if not, the medium will subsist similarly,[2] if indeed they are equivocal, the medium will be equivocal, if however as in genus[3] the medium will be similar. For instance, why is there alternate proportion? for there is a different cause in lines, and in numbers, and the same (medium) so far as they are lines, is different,* but so far as it has an increase of the same kind,† it is the same, the like also occurs in all things. There is indeed a different cause in a different subject, why colour is similar to colour, and figure to figure, for the similar in these is equivocal, for here‡ perhaps it is to have the sides analogous, and the angles equal, but in colours it consists in there being one sense (of their perception) or something else of the kind. Things however analogically the same, will have also the same medium by analogy, and this is so from cause,§ and that of which,‖ and to which¶ it is the cause following each other; but by assuming each singly,* that of which it is the cause is more widely extended, as for the external angles to be equal to four, is of wider extension than triangle or square, but equal† in all, for whatever have external angles equal to four right, will also have the medium similarly.‡ The medium however is the definition of the first extreme,[4] wherefore all sciences are produced by definition, thus to shed the leaf, is at the same time consequent to the vine, and exceeds,§[5] and to the fig tree, and exceeds, yet does not exceed all (plants), but is

* From the same medium quoad numbers.
† Multiplication. Vide Euclid, book v.
‡ In figures.
§ i. e. the middle.
‖ The major extreme.
¶ The minor extreme.
* The several species of the minor.
† With the general subject.
‡ They reciprocate.
§ Magis commune est. Buhle.

[1] Because problems ought to be "per se," not from accident.
[2] To the extremes.
[3] They are synonymous.
[4] Vide Mansel, Appendices B. and H., and cf. upon the method of interpretation to be used here, Anal. Post. i. 4, and i. 5. Aristotle intends by the middle being the definition of the major extreme, that it is so of the property which is demonstrated. For instance, why does it thunder? or why is there a noise in a cloud? because fire is extinguished. What is thunder? An extinction of fire in a cloud; here the medium is the definition of the major extreme, thunder, and not of the less, that is, of a cloud.
[5] Vide Waitz, vol. ii. p. 426-7, and the Port Royal Logic, p. i. ch. vi., also Mansel, App. A.

equal to them. If then you take the first middle[1] it is the definition of shedding the leaf, for the first will be the middle of one of them, because all are such,[2] next the middle of this* is, that sap is congealed, or something else of the sort, but what is it to shed the leaf? it is for the sap to be congealed, at the junction of the seed.

2. The major term ought to equal the minor in extent, although it ought to exceed the individuals *comprehended.*

* The cause of a plant having broad leaves.

In figures, to those who investigate the consequence of the cause, and of what it is the cause, we may explain the matter thus: let A be present with every B, and B with every D, but more extensively, B then will be universal to D, I call that universal which does not reciprocate,† but that the first universal, with which each singular does not reciprocate, but all together reciprocate, and are of similar extension. B then is the cause why A is present with D, wherefore it is necessary that A should be more widely extended than B, for if not, why will this‡ be rather the cause than that?§ If then A is present with all those of E, all those will be some one thing different from B,‖ for if not, how will it be possible to say that A is present with every thing with which E is, but E not with every thing with which A is? for why will there not be a certain cause as there is why A is present with all D? wherefore will all those of E be one thing? We must consider this, and let

† Cum latius sit. Buhle.

3. If the same is predicated of things differing in species, it can be demonstrated by diverse middle terms.

‡ B.

§ A.

‖ viz. D.

[1] The first universal subject in which the property is inherent—e. g. a plant with broad leaves, in which the falling off of leaves is present.

[2] i. e. The universal subject will be the cause of the leaves falling, as to the vine, fig tree, &c. because all vines and fig trees are plants with broad leaves. Vide Biese i. p. 317.

Ex. 1. Whatever is (B) without bile is long-lived (A)
Every quadruped (D) is without bile (B)
∴ Every quadruped (D) is long-lived (A).
Every animal of a dry complexion (C) is long-lived (A)
Every bird (E) is an animal of a dry complexion (C)
∴ Every bird (E) is long-lived (A).

* As B and C.
† Of the same property as of A.
‡ D and E differ in *species*.
§ i. e. an indemonstrable proposition.
‖ Example (1.)
¶ Each under the other.

there be C, hence there may be many causes* of the same thing,† but not to the same in species,‡ for instance, the cause why quadrupeds are long-lived, is their not having bile, but why birds live long, their being of a dry complexion, or something else: if however they do not arrive immediately at an individual,§ and there is not one medium only, but many,‖ the causes also are many.¶

CHAP. XVIII.—*Observation upon Cause to Singulars.*

* As to D.
1. The middle term ought to be the nearest to the singular to which it is cause.
† As B.
‡ A.
§ In D.
‖ Example (1.)

WHICH of the media is the cause to singulars,* whether that which belongs to the first universal, or that to the singular? Evidently the nearest to the singular to which it is cause.[1] For this is the cause why the first,† under the universal,‡ is inherent,§ C is the cause that B is inherent in D, hence C is the cause why A is inherent in D, but B is the cause why it is in C, yet to this itself is the cause.[2]‖

CHAP. XIX.—*Upon the Method and Habit necessary to the ascertainment of Principles.*

¶ Taylor and Buhle annex

CONCERNING syllogism then and demonstration, what either of them is, and how it is produced, is clear, and at the same time about demonstrative science, for it is the same:¶[3] but about principles, how they become

[1] The medium is to be assumed, proximate to the subject rather than to the property. Habet et Διότι suos gradus, quia potest esse causa proxima quæ non est prima h. e. per se nota et indemonstrabilis: cujus ideo præfertur, evidentia, quia (contra quam ceteræ) sua luce est conspicua, et nihil indiget aliena. Quare, quæ hanc adhibet causam demonstratio, et habetur et nominatur "potissima." Aldrich. Cf. also Whately and Hill.

[2] As the puration of bile is the cause to itself of longevity. Taylor.

Ex. 1. Whatever is without bile is long-lived
Every quadruped is without bile
∴ Every quadruped is long-lived: but
Every horse is a quadruped
∴ Every horse is long-lived.

[3] The methods of explaining demonstration and demonstrative science

known, and what is the habit which recognises them, is manifest hence to those who have previously doubted it.

this sentence to the preceding chapter. Bekker and Waitz as here.

That it is then impossible to have scientific knowledge through demonstration, without a knowledge of first immediate principles, has been elucidated before,[1] still some one may doubt the knowledge of immediate principles, both whether it is the same or not the same,* also whether there is a science of each or not,† or a science of one, but a different kind (of science) of another, and whether non-inherent habits are ingenerated,‡ or when inherent are latent.[2] If then, indeed, we possess them,§ it is absurd, for it happens that it (the principle) escapes those who have a more accurate knowledge than demonstration,[3] but if not having them before, we acquire them, how can we know and learn without pre-existent knowledge? for this is impossible, as we said also in the case of demonstration. It is evident then, that they ‖ can neither be possessed, nor ingenerated in the ignorant, and in those who

1. Of the necessity and method of obtaining principles of science—certain questions relative to habits solved.

* With a knowledge of the conclusion.

† i. e. of the principle and of the conclusion.

‡ i. e. are acquired. Cf. Eth. Nic. lib. ii. ch. 1, 3, 5, and lib. iii. 5; also see Categ. ch. vi., and de Animâ, ii. 1, and ii. 5.

§ i. e. by nature.

‖ The habit of principles.

are identical therefore sometimes, as in this chapter, demonstration is assumed for demonstrative science.

[1] Vide book i. ch. 2. We have already noticed the two senses in which ἀμεσος is used by Aristotle; here it is applied to a proposition not proved by any *higher* middle term; i. e. an axiomatic principle, which constitutes the first premise of a demonstration: cf. An. Post. i. 2. In An. Post. i. 13, it is applied to a premise immediate as to its conclusion. Vide Mansel; Aldrich, p. 104, note.

[2] As in infants. Aristotle considered the mind as a piece of blank paper, on which nothing was written but natural inclination (τὸ πεφυκος). One difference between disposition (δίαθεσις) and habit (ἕξις), drawn in the Categories and de Animâ, (vide marginal references,) consists in considering habit more lasting than disposition, the former applying to the virtues, etc., the latter to heat, cold, health, etc., which last undergo more rapid mutation. The relation between δύναμις, ἐνέργεια, and ἕξις, given by Aspasius, as quoted by Michelet, is as follows: *Facultas* a naturâ insita jam est potentia quædam, sed nondum nobis ut loquimur potentia, cujus ex ipso vigore *operatio* profluat; hanc demum potentiam philosophus *habitum* vocat.

[3] That is, the thing which is known, or the possession of the principle itself, is concealed from children, who having (suppose) a knowledge of axioms, possess thereby a knowledge more accurate than demonstration. Cf. Waitz.

have no habit, wherefore it is necessary to possess a certain power, yet not such an one as shall be more excellent according to accuracy than these. Now this appears inherent in all animals, for they have an innate power, which they call sensible perception,* but sense being inherent in some animals, a permanency of the sensible object is engendered, but in others it is not engendered.† Those, therefore, wherein the sensible object does not remain, either altogether or about those things which do not remain, such have no knowledge without sensible perception, but others when they perceive, retain one certain thing in the soul.‡ Now since there are many of this kind, a certain difference exists, so that with some, reason is produced from the permanency§ of such things,‖ but in others it is not.¶ From sense, therefore, as we say, memory is produced, but from repeated remembrance of the same thing, we get experience, for many remembrances in number constitute one experience. From experience, however, or from every universal being at rest in the soul,* that one besides the many, which in all of them is one and the same, the principle of art and science arises, if indeed it is conversant with generation,† of art, but if with being, of science.[1] Neither, therefore, are definite habits inherent,‡ nor are they produced from other habits more known, but from sensible perception, as when a flight occurs in battle, if one soldier makes a stand, another stands, and then another, until the fight is restored.

2. Animals possess sensible perception.

* αἰσθήσις. Cf. Eth. b. vi. ch. 2 and 11; de Animâ, b. ii. 5, et seq.; iii. 1.

† As insects. Vide Trendelen. de An. p. 170, 174.

‡ So Taylor and Buhle; but Waitz and Bekker read ἔτι. Cf. Brundisius.

§ Waitz and Bekker read μονῆς, but Taylor and Buhle, μνήμης.

‖ As in men.

¶ As in brutes.

* i. e. remaining.

† With things perishable.

3. In what way we arrive at a certain art or science from singulars subjected to the senses.

‡ i. e. the habits by which principles are known.

[1] Cf. Trendelenb. c. i. p. 137; Aldrich, Hill, and Mansel upon Induction and Method; Zabarella upon the last; and Whately upon the Province of Reasoning. The "methodus inventionis" can only be a process of inference, for no arrangement of parts is possible before they have been discovered, the discovery of general principles from individual objects of sense, if limited to the inferential process itself, will be induction. The term, however, is sometimes extended so as to include the preliminary accumulation of individuals: in this under sense it will embrace the successive steps given by Aristotle here, of αἴσθησις μνήμη, ἐμπειρία, ἐπαγωγη. Mansel. Vide also Poetic, ch. xvi.; De Anim. Proem. 167.

But the soul has such a state of being, as enables it to suffer this,* what, however, we have before said, but not clearly, let us again explain. When one thing without difference abides, there is (then) first, universal in the soul,[1] (for the singular indeed is perceived by sense, but sense is of the universal, as of man, but not of the man Callias,) again, in these† it stops, till individuals‡ and universals stop,§[2] as such a kind of animal, until animal,‖ and in this¶ again (it stops) after a similar manner.* It is manifest then that primary things become necessarily known to us by induction, for thus sensible perception produces the universal. But since, of those habits which are about intellect, by which we ascertain truth, some are always true, but others admit the false, as opinion, and reasoning,[3] but science, and intellect, are always true, and no other kind of knowledge, except intellect, is more accurate than science, but the principles of demonstrations are more known, and all science is connected with reason, there could not be a science of principles: but since nothing can be more true than science except intellect,

* So as to retain many successive images.

† In these most special species. Taylor.

‡ ἀμερῆ, individua. Buhle.

§ In the soul.

‖ Supply, is permanent in the soul.

¶ Animal.

* Until something else is permanent in the soul, as "living."

[1] That is, the first universal notion, or that which remains of those several things which are perceived by the senses, and which do not specifically differ. From first universal notions, another is formed, comprehending those things which the several singulars have in common, until summa genera are arrived at. The universal, of course, is equally and without difference found in many particulars.

[2] The universals are so called (ἀμερη) because they are inherent in singulars, not partially, but wholly, every where totally present with their participants: thus the whole of animal is in one man.

[3] Of the powers of the soul, some are irrational and disobedient to reason, as the nutritive, others are capable of being obedient to reason, as anger and desire. But other powers of the soul are rational; and of the rational, some are always true, as intellect and science, others are sometimes true, as opinion and λογισμός, i. e. reasoning about practical and political affairs, and things generable and corruptible, which are in a perpetual flux, and are subject to infinite mutations. For intellect, properly so called, is that power or summit of the soul which energizes about things that possess an invariable sameness of subsistence. Taylor. Vide also Trendelenb. de An. iii. c. 4—6; Biese i. p. 327; Rassow, p. 73. And cf. Eth. Nic. b. i. c. 13, Bohn's ed., where see Browne's note; Poetics, c. 16; Magna Moral. i. 34; and Eudem. vi. et lib. v. c. 3, et seq.

4. Intellect alone conversant with, and itself the principle of science. All science through demonstration knows the objects of science.

intellect will belong to principles, and to those who consider from these it is evident also, that as demonstration is not the principle of demonstration, so neither is science the principle of science. If then we have no other true genus (of habit) besides science, intellect will be the principle of science: it will also be the principle (of the knowledge) of the principle, but all this subsists similarly with respect to every thing.

END OF VOL. I.

ai
sir

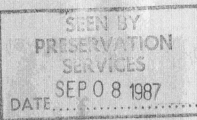

Printed in the USA
CPSIA information can be obtained
at www.ICGtesting.com
LVHW022111110923
757664LV00007B/232

9 781014 200167